THEORIES
FOR
EVERYTHING

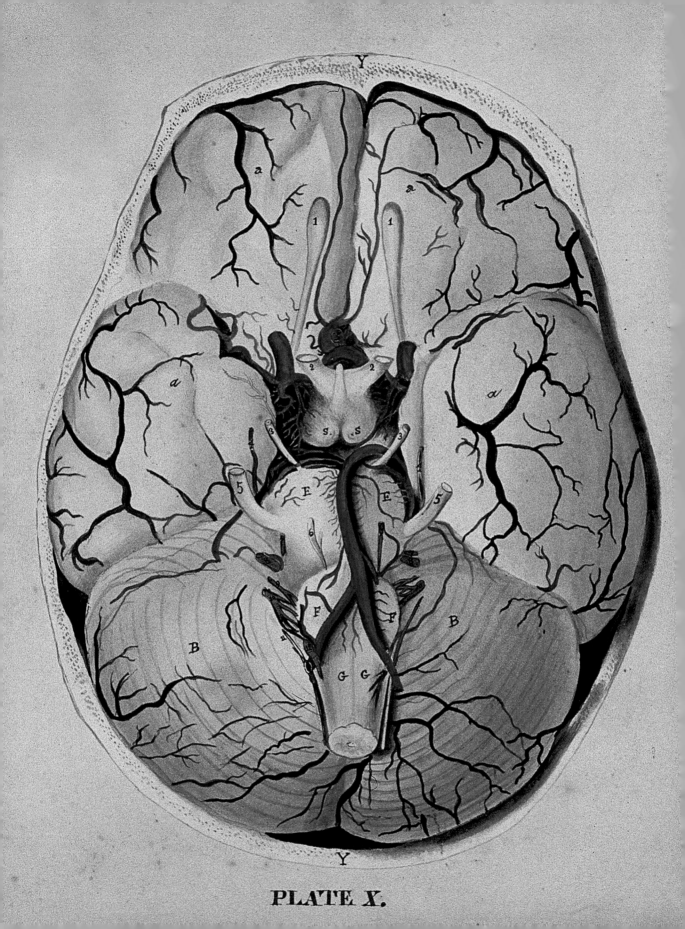

PLATE X.

THEORIES

AN ILLUSTRATED HISTORY OF SCIENCE

FOR

FROM THE INVENTION OF NUMBERS TO STRING THEORY

EVERYTHING

IN MEMORY OF JOHN LANGONE

~

We shall not cease from exploration
And the end of all our exploring
Will be to arrive where we started
And know the place for the first time.
—T. S. Eliot, "Little Gidding," *Four Quartets*

ATLAS COELESTIS,
seu
HARMONIA
MACROCOSMICA

Contents

LEFT: "Macrocosmos" The frontispiece of Andreas Celarius's 1661 *Harmonia Macrocosmica* envisions Urania, muse of astronomy, with Danish astronomer Tycho Brahe, seated at left. Copernicus seated at right, Ptolemy standing with book, Copernican scholar Philips Lansbergen standing far right, and to his right, Castillian King, Alfonso el Sabio.

INTRODUCTION

When we turn on the radio or TV; when we receive a vaccination to prevent disease; when we recognize that although the sun seems to rise and set, it's actually the Earth and not the sun that is moving—in all these moments, we are reaping the benefits of thousands of years of human efforts to comprehend Earth's physical and biological phenomena. While mysteries do remain, we have come to know a great deal about the nature of the planet on which we live as well as the universe beyond. The pursuit of such knowledge we call science, a word whose Greek root means not only "to know" but also "to discern" or "to separate one thing from another." The object of science is not simply to discover facts but to find general truths and articulate fundamental laws. Scientist call such intellectual constructs "theories."

In science, "theory" does not mean "speculation" or "idea," as it does in everyday conversation. A scientific theory is a presentation of fact. It has been arrived at by what is known as the scientific method, an accepted procedure of logic by which scientists test a hypothesis through careful observation, experimentation, and measurement. A hypothesis, or a set of hypotheses, that has withstood every attempt to prove it false may be called a theory. Thus the theories of gravity or evolution are not conjectures. They describe fundamental facts about life on Earth just as do Newton's laws of motion, Boyle's law of gases, Mendel's laws of heredity, and the law of conservation of energy.

Can a theory be proved false? If science finds contradictory evidence, and if that evidence, once tested, proves sound, then a theory will either be changed, if it can be, to accommodate the new evidence or it will be discarded. A theory must be potentially falsifiable—that is, made up of assertions that in principle can be proved wrong by evidence—since, as opposed to conjectures or ideas, a theory's truth must be able to be tested so that it can be proved or disproved.

Although science as we know it—a distinct discipline ruled by formal methods of investigation—has existed for only a few hundred years, our present knowledge incorporates ancient contents. We might not even recognize some of its sources as science, for science itself has changed the way we look at the world and knowledge. As a survey of the histories of scientific theories, then, this book may also be seen as a history of the way in which humans have come to see and understand the world.

This kind of knowledge rarely arrives in dramatic eureka moments of unanticipated discovery. Just as rare is the unerring path from hypothesis to breakthrough discovery. Science may appear to be a continuous process in which each generation improves upon the previous one's insights—an unbroken sequence of revelations that lead to greater enlightenment—but it's always more

messy than that. The journey to most insights often includes countless blind alleys and ideas that are wrong or only partially right but that are vigorously defended. In their apparent correctness, such ideas can sometimes obscure the truth.

The sudden emergence of a single set of concepts or the arrival of one uncommonly brilliant thinker does not typify normal scientific progress. Great minds more often than not synthesize the work of

IDEA

REVOLUTION

Some theories, like the two expressed by Albert Einstein, send ripples of inspiration and redefinition through every field of science and beyond.

many. Isaac Newton, a man with a great mind and a capacious ego, wrote that "if I have seen farther, it is by standing on the shoulders of giants." If the other giants do not often have their names listed beside the more familiar names of Newton, Faraday, or Einstein, they nonetheless helped make their scientific journeys possible.

Science has no doubt influenced history, but the reverse is also true. Commerce, cultural exchange, voyages of discovery, war, religion, and art have all had their effects on the development of science.

So has technological innovation. This book does not purport to be a history of technology, but throughout are examples of instruments, tools, and techniques that have helped propel the scientific process. The telescope and microscope gave scientists glimpses into worlds as yet unseen. Electrical generators, x-ray machines, and computers facilitated discoveries that would have been impossible without them. Some innovations caught science unawares. Both gunpowder and the steam engine altered the course of history before the science of either one was fully understood. On the other hand, the invention of the radio and electric generator came out of advances in science.

Innovation and invention have always moved and been moved by science. Two million years ago, *Homo habilis,* a distant ancestor of humans, developed tools of wood and stone. The regularity of these artifacts shows that Stone Age humans understood the value of similar techniques that produced consistent results.

Until relatively recently, human beings were hunter-gatherers. In around 8000 B.C., as the menacing glaciers of the last ice age receded, humans began to develop a talent for planting and raising crops and corralling wild animals. Gradually, humans domesticated both plants and animals. Through much trial and error, and across several parts of the world in succeeding centuries, they learned to develop new hybrids and breeds.

By 6000 B.C., inhabitants of the Fertile Crescent in the Middle East had succeeded in breeding more productive kinds of wild barley and wheat. People in what is now Mexico were in the process of domesticating *teosinte*, the wild ancestor of modern maize. In cultures arising in present-day Peru, central Africa, and eastern China, people were raising animals. The success of this agricultural revolution as it spread across the Earth altered the future of all human cultures.

People began to give up their nomadic existences and live in permanent habitations. These grew into cities. As stable population centers arose, it became more efficient to share resources. Sharing resources also meant sharing and comparing knowledge. In these ancient settings, in such places as Babylon and Mesopotamia, the first rudimentary sciences flourished.

The need to account for stores of grain or head of cattle, to measure and record the weight of a bushel or the size of a plot of land led to numbering systems. At first no more than symbols cut into clay, these numbering systems eventually grew into a written number system. By about 2400 B.C., Sumerians in Mesopotamia had developed a system of meaning based on the position of symbols. That method, called positional notation, made counting and mathematics considerably easier and, in turn, allowed mathematical thinking to become more complex.

The Mesopotamian numbering system, and later versions that developed from it and spread through the region, used a base of 60. Although our arithmetic uses a base-10, or decimal, system, the vestiges of the ancient base-60 system are still everywhere in our daily lives. We have 60 minutes to the hour, 60 seconds to the minute, and 360 degrees to the circle, thanks to this 4,000-year-old Middle Eastern practice. What none of the great Mesopotamian cutures— the Sumerians, the Babylonians, or

the Chaldeans—developed, though, was the concept of zero and a cipher to represent it.

As early as 1800 B.C., more than a thousand years before the first Greek philosophers, Mesopotamian thinkers had developed a sophisti- cated geometry and could solve the equivalent of equations with powers of two. Moreover, they compiled tables of what are now termed Pythagorean triples, numbers that could represent the length of the sides of a right triangle. A general theorem stating the relationship of those lengths—known as the Pythagorean theorem, after the sage Pythagoras—would not arrive until the time of the Greeks.

Numerical patterns, of course, were largely a creation of the human mind. But there was another, far more fundamental source for pat- terns of regularity in human life: the daily course of the sun and the nightly rotation of the moon and stars. Because the position of the sun and the orderly progression of the seasons affect human life directly, they were the subject of early and careful record keeping. Hence astronomy became the first highly organized science.

By 3000 B.C., if not earlier, the Egyptians had developed a 365-day calendar. Their year began with the annual flooding of the Nile, an event of paramount importance for agriculture. The zodiac—a chart of the positions and movements of stars—was formulated and system- atically described around 1600 B.C. by the Chaldeans. By 750 B.C., the Babylonians were recording solar and lunar eclipses. During the same period, the Chinese were keeping detailed and sophisticated astro- nomical records that would prove useful to astronomers of the 19th and 20th centuries as they were confirming comet cycles.

The work of astronomy not only occupied a great deal of intellectual effort but also frequently called for a stupendous amount of physical labor in erecting what were likely the first observatories. For exam- ple, about 2500 B.C., workers in the region of present-day Stonehenge, England, transported blocks of stone, 14 feet long and 30 tons in weight, from up to 200 miles away in order to build a circle of stone columns on the nearby Salisbury Plain. Whether Stonehenge served an astronomical purpose in the

STONEHENGE

Some have envisioned ancient rituals taking place at Stonehenge, on England's Salisbury Plain, as in this early 19th-century art. Superstitions aside, detailed knowledge of the natural world was essential to building the great stone circle.

modern sense is uncertain. (Our present distinction between the exact science of astronomy and the pseudoscience called astrology did not then exist, and would not for thousands of years.) But dutiful celestial observations were made, even if with the intent of finding some presumed portent of good or ill in the heavens.

Around the sixth century B.C., however, a new kind of thinking, one that would fundamentally alter the course of human development, arose in the burgeoning city-states of Greece. A bit of knowledge we take for granted will illustrate this new thinking:

Stretch a string between two points and pluck it. It creates a sound. Halve the length of the string and pluck once again. Now the note sounds the same but its pitch is different—higher. Halve the string again, and once again the note sounds the same but higher still.

Sometime in the sixth or seventh century B.C., it was discovered that by halving the length of a string, the pitch when it's plucked is exactly an octave higher. (We know now that the string is vibrating at twice the frequency.) The same ratio worked with the length of pipe in a flute. The Greeks realized they could further subdivide the octave: At two-thirds its length, the tone is one musical fifth higher; at three-quarters its length, a musical fourth higher.

Although they developed a different musical scale, the Chinese came to the same realization at about the same time. They also found a practical use for their new knowledge. They replaced measurements based on parts of the human body with those based on the lengths of pitch pipes. The volume of a bowl used for measuring grain was based on the pitch of the empty bowl when struck. In old Chinese, the word for grain measure also means wine bowl and bell.

The Pythagoreans were not quite so practical, but the idea that sound could be described mathematically was one of a number of discoveries that led toward a realization that natural phenomena could be subject not only to speculation and observation but quantitative analysis. The era of classical Greek science was about to begin.

It was in the Ionian city of Miletus, in the early sixth century B.C., that natural philosophy was born. The study broadened in interest and influence, and this great creative period lasted until early in the first century A.D. The names associated with this phase of the history of science—Thales, Anaximander, Heraclitos, Pythagoras, Parmenides, Socrates, Plato, Hippocrates, Eudoxos, Aristotle, Euclid, Ptolemy, Archimedes—recall men whose originality established the basis of sciences as diverse as astronomy, geology, geography, biology, medicine, geometry, physics, and psychology.

Much of their work was preserved, revised, and advanced by scholars, scientists, and mathematicians of the Islamic world, with its capitals of industry and learning in Baghdad and Cairo. The explorers of the Renaissance—not only those aboard ships but also those in studies and libraries—built upon discoveries made before them. The introduction of the printing press gave their age its own spirit of adventurous experiment and speculation. Voyages of discovery would widen the worlds of science just as would the telescope and microscope, and all these discoveries would require new methods of investigation.

Science, as we now know it, with its distinct fields of study, began to develop during the 16th and 17th centuries. By the 19th century, however, it became apparent that the dividing lines between sciences might be less sharp than earlier thought. The forces of heat, light, electricity, and magnetism were found to be nearly identical. The forces acting on molecules and atoms seemed similar to those among planets and stars. With the discovery of DNA molecules in the 20th century, it was clear that living things, too, were subject to some of the same laws that ruled the cosmos. Is there a theory that unified it all? That question remains in the 21st century, along with the mysteries arising from new discoveries: viruses, prions, ancient cells living deep in the oceans.

Each science has its own compelling story of discovery. And that is why this book is divided into six narrative histories: The Heavens, The Human Body, Matter and Energy, Life Itself, Earth and Moon, Mind and Behavior. All of these histories share common roots in ancient Greek and medieval Islamic science, math, and philosophy. For that reason, the reader will soon become familiar with the natural philosophers and scientists whose names appear and reappear. Plato

NEWTON AND THE APPLE

Whether or not an apple fell on Isaac Newton's head, his observations and measurements of the natural world informed his work in mathematics and mechanics—and enlightened all scientists coming after him.

and Aristotle, for instance, contributed insights that shaped scientific thought in many fields, as did Galileo, da Vinci, Newton, Bacon, Descartes, Lavoisier, Lyell, and Faraday. Essays in each chapter will focus on key milestones in theory and in the understanding of the biological and physical world. Fact boxes and timelines—biographical and historical—will highlight or summarize important events and developments. Finally, cross references will indicate the points where one story and another converge, which is, finally, what scientists themselves are always seeking.

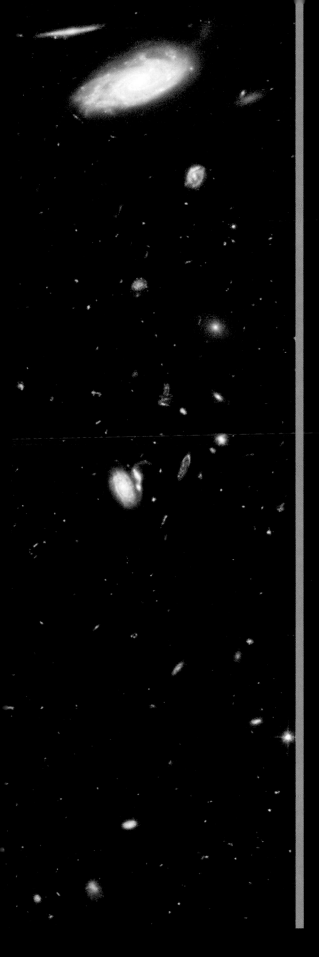

1

The Heavens

GAZE SKYWARD ON ANY CLEAR NIGHT from a dark-sky site and you'll see a myriad of stars, planets, and faint-fuzzy patches of light. As the night progresses, you'll spy new stars popping into view in the east, while others disappear below the western horizon. From your human vantage point, it's hard not to imagine the sky as a large, hollow, spherical shell that slowly turns around a stationary Earth at its center. After all, the stars appear to be fixed to this perpetually rotating sphere, never moving with respect to one another. Anomalies such as comets, meteors, and eclipses occasionally break the perceived cosmic order, while five "wandering stars," or planets, dance across the starry backdrop. Ancient Greek astronomers believed this celestial sphere was a crystalline orb, embedded with jewels—that is, the stars—while some native cultures believed the stars to be campfires tended by their ancestors.

Today we know that Earth is not at the center of a great celestial sphere. Instead, Earth's motion about its axis makes the stars, sun, moon, and planets appear to rise and set in our sky. As we explore the work of ancient astronomers, it is important to keep in mind that humans have flourished for more than 2.5 million years. Assuming 25 years per generation, roughly 240 generations have lived through known history, but more than 100,000 generations of humans span what we now consider pre-history. The intellectual activity of humans during that long period is relatively unknown. Artifacts survive, but they provide little more than glimpses into the knowledge base that represents the intelligence of our prehistoric ancestors.

Ancient remains do confirm, though, that the foundations of observational astronomy go back thousands of years. Ancient monuments—stone circles such as Stonehenge in England or Maya pyramids such as Chichen Itza in Mexico—are testaments to the importance granted to the starry heavens by prehistoric cultures.

Every ancient culture developed its own tale of how the universe began. In most cultures, the priests were the keepers of astronomical knowledge, which they used to advise their people as to when to plant and when to harvest. In ancient Egypt, for example, the position of certain stars was used to predict when the Nile would flood, a key event around which any agricultural activities had to be planned. Astronomical occurrences, such as eclipses, planetary conjunctions, or the appearance of a comet, were usually thought to be portents of earthly events to come.

BABYLONIAN SKIES

Some of the earliest stargazers were shepherds, who spent nightly hours watching their flocks and kept their eyes on the sky for signs of the changing seasons and the times when they should shift their flocks onto new grazing land. Viewing the heavens, they connected the dotlike stars to form patterns and images: bears and serpents, kings, queens, and more. They developed elaborate stories about the characters. Soon their gods and heroes were acting out their cultural legends in the skies over their heads.

Early stargazing eventually gave way to observation and record-keeping. Some of the world's oldest records of sky events come from the Chinese, who recorded

3000 B.C. – A.D. 150

ca 3000 B.C.
England's Stonehenge is built in alignment with the sun.

2686-2345 B.C.
The great pyramids of Egypt are built. They are thought to have some astronomical significance based on their positioning.

1361 B.C.
Chinese astronomers make the first recording of a lunar eclipse.

ca 750 B.C.
The first almanacs are created by Babylonian astronomers based on cycles of the moon.

BABYLONIAN BOUNDARY STONE

Ancient Babylonian *kudurrus*, as this black limestone sculpture is called, marked property lines. Found in Susa, Iran, this kudurru represents King Melishishu II of the 12th century B.C. presenting his daughter (holding a harp) to Nanai, goddess of health and medicine.

ca 340 B.C.
Greek philosopher Aristotle teaches that everything in the universe moves harmoniously around the Earth.

ca 270 B.C.
Aristarchus of Samos proposes a heliocentric universe, sun at the center and Earth one of the planets orbiting it.

ca 240 B.C.
Earliest known record of Halley's comet is made by Chinese astronomers.

ca A.D.**150**
Ptolemy lists 48 constellations in his star catalog and promotes model of geocentric universe.

the appearance of a brightening star, or nova, in 2679 B.C. and of a comet in 2316 B.C. Chinese astronomers also recorded, in the 11th century B.C., that the sun was near the star Beta Aquarii at the winter solstice, some 40 degrees from the position it occupies in the sky today, near the star Gamma Sagittarii.

The Babylonians routinely charted the movements of the sun, the moon, and the planets, which played an important role in their myths of creation as well. From the Old Babylonian period, dating from 1700 to 1600 B.C. and beginning with the reign of Hammurapi, epic poems recount tales of creation. One of these, *Enuma Elish,* refers to the phases of the moon and to 36 stars whose movements and appearances corresponded to various times of year. According to the epic, Marduk, the chief deity of the Mesopotamian pantheon, "fashioned stands for the great gods" and "set up constellations corresponding to them." He also "designated the year and marked out its divisions" and "apportioned three stars each to the twelve months."

At about the same time, astronomers were making the first observations of the planet Venus. Ammisaduqa, grandson of Hammurapi, ruled in Babylon around 1600 B.C. Observations of the rising and setting times of the planet Venus were made over a 21-year period during his reign. That information was eventually recorded in cuneiform, an early form of writing, on artifacts known as the Venus

tablets of Ammisaduqa. While historically significant, these observations were not particularly accurate. In fact, several records hold idealized rising and setting times based not on observation at all but on evolving theoretical calcuations. At the time, the Babylonians were formulating theories on how Venus moved through the sky. They used those theories to predict when and where the planet would appear or disappear on the morning or evening horizon.

Despite such inaccuracies, the Babylonians contributed significantly to the development of science. Astronomical observations were part of the Babylonian social system, holding both practical and religious significance. Even when individual observations weren't correct, patterns emerged through analysis of a long series of observations, offering a picture of how an object might move through the night sky. Such broad views went a long way in helping to develop theories of the motion and possibly even the origins of celestial objects.

Ancient scientists began to make connections between events on Earth and in the sky. In these early times, no practical distinction was made between astronomers making observations and astrol-ogers making predictions. If Jupiter shone brighter than normal and a flood occurred at about the same time, the next occurrence of a bright Jupiter was interpreted as a sign of an impending flood.

During the more than 400 years of the Kassite dynasty, which ranged from 1570 to 1155 B.C., a group of scribes created roughly 70 tablets,

---

THE MOON

It takes 27.322 days for the moon to orbit the Earth. The moon goes through several phases, where its shape appears to change: full moon, waxing gibbous, first quarter, waxing crescent, new moon (no moon), waning crescent, last quarter, and waning gibbous. The moon's orbital period is equal to its rotation period, and for that reason, the same side of the moon faces the Earth at all times.

collectively called *Enuma Anu Enlil*. These works contained literally thousands of omens for reading the skies. Temple astrologers would make observations, refer to the tablets for insight, then deliver their forecasts to the king.

The preeminent Babylonian astronomical text comes in the form of several clay tablets called *Mul Apin*, named for the opening words of the poem, which have been translated from the Sumerian to mean "Plow Star."

The *Mul Apin* tablets, the most important astronomical text coming from the Babylonians, contain a series of lists, beginning with the names of stars and constellations and continuing with the times that constellations and stars rise at the horizon, stars and constellations with simultaneous rising and setting times, and time intervals between subsequent rising times of certain constellations in the morning sky.

The oldest existing copies date from 700 B.C., but the text itself is a compilation of material, including text from both the Venus tablets and the *Enuma Anu Enlil*, so the original may be much older than that. The *Mul Apin* text was continually copied up to Hellenistic times, and surviving versions vary little one from another.

THE HEAVENS IN ANCIENT GREECE

The creation of the oldest copy of the *Mul Apin*, scholars believe, dates to a time roughly coinciding with the original composition of the great oral epics of Greek literature,

ANCIENT IMAGERY

Behind this Babylonian view of heaven, sky, and Earth may be their ancient myth that identifies Enlil, god of the sky, as the offspring of a union between An, god of the heavens, and Ki, goddess of Earth.

the *Iliad* and the *Odyssey*. With his references to constellations and the myths associated with them, Homer suggests that Greek astronomical knowledge was not as sophisticated as that of the Babylonians. Even as late as the seventh century B.C., Hesiod's *Works and Days* shows that the Greeks simply correlated the rotation of the heavens with the seasons. "When the Pleiades and Hyades and strong Orion set," wrote Hesiod, naming constellations that dropped below the horizon as spring approached, "remember it is seasonable for sowing."

The Greeks built upon Egyptian knowledge of the changing sky. Herodotus, the Greek historian who lived in the fifth century B.C., wrote admiringly that the Egyptians composed their year of 12 months, each with 30 days. "It is said that the Egyptians were the first of all men to discover the year, to which they gave twelve parts making up the [four] seasons," he wrote. "And herein the Egyptians reckon, as it seems to me, more sensibly than the Greeks, in so far as the Greeks put in an intercalary month every third year to keep the

CALENDARS

Early Babylonian calendars were based on the lunar month—the period between two successive full moons, amounting to 29.5 days. This cycle produced a lunar year of 354 days, days short of the length of an average solar year, which is observed to be 365.24199 days.

The ancient Egyptians were the first to base a calendar on the solar year. Life in Egypt revolved around the flooding of the Nile. Sirius, the brightest star in the night sky, shone just before sunrise at the time of year that the Nile would flood. The Egyptians used this event to set their calendars. The Maya were also concerned with keeping time, but they didn't correlate their calendar to the length of the year. Instead, they devised a system to count time well into the past or future. Modern calendars stem from the 8th century B.C. These led to the Roman Julian calendar,

This 7th-century B.C. Babylonian calendar lists lucky and unlucky days.

introduced by Julius Caesar in 46 B.C. The Julian calendar reached its final form around A.D. 8 under the Emperor Augustus. It was still off by 11 minutes and 14 seconds, and because of its design, its error accumulated over the centuries.

In 1582, Pope Gregory XIII reformed the calendar in two steps. First, he eliminated a ten-day discrepancy so that the date of March 21 would fall on the vernal, or spring, equinox. He did this by proclamation throughout the Holy Roman Empire, decreeing that the day after October 4, 1582, would be October 15.

Next, he changed the rule for determining leap years. Henceforward, all years divisible by four except century years divisible by 400 were to be leap years, with an extra day in February. This created an average Gregorian year of 365.2425 days, correct to about 1 day in 3,300 years.

seasons right, whereas the Egyptians reckon their twelve months at thirty days each and add in every year five days outside the number."

The Egyptians developed sun and water clocks, and had by the 13th century B.C. already identified 43 constellations and 5 planets—Mercury, Venus, Mars, Jupiter, and Saturn. To all of these they gave their own mythic interpretations. Mars was "the gleaming Horus," connected to the shape-shifting god most often represented as a falcon. Venus was first considered the planet of Osiris, god of the underworld, then gained its identity as the Morning and Evening Star, as Egyptians came to understand the planet's motion through our sky.

The Roman author Cicero wrote during the first century B.C. that the Egyptians called Venus and Mercury "companions of the sun," a moniker we now understand physically, since Venus and Mercury are closer to the sun than Earth and therefore never stray far from it in our earthly view.

In the first century B.C., Greek historian Diodorus Siculus wrote that in Thebes, one of ancient Egypt's grandest cities, priests could predict eclipses—an intellectual feat requiring a high degree of mathematical competence and astronomical knowledge.

Greek thinkers borrowed ideas from both the Babylonians and the Egyptians and formulated the earliest version of what we could call a science of astronomy. Thales of Miletus is said to have predicted a total eclipse of the sun, which some now date to May 28, 585 B.C.

According to Herodotus, the sun eclipsed, as predicted, amid a battle between two rival city-states. The daytime night, and Thales's startling foreknowledge, ended the war and secured him a place of honor in the writings not only of Herodotus but also of Plato and Aristotle.

Thales likely owed much of his astronomical acumen to the Babylonians, who, during the reign of Nabonassar, in the eighth century B.C., dramatically advanced their skills in astronomical observation. Their careful records of years of eclipses revealed patterns, particularly a cycle of roughly 18 years (223 lunar months). Babylonian methods predicted lunar eclipses fairly accurately, but not solar. Perhaps Thales mixed his knowledge with good luck.

Aristotle, the most famous and productive student of the philosopher Plato, insisted that observation must be the guiding principle in the study of nature. In two of his works, *De Caelo (On the Heavens)* and *Meteorologica (Meteorology)*, Aristotle explained the apparent motions of the stars, the planets, and the moon.

His model, developed in the fourth century B.C., assumed many features that scientists since have proved to be untrue: His was a geocentric, or Earth-centered, model of the universe; it assumed that everything in the heavens moves in perfectly uniform circular motions; and it did not take into account the physics at work when bodies with mass interact.

Aristotle's observations led to a complicated cosmological model of

56 spheres centered on a stationary and unmoving Earth. If Earth were spinning, he reasoned, an object thrown upward wouldn't drop back to the point from which it was thrown. Aristotle also reasoned that if Earth rotated around the sun, the stars would display an annual shift in position. To the naked eye, no such change is apparent, because the stars are so far away, but today's astronomers actually measure this slight shift, called stellar parallax, and use it to calculate the distances between Earth and heavenly objects that are relatively nearby.

Aristotle made detailed astronomical observations, and while he used them to construct an inaccurate cosmological model, he also did come to some conclusions that have proved correct and useful for future science.

Aristotle recognized that the Earth must be a sphere. He came to this conclusion because, among other things, it casts a curved shadow on the moon during a lunar eclipse. From this hypothesis, he calculated the Earth's diameter, coming up with an answer equivalent to about 5,100 kilometers.

Although Aristotle's calculations were way off, those of a third-century Greek, Eratosthenes, came much closer to being accurate. He determined Earth's size by noting that the length of a shadow cast by the sun at noon on the summer solstice was different in Alexandria

than in Syene (now Aswan), Egypt. Knowing the distance between Alexandria and Syene, Eratosthenes calculated Earth's diameter to be roughly 8,326 miles, which is remarkably close to today's measurement of approximately 7,926 miles.

The next great classical Greek astronomer, Aristarchus of Samos, lived from around 310 to 230 B.C. He is best known for estimating the distance from the Earth to the sun and moon. He cataloged some 675 stars and hypothesized that Earth rotates about a tilted axis. Aristarchus is also credited with proposing the idea of a heliocentric, or sun-centered, model of the universe. According to his model, the stars and sun were fixed and motionless, held on an enormous sphere with the sun at its center, while the Earth revolved inside this sphere in a circular orbit. Few agreed with this model, and in fact some considered it an act of impiety. It would be another 1,700 years before a sun-centered model returned to the forefront of Western science, thanks to Copernicus.

Building on Aristarchus's work in the second century B.C., Hipparchus described the slow shift of Earth's axis of rotation and developed mathematical models for the motion of the sun and moon. Hipparchus is best known, though, for developing a method to measure the visual brightness of stars. He divided stars into six categories, dubbing the brightest ones first-class or magnitude 1 stars. The faintest were sixth-class or magnitude 6, barely visible to the human eye. Using this brightness scale, Hipparchus cataloged some 850 stars.

Modern astronomers still use this basic scale today, but it has been extended to accommodate other objects, including the sun, and to include heavenly objects that are much fainter than Hipparchus could ever have seen with the naked eye. On Hipparchus's original scale, magnitude 1 stars are roughly 100 times brighter than magnitude 6 stars. The brighter

EARLY ASTRONOMERS

The first night-sky observers

ca 624 B.C.
Thales of Miletus is born.

585 B.C.
The solar eclipse predicted by Thales of Miletus takes place on May 28.

ca 547 B.C.
Thales of Miletus dies.

432 B.C.
Meton and Euctemon observe the summer solstice in Athens.

ca 384 B.C.
Aristotle is born in Stagira, Greece.

367 B.C.
Aristotle joins the Academy of Plato in Athens.

350 B.C.
Aristotle completes his work *On the Heavens*.

322 B.C.
Aristotle dies in Chalcis, Greece.

ca 310 B.C.
Aristarchus of Samos is born.

ca 285 B.C.
Aristarchus begins his studies at the Lyceum.

190 B.C.
Hipparchus is born in present-day Iznik, Turkey.

ca 150 B.C.
Hipparchus completes his *Commentary on Aratus and Eudoxus*.

ca A.D. 100
Ptolemy is born.

ca A.D. 150
Ptolemy completes his *Almagest*.

A.D. 170
Ptolemy dies.

PTOLEMY

In the second century, Ptolemy developed a geocentric model of the solar system that predicted the motions of the planets, sun, and moon to within one degree.

1543 – 1705

1543
Nicolaus Copernicus publishes his theory of a sun-centered universe.

1572
Tycho Brahe observes a new star, or supernova, traveling outside of Earth's atmosphere, providing evidence that the heavens can change.

1608
Dutch eyeglass maker Hans Lippershey creates the first refracting telescope, an invention destined to revolutionize astronomy.

1609
Johannes Kepler publishes his first works describing the laws of planetary motion.

an object, in other words, the smaller the number representing its visual magnitude. The modern scale also defines a jump of five magnitudes as a brightness difference of 100, but it uses negative numbers to describe very bright objects. The star Sirius, for instance, registers at magnitude −1.42; the sun at magnitude −26.5. Instruments such as the Hubble Space Telescope can detect objects fainter than magnitude +28, which is 440 times dimmer than anything we could detect with the unaided eye.

The last of the great ancient Greek astronomers was Claudius Ptolemaeus, known as Ptolemy, who lived from A.D. 100 to 170. Ptolemy developed a geocentric model of the solar system which, like Aristotle's model, put Earth at the center of the universe but which, unlike Aristotle's model, predicted the motions of the moon, sun, and planets with considerable accuracy—to within one degree. Apollonius of Perga had proposed a similar model in the third century B.C. Hipparchus expanded on it, and Ptolemy completed it.

In Ptolemy's vision of the universe, the planets move in circles called epicycles, and each epicycle moves around Earth in a circular orbit called the deferent. But these simple circles didn't quite match the motions seen in the sky. To compensate, Ptolemy put Earth slightly off center. He also plotted points, called equants, from which the center of each epicycle would appear to move at a constant speed.

In the end, the Ptolemaic model was an intricate system of several dozen circles of various sizes rotating at different rates. It served as the standard picture of the heavens for centuries. Over time, though, as astronomers compared model based predictions with actual observations, more and more errors were discovered, and the Ptolemaic model came to be regarded as a relatively inaccurate. Even with the errors, though, there was no better model to predict planetary motion. Ptolemy's ideas dominated astronomical thought for nearly 1,500 years.

Ptolemy's greatest labor was a work titled *Almagest,* a Latin rendering of the Arabic for *The Great Book.* Written around A.D. 150,

ASTROLABE

The astrolabe, dating back to the sixth century, gave astronomers a way to calculate the position of the sun and the stars relative to the horizon and the meridian. Astrolabes were widely used by early sailors until sextants, superior navigation tools, replaced them.

1610
Galileo Galilei describes his findings of sunspots, moon craters, and four moons of Jupiter, proving that not everything in the universe orbits the Earth.

1687
Sir Isaac Newton publishes his *Principia,* introducing his theory of universal gravitation and his three laws of motion.

1705
Edmund Halley's calculations predict a recurring comet. When the comet returns as predicted in 1758, it is named in his honor.

See page 318 for more information about Ptolemy.

Almagest is the only complete and comprehensive text of ancient Greek astronomy that has survived to modern times. The original works of many great classical astronomers, including Aristarchus and Hipparchus, have been lost, and it is thanks to Ptolemy's *Almagest* that we know of their work and accomplishments as well as those of Ptolemy himself.

THE COPERNICAN REVOLUTION

Ptolemy's picture of an orderly, geocentric universe prevailed up into the 16th century, when the religious, political, and intellectual upheavals of the Renaissance created the culture within which our modern view of the universe began to take shape. The impending shift in scientific thought had an unlikely instigator, Nicolaus Copernicus. By all accounts a quiet and sensitive visionary, Copernicus dared to set forth a view of the universe that was radical for its time and revolutionary in its influence.

Copernicus was born into a prosperous family in Torun, Poland, on February 19, 1473. His father was a merchant, his mother a member of a wealthy family. When he was ten, his father died, so his maternal uncle— a Catholic bishop and an academic named Lukasz Watzenrode—took young Nicolaus under his wing. At the time Columbus was sailing across the Atlantic, Copernicus was a student at the University of Cracow. He also attended the University of Bologna, Italy, where he studied canon (or church) law and medicine, and began exploring the science of astronomy. He became a doctor of canon law in 1503 from the University of Ferrara and began practicing medicine at the court of his uncle, now a bishop in Heilsberg, East Prussia. Royals and high-ranking members of the clergy sought his medical services, but he preferred to spend his time aiding the poor.

Although his training was in law and medicine, Copernicus's main interests were astronomy and mathematics. He read the work of the ancient Greeks, and in March 1513 he purchased 800 building stones and a barrel of lime, intending to build his own observatory. One year later, he had clearly formulated his own ideas of the universe and had written his first astronomical treatise, titled *De hypothesibus motuum coelestium a se constitutis commentariolus,* or *Commentary on the Theories of the Motions of Heavenly Objects from Their Arrangements.* He chose not to publish the manuscript but simply circulated it among friends.

Perhaps he knew how disturbing his new ideas would be to the larger world. The *Commentary* was Copernicus's first expression of the idea, new and threatening in his day, that Earth moves in a circular orbit around a stationary sun. It was an idea that would soon not only spark a paradigm shift in scientific thought but also mirror an entire ideological revolution.

Just two years earlier, in 1512, Martin Luther had received his doctoral degree in theology. Luther was teaching at the University of Wittenberg, Germany, at the same

time that Copernicus wrote the *Commentary*. A studious and penitent young man, Luther immersed himself in the study of the Bible and the early church. His studies led him to the conclusion that the Catholic Church had lost sight of several core tenents of Christianity, particularly the doctrine of justification by faith alone, or the idea that a person can gain the grace of God by way of belief, not actions—and especially not through indulgences, or monetary payments to church officials. At the time, indulgences were being sold by Catholic prelates as a way to pay for the renovation of Saint Peter's Basilica in Rome.

Luther and his followers pushed for church reform at the same time that Copernicus quietly refined his heliocentric model of the universe. As different as these two men's work might seem, their revolutionary ideas ultimately harmonized.

The classic geocentric model of the universe included the assumption that the most perfect region was the celestial region above the moon, represented in the outermost spheres, and that the spheres closer in toward Earth at the center represented less perfect states of being. This seemed to confirm the Christian model of heaven above, hell below. To revise this model was not only to challenge Aristotle and Ptolemy but also to challenge the church and Christian doctrine.

Copernicus had firm connections to the church himself: His uncle was a bishop, and he himself had become a canon, an official of the church, at the age of 24. He understood full well that his astronomical observations contradicted church doctrine, and yet he vehemently, quietly, argued against a geocentric universe. "We revolve around the Sun," he wrote in his *Commentary,* "like any other planet." And indeed his work was well received, even praised, by the papal court. On the strength of it, Pope Leo X invited Copernicus to come to Rome to assist in reforming the calendar.

Copernicus knew full well that his ideas might draw contempt from scholastic theologians and laypeople alike. He spent 16 years silently refining the model that he had first described in his *Commentary.* By 1530 he had completed it, but he still would not authorize its publication. The work *De revolutionibus orbium coelestium (On the Re-*

volutions of the Heavenly Orbs) was finally printed in Nuremberg, Germany, in the year Copernicus died, in 1543.

De revolutionibus presented a working geometric model of the observed motions of the planets— the very thing that Babylonians and ancient Greeks like Aristarchus had sought to construct. By presenting a working model with the sun at its center, Copernicus shattered the common view of the place of Earth and humankind in the larger universe. No longer was Earth the focal point, steadfastly anchoring the universe at the center while the heavens rotated slavishly around it. Instead, Earth was just another planet, moving according to physical laws shared with other planets circling the sun.

Copernicus's ideas brought scientific thinking closer to our modern understanding, but they did have their limitations. Like Ptolemy's, the Copernican system assumed that the planets moved in circular paths at uniform speeds. It added in the new idea, however, that the closer a planet is to the sun, the faster it revolves. Earth, for example, travels faster in its orbit than do the planets lying farther out from the sun. This new hypothesis helped Copernicus explain why some planets appear to reverse themselves in their progress across our skies, an optical illusion that astronomers then and now call retrograde motion.

The Copernican model was more elegant than the Ptolemaic one, but his assumption of uniform circular planetary orbits ultimately proved his system, like Ptolemy's, an inaccurate predictor of the motions and positions of the planets, amounting to errors as large as two degrees—that's four times the diameter of a full moon!

REFORMING THE REVOLUTION

Acceptance of the Copernican model was slow. By the end of the 16th century, some 60 years after the publication of *De revolutionibus*, there were still very few intellectuals who would publicly admit to believing that Copernicus was right. Even Galileo Galilei, ultimately known as the spokesman for a heliocentric universe, would not yet publicly support Copernicanism. In a 1597 letter to Johannes Kepler, a fellow astronomer, he admitted that he feared the censure that such a declaration would bring. Ten years later, though, the views coming through his telescope convinced him to defend the sun-centered model openly.

Galileo Galilei was born on February 15, 1564, in Pisa, Italy, the son of a musician and tradesman. He studied medicine at the University of Pisa, but his first love was mathematics. He eventually became a professor of mathematics, first in Pisa and then Padua, in 1592, a position he held for 18 years.

Contrary to popular belief, Galileo did not invent the telescope. In Venice in the summer of 1609, Galileo heard about a Dutchman who had developed a "spyglass" that made things appear closer. The device consisted of a tube into which were inserted two curved pieces of glass. At the time, it was well known that curved glass, like a curved mirror, can distort an image. Galileo surmised that the rumored device used two pieces of curved glass to increase the distortion. He had to test the concept for himself, and he built his own version of a spyglass, or refracting telescope. By August of the same year, Galileo was in Venice, demonstrating the telescope that he had constructed.

NICOLAUS COPERNICUS

Astronomer, heliocentric theorist

1473
Born on February 19, in Torun, Poland.

1491-1494
Studies liberal arts at the University of Cracow.

1496-1500
At the University of Bologna, Italy, studies under Domenico Maria de Novara, master astronomer; witnesses and assists on many celestial observations.

1501-1503
Studies medicine at the University of Pauda, Italy.

1503
Receives a doctorate in canon law from the University of Ferrara, Italy.

1504
Begins collecting observations and gathering ideas relating to his theories on the motions of the universe.

1507
Circulates his *Commentariolus*, first expression of his heliocentric model of the universe.

1522
Delivers a treatise on the minting of coinage at the Congress of the Estates of Royal Prussia at Grudziadz.

1539
Receives a visit from Georg Joachim Rheticus, professor of mathematics from Wittenberg, who is eager to learn of his heliocentric theory and to assist him in publishing a longer treatise describing it.

1543
Copernicus's most important treatise offering evidence for the heliocentric model of the universe *De revolutionibus orbium coelestium* is published in Nuremberg.

1543
Dies on May 24 in Frauenburg, East Prussia, present-day Frombork, Poland.

GALILEO AND THE TELESCOPE

Through his newly built telescope, Galileo Galilei observed in 1610 four points of light that appeared to move around Jupiter. He had discovered the four largest moons of Jupiter: Io, Europa, Ganymede, and Callisto. This 19th-century engraving portrays Galileo sharing his observations with a host of Venetian councilors.

GEOMETRY OF THE HEAVENS

Galileo's *Sidereus nuncius (The Starry Messenger)* outlined his discovery of Jupiter's moons and shattered the Aristotelian belief that all celestial objects move around the Earth.

Galileo's telescope made objects appear roughly 30 times closer than they did to the unaided eye. One of the first objects he looked at was the moon. The markings and pockmarks visible from Earth, surmised Galileo, came from peaks, valleys, and features that he called *maria,* or seas, on the moon's surface. By viewing the moon through the telescope, he measured the length of shadows cast by lunar mountains and used them to calculate their height. He also trained his telescope on the fuzzy band of light that stretches across the nighttime sky, the Milky Way, and confirmed that it was composed of innumerable stars, too faint to see with the unaided eye. Finally Galileo pointed his telescope toward the planets. When he viewed bright Jupiter, he found what he thought were four more planets circling around it. Today we know these objects as the Galilean moons, as scientists call the four largest satellites of Jupiter.

Galileo's observations contradicted the Aristotelian assumption that heavenly bodies and their movements were perfectly geometrical. The moon, for example, had irregular features similar to those found on imperfectly shaped Earth.

Galileo's observations of Jupiter also gave support to the heliocentric model of the universe. Some critics had argued that Earth could not be moving, since it never moved away from the moon. But when Galileo saw moons orbiting Jupiter, which in turn was orbiting the sun, he conjectured that Earth and its moon could travel around the sun together as well. The very

existence of the Galilean moons, circling around Jupiter, also shattered the belief that all celestial objects moved around the Earth.

On March 12, 1610, only a few months after he built his telescope, Galileo published his observations in *Sidereus nuncius,* or *The Starry Messenger.* Other than the title, the book was written in Italian and not Latin, making it accessible to a wider audience in Italy. The book became a huge success. Within five years, it had even been translated into Chinese. Galileo continued to make observations, chipping away at traditional assumptions about the universe. On the surface of the supposedly unchanging, perfect sun, he discovered dark blemishes, marks on the sun's "surface" or photosphere that we now call sunspots. Many argued that these spots were actually satellites of the sun, not surface features. Galileo's regular observations allowed him to chart the motions of the sunspots. He correctly believed that as the sun rotated, the spots rotated with it.

Views through his telescope also revealed what he thought might be appendages on Saturn: mysterious lumps that occasionally disappeared, only to reappear many months later. Not until 1659, 17 years after Galileo's death, did observers note that a thin, flat ring surrounded Saturn. The Dutch physicist Christiaan Huygens put forth this new idea in his book *Systema saturnium,* published in 1659. Huygens's many years of detailed observations allowed him to deduce that Saturn had a thin ring system detached from its globe. As Earth and Saturn both orbit the sun, the angle at which we view the rings changes. When the rings are edge on, as viewed from Earth, they vanish. When Saturn tilts toward or away from us, the rings appear as lobes on either side of the planet's disk. Thus Huygens used observation and logic to clarify Galileo's suspicions of appendages on Saturn.

Galileo also used his telescope to discover that Venus, like the moon, passes through phases in which its shape appears to change. We see Venus, as we see the moon, at different angles relative to the sun, and thus the sun's rays illuminate different portions of the planet over time. Those portions in our field of vision not struck by the sun's rays disappear against the dark night background. From our earthly viewpoint, Venus appears to cycle through phases from crescent to full, although when full, Venus is positioned on the far side of the sun and cannot be seen from Earth.

After four years of observing the sky through his telescope, Galileo became convinced Copernicus was right, and by 1613 he publicly declared himself a Copernican. He did so at a time of intense religious fervor in the Roman Catholic Church. Decades before, in 1542, Pope Paul III had established a council of cardinals to protect and support the faith. The resulting Inquisition meant that

GALILEO GALILEI

Astronomer, physicist

1564
Born in Pisa, Italy, on February 15.

1581
Begins studies at the University of Pisa, Italy.

1592
Granted chair of mathematics at the University of Padua.

1604
Begins experiments with accelerated motion on an inclined plane.

1609
Improves the telescope and becomes first to use it for serious astronomical observation.

1610
Using telescope, observes four moons of Jupiter and, later, the phases of Venus.

1613
Publishes *Letters on the Solar Spots,* in which he supports the Copernican system.

1616
Forbidden by officials of the Catholic Church to teach that a heliocentric model of the universe is true.

1616-1618
Charts the motions and eclipses of the moons of Jupiter.

1632
Publishes *Dialogue on the Two Chief World Systems,* a staged debate over the Ptolemaic and Copernican models of the universe.

1633
Tried by the Holy Office of the Inquisition; found guilty of heresy, he publicly renounces the heliocentric theory of the universe.

1642
Dies on January 8 in Arcetri, Italy.

Catholic officials continually sought out heretics and combed through published work to censor any writing that threatened Christian dogma.

In 1616 church officials deemed the Copernican view of the universe heretical. Archbishop Roberto Bellarmino warned Galileo to stop teaching the heliocentric model as fact. Copernicus's book was officially "suspended until corrected." The Index, the division of the Inquisition charged with examining books, found objectionable passages in *De revolutionibus,* primarily in places where Copernicus either reinterpreted Scripture to favor a sun-centered model or declared the model absolutely true.

For the next several years, Galileo turned his attention to other areas of science. In 1623 his friend Maffeo Barberini became Pope Urban VIII and soon gave Galileo the go-ahead to write on heliocentrism, provided he describe the model as a supposition, not a fact. The resulting book, *Dialogue on the Two Chief World Systems,* appeared in 1632. Galileo framed it as a conversation among three people: Salviati, proponent of the Copernican system; Simplicio, stalwart defender of the Aristotelian system; and Sagrado, a Venetian nobleman learning from them both.

Galileo was soon summoned to Rome, his friend no longer willing to support him, his ideas, or his freedom to publish. Catholic officials suspected that Galileo had acted deceitfully in dealing with the pope, even mocked him in the text. After a lengthy trial, on June 22, 1633, at the age of 70, Galileo was found guilty of heresy. He was forced to recant, his book was banned, and he was confined to his villa in Tuscany, where he died on January 8, 1642—99 years after the death of Copernicus.

During the same era as Galileo, a young Dane was watching his first eclipse of the sun, an event that would set young Tygrc Brahe on a lifelong path to observe and record events in the night sky.

Tycho (the Latinized form of his first name) Brahe was born to nobility on December 14, 1546, in what was then Skåne, Denmark, now part of Sweden. At age 13, he began studying at the Lutheran University of Copenhagen. His uncle and guardian wanted him to practice law, but a solar eclipse so fascinated Tycho that he devoted himself to astronomy ever after, following his passion in secret. He would spend his allowance on astronomy books and sneak out late at night to observe the sky.

In the summer of 1563, Tycho watched the conjunction, or apparent meeting, of Jupiter and Saturn. Night after night he charted the paths of the two planets as they moved closer to each other in the sky, nearly merging into a single point on August 24. As he made his observations, he became increasingly aware of large errors in the astronomical tables that had been developed using Ptolemy's model of the universe. He set out to correct these errors.

Upon the death of his uncle in 1565, Tycho began openly studying astronomy at the University of

TELESCOPES

Telescopes have advanced greatly since Galileo's day. In addition to optical telescopes that use relatively simple lenses and mirrors, we now use radio, x-ray, gamma-ray, and infrared telescopes to study almost every wavelength of radiation.

Wittenberg. With a personality said to be abrasive and arrogant, the brash 20-year-old engaged in a duel that cost him part of his nose, and for the rest of his life, he attached a metal nose prosthesis to his face with wax.

On November 11, 1572, Tycho noticed that a "new and unusual star, surpassing the other stars in brilliance," was shining directly over his head. We now know that this new star was a brilliant supernova—an extremely large, exploding star—in the constellation Cassiopeia. It shone spectacularly for 18 months, reaching a magnitude of –4.

The phenomenon of Tycho's star, as historians have come to call it, would puzzle any astronomer who believed in the Aristotelian view of a perfect, unchangeable, and unchanging heaven. In this classical view, such new stars and any other objects appearing and disappearing in the heavens, like comets, must reside in the lower, imperfect spheres, closer to Earth than the moon. Tycho's discovery suggested otherwise.

A dedicated observer, Tycho watched the star for more than two years and collected data from other observers across Europe. He found that the star's position didn't change; it was in the same place in Cassiopeia, regardless of where observations were made. Tycho therefore surmised that this brilliant star had to be part of the outer perfect sphere, not the imperfect one located between Earth and the moon. Such observations forced him to reevaluate the geocentric

model. He wrote his results as a small book, *De Stella Nova (On the New Star),* published in 1573, when Galileo was only nine years old.

Fame followed Tycho Brahe and his star. In 1576 King Frederick II of Denmark offered him an observatory on the island of Hven, in the Danish Sound. With funds from a patron, Tycho built two castles, first Uraniborg (Castle of the Heavens) and later Stjerneborg (Castle of the Stars). Here he lived for more than 20 years, observing the night sky with a myriad of grand instruments including sextants and the great mural quadrant.

While on Hven, Tycho tried to measure stellar parallax—the slight shift in a star's position. When he

OBSERVATORY

Quadrants await Tycho Brahe and Johannes Kepler on the terrace of Belvedere Castle in Prague.

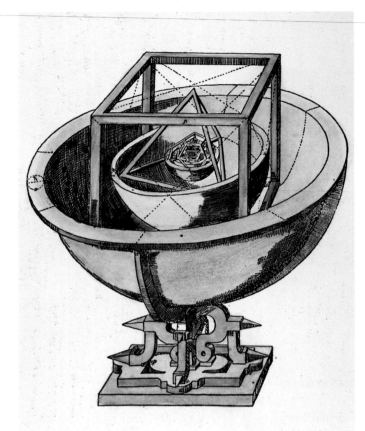

MODEL OF THE HEAVENS

Johannes Kepler devised a complex mathematical model of the solar system, with series of nested spheres and geometric spacers between them, as displayed in this colored woodcut from his book *Mysterium Cosmographicum.*

failed to detect any, he concluded that Earth was stationary and therefore declared the Copernican model to be wrong. Today we know that stellar parallaxes caused by Earth's orbit of the sun can indeed be observed and measured, but that they are 100 times smaller than anything Tycho Brahe could have detected with the instruments he had. He did succeed, though, in measuring the positions of 777 stars, all without the aid of a telescope. His meticulous habits of observation and the large instruments he designed for himself provided a high degree of accuracy, to within one minute of arc, or one-sixtieth of a degree.

When Frederick II died in 1588, Tycho's tempestuous personality lost him the support of the new king. He packed up his instruments and record books and moved into a new position as the imperial mathematician to Rudolph II, the Holy Roman Emperor, in Prague.

With his years of data, Tycho Brahe intended to develop his own Tychonic model of the universe. He hired several astronomers and mathematicians to do calculations. One of them was Johannes Kepler. Both scientists were destined to become significant in the history of astronomy. In November 1601, eight years before Galileo had even built his telescope, Tycho Brahe collapsed. From his deathbed, he persuaded Rudolph II to hire Kepler as his replacement.

Kepler couldn't have been more different from Tycho. The oldest of six children, he was born December 27, 1571, to a poor Protestant family in the town of Weil in what is now southwestern Germany and in what was then a predominantly Catholic region. His father was unreliable and lazy, his mother was of questionable moral character. In her later years, she was accused of witchcraft, and Kepler successfully defended her in a lengthy trial.

A sickly, quiet, studious child of meager means, Kepler attended the pauper's school, where he excelled. Winning a scholarship in 1587, he attended the University of Tübingen, where he studied theology. A highly religious Lutheran, Kepler celebrated the work of God in the mechanics of the universe. He considered the study of the motions of the planets akin to seeking the mind of God. Leaving Tübingen, he began teaching at a Lutheran school in Graz, Austria.

While working as a professor of mathematics and morals, Kepler elaborated on the Copernican system. He proposed that spacers shaped like geometric solids—a cube, a tetrahedron, a dodecahedron, an icosahedron, and an octahedron—separated the orbits of the six known planets (Mercury, Venus, Earth, Mars, Jupiter, and Saturn). His calculations showed that these five polyhedra accounted for the different distances of the planets from the sun. He also saw in his theory the heavenly rationale for there being six planets, since there were only these five perfect solid forms.

In 1596 Kepler published his complex mathematical model in *Mysterium cosmographicum,* or *The Cosmographic Mystery.* But even after that, he wasn't satisfied with his model. He needed better data, so he sent copies of the *Mysterium cosmographicum* to the preeminent observers of his time, Galileo Galilei and Tycho Brahe. He appealed to Galileo for moral support, but in 1597 even the great Italian astronomer lacked conviction in the Copernican model, and Kepler's appeal for an intellectual ally went unanswered. It would be another 16 years before Galileo decided in favor of Copernicanism.

As a Lutheran, life for Kepler in Austria was hard. When Tycho Brahe invited him to come to Prague in 1600, Kepler eagerly left Graz for a chance to work with the famous observer. Unfortunately, their personalities were diametrically opposed, and they had a hard time working together. Tycho was trying to develop his own model of the universe, so he was reluctant to share any of his observations with Kepler. Fortunately, though, Tycho did eventually recognize Kepler's genius and, just before he died, gave his equipment and observation books to Kepler, urging him to further develop a Tychonic model of the universe.

TYCHO BRAHE

Astronomer, mathematician

1546
Born on December 14, in Skåne, Denmark.

1559-1562
Studies rhetoric and philosophy at the University of Copenhagen; after witnessing a solar eclipse, becomes interested in astronomy.

1564
Constructs his first astronomical instrument, a wooden pair of calipers.

1566
Loses part of his nose in a duel with another student; later requires a metal prosthesis.

1572
Witnesses a new bright star, or supernova, in the constellation Cassiopeia, which provides evidence of change in the heavens.

1576
Receives an observatory on the island Hven from king Frederick II; the island becomes Tycho's center for astronomical observations.

1582
Great mural quadrant built in castle observatory on Hven.

1598
Publishes *Astronomiae instauratae mechanica,* or *The improved mechanical astronomy,* in which he describes machines he invented to study the stars.

1599
After traveling several years, settles in Prague as the imperial mathematician in the court of Emperor Rudolph II.

1600
Employs Johannes Kepler as an assistant, then leaves Kepler the task of continuing his studies after his death.

1601
Dies on October 24 in Prague.

NEW THEORIES

Johannes Kepler explains his three laws of planetary motion to his sponsor, Rudolph II, who was king of Bohemia, king of Hungary, and Holy Roman Emperor in the late 15th and early 16th centuries.

Kepler paid particular attention to Tycho's observational data on Mars. Despite 2,000 years of belief in Aristotle's theory of perfect circles and uniform motion, Kepler correctly deduced that the orbit of Mars was an ellipse and that its motion was not uniform. He also confirmed that a planet's orbital speed changes in relation to its proximity to the sun. As its orbital path comes nearer to the sun, it travels faster; as it moves farther away, it travels more slowly. In the work entitled *Astronomia nova (New Astronomy)*, published in 1609, Kepler outlined these principles, now considered the first two laws of planetary motion.

Kepler continued to study astronomy and to refine the Copernican model of the universe. In 1619, he published *Harmonice mundi (Harmonies of the World)*, in which he outlined the third law of planetary motion: The square of a planet's orbital period (the time it takes for one revolution) is proportional to the cube of its average distance from the sun. It's important to remember that Kepler

JOHANNES KEPLER

Founder of celestial mechanics

1571
Born on December 27 in Weil der Stadt, Germany.

1589
Graduates from University of Tübingen.

1594
Begins teaching mathematics and astronomy at the Protestant school in Graz, Austria.

1596
Publishes defense of the Copernican system.

1600
Invited by Tycho Brahe to join his court at castle Benáthy.

1601
Succeeds Tycho Brahe as imperial mathematician in the court of Emperor Rudolph II.

1604
Observes significant supernova, which is later named Kepler's star; publishes work on vision and light.

1605
Announces his first law of planetary motion.

1609
Publishes *Astronomia nova*, describing his first two laws of planetary motion.

1610–1611
Corresponds with Galileo Galilei about Jupiter's moons, optics, and the telescope.

1619
Publishes *Harmonice mundi (Harmonies of the World)*, which includes, among other things, his third law of planetary motion.

1630
Dies on November 15 in Regensburg, Germany.

derived his three laws from Tycho Brahe's data and not from any preconceived notions or theories.

Copernicus, Galileo, Tycho, and Kepler lived during times of great intellectual, cultural, and religious change. Their work transformed our view of the universe, from the long-held geocentric model—perfect spheres, uniform motion, and an unchanging hierarchy analogous to the divine order—to a dynamic heliocentric model, with ellipses, moons, pockmarks, and all. At the same time, both Galileo and Kepler were making astrological forecasts— a dichotomy that illustrates the changing times in which they lived, an era in which religion, mysticism, and science were all intertwined.

ON THE SHOULDERS OF GIANTS

In 1642, the same year that Galileo

NEWTON'S LAWS OF MOTION

In his landmark work, *Philosophiae naturalis principia mathematica*, Isaac Newton outlined three laws of motion and a universal law of gravitation.

The first law of motion, the inertial law, is more commonly known by the phrase the conservation of momentum. This law states that a body will continue at rest or in uniform motion in a straight line unless acted upon by some other force. In other words, an object will keep doing what it is doing unless an outside force compels it to change.

The second law of motion, the force law, says that the momentum of an object can change only if an outside action influences it. The amount and direction of that change is directly proportional to the outside force and inversely proportional to the object's mass: force equals mass times acceleration ($F = ma$).

Colliding billiard balls illustrate many of Newton's concepts of motion.

The third law, the reaction law, states that for every action there is an equal and opposite reaction. This theory implies that all forces occur in pairs that are mutually equal to and opposite each other. Newton used these laws, together with the laws of planetary motion discovered by Johannes Kepler, to analyze planetary orbits.

Finally, Newton's universal law of gravity states that all objects universally attract one another, and that the amount of gravitational force exerted is proportional to an object's mass and inversely proportional to the square of the distance between the two objects of attraction.

This theory is expressed in the equation $F = Gm_1m_2/r^2$, where F is the force of gravitational attraction between two spherical bodies, m_1 and m_2, whose centers are separated by a distance, r, and where G represents the gravitational constant.

Galilei died, the English Civil War began and Isaac Newton came into the world, destined to influence all future studies of the Earth and the heavens.

At Woolsthorpe Manor in Lincolnshire, England, Newton was born on December 25, 1642—and also on January 4, 1643, an anomaly with its origins in the state of calendars at the time.

In 1582, the Gregorian calendar, which we still use today, was put into use by papal decree. The old Julian calendar (named after Julius Caesar, who had introduced it throughout the Roman Empire) was based on an estimated length of the solar year that was off by 11 minutes. After 1,600 years, this small annual error had grown to an error of days. Pope Gregory XIII commissioned a panel of astronomers and mathematicians to create a new, improved calendar. When they were finished, the pope decreed—in an effort to correct the accumulated error—that the day after October 4, 1582, would be October 15. Newly Protestant England refused to listen, however, and continued to follow the outdated Julian calendar. So December 25, 1642, in England was January 4, 1643, in Catholic Europe. England and its colonies would not officially admit the superiority of Gregory's calendar until 1752, and not until after the Bolshevik Revolution of 1917 was it accepted in Orthodox Russia.

Newton's father, an illiterate though comfortable yeoman farmer, had died three months before young Isaac was born. When he was three, his mother remarried and moved to North Witham, leaving her son behind in Woolsthorpe under the care of her parents. In later life, Newton admitted to feeling resentful and angry at being abandoned. Years later, he confessed to "wishing death and hoping it to come." All in all, he led a rather solitary life. He was always inquisitive and mechanically inclined, however, and loved to read and experiment. In 1653, when he was 11

ISAAC NEWTON

The great English physicist

1642
Born on December 25 at Woolsthorpe Manor in Lincolnshire, England.

1661
Matriculates at Trinity College, Cambridge; exposed to philosophy and ideas, he begins to question the physics and mechanics of the world around him.

1665
Moves back to Woolsthorpe, when the plague hits Europe; Trinity College closes temporarily, .

1666
At Woolsthorpe, works out groundbreaking ideas in three areas: calculus, light and optics, and universal gravitation.

1672
Elected fellow of the Royal Society of London.

1672
Sends Henry Oldenburg, secretary of the Royal Society, his first "Letter on Light and Colors," which is read to society members and criticized by the eminent English physicist Robert Hooke.

1679
Begins a correspondence with Robert Hooke on the problem of planetary motion.

1687
Publishes his single greatest work, the *Philosophia naturalis principia mathematica*, outlining his laws of motion and the law of universal gravitation.

1703
Elected president of the Royal Society of London.

1704
Publishes *Opticks*, in which he describes experiments and discoveries concerning the nature of light.

1727
Dies on March 20 in London.

LOST GENIUS

Part of a series of paintings that depict imaginary monuments of illustrious Englishmen, *Allegorical Monument to Sir Isaac Newton* shows Minerva and the Sciences weeping at the urn holding Newton's remains.

years old, Newton entered grammar school in Grantham, England. It was here that the young genius discovered his particular talent for building machines.

After reading *The Mysteries of Nature and Art* by John Bate and finding himself preoccupied by time and motion, Newton built a working model of a windmill, pow-

1800 – 1923

1800
With a prism and a thermometer, William Herschel performs first study of sunlight's spectrum and discovers the invisible infrared energy beyond the color spectrum.

1843
German astronomer Heinrich Schwabe describes his discovery of the sunspot cycle.

1868
William Huggins uses absorption lines to measure redshifting in stars, which gives the first indication of how fast stars are moving.

ered by a mouse running on a treadmill. He also designed and flew kites with lanterns attached to their tails, which frightened people. He boarded in the household of the local apothecary, a setting that fostered his interest in chemistry and alchemy.

At 19, Newton entered Trinity College, Cambridge, designated as a subsizar, a student receiving free board and tuition in exchange for menial service. His lowly social situation turned Newton even more inward. He avoided his fellow students and tutor, preferring to spend hours in his rooms studying, 18 hours a day, 7 days a week. Studiousness became a lifelong habit, and by the end of his days, Newton amassed a library of 1,600 to 1,800 volumes.

The core curriculum at Trinity College leaned distinctly toward an Aristotelian point of view. Newton adopted an attitude best expressed in the popular saying that he wrote into his notebook: "Plato and Aristotle are my friends, but my best friend is truth."

A year into his studies, Newton began studying mathematics. It was not long before he had begun developing his own ideas, the seeds of calculus, the mathematical science for which he is renowned.

The black plague overwhelmed England in 1665, and the doors to Trinity College closed for two years. Newton returned to Woolsthorpe. There he spent his days in mathematical and philosophical thought. It was during this time that Newton developed calculus, investigated the nature of light, and began conceiving his ideas about the physics of motion. During this period as well, the famous apple is said to have fallen, causing the flash of insight about gravity and the orbit of the moon.

According to the legend Newton told in his later years, he was walking in the orchard at Woolsthorpe when he saw an apple fall. He wondered if the force that draws a falling apple to the ground could be the same force that draws the moon toward Earth and keeps it in its orbit. He deduced that the strength of this force decreased as the square of the distance between the two objects in question increased, whether those objects were an apple and Earth or the moon and Earth.

1901
German physicist Karl Schwarzschild begins work on the foundations of black hole theory.

1905-1907
Ejnar Hertzsprung creates a standard of measurement for the brightness of stars, showing the relationship between color and magnitude.

1923
Edwin Hubble discovers a variable star in the Andromeda nebula (or galaxy) and proves that galaxies exist outside our own.

HALLEY

Eminent British astronomer Edmund Halley played a key role in spurring on Isaac Newton to write the *Principia*. Not only did Halley encourage Newton to publish his work, he also funded its printing.

See page 229 for more information on Stephen Hawking.

Newton spent a long time trying to figure out how this force worked, but the final resolution would not come for another 20 years.

When Newton returned to Trinity College, he shared his findings with his mentor, Isaac Barrow, who had already recognized his student's genius. Approaching retirement, Barrow lobbied for Newton to take over his position, and in 1669, Newton was appointed the Lucasian Professor of Mathematics at Trinity College, Cambridge, the same position held by physicist Stephen Hawking today.

By 1671, Newton had built the first reflecting telescope and had published papers on light and color. These papers generated a great deal of controversy, in particular evoking criticism from the eminent English physicist Robert Hooke (1635-1703), who attacked Newton's findings because they contradicted some of his own work on the science of color. Angered, Newton retreated further into himself and vowed never to publish again.

He continued to hone his theories in isolation until Edmund Halley, another English physicist, visited him in 1684. Just two years before, a very bright comet had appeared in the night sky. Halley wondered if this comet was the same that had been seen in 1531 and in 1607. All three circled the sun in the opposite direction from the planets. He needed an accurate method of calculating the orbits he observed, to prove whether the comets were one and the same.

A few months earlier, Halley had met with two distinguished scientists, both fellow members of the honorific Royal Society in London: Christopher Wren, the noted architect of St. Paul's Cathedral, and Newton's early rival, Robert Hooke. The three men had had a heated discussion about the laws governing the motion of planets in their orbits, in the midst of which Hooke declared that he had derived proof from Kepler's laws that gravity was the force emanating from the sun that moved the planets in their orbits. But Hooke refused to share that proof.

Irritated, Halley decided to visit Newton in Cambridge, and their meeting spurred some of the greatest scientific work of all time. Halley asked Newton to consider what shape a planetary orbit would have if the force of attraction toward the sun were equal to one divided by the square of that planet's distance from the sun. Newton immediately replied, "An ellipse."

Astonished that Newton so easily claimed to have mathematically derived Kepler's third law, Halley asked Newton how he knew that the orbit was an ellipse. Newton replied that he had calculated it three years earlier and began looking for his written calculations. Unable to find them, Newton promised to reconstruct the work and send it.

Three months later, the proof arrived at Halley's home in Islington, near London. Halley urged Newton to publish it, but Newton felt the work was incomplete. "Now that I am upon this subject, I would gladly know the bottom of it before I publish my papers," he wrote Halley in January 1685. Newton spent the next 18 months, day and night, working on the problem. He often forgot to eat and slept only a few hours at a time. The result was his masterpiece, *Philosophiae naturalis principia mathematica*, or *Mathematical Principles of Natural Philosophy*, commonly referred to simply as the *Principia*. This book by Newton held discoveries that forever changed how we view the world around us.

Published with funding from Halley in 1687, the *Principia* outlined a new physics of motion and the concept of gravity. Newton made a great leap of thought by assuming, then proving, that the laws of motion are the same on Earth as they are in the heavens. Newton provided mathematical proof that we inhabit an orderly and knowable universe. Discovered and expressed more than 300 years ago, the basic tenets of Isaac Newton's laws of motion and universal gravitation are still used by today's scientists to calculate orbits and send spacecraft to other planets.

Newton's work united many previously isolated astronomical observations, discoveries, and theories. His work culminated the search begun by the ancient Greek philosophers many centuries before. In a letter to Robert Hooke dated February 5, 1675, Newton wrote, "If I have seen further [than others,] it is by standing upon the shoulders of giants." The comment predates the *Principia*; it referred to Newton's optical theories and was probably a thinly veiled jab at Hooke's contorted posture and small stature. It can be

EDMUND HALLEY

Astronomer, comet discoverer

1656
Born on November 8 in Haggerston, Shoreditch, near London, England.

1673
Studies at Queens College, Oxford.

1676
Voyages to the island of Saint Helena in the South Atlantic to catalog the stars of the Southern Hemisphere.

1678
After publishing his catalog of southern stars, is elected a fellow of the Royal Society.

1684
First visits Isaac Newton, marking the beginning of his important role in the study of gravitation.

1686
Publishes the first meteorological chart: a map of the world showing prevailing winds.

1698
Commands the ship *Paramour Pink* on the first sea voyage specifically planned for scientific purposes.

1701
Publishes the first magnetic chart of the Atlantic and Pacific regions.

1704
Appointed Savilian Professor of Geometry at Oxford.

1705
Publishes *Synopses of the Astronomy of Comets;* accurately predicts return of comet later named for him.

1720
Succeeds John Flamsteed as astronomer royal at Greenwich Royal Observatory.

1742
Dies on January 14 in Greenwich, England.

read to have greater meaning and application to Newton's work as a whole, however. Without Pythagoras, Copernicus, Galileo, Kepler, Brahe, and others, Newton would not have stood nearly so tall.

Isaac Newton became Sir Isaac in 1705, when Queen Anne knighted him. The latter half of his life was darkened by controversy, but his reputation withstood the fray. Sir Isaac Newton died on March 20, 1727, in London. He was buried with great ceremony in Westminster Abbey. A loner all his life, he affected millions with his work, as he left behind a legacy of physical laws and mathematical methods that proved essential to modern science and technology.

EARLY PLANET HUNTERS

Eleven years after Newton died, Friedrich Wilhelm Herschel was born to a modest though musical family in Hanover, Germany. As a child, Wilhelm (anglicized to William) spent long hours gazing at the night sky with his father. Astronomy fascinated him, but he found his first calling in music. In 1757, Herschel moved to England, where he first taught music and then, nine years later, accepted a position as the organist in the Octagon Chapel in the city of Bath.

Through his years of teaching and playing music, Herschel never lost his interest in the night sky. For a while it was nothing more than a casual stargazing hobby, but in 1773, at the age of 35, Herschel decided to build telescopes. He converted practically all the rooms in his house to workshops.

On March 4, 1774, Herschel gazed for the first time through his newly completed 5.5-foot reflecting telescope. The object in the eyepiece was the Orion Nebula. This moment marked the beginning of William Herschel's history-making astronomical career.

Herschel built several more telescopes, the largest measuring 40 feet in length and including a 49-inch mirror. On March 13, 1781, he spotted an object through one of his scopes. "In examining the small stars in the neighbourhood of HGeminorum, I perceived one that appeared visibly larger than the rest," he wrote in his notes. He thought he was viewing a comet.

After watching the object over several nights, he realized it was a new planet, visible as it moved out beyond the orbit of Saturn. In fact, William Herschel had discovered Uranus: the first new planet identified in recorded history.

He originally named the planet Georgium Sidus, or Georgian Star, to honor the king of England, George III. Later, however, he decided to adopt the name Uranus instead, in keeping with the tradition of naming planets after the gods of Greek mythology. The following year, the king appointed Herschel his royal astronomer. With the post came a modest pension, so Herschel no longer had to work as a musician. He devoted himself exclusively to astronomical research.

The idea that more than six planets might exist in the solar system

goes back nearly 200 years before the discovery of Uranus. In his quest for clockwork mechanisms moving the planets, Johannes Kepler discovered a disproportionately large gap between the orbits of Mars and Jupiter. For a highly religious man like Kepler, it seemed odd that God would have left so much empty space. He toyed with the idea that the gap in fact contained the orbit of an undiscovered planet.

A century later, Isaac Newton—who was also a highly religious man—likewise assumed the universe to be a stable system operating with predictable and well-defined mechanics. The gravitational forces brought into this system by massive Jupiter and Saturn had the

The French Royal
Observatory (shown
here, circa 1815-20)
was just one of the
observatories where
astronomers were
enlisted to participate
in the search for a
planet between Mars
and Jupiter.

professor of astronomy at Oxford University, published his work *Astronomiae elementa,* which outlined the idea that planetary orbits occur at regular intervals. In 1766, Johann Daniel Tierz (Latinized to Titius) revised Gregory's figures, and in 1772 the idea reached the German astronomer Johann Elert Bode. Building on Gregory's work, Bode developed a mathematical equation to express the interval at which planets would occur, now called Bode's law.

Through this work, Bode had become convinced that another planet orbited the sun between Mars and Jupiter. When Herschel discovered Uranus nine years later, the planet's orbit matched its predicted distance from the sun, according to Bode's law. And now the search to find a missing planet between the orbits of Mars and Jupiter was on. Baron Franz Xaver von Zach, court astronomer for the duke of Gotha, gathered together a group of German astronomers and enlisted investigators in observatories across Europe in the search.

Unaware of the concerted effort to find the presumed planet, Giuseppi Piazzi of Palermo, the main city of Sicily, was making his customary nightly observation of the stars on January 1, 1801, when he spotted an eighth-magnitude object. The celestial object appeared to show movement relative to the position of other stars over successive nights. But this was no star, Piazzi realized. He had discovered another member of the solar system. Distance calculations put it between the orbits of Mars and

potential to disrupt the overall structure, so they were banished by divine design to the outer recesses. For Newton, the gap between Mars and Jupiter provided evidence of how God had carefully created a stabilized system.

In the early part of the 18th century, 15 years after publication of the *Principia,* David Gregory,

THE LIFE OF STARS

Stars are gaseous balls of hydrogen and helium that emit radiation. They hold the basic building blocks of all matter within their cores. As the American astronomer Carl Sagan once said, "We are all star stuff."

The path taken by a star depends on its size and therefore its gravitational pull. Material streams into the core of a forming star; temperature and pressure increase. Once temperatures are high enough to ignite nuclear reactions, a star is born. New stars survive as long as they can fend off the relentless force of gravity that could collapse them.

Stars like our sun generate their energy by a proton-proton chain reaction that converts hydrogen into helium. A helium nucleus has roughly 0.7 percent less mass than the four hydrogen nuclei needed to create it, and the reaction converts that mass difference into energy. The sun transforms approximately 700 million tons of hydrogen into 695 million tons of helium every second. The remaining 5 million tons of matter are converted directly into energy, which radiates out from the core, counteracting the star's gravitational collapse. This gravity-radiation pressure balance is called hydrostatic equilibrium.

Once a star converts all of the hydrogen in its core to helium, the fire goes out. Without nuclear reactions there is no outward radiation pressure, and gravity begins to collapse the star. The core contracts and begins to heat up. Fresh hydrogen outside the star's core ignites to form a hydrogen-burning shell. The star is still contracting, which heats the shell and produces more energy. At this stage of its life, radiation pressure exceeds its gravitational collapse, and the star expands into a red giant, or even further into a supergiant. The star will spend the next few million years burning its hydrogen shell while its core gradually collapses and slowly heats up. If core temperatures reach 100 million kelvins (water boils at 373 kelvins), an explosion called helium flash occurs deep within the star's core, fusing three helium nuclei to form one carbon nucleus.

Eventually the helium is depleted, the core shuts down again, and a helium-burning shell surrounds the carbon core. At this stage the star is a bit unstable. It pulses and spews out gaseous matter that forms a ring or planetary nebula around its hot core. For stars as large as the sun, this is the end. The core slowly contracts to a carbon white dwarf and then, over thousands of millions of years, the white dwarf cools to a black dwarf.

When a star at least 20 times more massive than the sun converts all of its core helium to carbon, it begins to contract. When the core reaches 600 million kelvins, carbon burning begins in a flash that can rip the star apart. This cataclysmic supernova explosion thrusts the star's outer layers into space while its core contracts to a neutron star. If the star is even more massive, the core may contract into a black hole.

The Pleiades is a cluster of hot young blue stars located in the constellation Taurus (the Bull).

Jupiter. Piazzi named the object Ceres, after the goddess of the harvest, patron deity of Sicily.

Initially, Ceres was touted as the seventh planet in the solar system. But when Herschel viewed it through his large telescope, he discovered that Ceres was smaller than the Earth's moon. One year after Ceres was discovered, another small object was detected, orbiting at roughly the same distance from Earth. Heinrich Wilhelm Matthäus Olbers called the object he had discovered Pallas. Herschel calculated Pallas to be less than 111 miles across—far too small to be a planet.

In fact, Ceres and Pallas were asteroids, as Herschel called these small orbiting objects, neither planets nor stars. German astronomer Karl Ludwig Harding discovered another one, naming it Juno, on September 1, 1804; Olbers discovered Vesta three years later. To explain all these asteroids found where a missing planet should have been, Olbers proposed that the asteroids were fragments of a full-size planet that had once occupied the gap.

More than 60 years after the discovery of Uranus, a young British astronomer, John Couch Adams, began analyzing the planet's orbit. Herschel had serendipitously discovered Uranus in 1781, but a century earlier astronomers had seen and charted the planet as a star. Their early observational data, along with more than 60 years of data recorded since the identification of Uranus as a planet, yielded an orbit that wasn't following Newton's laws of motion.

One way to account for this discrepancy was to hypothesize the gravitational attraction of an undiscovered planet outside the orbit of Uranus. Adams calculated where the orbit and position of such a planet might be, and in October 1845 he sent his calculations off to astronomers at the Royal Observatory in Greenwich. Not taking the prediction seriously, Sir George Biddell Airy, the royal astronomer, put the papers aside. Meanwhile, French astronomer Urbain-Jean-Joseph Leverrier made the same calculations and enlisted the help of Johann Galle of the Berlin Observatory to confirm them. The

SPOTTING PLUTO

A 24-year-old Clyde Tombaugh proudly displays his home-built nine-inch Newtonian telescope. One month before this photo was taken, Tombaugh had discovered the planet Pluto.

would two people perceive the same event if one was moving and the other was not?

In 1905, Einstein introduced his theory of special relativity, which held that the laws of physics are the same for all observers, provided that their motion is uniform. Imagine sitting on a train, asleep. You wake up, look out the window, and see the train next to you slowly moving. For a moment, you can't tell if your train or the other one is moving. According to the principle of relativity, there is no experiment you can perform to decide if your train or the other train is moving.

See pages 205-06 for more information on joules.

All motion is relative. There is no way that by measuring the motion of objects you could tell whether the other train was at rest or moving at a steady velocity. Special relativity, in essence, makes the concept of being at rest meaningless. By the same token, the measurement of the speed of light relative to any observer will always have the same result, regardless of the observer's motion relative to the light source.

For objects at low speeds over short distances, Einstein's special theory produces the same predic-tions as Newton's laws of motion. It is only for objects moving very long distances or at very high velocities (near the speed of light) that predictions based on the two theories diverge. Newton's theory dealt with space and time separately, but it unified motion and gravity. Einstein's theory unified the three dimensions in space with the dimension of time.

Einstein's special theory of rela-tivity also produced a formula that connected energy with mass and the speed of light, $E = mc^2$ (E is energy, measured in a unit called joules; m is mass in kilograms; and c is the speed of light in meters per second). According to this equation, all matter in the universe is a form of energy, and all energy has mass.

In 1915, Einstein put forward a more general theory of relativity, which tackles the case of observers in an accelerated frame of reference and provides a new description of gravity. He questioned Newton's concept of gravity as an attractive force, proposing instead that gravity bends or curves the fabric of space-time. This curvature controls the natural motions of bodies in space.

1957 – 1995

1957
Russian satellite Sputnik 1 is launched, inaugurating the space race between the United States and the Soviet Union.

1961
Russian astronaut Yury Gagarin becomes the first human to orbit the Earth.

1965
Background radiation is discovered; scientists determine that it is the remnant of a "big bang" that took place when the universe began.

1967
Jocelyn Bell Burnell and Antony Hewish discover the first pulsar, a rapidly spinning neutron star that emits radio waves.

MATH FOR FUN

"When I have no special problem to occupy my mind," Albert Einstein once said, "I love to reconstruct proofs of mathematical and physical theorems that have long been known to me. There is no goal in this, merely an opportunity to indulge in the pleasant occupation of thinking."

Imagine space-time as a rubber sheet stretched across a frame. Place a bowling ball in the center, and the space-time rubber sheet bends, stretches, and curves to accommodate the mass of the ball.

Now imagine rolling a golf ball in a straight line across the sheet. If its velocity is high enough, the golf ball may escape the bowling ball's gravity well. If its velocity is slow, the golf ball rolls toward the bowling ball, trapped in its gravity well. If the golf ball's velocity is somewhere in between, it may slingshot around the ball and travel in a direction that is 90 degrees (or some angle in between) from its original line of motion. Matter curves space-time, while space-time determines how matter moves.

Einstein predicted that light from a distant star would bend as it passed the sun's large mass. Sir Arthur

1969
The Apollo 11 mission lands on the moon; Neil Armstrong and Buzz Aldrin become the first men to explore the lunar surface.

1979-1989
NASA Voyager probes return close-up images of Jupiter, Saturn, Uranus, and Neptune.

1990
The *Magellan* probe reaches Venus and maps nearly 98 percent of the planet's surface with radar.

1995
Astronomers discover the first planet outside our solar system.

See page 64 for more information about Stanley Eddington.

BINARY STAR

A binary (or double) star is a pair of stars that orbit around a common center of gravity. Astronomers speculate that up to half the stars in our Milky Way galaxy are part of binary star or even multi-star systems.

Stanley Eddington, an astrophysicist, set out to prove it. On May 19, 1919, a total solar eclipse occurred in West Africa. As the sun darkened, the stars came into view. Eddington shot several photographic plates of stars near the limb of the darkened sun. He examined the images, measuring each star's position, looking for a change of one second of arc. For useful results, Eddington needed an image that included stars not only near the sun but also farther away. He was lucky: The eclipse occurred in a region of the sky containing the distant Hyades star cluster, "by far the best star-field encountered," as Eddington put it. Otherwise, it might have been years before Einstein's prediction was proved correct.

The general theory of relativity was also confirmed when Einstein used it to calculate slight deviations in Mercury's orbit. Johannes Kepler knew that Mercury's orbit was elliptical, but he didn't envision how the orbit's axis sweeps around in a movement called precession. Astronomers recognized that Mercury's orbit was advancing faster than Newton's laws predicted.

Einstein tackled the problem by first calculating how much the sun's mass curves space-time in the region of Mercury's orbit, then calculating how Mercury moves through that region. He discovered that Mercury's orbit was slipping forward due to the curvature of space-time. Today we know that the orbits of Venus, Earth, and the asteroid Icarus all slip forward due to the curvature of space-time near the sun.

Another result of Einstein's general theory is the concept of gravity waves. Einstein predicted that the force of gravity exerted extremely weak and wavelike disturbances that propagate at the speed of light. Similar to waves on the ocean, gravity waves are ripples in the fabric of space-time, generated when a mass is accelerated, oscillated, or violently disturbed. One of the weakest forces of nature, the only gravity waves that can be detected are those produced by highly massive objects, such as close binary star systems with massive neutron stars, black holes, and supernovas.

STAR LIGHT, STAR BRIGHT

In the early 19th century, astronomers were focusing on the solar system, observing and cataloging the positions and magnitudes of stars, continuing work that had begun in antiquity. Star explosions observed by Tycho in 1572 and Kepler in 1604 led to the premise that stars could change, but astronomers learned little more about stars for centuries.

In 1814 Joseph von Fraunhofer, an optician living in Munich, developed the first simple spectroscope, an instrument that separates light. Sunlight entered the spectroscope's narrow slit and then passed through a prism, which refracted the light into a solar spectrum with some 600 dark lines. Fraunhofer's discovery aroused widespread interest among physicists and chemists as well as astronomers.

Gustav Kirchhoff, a German physicist, and his colleague Robert Bunsen, a chemist, discovered in 1859 that each set of those dark

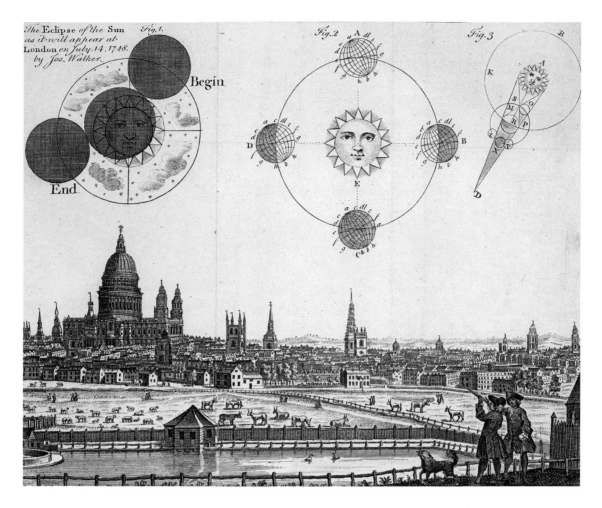

The Eclipse of the Sun as it will appear at London on July 14. 1748. by Jos. Walker.

Fig.1

Begin

End

Fig.2

Fig.3

lines was associated with individual chemical elements. They identified the lines of many metals and discovered two new elements in the process: cesium and rubidium, names derived from the Latin for bluish gray and red.

In subsequent experiments, Kirchhoff began to understand how the lines were produced. He passed the sun's spectrum through a yellow sodium flame, expecting the bright flame would fill the dark sodium line in the solar spectrum. Instead, the line became darker. Kirchhoff inferred that the sun's atmosphere, like the sodium flame, contained sodium vapor that absorbed the yellow wavelength of light. Today, we call these dark spectral lines absorption lines.

Kirchhoff's sense of absorption lines required the existence of a hot-gas atmosphere surrounding the sun. Laboratory experiments had shown that white-hot objects or molten metals produced a continuous white-light spectrum. Yet surface features such as sunspots, bright patches called plages (or, formerly, bright flocculi), and ever-changing filaments seemed to be atmospheric in nature, not arising from an extremely hot solid object

HERSCHEL

NEWTON
1643–1727

The Griffith Observatory in the Hollywood Hills above Los Angeles, California, includes a monument to the great astronomers of world history.

or liquid metal. Over time, experimental physicists discovered that hot gases under high pressure also produce a continuous spectrum.

As astronomers pointed their ever increasing arsenal of instruments toward the sun, more questions arose about the nature of our star. Many were astonished, during a total solar eclipse, to observe a bright, white, filamentary corona surrounding the moon's dark disk. At the same time, larger instruments detected solar prominences, plumes of gas erupting as bright projections beyond the sun's limb. Were these features on the sun or part of an atmosphere around the moon? Continued spectroscopic observations, as well as advances in physics, gradually revealed they were the result of physical processes occurring in different layers of the sun.

In 1866 Joseph Norman Lockyer, British amateur astronomer, found a simple way to observe the sun in detail. He projected a telescopic image of the sun onto a screen with a thin slit in front of a spectroscope. He could move the slit so that light from different solar features would pass through. The strength of the spectral lines when he looked at dark sunspots was weaker than when he looked at areas just outside them. Since spectral line strength varies with temperature, Lockyer concluded that sunspots were cooler regions.

He also scanned the sun's limb for prominences. Lockyer theorized that these apparent red flames were actually hot gas, which would emit a distinctive spectral pattern of bright lines. While observing from his Wimbledon backyard, he found what he was looking for. "I saw a bright line flash into the field," he recalled. He analyzed the characteristics of the line and concluded that the solar prominences were composed primarily of hydrogen.

In August 1868 Pierre Jules Cesar Jansen, a French astronomer, noticed a bright yellow line in the spectra of the sun during an eclipse. Two months later, Lockyer also detected the line. No such pattern had ever been observed, so Lockyer concluded that it must be caused by an element not found or identified on Earth. British chemist Edward Frankland later named the element helium, after *helios*, Greek for sun.

The latter half of the 19th century saw the construction of many new observatories and the regular use of photography in astronomy. The first photograph of the moon was a daguerreotype, taken in 1840 by English astronomer John William Draper. His son, American astronomer Henry Draper, photographed the spectrum of the bright star Vega in the constellation Lyra in 1872 . As more stellar spectra were gathered, scientists were amassing a picture of the general composition and temperature of a wide variety of stars.

Building on the work of Italian astronomer Pietro Angelo Secchi, Draper developed a system that classified stellar spectra into 16 groups. Upon his untimely death in 1882, Draper's widow funded the continuation of his work at the Harvard College Observatory. Edward Charles Pickering, the observatory's director, began a spectroscopic survey of the entire sky. Pickering hired many assistants to work on the project, the majority of whom were women. By the late 1880s, when women were not yet able to vote, upwards of 15 women worked at the observatory. For 25 cents an hour, they analyzed thousands of photographic images of stars and stellar spectra, doing complex computations to ascertain the position and composition of each star.

After Pickering's death, one of these women, Annie Jump Cannon, continued to review photographic plates containing stellar spectra. She would analyze the spectra, then call out each star's classification to an assistant, who would record it. She became exceptionally quick and accurate at the work, classifying up to three stars a minute. Working from 1915 to 1924 on what would be called the Henry Draper Catalog, Cannon compiled and ordered the spectra of some 225,300 stars. Her classification system—O, B, A, F, G, K, M, inspiring the mnemonic phrase "Oh, Be A Fine Girl/Guy, Kiss Me!"—is still taught to astronomy students today.

By 1910, Cannon's classification was widely accepted. Astronomers began wondering if a star's intrinsic brightness could be related to its spectral type. In 1911, astronomers Ejnar Hertzsprung and Hans Rosenberg plotted that relationship for members of the Pleiades and Hyades star clusters in the constellation of Taurus, the bull. Princeton astronomer Henry Norris Russell soon did the same for stars whose distance measures were fairly reliable.

The result of their shared work is the Hertzsprung-Russell diagram, which demonstrates relationships between a star's spectral type (an indication of its temperature) and its brightness or luminosity.

Luminosity is charted along the vertical axis, temperature along the horizontal. Stars in the upper left are hot, young, giant blue stars; while those in the upper right are cooler red giants and supergiants near the end of their lives. Stars in the lower left are white dwarfs: hot, small stars that are very faint and at the end of their life cycle. Down the middle of the diagram, from the upper left to the lower right, runs the main sequence, where roughly 90 percent of all stars are positioned.

Astronomers still had little idea of how a star shines, though. By 1917, Eddington was working on a theory of a star's energy production and evolution. With a strong background in astronomy, physics, and mathematics and with knowledge of atomic physics and the special theory of relativity, Eddington was able to demonstrate that heat is transported by radiation in stars. He also reasoned that at the high temperatures found in stellar interiors, electrons would be stripped from their nuclei, forming what physicists today call a plasma.

Finally, Eddington grasped the relationship between a star's mass and its luminosity. He argued that its mass is converted to energy, according to Einstein's expression, $E = mc^2$. He outlined his findings in his 1926 book, *The Internal Constitution of the Stars*. Eddington believed that stars converted hydrogen to helium, but the knowledge of subatomic physics was insufficient to provide a mechanism for this conversion.

It wasn't until late 1939, when Hans Albrecht Bethe published his paper "Energy Production in Stars," that scientists knew about stars' energy sources. Bethe suggested that more than 98 percent of the sun's energy comes from the conversion of hydrogen into helium. He was right: Every second the sun converts 700 million tons of hydrogen into 695 million tons of helium. The remaining five million tons of matter (roughly 600 times the weight of water flowing over Niagara Falls in one second) converts to pure energy.

COSMIC CONUNDRUMS

While Eddington and Bethe were probing stars' internal furnaces, Edwin Powell Hubble was setting the stage for a new cosmology. The son of a lawyer and insurance agent, Hubble was born in Marshfield, Missouri. He entered the University of Chicago in 1906; attended Queens College, Oxford, as a Rhodes scholar; and returned to Chicago for his Ph.D. in 1914, studying faint nebulae at Yerkes Observatory. After two years in the U.S. Infantry during World War I, Hubble joined the staff of Mount Wilson Observatory. There he remained for the rest of his career, using a 100-inch telescope to observe and classify nebulae.

At the time there were two theories as to the nature of the faint fuzzy patches visible through tele-

MESSIER CATALOG

The Messier catalog is a list of some 109 permanent deep-sky objects, including galaxies, nebulae, and star clusters. A helpful guide to non-professional astronomers, the catalog was compiled by Charles Messier and Pierre Mechain between 1717 and 1786.

scopes, first cataloged by Charles Messier and then by William Herschel. One camp believed they were clouds of interstellar gas in the Milky Way; the other camp thought they were galaxies outside the Milky Way. It turns out that both were right, for both kinds of objects fall into the group broadly classified as nebulae. In 1922, Hubble was the first to classify diffuse nebulae of the Milky Way, distinguishing them as either reflection or emission nebulae. On October 4, 1923, Hubble resolved stars in what is known today as the Andromeda galaxy. Four months later he discovered a Cepheid variable star in Andromeda.

First identified by the British astronomer John Goodricke in 1784, Cepheid variables are large, pulsating yellow stars whose brightness can range from 0.1 to 2 magnitudes. Their periods of pulsation, bright to faint to bright again, can range from 2 days to 60.

In 1912 Henrietta Swan Leavitt, one of Pickering's assistants, was determining the number of Cepheid variable stars in the Small Magellanic Cloud, a satellite galaxy of our own Milky Way. Looking at photographic plates taken in Peru, Leavitt noticed that the periods of Cepheid variable stars related to their average brightness: Stars with longer

CATALOGING THE STARS

Curator of photographs at the Harvard College Observatory, Annie Jump Cannon cared for 300,000 photographic plates, which she used to classify the spectra of some 225,300 stars.

periods were brighter than those with shorter periods. Since all the stars in the Magellanic Cloud were about the same distance from Earth, their intrinsic brightness had to relate to their periods, not their distance away.

American astronomer Harlow Shapley recognized the importance of this period-luminosity relationship. He began searching for stars in globular clusters—large globes of densely packed stars holding tens of thousands to a million stars each. Shapley called the Cepheid

variables "lighthouses" and used them to determine the distance of globular clusters from Earth. Hubble used the findings on Cepheid variables to prove that the so-called nebulae were actually galaxies far beyond any object in the Milky Way. Observing Cepheid variables in Andromeda, he was able to derive its distance from Earth as 490,000 light-years.

Hubble's observations of galaxies had even greater implications because of Einstein's general theory of relativity. Astronomers at the

THE BIG BANG

The big bang theory is often portrayed as the definitive model for the formation of our universe. In fact, it is an assumption based on what has been observed in the universe. The theory began to take shape with Alexander Friedmann and Abbé Georges Lemaître in the 1920s; it was later revised by George Gamow in the 1940s. The name "big bang" stems from a sarcastic comment made in the 1950s by astronomer Fred Hoyle, who expressed doubts about the theory.

Artists can only speculate as to how the big bang appeared or what black holes look like.

atomic nucleus. As the universe expanded, the gamma rays' wavelengths grew longer, which lowered their energy and cooled the universe. While this ferment of hot gas and radiation continued to cool, nuclear particles and then atomic nuclei formed. The protons, neutrons, and electrons that make up the structure of matter in our universe were created during the first four seconds after the big bang.

Within 30 minutes' time, all these nuclear reactions had stopped. Roughly 25 percent of the universe's mass was helium, 75 percent hydrogen—the same helium-hydrogen ratio found in the oldest stars today. A million years later, the universe had cooled and nuclei and electrons combined into atoms. Photons from this time still appear today: We call them cosmic background radiation.

Because the physics of the universe before the big bang is unknown, cosmologists begin their speculations by asking what the universe was like a few ten-millionths of a second after. At this time, the universe was filled with high-energy gamma rays at temperatures of ten billion kelvins and at densities close to that of an

SKY SURVEY
Edwin Hubble examines the 48-inch telescope at the Palomar Observatory in San Diego County, California. He is making final preparations for the 1958 sky survey sponsored by the National Geographic Society, which resulted in the first definitive photographic atlas of the heavens.

time questioned whether the universe was static, expanding, or contracting. Hubble measured the spectra of 46 galaxies and found that their spectra had been displaced toward the red end of the spectrum, or redshifted.

To understand redshift, imagine yourself sitting at a railroad crossing, waiting for an oncoming train to pass. As the train approaches, its whistle has a higher pitch; as it pass-es by, the pitch lowers. The whistle is sending out a steady tone whose sound waves move out in a circle. The change in pitch arises from the train's motion. As the train moves, the center of each new sound wave moves with it. The whistle's sound waves bunch up in the train's direction of motion (higher frequency) and spread out behind (lower frequency). The phenomenon is called the Doppler effect, named after

Christian Doppler, the Austrian physicist who first described it, in 1842. Six years later, French physicist Hippolyte Fizeau suggested that light waves would behave the same way—and he was correct.

In 1929, Hubble announced that the universe was expanding. He offered proof of the theory pub-lished two years earlier by Georges Henri Lemaître, a Belgian-born Catholic priest and astronomer who had come to the same conclusion, using the framework of Einstein's general theory of relativity.

The primary opposition to Lemaître's theory was the steady-state theory proposed by Fred Hoyle

NEBULAE

Spend time watching the delicate tendrils of cirrus clouds intertwine under the force of winds in the upper atmosphere, or the billowing formation of cumulus clouds on a hot afternoon, and you'll better understand nebulae.

The word "nebula" derives from the Latin word for cloud. These regions of interstellar gas and dust may become huge, billowing mole-cular clouds where new stars form, or they may be the graceful result of a star's violent death. Nebulae provide the building blocks for stars, galaxies, and planets, while their composition and delicate patterns reveal the nature of stars forming in their interiors or of star death, which may have formed them.

The emission nebula NGC 281, in Cassiopeia, includes a small open cluster of stars.

There are three types of nebu-lae: reflection, emission, and absorption. Reflection nebulae glow by the scattered starlight of nearby stars. Dust particles within the gas cloud disperse starlight, giving the nebula a faint glow. Most reflection nebulae appear blue, because the shorter waves of blue light are scat-tered more efficiently than longer-wavelength red light. Because the glow of reflection nebulae is rather faint, most of them can be detected only by making long photo-graphic exposures of the sky.

Emission nebulae are hot, discrete clouds. Made primarily of ionized hydrogen, they origin-ate when ultraviolet radiation, released from young stars, removes electrons from hydrogen atoms—a process called photoionization. Emission nebulae glow with the light of excited atoms and ions, similar to the excitation of atoms of gas inside a neon sign. The process of photo-ionization takes quite a bit of energy, so only the hottest stars can produce ultra-violet photons in the numbers needed to make the nebulae glow. Emission nebulae usually occur around hot, young, blue stars.

Visible as dark regions along the Milky Way, absorption or dark nebulae are dense clouds of gas and dust that have neither hot, young stars within their envelope to ionize the gas nor nearby stars whose starlight they could reflect. Instead, we see dark nebulae as silhouettes against the backdrop of the Milky Way or bright nebulae.

The smallest dark nebulae are called "Bok glob-ules," named after the Dutch-American astro-nomer Bart Bok, who first studied these objects in the 1930s. They are less than three light-years in diameter, with a mass between 10 and 100 times the mass of the sun.

and others in 1948. In fact, it was Hoyle who first sarcastically dubbed Lemaître's theory the "big bang." The name stuck.

The steady-state cosmological model asserts that the universe has no beginning and will never end. It employs the idea of a "flat" universe in which space expands at a constant rate. In a steady-state model, all points in the universe appear the same at any given time. This implies a constant average density of matter in the universe. To compensate for expansion, matter must be continually created at a constant rate.

According to the big bang model of the universe, all matter and radiation originated in a theoretical point where density, the force of gravity, and the curvature of space-time are all infinite. This point, called a singularity, has no radius or size. The force of gravity is so great that the fabric of space-time curves in on itself. The laws of physics as we know them do not exist in a singularity.

Some assume that this theory means that an explosion happened at the "center" of the universe or at some point "over there," then everything expanded to fill the space. That interpretation is wrong. The big bang theory actually involves the entire universe: time, space, everything. In one instant, all space and time rapidly began to expand or inflate—and it isn't over yet; the universe is still expanding. Picture the expansion like raisin bread dough. The dough is the fabric of space-time, and as it rises, the raisins (galaxies) move away from each other in all directions.

The debate between these opposing theories raged for 20 years. Then, in 1965, two engineers with Bell Labs accidentally discovered residual background radiation from the early universe. The very existence of this cosmic microwave background, or CMB, radiation had been predicted in the big bang theory.

In 1989, NASA launched the Cosmic Background Explorer (COBE) to map this radiation over the entire sky. COBE found tiny differences in background radiation, fluctuations no more than 30 millionths of a degree warmer or cooler than average. These indicated structures that existed around the time when the first galaxies were forming, further validating the big bang theory.

Launched on June 30, 2001, NASA's Wilkinson Microwave Anisotropy Probe (WMAP) charts signals that inform us of the conditions of the early universe. WMAP measures small variations in the temperature of the cosmic microwave background, revealing the size, matter content, age, geometry, past, and perhaps even future of the universe.

After three years of continuous observations, WMAP found evidence to support the concept of not just an expanding but an accelerating universe at the time of the big bang. In the very first moments following the birth of the universe, in a mere fraction of a second, WMAP observations suggest the universe grew by a factor of 10^{50}—that's a 1 with 50 zeros after it!

DOPPLER SHIFT

This principle describes the shift in frequency of electromagnetic waves emitted from an object based on its movement relative to an observer. When the object moves away, causing a lower frequency, it is known as a redshift. Likewise, when the object moves closer, causing a higher frequency, it is known as a blueshift.

As time passed, the force of gravity began slowing the expansion down. With all of the visible matter (matter that we can see, such as stars, nebulae, galaxies, etc.) and dark matter (invisible matter whose existence is inferred by its gravitational presence) in the universe, you would think that gravity is still applying the brakes. But that is not the case.

In the mid-1990s, two separate research teams—the Supernova Cosmology Project and the High-Z Supernovae Search team—set out to measure this deceleration. Both teams used very distant supernovas to measure the expansion rate, and what they found was startling.

The supernovas appear farther away than they should be, according to current theories. These findings suggest that the rate of expansion of the universe is speeding up, not slowing down! If the expansion of the universe is

THE CURVATURE OF SPACE-TIME

Newton assumed that the geometry of the universe was flat; Einstein made no such assumption. In fact, his general theory of relativity predicts that the entire universe is shaped with a general curvature.

There are three possible geometric shapes for the universe. It is hard for us to imagine the actual shape of these configurations, but we can picture them in two-dimensional space, as if drawn on a flat piece of paper.

The first shape, called a closed universe, has a positive curvature. This configuration has a finite volume with no edge and looks spherical in two dimensions—imagine a flat photograph of Earth. As on the surface of the Earth, in a closed universe you could travel in a straight line and eventually end up where you started. With enough mass, eventually the expansion of such a universe would

The positive curvature of a closed universe produces a universe of finite volume and no edge.

stop, and it would begin to contract gravitationally, ultimately shrinking down to a point where space and time are infinitely distorted. This endpoint, the opposite of the big bang, is called the "big crunch." Some speculate that the universe oscillates between expansion and contraction in a process dubbed the "big bounce."

The second possible shape, an open universe, has negative curvature. Taking the the shape of a hyperboloid with negative curvature, it bends away from itself. It would appear like a saddle in two dimensions. Gravity would be too weak to halt its expansion.

The third possible geometric shape, called a flat universe, has zero curvature. Here, too, the universe is infinite and expansion would continue forever, albeit proceeding a bit more slowly than it would in the case of an open universe.

accelerating, some type of antigravity force has to be driving it. Some scientists believe that "dark energy," radiating from deep space, provides the repulsive force.

Albert Einstein first proposed such an antigravity force in his theory of general relativity. Called the cosmological constant (not to be confused with the Hubble constant), this repulsive force was a mathematical fix that helped balance the universe against its own gravity. Simply put, general relativity predicted that the universe must either expand or contract, but Einstein thought the universe was static. Adding this antigravity cosmological constant brought balance to the equation.

After Lemaître proposed and Edwin Hubble observed the expansion of the universe, Einstein removed the cosmological constant from his conception of the universe and its physical laws. He regretted adding the term to his original equation and said he thought of it as his "greatest scientific blunder."

Now it seems he may have been on the right track after all. Recent observations by the Hubble Space Telescope and WMAP have found that the bulk of the universe is made of dark energy. Current estimates of the universe's mass-to-energy budget place dark energy at roughly 70 percent, while visible and dark matter make up less than 30 percent. In short, most of the universe is made of something we know virtually nothing about.

The nature of dark energy is important to the fate of the universe. If dark energy is stable, the universe will continue to expand and accelerate forever. If dark energy is unstable, the universe could ultimately come apart. Dubbed the "big rip," this doomsday scenario portrays the universe accelerating to speeds that rip apart the fabric of space-time to a point where even atoms are torn apart. On the flip side, if dark energy is dynamic, it could gradually decelerate and transform itself into an attractive force, sucking the universe back in on itself and moving toward a "big crunch" or implosion, the opposite of a big bang.

FROM HEAVENLY SPHERES TO COSMIC IMPLOSION

From antiquity through the Renaissance, astronomers spent their time cataloging observations, relating them to earthly events, and devising geometrical models to reproduce the movements that they observed. Kepler's laws of planetary motion spurred investigations into the forces behind these motions. Newton's laws of gravity unified many disparate theories, illustrated cause and effect, and showed that physical laws are the same on Earth and in space.

Newton's laws also gave mathematicians and scientists a sense of certainty. In the early 19th century, tiny cracks began to appear. By the 20th century, Einstein's theories of special and general relativity clearly showed that any apparent certainty in Newton's laws might apply in our own mundane lives but did not pertain in the worlds of the very large or very small—the realms where science was now making its boldest discoveries.

THE HUBBLE VIEW
The Hubble Space Telescope was launched in 1990. It orbits the Earth every 97 minutes at an altitude of about 600 kilometers. Its instruments include cameras and spectrographs as well as mirrors, which focus and magnify light.

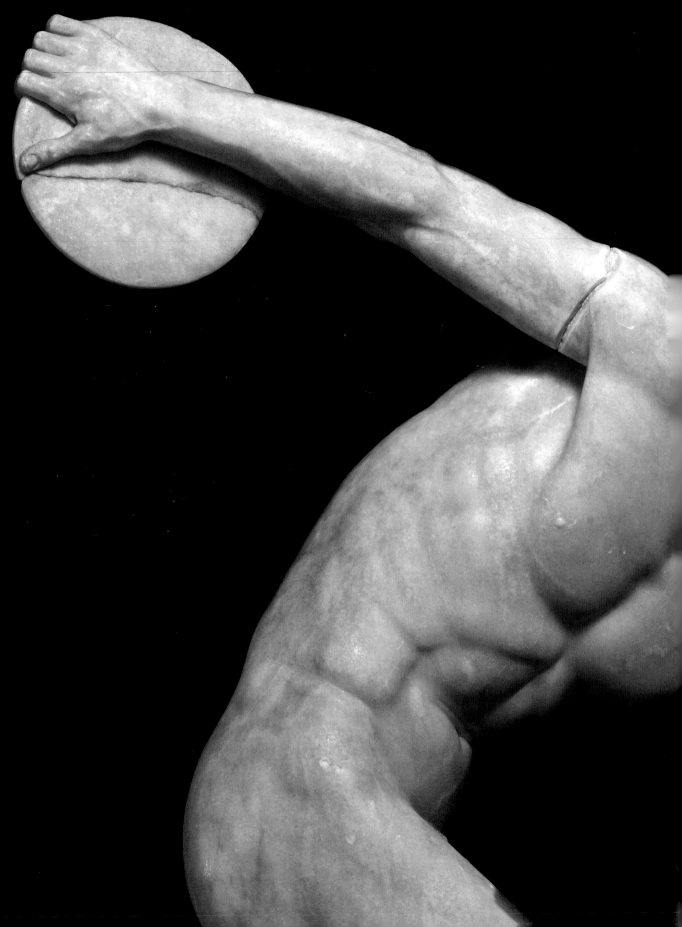

2

The Human Body

JUST AS THE COPERNICAN REVOLUTION installed the sun as the center of the universe, it might be said that centuries of biological and physiological revolutions have put the human body at the center of another closely related universe, one that began with the precursors of life in stellar dust and evolved into a remarkably complex collection of atoms, cells, molecules, amino acids, and proteins. Each human body is indeed a wondrous biological galaxy, far more than a mere bundle of flesh and bones and blood. Its many components are seen and unseen, and its intricate mechanisms of diverse nature, a puzzlement for thousands of years, are still being scrutinized.

Aided by today's sophisticated technology, knowledge about the human body has surfaced at a pace that could not have been believed by the ancients. Still, spurred by insight and intuition, along with real, albeit rudimentary, science, there was among them no lack of theorizing about the makeup and function of the body's parts and the nature of the diseases that could plague them. A few of their theories have proved to be remarkably accurate, others woefully erroneous.

"I consider the Body as a System of Tubes and Glands," observed the English essayist

Joseph Addison in 1711, "or, to use
a more Rustick phrase, a bundle of
Pipes and Strainers, fitted to make
a proper Engine for the Soul to
work with." Ralph Waldo Emerson
used equally image-laden language.
"The human body," he wrote, "is
the magazine of inventions, the
patent office, where are the models
from which every hint is taken.
All the tools and engines on earth
are only extensions of its limbs and
senses."

THE DAWN OF MEDICINE

Comparing the amalgam that is the
human body to a piece of intricate
machinery—and the brain to a
computer, as we in this electronics-
oriented society so often do—is
understandable. We are, after all,
formidable engines of phenomenal
organic energy, masterpieces of
mechanical and architectural
design and efficiency. But to primitive peoples, whose association with
machinery was limited to say the
least, the body was a standing miracle, a work of magic whose mysteries were tediously unraveled bit by
bit through observations of human
remains opened by battle wounds

and decomposition, and through
examination of dead animals.
Indeed, it is perhaps no stretch to
suggest that knowledge of anatomy,
albeit rudimentary, got a kick-start
at cook-fires and meal sites where
bones, blood, meat, organs, and
entrails were laid bare for all to see.

Egyptian priest-mummifiers,
2,000 and more years before
Christ, expanded anatomical
knowledge, if only for their own
purposes. Their methods of
preparing the human body for
burial were elaborate, though
crude. First, they drew the brain
out through the nostrils with an
iron hook; next, they cut slits in
the limbs and removed the muscles; then they stuffed the empty
skin with resin-soaked papyrus.
Organs, viscera, and heart arteries
were extracted through an incision
in the left flank. (Early on, the
heart was left behind, but this
practice changed later.)

While early Egyptian priests
mummified some 70 million
corpses, according to one source,
they handed down only fragments
of what they must have learned
from their many eviscerations.

2600 B.C. – A.D. 145

ca 2600 B.C.
Imhotep, ancient
Egyptian healer,
describes numerous
ailments, including
tuberculosis and
appendicitis, and
lists remedies.

ca 1550 B.C.
The Ebers Papyrus
documents Egyptian
medical practice and
knowledge, ranging from
arthritis and diabetes to
parasitic infections and
crocodile bites.

ca 1400 B.C.
Ayurvedic medicine
originates, a traditional
Hindu system that takes
a holistic approach,
rooted in early
Vedic culture.

REMEDIES
The Egyptian Ebers Papyrus (ca 1550 B.C.), which lists some 700 remedies, is thought to have been dictated to a scribe by a head pharmacist as he directed the gatherers and preparers of drugs, as depicted in this painting.

What they did leave behind, however, was a trove of medical papyri that attests to ancient Egypt's place in the history of medicine. The seeds, if not the full flowering, of medicine were certainly to be found in the hieratic script, or abridged hieroglyphics, used by the priests.

One of the most important of these ancient texts was the so-called Ebers Papyrus, allegedly buried between the legs of a mummy and acquired in 1872 by the German Egyptologist Georg Ebers. Dating to around 1550 B.C. it was a scroll more than 65 feet long, covered with columns

ca 420 B.C.
Greek physician Hippocrates begins to study the human body, greatly advancing the science of medicine.

ca 220 B.C.
Erasistratus of Ceos describes the divisions of the brain and the nervous system.

ca A.D. 100
Rufus of Ephesus accurately describes the pulse and diseases of the kidney and bladder.

ca A.D. 145
Greek physician Claudius Galen refines the theory of the humors, a theory of human health and disease that prevails for 1,400 years.

HIPPOCRATES

The legendary Greek Hippocrates served as the model of the caring, dedicated, analytical physician who considered disease subject to knowledgable treatment.

of closely packed script. Its introduction suggested its value as an early scientific document. "Here," it read, "begins the book on the preparation of medicine for all parts of the body."

The Ebers Papyrus was encyclopedic in scope, more than a hundred pages full of incantations against disease but also, more important, detailed lists of a variety of diseases, case histories, and some 700 remedies. Here, one could read of painful swellings, arthritic "hardening of the limbs," parasitic infections, tumors, diabetes, birth control, and treatments for ear, eye, and nose disorders, burns, and crocodile bites.

While the ancient Egyptians were on the verge of achieving some significant medical breakthroughs—and as impressive as their medical papyri were, considering the time they were written—they were by no means experts in actual anatomy and physiology. The experts would arrive hundreds of years later, when opening and exploring of the human body became not a religious rite of preservation but a scientific method aimed at truly understanding the body and its workings. Moreover, joining the priests and physicians in the investigation and in pursuing the healing arts was a band of natural philosophers who regarded medicine as a branch of their discipline.

One of these philosopher-scientists was Alcmaeon, around 500 B.C. a pupil of Pythagoras and the philosopher and mathematician who is credited as the first to suggest that the brain was the center of the body's "higher activities." Men like Alcmaeon broke with the traditional train of thought, which regarded disease as a matter of fate, astrological accident, or supernatural influence.

An innovator who tried to view illness in exclusively physical terms, Alcmaeon was probably the first to dissect the human body. He theorized that disease was caused by a fundamental imbalance between certain opposed qualities in the body such as heat and cold or wetness and dryness. He accepted Pythagoras's view of the centrality of the brain, adding that it was the origin of the nerves. He discovered the optic nerve and the part that later became known as the Eustachian tube, which connects the throat and nose to the middle ear; he suggested that the head of a fetus develops first.

Alcmaeon's name may not be widely known among laypersons, but that of Hippocrates certainly is. Hippocratus may well be the most celebrated physician of antiquity; he is generally known as the father of medicine. Very little is actually known of Hippocrates's life, and the writings that are attributed to him may well have been the work of several individuals of different periods; they are thus often referred to simply as the Hippocratic Collection.

No matter, for Hippocrates, whether a shadowy figure or a heroic legend, was devoted to observing his patients and gathering the information necessary to understand disease. The art of healing was his forte, aided and abetted by the power of nature.

Like Alcmaeon, Hippocrates believed in the central role of the brain. He recognized the value of rest, of boiled water when irrigating a wound, and of cleansing of the hands and nails of the physician. With a keen eye and a deep regard for his patients, he may be the physician who originated the practice of bedside medicine. "Wherever the art of medicine is loved," he wrote, "there also is love of humanity."

Apart from such sentiments, and his belief that the physician is the servant of his art, what truly distinguished Hippocrates from his predecessors was his complete disregard of presumed spiritual causes of disease and rejection of the assumption that the gods were the only causative agents. Rather, Hippocrates saw

ANCIENT ANATOMY

In ancient India, knowledge of human anatomy was limited because Hindus were forbidden to cut into a dead body. An ancient text suggested that a dead body be laid in a river for seven days, after which parts could be detached from the body without cutting.

that disease was a natural event that could be understood in practical terms.

Treatment methods followed the prevailing concept of the day: the theory of the four bodily humors, or humoral pathology, which considered all diseases to be disorders of bodily fluids. The word "humor" was long used to describe any fluid found in plants and animals. According to the theory, health stemmed from the equal influence of the four bodily

THE THEORY OF HUMORS

One of the most persistent of all scientific models, the theory of humors, also called humoralism, may have originated in the fifth century B.C. with Empedocles, the Greek philosopher and statesman who was also reputed to be the founder of rhetoric. True to that other art, the theory of humors smacks of the powers of persuasiveness and exaggeration—yet it held sway for centuries.

Essentially, the theory said that all diseases could be explained by reference to four principal bodily fluids, or humors: blood, phlegm, choler (yellow bile), and melancholy (black bile). The fluids corresponded to the four elements—blood to fire, phlegm to water, yellow bile to air, and black bile to earth—which, to Empedocles, were the "four-fold root of all things." Also paired with the fluids were the four seasons and their characteristics, which were believed to have a specific influence on the formation of each of the humors. Winter represented old age and was associated with phlegm; spring: childhood, heat, and blood; summer: youth, dryness, and yellow bile; and fall: adulthood, chilliness, melancholy, and black bile.

An excess of any one fluid was believed to affect mind or body, thus the expressions sanguine, choleric, phlegmatic, and melancholic, referring to

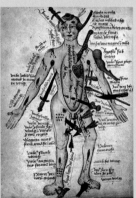

A 16th-century German battle guide displays many wounds.

mood or behavior. For example, an excess of blood (hot) made one sanguine; too much phlegm (wet and cold) made one sluggish and unemotional.

Food, too, played a role in this formula: Cold foods produced phlegm, warm foods produced yellow bile and hence "warm" diseases. An imbalance of the humors was the cause of any disease. The treatment to restore the balance was enantiopathy, the countering of an overabundance of one humor with the overabundance of another, such as using cold to treat a fever.

The Doctrine of the Four Temperaments, as humoralism was also called, left its legacy in the concept of homeostasis, still accepted today, whereby the body's biological systems try to maintain an equilibrium by adjusting its physiological processes when there are changes in the external environment.

The humoral theory was supported by the founder of experimental physiology, Claudius Galen, whose influence dominated medical science from the 2nd to the 16th centuries. The Swiss alchemist Paracelsus was among the first to debunk the theory with his view that diseases had an environmental, not a humoral, base. It was finally buried for good in the 1800s, when Rudolf Virchow posited his theory of cellular pathology, stating that disease was due to cells run wild.

humors, which were analogous to the four elements of Greek physics: earth, air, water, and fire. An earlier theory of Pythagoras on the functional significance of numbers in an objective world, which saw significance in the number four as the number of basic elements—had a place as well in humors theory and ancient methods for treating disease.

In an arcane formula, the elements were associated with the seasons, the winds, and, in turn, the four humors. These humors were blood, phlegm, black bile, and yellow bile. According to the theory, they were associated with four major organs—heart, brain, liver, and spleen—and ultimately with the four seasons and the four ages of man: childhood, youth, maturity, and old age.

As arcane as this medical theory might seem, its underlying assumption was straightforward: Any deviation from perfect balance among the four humors produced disease. An excess of phlegm, for example, could cause epilepsy, according to this theory. Treatment consisted of attempting to restore balance by trying to restrain the overactive humor while encouraging the others.

Incredibly, humoral pathology turned out to be one of the most durable theories in the history of human thought, influencing generations of physicians well into the 18th century before it was abandoned—but not before it firmly established the view held even today that equilibrium is imperative to health. This concept is now known as homeostasis, the ability of an organism to maintain internal equilibrium by adjusting its physiological processes.

ARISTOTLE AND GALEN

After Hippocrates, perhaps the greatest of the classical period's men of science who contributed to our understanding of the human body was Aristotle, the philosopher, whose theories influenced not only logic, metaphysics, politics, physics, mathematics, and astronomy, but also the nascent sciences of biology, zoology, embryology, physiology, and comparative anatomy. Not a physician, but the son of one, Aristotle has been called the father of modern science and anatomy.

With respect to the latter, Aristotle's contributions to what we know about the human body came not from its dissection but from the dissection of the bodies of animals. His studies of marine life are astonishing in their close observations, even if some of the conclusions he draws from them about human anatomy would later be proved wrong. He argued, for example, that the body's control center lay in the heart, and that the purpose of breathing was to remove heat from the body. Arteries were full of air, not blood, Aristotle and his fellow ancient Greeks believed.

Still, some of his insights were remarkable. By examining fowl, he disproved the widespread belief that an embryo was fully formed from its first day. His dissections demonstrated clearly that a chick's

ARISTOTLE

As part of his huge body of work on the natural world, Aristotle attempted analyses of the body's structures and functions.

heart did not develop until the fourth day after fertilization. Semen, he propounded, was the activating and formative agent of procreation, while the female supplied the material substance for the embryo in the form of an egg. Noteworthy, too, were Aristotle's descriptions of, and the names he gave to, some of the body's structures. He named the aorta; he diagrammed the male genitourinary system; he even made precise renderings of the dogfish placenta.

Perhaps one of his greatest contributions to biological science was a classification system by genus and species, which would form the baseline for distinguishing living species. He decided correctly, for example, that dolphins must be mammals, not fish, because they bear their young alive and then suckle them. And in a prescient commentary on the evolution of life, he wrote, "Nature proceeds little by little from things lifeless to animal life in such a way that it is impossible to determine the exact line of demarcation, nor on which side thereof an intermediate form should lie."

After Aristotle, a procession of lesser-known Greek and Roman physicians and non-physicians, surgeons, anatomists, writers, and translators of works on medicine continued studying the body, offering a rash of theories known today primarily just to historians of medicine. One theory saw irri-

GALEN

As a doctor to gladiators who had been wounded in the arena at Pergamum, 2nd-century Greek physician Claudius Galen built the foundation of our understanding of human anatomy and physiology.

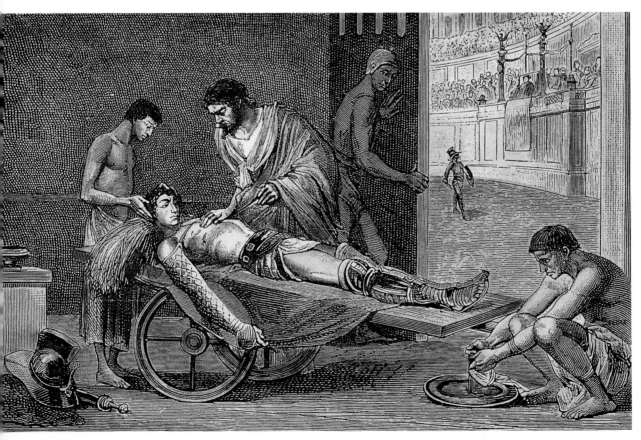

tation as a cause of disease; others saw disease as disturbances of the body's liquid, solid, or gaseous components; yet another attributed disease to an increase in blood flow to a body part. Among all these there were, however, some noteworthy findings.

Erasistratus, for instance, an anatomist who may have been a grandson of Aristotle, conceived of the heart as a pump and nearly stumbled on the mechanism of the circulatory system. (He got it wrong, though: He theorized that blood moved from the liver to the heart and lungs via the arteries and veins.) He was the first to distinguish between sensory and motor nerves, and he named the trachea. More important, he challenged the theory of humors.

Rufus of Ephesus, a Greek physician who lived in the first century A.D., during the reign of the Emperor Trajan, wrote accurately on the pulse and heartbeat. He authored an influential treatise on bodily parts, including a careful study of the lens of the eye.

But it was the second-century Greek physician Claudius Galen, regarded as the founder of experimental physiology, whose authority, for better and worse, would endure, largely uncontested, well into the 17th century. Court physician to the Emperor Marcus Aurelius and doctor to gladiators—a post that undoubtedly exposed him to numerous kinds of gaping wounds and trauma—Galen was probably the greatest of ancient physicians after Hippocrates, an enormously skilled and brilliant experimentalist and clinician, although egotistical to the point of being obnoxious, according to his contemporaries.

Because human dissection was considered indecent and taboo during his time, Galen carefully dissected monkeys, apes, hogs, even an elephant, and transferred his observations by analogy to humans, a practice that quite often produced erroneous results. For example, he concluded that blood was manufactured in

CLAUDIUS GALEN

Founder of experimental physiology

ca A.D. 129
Claudius Galenus, or Galen, is born in Pergamum, Mysia, Anatolia (now western Turkey).

145
Begins to study medicine at Smyrna (now Izmir, Turkey), and eventually travels to Alexandria, Egypt.

157
Returns to Pergamum to act as physician to gladiators, where he gains experience treating open wounds and performing surgery.

162
Travels to Rome, where he gives public anatomy lectures and demonstrations and quickly rises to fame.

168
Joins Lucius Verus and Marcus Aurelius on their military campaign in Italy.

169
Returns to Rome after Lucius Verus's death.

191
Fire destroys many of his writings; he writes more in decades to come.

ca 216
Estimated end of life; little is known about his date or place of death.

Influence

ca 850
More than 100 of his manuscripts translated into Arabic, greatly influencing Islamic medicine.

1543
Andreas Vesalius publishes *Fabrica*, correcting many flaws in Galen's anatomical teachings.

1628
William Harvey rejects Galen's teachings and accurately describes the circulatory system.

the liver from material provided by the stomach. He confused nerves with tendons, and he assumed that because certain structures and blood vessels existed in animal, they must be present in humans. But his methods were logical, and much of what he accomplished (helped along by any stray human skeleton he stumbled on in the countryside) provided a point of departure for the development of modern medicine.

A prolific writer, Galen detailed his findings, the more accurate of which are enough to awe even today's practitioners. He gave us precise descriptions of the skeleton and skull, correctly explained the mechanism of respiration, and proved experimentally that arteries carry blood not air, thus upsetting an ancient accepted theory. He outlined the difference between pneumonia and pleurisy. He was the first to describe the cranial nerves and the sympathetic nervous system.

He overturned ancient beliefs by demonstrating that the larynx, not the lungs, generated the voice. He showed that paralysis could be induced in his animal subjects by cutting their spinal cords. In his work and writing, Galen managed to combine into a coherent whole the medical ideas and achievements of his predecessors, especially Hippocrates and Aristotle. He embraced the theory of the four humors but expanded it, devising his own theories of disease, both physical and mental.

Galen taught that different combinations of the four humors—mixed in with the conditions of cold and warmth, humidity and dryness—formed one's temperament as well as one's physical condition, and that a perfectly proportioned combination of all the ingredients made an individual ideal in both mind and body. Thus a person could be blood sanguine (optimistic), yellow-bile choleric (easily angered, ambitious, and vengeful), phlegmatic (unexcitable), or melancholic. The word "melancholy" actually comes from the Greek for black bile.

THE MIDDLE AGES

Galen spoke with such authority that not many in his time dared to

900 – 1573

ca 900	**ca 1000**	**ca 1025**	**1040**
Muslim physician Rhazes teaches that a balanced diet and physical activity play vital roles in health and disease.	Arab scientist Alhazen investigates many aspects of the human body, notably the eyes and vision.	Persian physician Avicenna composes his encyclopedia of medical knowledge, *The Canon of Medicine*.	Petrocellus of Italy writes *Practica*, an extensive early medical work.

question his views and findings. Indeed, such reticence continued well into the 16th century. Fortunately, a few independent thinkers emerged in the interim, among them visionary Jewish physicians and Arab scholars known especially for their skills in chemistry and in devising new remedies. While they made their own mistakes, these early scientists struggled to systematize the human body, to understand the organic causes of disease, and to preserve and improve on the best of the Greek tradition. They appreciated many of Galen's contributions yet came to criticize his dogmatism and recognize his errors, thus helping to reverse any overconfident adherence to his ideas.

One Islamic seeker of truth was a physician with the formidable name, Abu Bakr Muhammad ibn Zakariya ar-Razi, known in the West as Rhazes. A ninth-century Persian who was chief physician at Baghdad's leading hospital, Rhazes was an empirical scientist. He believed in experimentation and practiced exacting observation of his patients. Rhazes recognized

AVICENNA
ex Codice antiquo Galeni.

See page 171 for more information about Muslim contributions to science.

that a balanced diet and exercise played key roles in maintaining health and resisting disease—far more important, in his estimation, than an overreliance on any sort of treatment based on the theory of humors. His theory of therapy, if it can be called that, could be expressed in just a few words: "In treating a patient," Rhazes wrote,

1347-1351
The bubonic plague kills a third of the population of Europe.

1536
Venetian anatomist Niccolo Massa describes cerebrospinal fluid.

1543
Flemish physician Andreas Vesalius publishes his treatise, *De humani corporis fabrica (On the Fabric of the Human Body)*.

1573
Italian physician Girolamo Mercuriali publishes *De nervis opticis*, in which he describes the anatomy of the optic nerve.

INSIDE VIEW

Avicenna's view of human anatomy, although imaginative, showed insight in many areas.

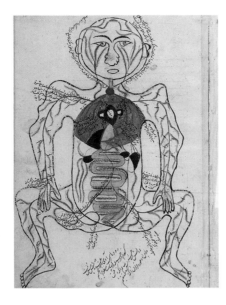

SALERNO

The first medical school in the West was established in Salerno, Italy, as the study of medicine flourished in Islamic realms. The Salerno school gave rise to other great medical schools including those in Padua and Bologna, Italy, and in Montpellier and Paris, France. By 1200, the Montpellier school had become the top medical school in Europe.

"let your first thought be to strengthen his natural vitality."

With foresight unmatched by that of his predecessors and many of his contemporaries, Rhazes understood that health and disease could never be described empirically by a formula that relied on simple liquids and the elements of air, fire, water, and earth. Consideration of many individual cases led Rhazes to recognize that neither causes nor cures were absolute or identical, case to case. "When the disease is stronger than the patient," wrote Rhazes, "the physician will not be able to help him at all, and if the strength of the patient is greater than the strength of the disease, he does not need a physician at all. But when both are equal, then one needs a physician who will support the patient's strength and help him against disease."

More dubious of Galen was another Persian, Ibn Sina, better known as Avicenna, who lived from A.D. 980 to 1037. Called the "prince of physicians," Avicenna was an outspoken empiricist who insisted that theories must be confirmed by experience. He argued against the blind acceptance of any authority. Although a Galenist in theory (as were most Arab physicians), he was closer to Hippocrates in his careful, systematic approach to diagnosis. His hundreds of written works justify the princely appellation given him: He produced an extraordinary scientific encyclopedia with compendia on the fundamentals of medicine, hygiene, drugs, and contagious diseases. He articulated the difference, for example, between measles and smallpox.

One heartening side of the practice of medicine developed in the 12th and 13th centuries as hospitals, run by the Catholic Church for the relief of the sick, evolved into seats of clinical learning, out-shining in reputation even the oldest medical school in the West, that of Salerno in Italy. In the halls of Europe's early dedicated medical schools—renowned institutions at Padua, Pisa, and Bologna in Italy, and at Paris and Montpellier in France—medieval medicine began to embrace the analytical legacy of Hippocrates and Galen.

In the 1300s, attendance at dissection demonstrations became a required part of any medical school's curriculum. (It is commonly thought today that there was an ecclesiastical prohibition against human dissection, but this is one of many modern-day myths about the Middle Ages.) The mysterious structures that lay

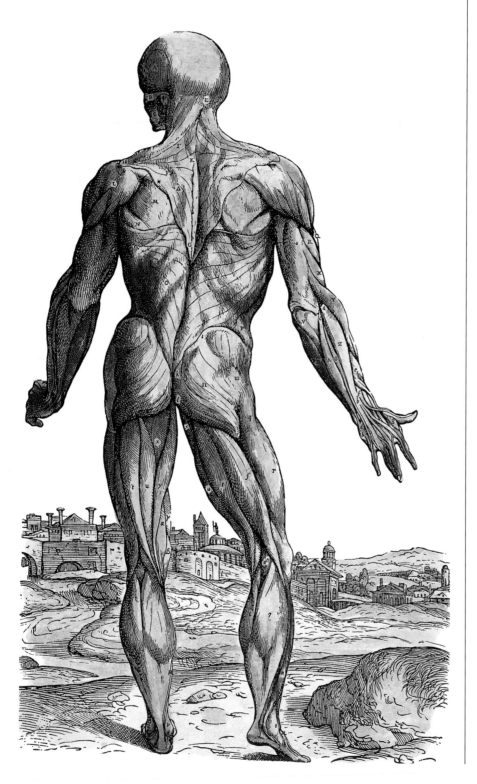

RENAISSANCE MAN
Flemish physician Andreas Vesalius made thorough observations and records of his dissections of human bodies. His 16th-century *De humani corpori fabrica* advanced general knowledge of the human body's functions and organs.

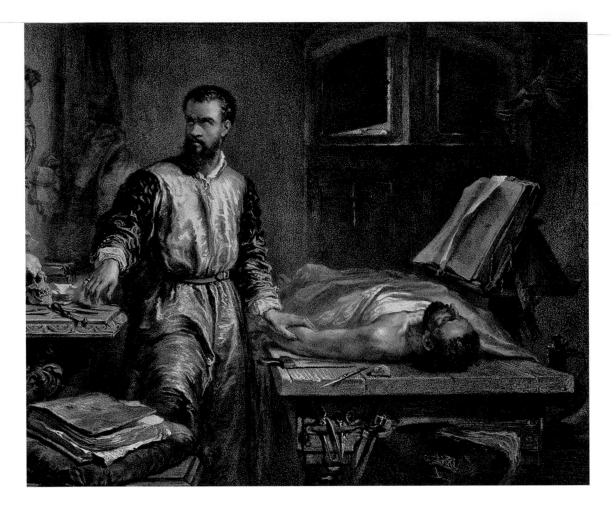

VESALIUS

At the University of Bologna in 1540 Andreas Vesalius initiated a course of human dissections that distinguished his work from Galen's. Three years later he published the results of this work in his *De humani corporis fabrica libri septem* ("The Seven Books on the Structure of the Human Body").

deep under the skin of the human body came to be examined with a degree of freedom that the ancients could not imagine.

ANATOMY AS ART

With the developing study of anatomy, along with the revival of art and literature, Renaissance scientists began to regard the body as a system of mechanisms. Bologna's Mondino dei Liucci drew on Galen's observations to write a handbook on dissection. Limited in theory by Galen's errors on the structure of the human frame, still dei Liucci recorded his observa-

tions upon opening the body's abdominal cavities, the chest, and skull. He even did post-mortems on two female cadavers to compare the size of the uterus in a virgin and in a woman who had borne children. So popular was his work that it remained the official textbook in medical schools for more than two centuries after it was written.

Leonardo da Vinci, true to the interpretation of the body as an intricate mechanism, turned his dissections into some beautifully detailed studies that, on the one hand, flowed from a mechanical engineer's mind, but, on the other, presented human anatomy as art. As good as da Vinci was, it took Andreas Vesalius to raise the study of human anatomy to a science.

Born in Belgium in 1514, Vesalius took to stealing corpses from the gallows, a practice that got him banned from France. Wherever he could, he gathered his "materials" and brought them back to his rooms for dissection and study. He performed the dissections himself, slicing through the body region by region, rather than—as most of his contemporaries did—leaving the chore to a student or a barber who followed the spoken directions of an instructor reading from Galen's error-prone accounts. Vesalius's cutting and prying revealed much, to be sure, but it was a dangerous, bloody business in those days when bacteria, viruses, and the diseases they cause were unknown. Corpses were often decayed and contaminated. Cleanliness in the dissecting room was impossible. But for Vesalius, solving the body's mysteries was worth the risk.

As a result, Vesalius left to the world an authoritative book of keen firsthand observations: *De humani corporis fabrica*, illustrated with memorable woodcuts by the Flemish artist Jan Stephanus van Kalcker. A monumental work and highly detailed, it revealed for the first time the importance of the skeleton not only for body support and movement but also as a shield for the fragile organs it housed.

The *Fabrica* served another purpose, one that no one had dared to consider as Vesalius had: It was a wake-up call to those who continued to base their anatomical knowledge on Galen's animal dissections. Vesalius was able to disprove, among other Galenic notions, that blood was manufactured in the liver, traveled to the right ventricle of the heart, and then passed somehow to the left ventricle, where it was mixed with air. Galen had not understood that blood circulated throughout

ANDREAS VESALIUS

Father of modern anatomy

1514
Born André Wesele Crabbe on December 31 in Brussels.

1529
Begins studies at the University of Louvain.

1533
Begins studying medicine at the University of Paris.

1537
Receives his bachelor's degree in medicine from the University of Louvain. Continues his medical training at the University of Padua, where he receives his doctorate of medicine. There, he immediately begins lecturing on anatomy and surgery.

1537
Publishes his first book, *A Paraphrase of the Ninth Book of Rhazes*.

1538
Begins to question respected anatomical writings based on Galen's teachings, and begins suspecting that Galen's human anatomy was based on study of apes' bodies.

1543
Publishes his most famous work, *De humani corporis fabrica (On the Fabric of the Human Body*, also known as the *Fabrica)*, which includes detailed drawings of the human anatomy.

1553
Starts private medical practice in Brussels.

1555
Publishes a revised version of the *Fabrica*, which includes important new ideas, such as a description of the vein valves.

1559
Leaves private practice; becomes physician to king of Spain.

1561
Writes *An Examination of Gabrielle Fallopio's Anatomical Observations*.

1564
Dies on October 15 on the Greek island of Zákinthos.

FAMOSO·DOCTOR   PARESELSVS·

PARACELSUS

Bold and boastful, the Swiss physician who called himself Paracelsus decried references to the humors as explanations of illnesses. He campaigned for a medicine based on studies of the body's chemistry.

the body, a fact that would be established a half-century after Vesalius's time when an English farmer's son, William Harvey, showed conclusively that blood pumped by the heart circulates from arteries into veins and back to the heart.

Anatomy had at last come into its own, and eventually all of Galen's inaccurate observations were corrected. As Vesalius himself wrote in his *Fabrica*, "How much has been attributed to Galen, easily leader of the professors of dissection, by those physicians and anatomists who have followed him, and often against reason. . . .

Indeed, I myself cannot wonder enough at my own stupidity and too great trust in the writings of Galen and other anatomists."

BURYING GALEN'S BODY

Despite the mounting evidence that Galen was too often on the wrong track, some of his mainstays, notably the theory of humors, continued to hang on. More chipping away was needed, and one of the most flamboyant characters to do just that was a Swiss physician and alchemist named Theophrastus Bombast von Hohenheim. He adopted as his nom de plume Paracelsus, an invented name that implied he was better even than an ancient physician and writer named Celsus.

The son of a physician, Paracelsus learned about metals and minerals in the mines and smelters of the Tirol region of the Alps. He learned astrology and folk medicine from gypsies, executioners, barbers, and midwives; and he learned medicine from his father's library and from a translator of Hippocrates. "I have been chosen by God to extinguish and blot out all the phantasies of elaborate and false works of delusive and presumptuous words," he roared in one of his writings, showing his typically grand sense of self-importance, "be they the words of Aristotle, Galen, Avicenna or the dogmas of any of their followers. After me, you Avicenna, Rhazes and the others. You after me, not I after you. Follow me."

Despite his lack of humility and his arcane pharmacopoeia, which contained bizarre concoctions—for instance, a mixture of gold filings, ground antimony, wine, and salt that was allowed to "digest" in horse dung for four months—Paracelsus was often on the mark. He did not deserve the reputation later granted him as a mountebank. His attack on the importance of humors was among his most impressive campaigns, suggesting what might be termed an environmental theory of disease.

He had already observed, as had Hippocrates, geographic differences in the experience of illnesses, but while working as a physician in a mining community, he saw many cases of lung disease. These observations suggested that not all disease was caused by internal fluid imbalances. Instead, Paracelsus believed, illness was caused by outside forces that enter the body and grow from a seed. The body was a chemical system, more complex than just a mix of four fluids, he argued, and each disease had a chemical cause and corresponding remedy. Thus medicine was a branch of chemistry, and to restore a person to health, it was essential to restore chemical equilibrium.

From this reasoning, there might be great therapeutic potential in inorganic as well as organic materials. Paracelsus introduced numerous medicines made from mercury, zinc, sulfur, and iron. Some of his cures were hopeless, but some worked remarkably well, albeit for the wrong reasons—such as his practice of administering iron salts to weak patients, since iron was associated with Mars, the

strong god of war. Today we know that iron deficiencies in the blood and body can cause anemia, or weakness. We know that muscular weakness can be attributed to a dietary deficiency of potassium, that zinc is essential to growth, and that manganese and chromium may help the heart. All it takes is a glance at the label on a bottle of multivitamins to see Paracelsus's hand in the mix, even today.

It might be argued that the achievements of Paracelsus and others of his time came about serendipitously, but they did manage to shake the foundations of establishment medicine as they pursued more careful analysis than their predecessors had. As Paracelsus put it, in a pronouncement that could be heard as the driving force of an entire cadre of medieval medical explorers, "If I want to prove anything, I shall not do so by quoting authorities, but by experiment and by reasoning thereupon."

Another pioneer who did so was the 17th-century Paduan professor Santorio, also called Sanctorius. Unlike Paracelsus, who leaned heavily on chemistry to explain medicine and physiological processes, Santorio and his followers connected physiologic occurrences to the laws of physics. He is perhaps best known for his theory of a physiology of metabolism, which he pursued by gathering careful experimental records and devising cunning methods to track temperature and pulse rate.

For three decades, Santorio meticulously weighed everything he ate and drank and compared

IN SEARCH OF CADAVERS
Grave robbing reached its height in Great Britain during the 18th and 19th centuries, when the supply of cadavers was insufficient for medical schools. Students often had to provide their own, so they turned to grave robbery. For fear of being arrested, students often hired "sack 'em up" men to do the job for them. Some resorted to murder.

HARVEY

To show how blood circulated, English physician William Harvey placed a tourniquet on a subject's arm. By tightening and loosening the tourniquet, and by stopping the flow at various points, he demonstrated that valves in the veins permit blood to flow in only one direction, toward the heart.

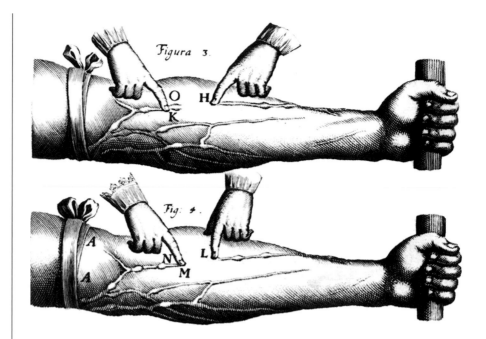

those amounts with the weights of his urine and feces, which he discovered to be considerably lower. Trying to account for the difference, he spent hours in a specially crafted weighing chair. He eventually came up with a theory of "insensible perspiration" to explain the missing mass. Although the explanation was misguided, Santorio's empirical methodology was still used centuries later.

HARVEY'S TRIUMPH

The mechanical concept of the human organism was supported by René Descartes, a French philosopher and mathematician of the 18th century. Wedded to a highly mechanical view of nature and its contents, Descartes argued that the human body was basically a set of mechanisms inhabited by a spirit— the "ghost in the machine," as it later came to be called. The first to

distinguish between matter and mind clearly, he argued that matter had to be regarded as divisible, and that the living body was governed by the laws of inanimate matter. The mind was different, indivisible, and ruled by laws other than those of the material world. He saw the heart as an engine, and his theory of muscular movement was based on a system of hydraulics.

Giovanni Borelli, an Italian professor of mathematics, made it his life's work to explain the movement of muscles and organs in light of the principles of levers, fulcrums, springs, and pumps. Examining the way the body adjusts and maintains its center of gravity directly over the feet, he considered it a system of weights and pulleys; he modeled the movements of walking, running, and jumping mathematically, describing systems of forces and counterforces. He used this biomechanical bent even to interpret the grinding, crushing action of the stomach during digestion.

The mechanistic view of the body found perhaps its most exaggerated statement in the work of another French theorist, Julien de la Mettrie. His 1747 book *Man the Machine* presented the extreme (and, for the time, shockingly atheistic) view that the body was entirely mechanical. Human behavior is basically a set of reactive responses to stimuli, proposed La Mettrie, and human thought is "secreted" by the brain, much as bile is produced by the liver. Running counter to this highly mechanistic view was a growing "vitalist" or "animist" theory of life, which argued that many functions of the human body could be explained only by the presence of a spirit or soul.

The growing perception of the heart as a throbbing, mechanical pump, ushered in a new era of medicine, beginning with the anatomist William Harvey's discovery of the circulation of the blood, which he described as a vital process that follows the laws of physics. Such an idea was outrageously radical at the time, in part because it ran counter to Galen's notion that the heart moved blood from the liver to the lungs. Indeed, Harvey spent a good deal of his career trying to convince his own profession of what we now accept as a fundamental physiological process, and it would take other researchers many years to confirm Harvey's theory after his death.

Harvey studied at the University of Padua. He may even have met Galileo Galilei, who was then a professor there. Harvey's monumental theory of blood in motion, which seems so simple today, came after many careful animal dissections, experiments with snakes, autopsies, and clinical observations. His discoveries would make physiology a truly dynamic science, and the theory he proposed bore many results.

WILLIAM HARVEY

Explorer of the circulatory system

1578
Born on April 1, in Folkestone, Kent, England.

1593-1599
Studies medicine at Caius College, Cambridge.

1600
Continues his medical training at the University of Padua, Italy, where he studies under the great anatomist Fabricius.

1602
Receives his doctorate of medicine at Padua.

1607
Elected a fellow of the Royal College of Physicians.

1610
Begins work on heart and circulation by dissecting animals.

1610-1623
Gives surgery lectures for the Royal College of Physicians in London.

1618
Appointed physician to King James I of England.

1625
Appointed physician to King Charles I.

1628
Publishes *An Anatomic Exercise of the Motion of the Heart and Blood in Animals*; becomes the first man to describe the circulatory system accurately.

1645
Appointed warden of Merton College, Oxford.

1651
Publishes *The Generation of Animals*, his work on comparative embryology.

1654
Elected president of Royal College of Physicians, but declines.

1657
Dies on June 3 near London.

THE HEART

The adult human heart averages 72 beats per minute at rest. During an average lifetime, the heart will beat more than 2.5 billion times. The human body contains about six quarts of blood, which circulates in the body three times every minute.

See pages 251-53 for more information about William Harvey.

Borelli had hypothesized that the heart functions like a piston in a pump cylinder, and he even calculated the amount of generated pressure that was required to move the blood around. Harvey demonstrated that the heart pumped the blood in a cycle, moving it through arteries to every part of the body and returning it through veins to the heart. He explained the role of the aortic and vein valves, and he proved that the pulse reflected heart contractions.

Coming up with all these facts, which today we take for granted, was a daunting task, even for someone of Harvey's skills. He had misgivings, believing that the work he had embarked on was too arduous even to contemplate, and he wrote that he was tempted to think that the heart's motion "was only to be comprehended by God." Later, after his discoveries, he worried about the impact that they would have, fearing that he would be injured "from the envy of a few" and that "mankind at large" would blame him for having overturned hallowed doctrine. When his work was over, he seemed to have come to grips with such insecurities, though, writing in his book *On the Motion of the Heart and Blood in Animals:* "Still, the die is cast, and my trust is in my love of truth, and the candour that inheres in cultivated minds."

As groundbreaking as Harvey's discovery was, there were still some loose ends. He had no microscope, so he was unable to visualize how blood got from arteries to veins, an essential part of the circulatory process. The answer would come some 30 years later, when Marcello Malpighi, an anatomy professor at both Messina and Pisa, drew on his expert skill at using the remarkable new instrument called the microscope.

A proponent of Harvey's theory of blood circulation, Malpighi speculated that if the circulatory system was indeed closed, some extremely tiny blood vessels must be present to allow the blood to get from the arterial system back into the venous system. Confirmation of this idea came while he examined the fine structure of human lung tissue through the microscope, where he saw clearly

1628 – 1900

1628
English physician William Harvey describes the circulation of blood through the human body.

1674
Dutch microscopist Antoni van Leeuwenhoek publishes the first accurate description of red blood corpuscles.

1735
English surgeon Claudius Amyand performs the first successful appendectomy.

visible, threadlike vessels that joined the arteries to the veins. We now call them capillaries. Harvey's theory was complete.

But the work did not end there. For many years after Harvey's triumph, inquisitive investigators turned their attention to blood itself and to the entire cardiovascular system. No one really knew what circulation was all about. Certainly Harvey did not know why blood circulated; and while Malpighi was the first to note lung circulation, he didn't understand why it happened. Oxygen, the vital component carried by the blood, was not recognized until its first discovery by the British theologian and chemist Joseph Priestley, in 1774, so theories about the purpose of blood circulation ranged far and wide. Some considered it a way to distribute heat through the body, while others proposed it as a cooling system.

It was a brilliant but less well known English physiologist and chemist, John Mayow, who used his knowledge of respiration to conclude that the point of breathing was to create an interchange of gases between the air and the blood. Something vital in the air, he reasoned, was getting into the blood, some "nitro-aerial spirit" that changed dark venous blood to bright red. Mayow could not have known it, but he was close to discovering oxygen and its essential role in the human body.

The early 1700s saw other blood-related discoveries, among them the earliest measurement of blood pressure in animals, a crude procedure in its early version. A tube was directly inserted into an artery. As the blood pulsed into the tube, the height to which it rose was noted. In this period the presence of iron was also discovered in the blood, a finding that no doubt would have thrilled Paracelsus.

One aspect of blood that had captured physicians' imaginations for centuries was the possibility of transfusing it from one person to another. References to the procedure date back to Egyptian papyri, and there are vague allusions to it in the writings of some Roman poets. Credible medical records give 1665 as a starting point, when an English physiologist named

See page 273 for more information about Joseph Priestley.

1796	**1842**	**1870**	**1900**
English surgeon Edward Jenner devises a vaccination for smallpox.	American physician Crawford Williamson Long performs the first surgical procedure using anesthesia.	Microbiologists Louis Pasteur, Joseph Lister, and Robert Koch establish the germ theory of disease.	Austrian-born American pathologist Karl Landsteiner identifies different blood types, later categorizing them as A, B, AB, and O.

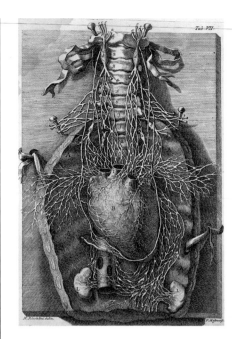

Richard Lower performed the first transfusion from one animal to another by connecting the blood vessels of two dogs. The feat was followed by a number of unsuccessful attempts to transfuse animal blood into humans. In 1667, for example, the French physician Jean-Baptiste Denis injected lamb's blood into three patients. One died shortly thereafter.

Direct person-to-person blood transfusions were later attempted. A few saw some degree of success, but all were just as risky as animal-to-human transfusions, given that no one had any idea of blood types, not to mention the composition of blood. That knowledge base changed dramatically in the early 1900s when the Austrian-American immunologist Karl Landsteiner identified separate blood types based on chemical markers, antigens that each cell carried on its surface. Some had antigen A, others had antigen B, and still others had both. Some had none at all; those he called O. If blood of one type was introduced into a person with another type, the patient's immune system would consider it an intrusion and attack.

Ten years later, Landsteiner would make another important discovery: He isolated the so-called Rhesus (Rh) factor in the blood. Named for the Rhesus breed of monkey that he used in his experiments, the Rh factor can cause a serious disease in a newborn whose blood grouping is incompatible with that of the mother's. People who have Rh-negative blood and receive Rh-positive transfusions produce antibodies to the new Rh factor, which can attack red blood cells.

In the early 18th century, new discoveries about blood quite naturally stimulated interest in the organ that drives it through the body, the heart. Little was known about the complicated structure and mechanisms of the heart. Few understood the significance of the heartbeat or the relationship between blood pressure and heart rate, and few were aware of the many diseases to which the heart was prone. It was not until 1809 that the mechanism of heart murmurs was described, some of the information coming from the physician's standard practice of applying an ear to the ailing chest.

In 1816, a remarkable invention made the sounds of the heart much more audible. The stethoscope was the brainchild of René-Théophile-Hyacinthe Laënnec, considered by many to be the father of thoracic medicine. His invention would transform the diagnosis and treatment of cardiovascular disorders, remaining essential to general medicine even after more sophisticated diagnostic technologies emerged.

Although an undisputed expert in diseases of the chest such as bronchitis, pneumonia, and pleurisy, Laënnec's name would go down in medical history for inventing the stethoscope and for the tale of how it happened. One of Laënnec's heart patients was a young woman of a zaftig build. Prudence prevented him from resting his ear on her ample bosom—or, in his words, "direct auscultation was rendered inadmissible by the age and sex of the patient." Drawing on principles of basic acoustical science, he rolled several sheets of stiff paper into a cylinder and placed one end over the patient's heart, the other over his ear. It worked admirably, amplifying the heart sounds beyond what Laënnec's ear alone could have heard. Soon improved models of various sizes, shapes, and materials had been produced, and with them a new medical term came into fashion: "mediate auscultation."

THE CAUSES OF DISEASE

Long before Laënnec was literally listening for the causes of heart disease, others had been using all senses to discover the cause or causes of diseases of all kinds. Aristotle summed up the nature of the quest that would go on for centuries after his death: "Conscientious and careful physicians allocate causes of disease to natural laws," he said, "while the ablest scientists go back to medicine for their first principles." But for all the theorizing about humors, chemistry, nature, indolence, and demons, the culprits attacking human health remained invisible—dependent, as the 18th-century British anatomist John Hunter observed, "on circumstances which are unknown, or appear to be accidental." One could dismiss Galen and his followers, and the other purveyors of

ANTONI VAN LEEUWENHOEK

First scientist to see microorganisms

1632
Born on October 24 in Delft, the Netherlands.

1648
After basic schooling in the town of Warmond, becomes an apprentice in a linen-draper's shop.

1652
In Delft, opens his own fabric business.

1660
Appointed chamberlain to the sheriffs of Delft; the position gives him financial means to pursue scientific interests.

1671
Begins grinding lenses and creating microscopes, at first to inspect cloth.

1673
First correspondence with the Royal Society concerning his microscopic discoveries; the relationship continues throughout the rest of his life.

1674
Discovers bacteria and protozoa, which he calls "very little animalcules," in rainwater and saliva.

1677
Observes and describes spermatozoa from both animals and humans.

1680
Elected a fellow of the Royal Society.

1683
Discovers and gives the first accurate description of human blood capillaries.

1716
Awarded a silver medal by the Louvain College of Professors for his advancements in science.

1723
Dies on August 26 in Delft.

THE GERM THEORY

Human diseases were not truly explainable until scientists grasped the importance of microorganisms. The Dutch microscopist Antoni van Leeuwenhoek, who discovered what he called animalcules, did not realize how close he had come to identifying bacteria and formulating a germ theory of disease.

For centuries the prevailing belief, along with the humoral theory, was that noxious bad air—miasma or vapors—was the causative factor. Astral influences were also cited, along with chemicals, poor nutrition, various other outside influences, and even permutations of the laws of physics.

The revolutionary theory that microscopic infectious agents could cause disease was not the brainchild of a single scientist. Rather, the germ theory evolved gradually through the thinking of several investigators, dating back to the 1500s, scientists who suspected that some unidentified entity was behind certain forms of illness. But credit for the germ theory should be granted to three men in the later 19th century: Louis Pasteur, Joseph Lister, and Robert Koch.

In experiments with fermentation, Pasteur showed that putrefaction in milk and wines was not the result of spontaneous decay (a popular belief) but microorganisms in the air, which contaminated liquids exposed to them. Heating milk to a certain temperature, he also found, would prevent it from spreading tuberculosis and typhoid, proof that the organisms' effects could be stifled.

Lister's contribution to the theory was the use of an antiseptic to kill germs, notably in surgical

French scientist Louis Pasteur proved microorganisms key to both wine and disease.

situations. While Pasteur had demonstrated the involvement of microbes in putrefaction, his own sterilization techniques were not suited for the operating suite. Lister, a surgeon, was on the other hand most scrupulous in his work habits, draining wounds, frequently changing dressings, and using silver sutures to keep wounds clean.

Aware that Pasteur's heat sterilizations did little for surgery, Lister turned to chemical antiseptics such as carbolic acid. He demonstrated that infections were caused by bacteria and could be controlled by antibacterials—and thus inspired a great advance in surgical medicine.

It was Robert Koch, however, who devised new ways of obtaining pure cultures of microorganisms in specially prepared, nutrient-rich media. Keenly aware of contamination at a time when surgeons were ignoring Lister—and when they still performed operations in street clothes without masks or caps—Koch demanded sterile laboratory conditions.

For cultures, he came up with the right combinations of gels and agar—the gelatinous material derived from marine algae and used as a medium for culturing bacteria—instead of Pasteur's bouillon. Koch's methodology paid off, and he isolated not only the anthrax bacillus but also the bacterium responsible for pneumonia. His researchers went on to identify the causative agents in typhoid and diphtheria, while he turned his attention to malaria. He was awarded the Nobel Prize in physiology or medicine in 1905, honored as one of the fathers of bacteriology and the germ theory.

catch-all theories, but the fact remained that whatever caused disease was ultimately debatable, complex, and probably many-faceted.

The idea of a germ as an infectious agent was not demonstrated until the 1800s, yet the belief that something external to the body was behind disease was not uncommon centuries earlier. As early as 1546, an Italian pathologist, Girolamo Fracastoro (also a geologist, astronomer, and poet), suggested that some sort of contagious, physical, non-living chemical agents caused infection, even epidemics such as that of foot-and-mouth disease. A more popular notion, however, one that would last for centuries (perhaps stemming from Hippocrates's suspicion of foul-smelling air), was the miasma theory.

The miasma theory held that noxious bad air or vapors touched off outbreaks of diseases like cholera. There was some degree of truth in this, since infectious illness can be transmitted through poor sanitation and pollution, which may give off putrid odors. But it was ultimately supplanted by what would come to be known as the germ theory of disease.

In fact, miasmas would be dismissed in 1854 by a London physician, John Snow, following a cholera outbreak in his city's Soho district. Snow suggested that cholera was waterborne and entered the body through contact with contaminated water. Furthermore, he said, if the handle of the Broad Street Pump were removed, the outbreak would stop. He was right.

But if cholera was waterborne, what was it that the water was actually carrying? Fracastoro had flirted with the answer in the 1500s. More than a hundred years later, so did a Dutch cloth merchant and dresser, who turned into a lens-grinder and microscopemaker par excellence, by the name of Antonie van Leeuwenhoek. He created instruments with such revolutionary levels of magnification that one day, while observing

LOUIS PASTEUR

Proponent of the germ theory

1822
Born on December 27 in Dole, France.

1843
Having received his bachelor's degree in science, enters École Normale Supérieure, a teachers' college in Paris.

1847
Works on molecular asymmetry, bringing together the principles of crystallography, chemistry, and optics, which become the basis for the new science of stereochemistry.

1849
Becomes professor of chemistry in Strasbourg, France.

1857
Becomes director of scientific studies at École Normale in Paris; begins work on fermentation and spontaneous generation.

1862
Elected to the Academy of Sciences.

1865
Develops a process of heating wine to prevent souring, now known as pasteurization.

1868
Elected member of the Royal Society.

1870
Publishes *Studies on the Diseases of Silkworms*.

1881
Produces anthrax vaccine.

1885
Produces rabies vaccine and saves the life of a nine-year-old boy who had been bitten by a rabid dog.

1888
Founds the Pasteur Institute, Paris.

1895
Dies on September 28 near Paris.

See pages 257-59 for more information about Antonie van Leeuwenhoek.

PORTAL TO A STOMACH

In 1822, 19-year-old Alexis St. Martin was shot in the stomach. Miraculously, he survived, and his wound healed with a permanent opening, through which physician William Beaumont could observe the actions of his stomach. Beaumont's experiments on St. Martin revolutionized our knowledge of digestion. Alexis St. Martin lived to be 83.

some drops of rainwater, he saw in them what came to be called animalcules: little creatures, thousands of times tinier than the tiniest fleas, that could be seen with the naked eye. These microscopic animalcules appeared to have tiny legs and tails, which allowed them to flit about in the water drops in which they lived.

Van Leeuwenhoek discovered other animalcules in saliva he scraped from his tongue when he was ill. They had similar structures to the creatures in the water drop, but they moved differently. Were they the bearers of his illness? Without doubt, van Leeuwenhoek had come within a hair's breadth of identifying the microorganisms that cause disease, and equally near to coming up with the germ theory.

He also examined his own semen under the microscope, and again he saw minuscule creatures, but this time they all looked alike, with identical tails attached to what appeared to be heads. Microscopic views of his blood revealed other tiny structures—what we now know as red blood cells.

At the suggestion of another Dutch scientist, van Leeuwenhoek reported the results of his labors to England's Royal Society, writing lengthy, meticulously illustrated letters. Over five decades, he sent nearly 200 such missives, and in so doing became one of the most celebrated medical investigators of the Western world.

Van Leeuwenhoek probably never knew how close he had come to identifying the major causes of disease, but within 150 years, others had developed a theory of germs and disease that explained how such microorganisms invaded the human body. Indeed, in the 19th century, the germ theory seemed to be everywhere, with related discoveries occurring in a number of different places.

In 1847 Hungarian obstetrician Ignaz Semmelweis meditated upon all he had seen as a young intern in Vienna. He came up with a shocking discovery: Maternity wards in hospitals had an appallingly high death rate from puerperal, or child bed, fever. Semmelweis's explanation for the phenomenon was one that had been overlooked by doctors and hospital staff: Surgeons often proceeded directly from performing autopsies to working with the expectant mothers, a sloppy habit that fostered infection.

Semmelweis's remedy was to institute among the staff the simple practices of hand-washing and disinfection with chlorinated lime, a substance akin to modern-day chlorine bleach. With these preventive measures, the mortality rate dropped nearly to zero.

Semmelweis could not explain the result, but we know today that he had found out how to keep the microbes at bay. Because the miasma theory was still alive, his argument for new practices was rejected as presumptuous. Discouraged, the young doctor left Vienna in 1850, ten years before Louis Pasteur demonstrated that anthrax—a specific disease—was caused by anthrax bacillus—a specific organism. Semmelweis died in an insane asylum.

Louis Pasteur is the French chemist and microbiologist who deserves much of the credit—along with Joseph Lister and Robert Koch—for the development and acceptance of the germ theory in the late 19th century. In a series of classic tests, Pasteur showed that the processes of fermentation and putrefaction in beer, wine, and milk were caused by germs.

These germs, he said, were not spontaneously generated by the decay processes themselves, a prevalent belief of the time, nor by oxygen alone. Rather, the fermentation came about when the liquids became contaminated with bacteria found in the air to which they had been exposed. After demonstrating this in a historic lecture at the Sorbonne in Paris in 1864, Pasteur remarked, "Never will the doctrine of spontaneous generation recover from the mortal blow of this simple experiment." Bacteriology had entered the medical lexicon.

Much was accomplished during these fertile years of the 19th century. Casimir-Joseph Davaine, a French physician, had identified the anthrax bacillus, a microorganism. Others had found that tuberculosis could be transmitted in cow's milk. Techniques had been developed in staining bacteria for analysis, and some were beginning to classify bacteria by form and structure. William T. Helmuth even wrote an "Ode to the Bacillus." "Oh, powerful bacillus," he penned, "With wonder how you fill us, Everyday! While medical detectives, With powerful objectives, Watch your play."

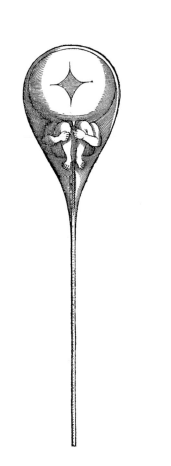

REPRODUCTIVE HYPOTHESES Although the homunculus—a little human contained within a spermatozoan—was by most scientists considered folklore, the theorists of human reproduction in the 17th century were divided between the ovists and the spermists.

Surgeons became more aware of the troubling, even fatal, potential of microorganisms. In the 1860s, severe infection and death by blood poisoning were common after surgery; barely half of all patients survived. Influenced by Pasteur's work, the English surgeon Joseph Lister had been studying inflammation and the discharge of pus after wounds. He suspected that germs carried in the air might be producing surgical infections.

In 1865, Lister decided to try disinfectant techniques on a boy with a bad compound fracture of the leg. He sprayed and bathed the

CELLULAR THEORY

In 1665 the English physicist Robert Hooke, who was also a mechanical genius, saw some odd structures in a piece of cork that he was observing under his microscope. He referred to them as "little boxes or cells, distinct from one another," but carried the work no further. It was not until 1838 that these little cells were recognized as the basic structural units of all plant life, grouping together to form vegetable tissues and containing within each one a nucleus soon to be found to play an important role in life. German scientist Theodor Schwann found that animals, as well as plants, are constructed of cells.

Cells and their myriad components not only hold all living things together, they direct the many forms life will take. In them are encoded both the purpose and the longevity of an organism; they sit at the heart of all biological investigation. The tiniest structural unit of living matter capable of functioning independently, a cell can be a complete organism, as in bacteria and protozoans, like amoebas, which feed by absorbing surrounding organic particles. Specialized cells group together and become organized into tissues and organs.

With the invention of the electron microscope, biologists were finally able to get a near-perfect look through the thin, porous membrane that wrapped the cell like a sausage casing. Inside the shadowy interior, they witnessed a teeming, industrious microworld, packed with the stuff of life itself. Nucleic acids direct the production of protein, carbohydrate/polysaccharides, and long chains of repeating nucleotides that make up the genetic code in the master chemical, DNA, and its companion, RNA. Inside the cell, too, are the gene-carrying chromosomes, slender molecules of two-stranded DNA, twisted together.

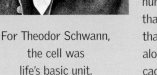

For Theodor Schwann, the cell was life's basic unit.

Each living thing, plant or animal, true to the genetic code by which it lives, has a distinctive, predetermined number of chromosomes, investigators found. White rats have 42, pea plants 14, corn 20, a fruit fly 8, and the rhizopod, a one-celled creature, an astonishing 1,500. Humans, if all is right, have 23 pairs of the DNA strands, corresponding with the number from each of the two parents, for a total of 46. Comparing the human chromosome count with that of the rhizopod was proof that the number of chromosomes alone did not account for the intricacy of the human being. Enzymes were there, too, more than 100,000 in each cell, chemical workhorses that speed up all the changes that take place regularly in our bodies. Without cell-regulated enzyme action, we would be unable to digest food, replace blood cells, build tissue, or even take a breath.

Perhaps the two names most closely associated with modern cell biology are those of James Watson and Francis Crick, who described the intricate molecular, chemical structure of DNA as a double helix, a twisted ladder capable of unhinging itself as it accomplishes the two essential activities in a cell's life: reproducing itself exactly by dividing in two by mitosis and manufacturing protein. Essentially, DNA turned out to be a biological missing link between living and nonliving matter. The cellular theory would be a quantum leap forward for biology and medicine and the understanding of living things.

Friedrich Nietzsche perhaps expressed it best: "There is more wisdom in your body than in your deepest philosophy."

wound with linseed oil and carbolic acid. (Now called phenol, it is the active ingredient in Lysol and other disinfectants; in Lister's day it had shown spectacular success in treating sewage.) Lister kept the cleansed wound covered for days, and the child recovered with no infection.

After several more successes, Lister published papers urging antiseptic methods. He argued that microbes caused infections, and that pus, considered a normal and desirable part of healing, was the product of septic infections. As usual, the old ways did not die easily: Into the 1890s, surgeons wore no masks or head coverings, and some still worked in street clothes.

Pasteur and Lister deserve much of the credit for the development and acceptance of the germ theory. They were joined by another pioneer whose contributions to bacteriology were just as important. Indeed, the theory's most comprehensive expression was found in the work of the German physician Robert Koch.

Koch, who had studied cholera in India and Egypt, was the first to isolate and obtain a pure culture of the anthrax bacterium that Pasteur had studied. He separated it from surrounding fluid. He observed that the microbe could not live in its normal form outside an animal host. To survive, it formed spores, which allowed it to remain in soils in a sort of hibernation state.

In 1882 Koch identified the bacterium that causes tuberculosis, an accomplishment that won him a Nobel Prize. He spent the rest of his life in a vain attempt to control the TB bacterium. Perhaps more important, he articulated the famous Koch's postulates: a sequence of conditions that must be met to identify an organism as the causative agent of a disease. Among his rules: The organism must be present in all cases of the disease; inoculation with a pure culture must produce the disease in susceptible animals; and from these infected animals, it must be possible to propagate the original organism in pure cultures.

THE CELL

Around the time that Malpighi was training his microscope on capillary circulation, others were using the same instrument to peer into animal and plant tissues. They were looking at cells, the tiny envelopes of living matter that make up everything that lives and the smallest structural units of an organism able to function independently. Cells had been observed and named as early as 1665 by British scientist Robert Hooke, who gave them their name, thinking that the microscopic structures he was seeing in bits of cork and green plants looked like monastic rooms.

Gradually, answers to some of the fundamental questions about the structure and purpose of these little compartments emerged. Scottish botanist Robert Brown was in the forefront of cellular research in the early 19th century, noticing, among other things, that when he examined bits of matter in a liquid under his microscope, they seemed to be jerking about

MICROSCOPES
A microscope uses a series of lenses to enlarge the view of small objects for observation and analysis. Many types of microscopes exist: simple and compound, electron, stereoscopic, polarizing, scanning optical, reflecting, acoustic, and scanning tunneling. Although he did not invent the microscope, Antoni van Leeuwenhoek is the first scientist associated with its analytic use.

See page 279 for more information about cell theory.

incessantly—the result of collisions with the unseen molecules of the liquid, now called Brownian motion. In 1831, Brown also observed that plant cells contain an inner component, which he named a nucleus. This observation would eventually take on huge significance for future investigators trying to understand cellular processes.

A few years later, Czech physiologist Jan Evangelista Purkinje first witnessed mitosis, or cell division, the process by which a cell divides, with active involvement of the nucleus, to form two daughter cells, each of which contains the same genetic material as the original. In addition, Purkinje described several different cell types within the protoplasm, or semi-fluid substance that fills cells and makes up their living matter.

But it was not until 1838 that the cell was recognized as the basic structural unit of all plant life. For this we can credit the German botanist Matthias Jakob Schleiden, who saw that vegetable tissues develop from and are constructed of groups of cells, with the nucleus playing the most significant part in each cell. It was a bold claim, but Schleiden could back it up with years of observations using powerful compound microscopes. He studied the way material streams around inside cells. Although he incorrectly decided that cells reproduce by budding off from the surface rather than by dividing, he did provide a firm foundation, at least in the study of plants, for what would become a comprehensive theory of cell biology. Its

See page 277 for more information about Jan Purkinje.

application to animal cells would arrive only a few months later, courtesy of a friend of Schleiden's, Theodor Schwann.

Schwann, a German physiologist, had done important work in a number of areas, including animal physiology, showing that embryos develop from a single cell, or fertilized egg. He had also he coined the term "metabolism" to describe how tissues are built from nutrient components. But his greatest contribution to science, which would prove to be the basis of modern cell theory, came in his 1839 book, *Microscopical Researches into the Accordance in the Structure and Growth of Animals and Plants.*

Cells and their derivatives, Schwann declared, make up all animals and plants. "There is one universal principle of development for the elementary parts of organisms, however different," he wrote, "and that principle is the formation of cells." This new idea swept away all lingering notions that the growth and maintenance of living organisms were governed by some vague principle, such as a collective vital spirit. To Schwann, the individual cell was the key to understanding physiology. "Each of the elementary parts possesses a force of its own, a life of its own," he wrote. "The whole organism exists only through the reciprocal action of the single elementary parts."

Each cell thus has a separate identity, but all behave for the common good. Today, we know that the human body's 50 trillion to 75 trillion cells carry out all of the functions of life, that most of them work to transform energy for the body. When a group of them get together, they form tissue; and when tissues collect, they become organs.

But how did cells come into being in the first place? Here Schleiden and many of his contemporaries returned to vitalism: They presumed that cells were guided by some vital force, distinct from chemical and other physical forces, and crystallized out of gelatinous raw materials.

This view was not held by the perceptive, questioning, Polish-born anatomist and pathologist Rudolf Virchow, however. In 1858, he attacked the vitalism theory, declaring unequivocally that "all cells originate from cells." No central life force shaped organisms, Virchow asserted. Living things were the "sum of vital units"— cells—"each of which possesses the full characteristics of life." With respect to disease, Virchow declared, it was simply a matter of cells run amok. Over time, he believed, cells respond to abnormal conditions by beginning to generate abnormal progeny that cause illness. He likened cells to autonomous citizens of a "social arrangement, or society," in which

THROUGH THE LENS

Theodor Schwann, the German physiologist who proposed that cells were the basic building blocks of life, drew the little units as he saw them through the microscope.

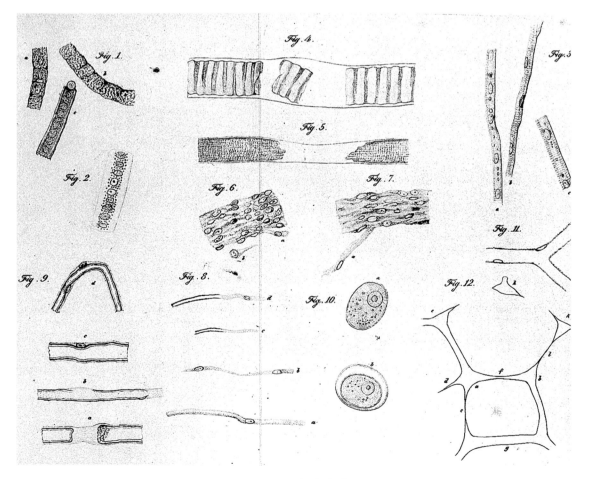

each individual should act to enhance the greater well-being of its neighbors and the whole organism. Sometimes they did not, though, and the resulting disorder caused disease. Many years later, some of Virchow's ideas would prove apt in explaining cancer, the ultimate cellular mutiny.

THE SCIENCE OF PREVENTION

Given their limited research tools and the resultant lack of solid information, any attempt by 19th-century scientists to connect cells to disease, however, was purely broad speculation, and could not go much beyond Virchow's hypotheses. On the other hand, as evidence for the role of microbes in causing disease mounted, researchers like Pasteur turned their attention to stifling the growth of the nasty animalcules in order to treat the diseases they spawned. Indeed, Pasteur seemed devoted to an even higher goal. "When meditating over a disease," he said during an 1884 address in Paris, "I never think of finding a remedy for it, but, instead, a means of preventing it."

A means of preventing it. These were key words, dependent on two essential factors: first, a science of immunology—studies on how and why disease takes hold of the body and on how the body wards it off,—and second, the preventive vaccines emerging from that study. Neither was well understood until Pasteur built on the work of his predecessor, Edward Jenner, to produce what would be one of

VACCINATION

In 1796, English physician Edward Jenner vaccinated eight-year-old James Phipps against smallpox and ushered in a new age of preventive medicine.

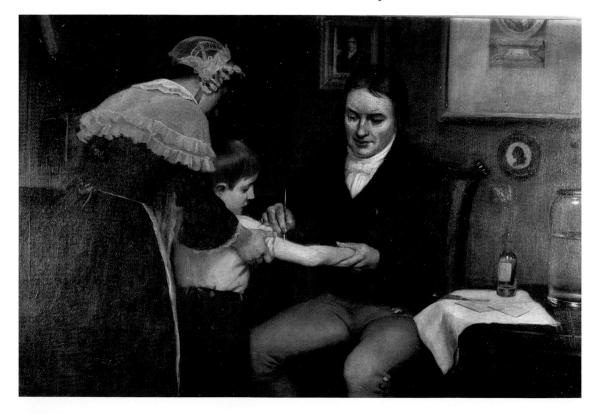

medicine's greatest triumphs: inoculation. First Jenner, an English country doctor, discovered vaccination in 1796. Whereas Lister was set on killing germs to save lives, Jenner harnessed them to do the same.

Jenner observed that people who had been infected with cowpox—a mild illness spread by milking cows—did not get smallpox, a prolific killer. Others had made similar observations in France and Germany, and Jenner began to think about the implications: Exposure to cowpox made one immune.

He decided to try a daring experiment: If exposure to cowpox protected people from smallpox, then why not take fluid from a cowpox pustule, transfer it to an uninfected person, and then expose that person to smallpox? As risky as it seemed, it was based on such keen and careful observations that Jenner must have had few doubts about success, or he would not have proceeded. He mentioned his plan to his former teacher, John Hunter, a British anatomist and surgeon whose experiments in lymphatics—the circulation of lymph fluid to remove bacteria from the body's tissue—and the formation of pus in infected tissue had been part of Jenner's education. "Don't think, try," Hunter advised him. "Be patient, be accurate."

Jenner's first subject was an eight-year-old boy, James Phipps. Cowpox pus was extracted from the hand of a milkmaid and carefully introduced into the boy in a procedure that Jenner termed vaccination, from the Latin word for cow, *vacca*. Two months later, Jenner inoculated the boy with what should have been a deadly quantity of smallpox, and the boy did not contract the disease. His name would not win the notoriety of Jenner's, but word of the successful preventive method in which he had played such a key role soon spread rapidly around the world.

The usual doubts and criticisms surfaced. "The skepticism that appeared, even among the most enlightened of medical men when

EDWARD JENNER

Inventor of the vaccination

1749
Born on May 17 in Berkeley, Gloucestershire, England.

1763
Apprentices to local surgeon Daniel Ludlow at the age of 14.

1773
Completes medical training at St. George's Hospital, London.

1772
Returns to Berkeley as local medical practitioner and surgeon.

1783
Develops method for purifying tartar emetic, a chemical used to treat parasitic diseases.

1789
For a scientific paper explaining the nesting habits of the cuckoo bird, elected fellow of the Royal Society.

1796
Successfully vaccinates eight-year-old James Phipps, protecting him from smallpox, with inoculation prepared from cowpox disease.

1798
Publishes "An Inquiry into the Causes and Effects of the Variolae Vaccinae," in which he describes the use of cowpox inoculation to prevent smallpox.

1804
Awarded special medal by Napoleon, honoring his medical achievement.

1809
For his knowledge of geology, earth science, and fossilization, elected member of the Geologic Society.

1819
Discovers the fossilized remains of what we now call a plesiosaur.

1823
Dies on January 26 in Berkeley, England.

my sentiments on the important subject of the cow-pox were first promulgated was highly laudable," a generous Jenner wrote later. "To have admitted the truth of a doctrine, at once so novel and so unlike any thing that ever had appeared in the annals of medicine, without the test of the most rigid scrutiny, would have bordered upon temerity."

Pasteur kept up the momentum that Jenner initiated. He had already disproved the leading theory of fermentation—that it was purely a chemical phenomenon—and had demonstrated that it was caused by microorganisms instead. He had also shown that if a sterile fluid was not exposed to germs from the air, no contamination would result. As a practical matter, he determined that heating milk to a certain temperature would keep it from spreading typhoid and tuberculosis germs. This method, which came to be called pasteurization, was quickly and broadly adopted—and certainly saved countless lives.

But the most spectacular of Pasteur's discoveries came in the 1880s. He had found that exposing chickens to a bit of cultured chicken cholera bacteria would prevent them from developing a serious form of the disease—much as Jenner had found that smallpox could be prevented by treatment with a vaccine of cowpox.

Pasteur further tested the idea by isolating a culture of anthrax, the deadly disease to which both animals and humans are susceptible. He used it to vaccinate two dozen sheep, then housed them with an equal number of untreated sheep and exposed them all to lethal doses of anthrax. All the unvaccinated animals died; all the vaccinated ones lived. The results made Pasteur internationally famous.

In 1868, he decided to try one of his preparations on a human being. The great chemist had been working on a vaccine for rabies, a fatal viral disease of warm-blooded animals that attacks the central nervous system. Pasteur's experiments with animals had shown success in preventing rabies, using the same technique he had employed with anthrax and cholera. He had to pass the disease from animal to animal, since at his stage of knowledge he could not isolate the virus. He was still experimenting with animals when a nine-year-old boy, Joseph Meister, was severely bitten by a rabid animal in a nearby town. Despite warnings from colleagues, Pasteur gave the boy a series of 13 injections. The child lived, and he did not contract rabies.

VIRUSES, A NEW SOURCE OF DISEASE

Now that certain bacteria were known to cause certain diseases, viruses were the next target. So small they could not be seen under ordinary microscopes, they even passed right through filters that trapped bacteria. Medical investigators suspected their existence, but all they could do to learn more about them was to inject substances believed to contain one into an animal and watch the effect. They also conducted experiments by implanting the suspect

SMALLPOX

In the 18th century, smallpox plagued much of the world with its devastating rate of infection and death. With Jenner's vaccine, the disease retreated and now has been nearly eradicated.

COWPOX

The cowpox disease has been known for centuries, known by the ulcers that form on cows' udders. When a human catches cowpox from a cow, the virus enters a cut or scratch and forms an ulcer. Researchers in the 1980s found that humans can catch cowpox from rodents as well.

THE IMMUNE SYSTEM

Whether a person acquires an infection, bacterial or viral, or manages to fight it off all depends on the state of the body's formidable natural defenses, the collection of cells and cell by-products that make up the human immune system.

On the front line are protein molecules, antibodies produced by white blood cells, which destroy or immobilize invading pathogens carrying other protein substances called antigens. The so-called antibody-antigen reaction is best observed when tissues are set upon by bacteria through an open wound in the skin. The body immediately activates its defenders and dispatches them to the wound, where they recognize the invaders as foreign and attack.

The immune system draws on specialized cells—lymphocytes that recognize antigens, for example, and phagocytic macrophages that engulf and destroy invaders. Lympho-cytes, which make up between 22 and 28 percent of all white blood cells in a normal adult, include two types of cell, B-cells and T-cells, which arise in the bone marrow and then mature. Then they flow into the bloodstream, lodging in a filmy network of connective lymphoid tissue in the spleen and in lymph nodes among other structures.

Central to the system is the lymph itself, a watery fluid that holds the white blood cells. Lymph circulates through the lymphatic system, an interconnected arrangement of channels, spaces, and vessels, and is delivered to the blood. Lymph nodes—small ovoid bodies that contain the

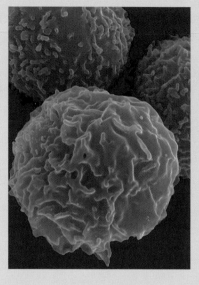

Precursor T- and B-cells (tinted blue and red, respectively) make up the immune system's lymphocytes.

lymphocytes—are distributed along the lymphatic vessels, where they filter the lymph of bacteria and other foreign particles.

Lymphocytes in the spleen perform the same function. A highly vascular lymphoid organ to the left of the stomach, the spleen filters foreign substances from the blood. It also stores blood and rids it of old cells.

The system works well, but it can sabotage itself through the phenomenon of auto-immunity—in effect, a civil war raging in the body. In some situations, T-cells turn against normal cells, treating them as foreign and causing a number of diseases such as Type 1 diabetes, pernicious anemia, rheumatoid arthritis, and lupus, which involves the skin, joints, and other bodily systems. Sometimes the beneficial activities of the immune response have to be suppressed by radiation or drugs to control autoimmune diseases or to prevent trans-planted organs from being rejected.

When a new kidney or heart is transplanted into the body, the immune system considers it foreign and sends its disease-fighting force out to reject the foreign tissue. Potent immunosuppressive drugs can halt the process, but they can weaken the body's defenses to such an extent that infective agents, as well as the grafted organ, go undisturbed. It is interesting to note that the rejection phenomenon is not set off in the case of pregnancy, when the fetus, with only half of its genes identical to the mother's, remains safe in the womb for up to nine months.

substances into fertile chicken eggs, then watching changes in the developing embryo.

Given their invisibility, why would anyone suspect that viruses existed in the first place? The answer was simply that there were numerous diseases for which no pathogen had been found, and the onset, progress, and resolution of these diseases suggested an agent related to microbes.

In the late 1800s, Dutch botanist Martinus Beijerinck performed a puzzling experiment that did not capture a virus but did suggest its presence. He squeezed the juice from tobacco plants infected with a disfiguring disease, tobacco mosaic. Examining it under the microscope, he could find no bacteria. Whatever was causing the problem was much smaller than any bacteria known at the time: Beijerinck called it a virus. (Jenner had referred to the material that caused cowpox as a "virus," but for him, the word simply expressed a virulent or poisonous substance.)

Filterable viruses, as they were now called—meaning they were capable of passing through a fine-pore laboratory filter—were leaving their footprints everywhere. The number of diseases they seemed to cause increased as the various liquids they hid in were scrutinized more carefully. The quest for viral illnesses became paramount to researchers.

In 1897 Paul Frosch, a German physician, showed that a filterable virus was the cause of foot-and-mouth disease in animals; it was the first time that a filterable virus

had been shown to be the agent of an animal disease.

But what of the role of viruses in human health and disease? The answer was already suggested by Pasteur's rabies experiment on young Joseph Meister, and more proof surfaced in 1900 in the laboratory of a U.S. Army pathologist, Walter Reed.

His target was yellow fever, an infectious tropical disease characterized by high fever and jaundice. Thousands of people had been killed in epidemics in the Mississippi Valley and throughout the Americas. Cuba was one of the

LOUIS PASTEUR

Few scientists have been as widely celebrated in their own times as Pasteur was in his. Typical of the enthusiasm was this cover illustration from a French magazine published in the year of his death.

A LOUIS PASTEUR

areas hit the hardest by yellow fever. The conventional theory was that the disease was spread by clothing or bedding infected with bacteria. That idea was scrapped when further investigation into patterns of the spread indicated an insect carrier, most likely a mosquito.

Concerned about the outbreaks, the U.S. surgeon general appointed a medical commission to attack the disease and named Reed to direct it. Reed believed that the best way to prove that a mosquito was the culprit was to experiment on human subjects, "to clear the field for further effective work." Human subjects were essential, since the disease did not affect animals. Dispatched to Cuba, Reed began investigating.

The experiment he organized was perhaps one of the most courageous scientific examples of the ends justifying the means. It was based on the speculation that a mosquito that had bitten a yellow fever victim could transmit the disease by biting a noninfected individual. Spanish immigrant volunteers would be paid $100 in gold, with a bonus of $100 if they got sick. U.S. soldiers who participated got paid nothing.

The methodology was crude, to say the least. Mosquitoes were placed in test tubes, which were then inverted on the arms of infected persons, allowing the insects to suck a blood meal. Two weeks later, presumably after the disease agent had matured inside the insect, the same tubes were inverted on the arms of healthy volunteers, and the mosquitoes sucked blood again. In the first experiments, two sub-

jects developed the disease, one a severe and near-fatal case, the other less so. Dr. Jesse Lazear, a scientist from Johns Hopkins University working on the project, was not so fortunate: He died of yellow fever, probably from an experimental bite.

Further experiments used different species of mosquitoes, and more than a score of cases of the disease were produced, 14 by infected bites and others by injection of filtered blood serum drawn from volunteers in the early stages of the disease. In all, some 30 volunteers contracted yellow fever; five died.

The experiment instigated a mosquito-eradication program that erased yellow fever from Cuba, and it proved that a filterable virus, or at least some sort of ultramicroscopic organism, was transmitted to humans via mosquito bites. But the experiment also triggered criticism. For one thing, the first experiments were apparently undertaken without obtaining any formal consent from the volunteers. Reed later drew up protocols that recognized the risks. There was also the matter of Reed's participation. He had agreed—as did Lazear—to experiment on himself; but in the long run he never did—as did Lazear, fatally—a decision that raised eyebrows among some of his colleagues.

Ethics aside (if that is possible in formulating any theory and practice in human health), the yellow fever experiments and the disease they wiped out were a sign of the future, when preventive measures against a range of viral diseases such as pneumonia, influenza, hepatitis

A and B, chickenpox, and measles would be a reality. Eventually no one would have to experience daily life greatly diminished by the threat of viral disease, as did an early American physician during a yellow fever scare in 1793: "Many never walked on the footpath, but went into the middle of the streets, to avoid being infected in passing by houses wherein people had died. The old custom of shaking hands fell into such general disuse, that many were affronted at even the offer of the hand."

One other noteworthy experiment that would implicate a virus in a disease was conducted after Reed's, in 1910, by Dr. Francis Peyton Rous, a New York pathologist. Rous injected chickens with a filtered liquid made from a sarcoma—a malignant tumor arising from connective tissues—found in another chicken. He repeated his experiment several times, and each time the results were the same: The injected chickens developed the sarcoma, proof that the extract, filtered free of cells, carried a virus

YELLOW FEVER

"Conquerors of Yellow Fever," a painting by Dean Cornwell, depicts the brain trust assigned to find a cause and cure for yellow fever. In civilian clothes at left stands Cuban physician Carlos Finlay; at the stairway, right, U.S. Army pathologist Walter Reed.

that was capable of transmitting malignancy. Dr. Rous's experiment, regarded as highly significant even today, met with great skepticism at the time, because the popular assumption was that the cancer cell itself was the only agent that could transmit cancer.

As productive as all this work was, it told scientists little about the makeup of a virus. Some years after Dr. Rous's experiment, however, American biochemist Wendell Stanley managed to purify and crystallize viruses, including the tobacco mosaic virus, and examine them, thus unmasking their molecular structure. In 1934 Albert Sabin, the American bacteriologist who would later develop a live-virus vaccine against polio, isolated a virus from the central nervous system of a person who had died of an inflammation of the spinal cord after being bitten by a monkey.

It would eventually become clear that the pathogens consisted of nothing but a tough envelope of protein, inside of which was packed nucleic acid. (Later researchers would learn that this structure was either genetic code–carrying DNA or RNA, wrapped in coils, which controlled cellular function and heredity.) This observation posed a serious problem. Viruses were clearly not alive in the way that bacteria and other cells are alive, yet they could grow and reproduce.

Hovering as these viruses did in a sort of gray world between life and nonlife, how, the researchers asked, did they survive? How did they infect? Viruses would not be photographed until the invention, in the 1940s, of the electron microscope, so researchers had only limited answers.

By the late 1930s it was known that the tiny agents that could sneak through bacterial filters needed a host cell to live, and to do this they took over its machinery, including its instructions for normal duplication. Tricked by the virus's commands, and with its own genetic information altered or blotted out, the hapless cell was either forced to manufacture thousands of new viruses instead of normal protein before destroying itself, or was so transformed that it produced endless copies of

1922 – 1960

1922
Insulin is first administered to diabetic patients by Canadian physicians Frederick Banting, Charles Best, and John MacLeod.

1928
Scottish bacteriologist Alexander Fleming discovers penicillin while experimenting with staphylococcus bacteria.

1940s
Chemotherapy is developed as an effective treatment for cancer.

1943
American microbiologist Selman Waksman isolates streptomycin, the first antibiotic effective against the bacterium that causes tuberculosis.

VACCINATIONS
In this contemporary wood engraving, the Third Gurkhas in India are vaccinated for cholera at the time of the 1893 epidemic.

its new, flawed self. A hijacked bacterium cell could lose all of its metabolic processes in a few minutes, a human mammalian cell in several hours.

Eventually researchers began to see that many viruses could lie quietly in cells until something—drugs, environmental pollutants, or some biochemical change—touched them off, instigating disease-causing changes in the cell's own genetic instructions. Ironically—although researchers could not have known it at the time—the virus that causes AIDS probably first leaped into the human population during these very years.

DRUGS AND ANTIBIOTICS

Battling, curing, and preventing human ailments caused by viruses and bacteria continued to hold center stage. But in Pasteur's time, antivirals were difficult to develop (as they still are today), given that

1953
American geneticist James Watson and British biologist Francis Crick unlock the double-helix structure and the function of DNA.

1954
The first successful transplant of an organ, a kidney, is performed on identical twin brothers by American surgeon Joseph Murray in Boston, Massachusetts.

1955
American physician Jonas Salk's vaccine for polio, discovered in 1952, is released in the United States.

1960
The first birth control pill, Enovid-10, is developed and marketed in the United States.

ANTIBACTERIAL SUCCESS

Finding compounds that killed bacteria could require endless trials or occur by accident, as in the case of the penicillin mold that killed the staph microbes in Alexander Fleming's culture dish.

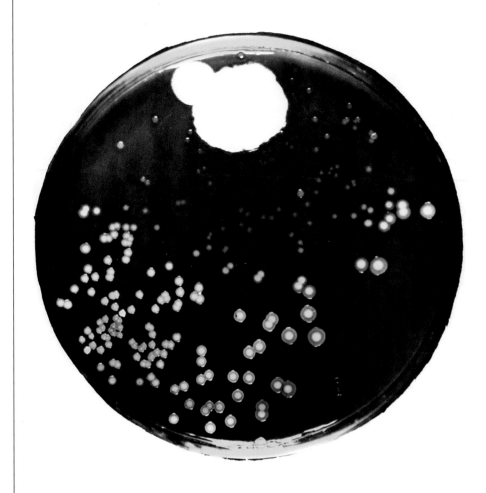

The beginning of Penicillin
Alexander Fleming

the enemy was both invisible and complex. Pasteur and others noted that some substances seemed to retard the growth of microbes, but some of those treatments also damaged the tissue that the germs were infecting. What was needed was a substance that attached specifically to bacteria and reacted to only specific molecules in a cell, something like today's highly specific

monoclonal antibodies. Such a thing did exist, but no one recognized it until German chemist and bacteriologist Paul Ehrlich, whose complicated side-chain theory of organic molecules significantly advanced the science of immunity and serum reactions.

Ehrlich pondered on the dyes used to make bacteria visible under the microscope. If a substance like these dyes could be found whose chemistry had the ability to kill germs, it might prove the basis for antimicrobial therapy. In 1910, after hundreds of experiments, Ehrlich's lab identified a compound—Number 606—that eliminated the spirochetes that cause syphilis, a sexually transmitted disease that was almost always fatal and that often caused insanity before death.

Soon, similar "magic bullets"—drugs or treatments that cure or prevent disease—were being discovered. Like so many others, one was found by accident. In 1928 British researcher Sir Alexander Fleming, experimenting with cultures of staphylococcus bacteria, inadvertently allowed one dish to get contaminated. Instead of being completely covered with the bacteria, however, the culture dish showed large areas where no staph microbes grew. Those spaces were infested by a mold that apparently produced a powerful bacteria-killer, soon identified as *Penicillium notatum*. The substance that Fleming named penicillin was in therapeutic use a decade later, after being developed by a number of biochemists. It soon became the prime antibiotic of the 20th century.

Long before penicillin was widely available as a drug, however, another class of compounds had proved effective, too. In 1932, Ehrlich's countryman Gerhard Domagk discovered a type of dye that killed streptococcus. It effectively cured both his own daughter and a son of President Franklin D. Roosevelt. The active ingredient, sulfanilamide (later brand-named Prontonsil), was isolated and used to create a number of compounds that inhibit bacterial growth. They are now known collectively as the sulfa drugs.

Despite all dazzling successes, one critical microbe stubbornly resisted antibiotic attack: the bacillus that causes tuberculosis, a common and often fatal disease that affects the lungs and other tissues of the body. A litany of researchers dating back to the 1600s had

ALEXANDER FLEMING

Discoverer of penicillin

1881
Born on August 6 in Lochfield, Ayrshire, Scotland.

1906
Receives degree from St. Mary's Hospital Medical School, University of London.

1918
After serving during World War I as a captain in the Army Medical Corps, returns to St. Mary's to teach and pursue research.

1921
Identifies and isolates lysozyme, an enzyme that exhibits antibiotic activity, found in certain animal tissues and secretions.

1928
While researching staphylococcus bacteria, realizes that a species of mold, *Penicillium notatum*, has killed all the bacteria surrounding it—the discovery of penicillin.

1928
Named Arris and Gale Lecturer at the Royal College of Surgeons.

1943
Elected a fellow of the Royal Society.

1944
Knighted in honor of his work in the medical field.

1945
Receives the Nobel Prize in physiology or medicine, sharing it with Ernst Boris Chain and Howard Walter Florey.

1948
Becomes emeritus professor of bacteriology, University of London.

1951-1954
Serves as rector of Edinburgh University.

1955
Dies on March 11 in London, England.

See page 103 for more information about Robert Koch.

WARTIME DRUG
Penicillin proved its value on the battlefields of World War II, where it fought infections that killed wounded soldiers in previous wars. After the war the drug went into mass production.

focused on the disease, including the English physician Benjamin Marten, who in 1720, proposed a theory of pulmonary tuberculosis based on the assumption that the causative agent was a microorganism. More than a century and a half later, Koch discovered the tubercle.

A host of treatments for tuberculosis were tried, from gold preparations to nerve surgery that paralyzed the diaphragm. Finally in 1943 Selman Waksman, a Russian-American biochemist and specialist in soil biology, isolated a mold that produced a substance called streptomycin that is lethal to tuberculosis bacteria. While not eradicated, one more of humankind's infectious threats was matched with a treatment.

THE VIRUS QUESTION, STILL UNSOLVED

Viral diseases still posed a greater challenge. Understanding them was a chore—and for some of them, it still is today. So, too, is formulating antiviral substances.

A viral infection may not necessarily mean disease. Some viruses, in fact, do no harm at all, and others might create symptoms so mild that they go unrecognized. Indeed, for every treated case of paralytic polio, there have been many hundreds of cases of the disease that went unnoticed. Having said that, it's important to note that HIV, the human immunodeficiency virus, alone infects millions worldwide and kills upward of three million in a given year.

BACTERIA AND VIRUSES

There are important differences between bacteria and viruses, but both share the ability to cause devastating diseases.

Bacteria are unicellular microorganisms that usually reproduce asexually but can sometimes reproduce sexually. They contain cytoplasm: semifluid, transparent living matter. Bacteria can be helpful—as when they decompose dead material or aid in digesting food in the intestines—but they can also be detrimental, becoming pathogenic, carrying and causing infection. Bacteria can be killed, or their growth hindered, by antibiotics, which can be administered orally, by injection, or topically.

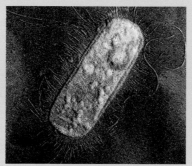

The ubiquitous *E. coli* bacterium can be useful, harmless, or severely poisonous.

Viruses are submicroscopic, tinier than bacteria, and not typically regarded as alive. They are constructed not of cytoplasm but of a core of DNA or RNA surrounded by a coat of protein. Despite this store of life's substance, a virus is incapable of surviving by itself—until it gets into a living cell, where it commandeers the cellular machinery, including instructions for duplication, and does its damaging parasitic work. Antibiotics are ineffective against viruses; antivirals, capable of destroying them or inhibiting their growth and reproduction, must be used instead.

It is far easier to make an antibiotic (or a vaccine against diseases caused by bacteria) than an antiviral. Early antimicrobials were relatively simple: penicillin from a mold, dilute carbolic acid, and other natural antibiotic substances. Eventually chemists produced semisynthetic and synthetic antibiotics: Streptomycin to treat tuberculosis, for example, and broad-spectrum ones such as Aureo-mycin, Terramycin, and Chloramphenicol, especially effective against typhoid fever. Vaccines and other preventive measures were developed against bacterial diseases such as typhoid, whooping cough, and tuberculosis.

Vaccines depend on the immune system's ability to remember a past encounter. Vaccines introduce a dummy enemy and prepare the immune system for disease-causing attacks. In a vaccine, the sham enemy is a weakened or killed virus, which triggers lymphocytes to reproduce and make anti-bodies but does not cause disease. When the actual disease comes along, the body is ready.

But some disease-causing microorganisms mutate so that they resist antibiotics. When they do so, the drug destroys more non-resistant bugs, which encourages the mutants to multiply and strengthen their drug resistance. Overprescribing antibiotics contributes to the appearance of resistant strains.

Vaccines have been developed against many viral diseases, including measles, influenza, rabies, herpes, and polio. Some antivirals stop the virus from entering cells by interfering with its receptor proteins, the molecular structures that bind with various substances. Others strip the virus of its ability to take over a cell, while still others target the virus's reproductive capacity.

Like antibiotics, antivirals can lose their efficacy, as when genes from differing strains of a disease combine to form a new, sometimes more virulent, strain. The virus that causes influenza, for example, is notorious for changing its stripes. A vaccine against one strain of influenza may not necessarily protect against another.

CAUSE OF AIDS

The human immunodeficiency virus (HIV), shown here enlarged 26,000 times, long eluded researchers seeking the cause of acquired immune deficiency syndrome (AIDS). It has thus far resisted antiviral treatment regimens.

As knowledge of viral genetics accumulated through the 20th century, scientists gained a better understanding of how viruses rearranged the host cell's internal chemistry. But several obstacles remained, one of the most formid-able that many kinds of viruses don't contain DNA, but only RNA, which acts outside the cell nucleus.

How, then, could such viruses affect the DNA of host cells? The answer lay in a cellular enzyme called reverse transcriptase, discovered by American virologist David Baltimore, who won the 1975 Nobel Prize in physiology or medicine for the achievement. Baltimore's research showed that reverse transcriptase allowed a strand of RNA to copy itself back into DNA, thus enabling a virus—now termed a retrovirus—to rewrite the chemical instructions in an infected cell's nucleus.

Many other viruses, like those that cause certain kinds of hepatitis, continued to confound science. Eventually the polio virus was virtually eliminated by vaccination. And in 1977, thanks to worldwide vaccination efforts, the last known case of smallpox, a killer that had stalked the Earth for thousands of years, was found and treated. The World Health Organization agreed that all the stocks of smallpox virus in labs all over the world should be destroyed (with the exception of two, one in the United States and one in the Soviet Union).

It was welcome news, but not everyone agreed. Baltimore, one of the scientists who believed all the

smallpox virus should be eliminated, summed up the dilemma: "It [the virus] only continues to exist because some people got sentimental over smallpox. Environmentalists, in particular, feel we should never eradicate a living species. Of course, it happens all the time, but this would have been conscious, and some people felt bad about it."

To be fair, a large group of virologists did not want an object of potential inquiry made unavailable. Further, should someone choose to use smallpox for a biological attack, the attacked nation would need a stockpile to prepare a vaccine and protect its people.

The hunt for antivirals produced successful vaccines against not only smallpox and polio but a number of other diseases, including influenza, measles, and mumps. But developing an effective vaccine against AIDS has been especially difficult because so far the immune system, for complex reasons, cannot control HIV the way it can other viruses. Laboratories around the world are currently researching gene therapy, an alternative that might work by sending a stripped-down version of the AIDS virus into damaged cells, carrying genetic components that can interfere with the growth of the real virus. "It works in the lab," Baltimore has said, "but it will be a while before we can know if it works in people."

Other challenges remain, compounded by the discovery of a warped protein called a prion, discovered by American neurologist

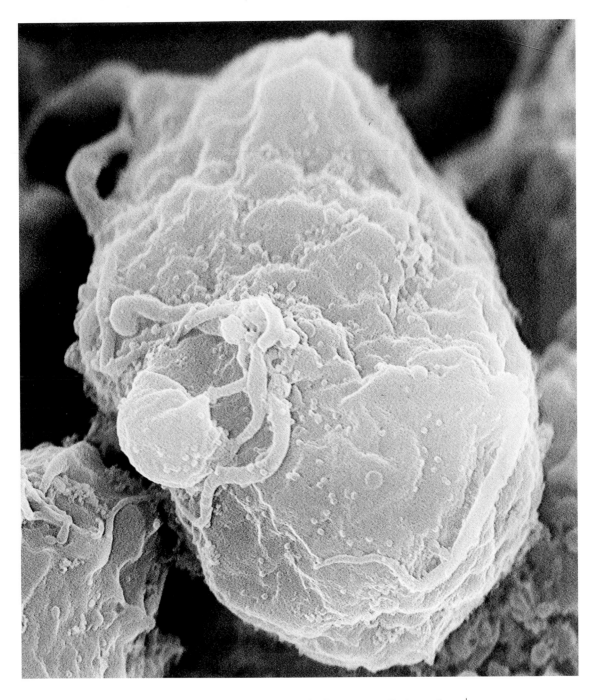

Stanley B. Prusiner. The prion, or possibly a hybrid particle called a virino, appeared to be responsible for certain horrible conditions such as scrapie (a neurological disease of sheep and goats) and mad cow disease, which temporarily brought the British beef industry to a halt in the 1990s. These findings prompted the first new principle of infection postulated since the 19th century. While the prion's existence is still questioned by some scientists, it remains the subject of intense investigation and may one day usher in new treatments and vaccines.

NUTRITION AND METABOLISM

As medicinal chemistry progressed from the mid-19th century on, many diseases came under some degree of control. A number of scientists now turned their focus on specific organic substances that appeared to be essential for normal growth and bodily activity. We know them today as vitamins.

Nutrition and metabolism—the chemical and physical processes within a living organism that are essential to the maintenance of life—aroused considerable interest. Probably the earliest concept of how vitamins fit into the picture came in 1881, when a Swiss physiologist, N. Lunin, found that a synthetic milk diet inhibited animals' growth, whereas on fresh milk, they thrived. Chemically pure foods, Lunin reasoned, lacked some unknown factor that was able to nurture growth and sustain life. Soon the term "vitamine" was coined, on the assumption that the mysterious substances were amines, a class of organic compounds. When it was discovered that these substances were not amines, the letter *e* was dropped, and "vitamin" became the accepted term. They had a name now—but what were they?

In time, vitamins were identified as substances that could be obtained naturally from plant and animal foods. To isolate, identify,

VITAMIN SOURCE

In order to provide an extra source of vitamin C, the small fruits called rose hips, which grow on many varieties of rose, have long been gathered and processed into syrup and, now, into vitamins.

and eventually synthesize these mystery substances required experiment upon experiment. The most fruitful efforts involved scrutinizing deficiency diseases, notably rickets, scurvy, beriberi, and pellagra.

Rickets, essentially a disease of children, had been known for some time and was a serious problem in England. It retarded bone growth, caused deformation and demineralization of the bones, and left children's bodies prone to bone fractures. After producing experimental rickets in animals by feeding them deficient diets, researchers found that sunlight and cod liver oil improved their conditions. The vitamin recognized as an anti-rickets agent in 1918 was isolated in 1932. It was named vitamin D, following the researchers' habits of using terms like "Factor A" and "Factor B" to describe the organic substances whose absence from the diet seemed to cause disease.

Scurvy, an ancient disease characterized by spongy, bleeding gums and weakness, was first described in the year 1250. In 1617 an English surgeon, John Woodall, urged the eating of lemons and limes as a preventive measure, an intuitive precursor to the research finding that scurvy was caused by a deficiency of vitamin C. Chests of the fruit were loaded on British ships, and sailors mixed the juice in their beer. "It was also their constant diversion to pelt one another with the rinds," wrote one physician, "so that the deck was always strewed and wet with the fragrant liquor. The happy effect was, that the admiral brought his sailors home in good health."

The floodgates opened in the 1920s, and vitamin after vitamin was recognized, isolated, and linked to diseases in cases of deficiencies. An antineuritis factor was found in rice polishings: We now know the substance as vitamin B-1. Milk enriched with vitamin D came on the market in 1925. Vitamin E was discovered in wheat germ in 1931, and vitamin C, or ascorbic acid, was synthesized in 1933. Market shelves did not yet groan under the weight of bottled vitamin supplements, but the discoveries opened people's eyes to the benefits of

a protective balanced diet that included milk, eggs, fresh fruit, and leafy vegetables. There was truth in Jonathan Swift's observation that "Kitchen Physic is the best Physic."

There's an interesting aside to the vitamin story. The committee responsible for nominating Nobel Prize recipients long ignored anyone who had discovered vitamins. The suspicion was that the committee was swayed by skeptics who felt they were hypothetical entities, unidentified organic nutrients used to explain a variety of disorders. As one scientist said of vitamins,

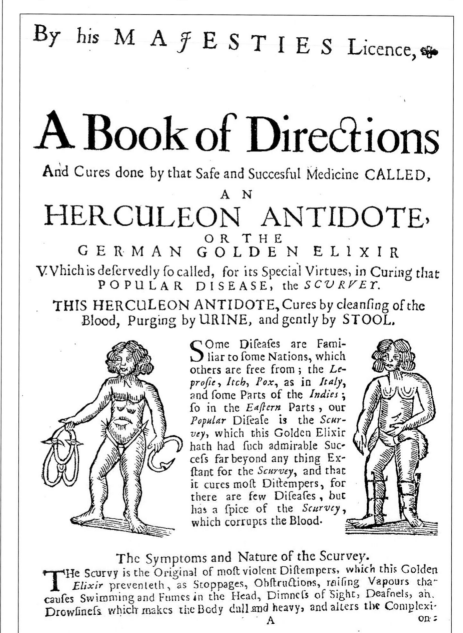

By his MAJESTIES Licence,

A Book of Directions

And Cures done by that Safe and Succesful Medicine CALLED,

A N

HERCULEON ANTIDOTE,

OR THE

GERMAN GOLDEN ELIXIR

VVhich is defervedly fo called, for its Special Virtues, in Curing that POPULAR DISEASE, the *SCURVEY*.

THIS HERCULEON ANTIDOTE, Cures by cleanfing of the Blood, Purging by URINE, and gently by STOOL.

SOme Difeafes are Familiar to fome Nations, which others are free from ; the *Leprofie*, *Itch*, *Pox*, as in *Italy*, and fome Parts of the *Indies* ; fo in the *Eaftern* Parts , our *Popular* Difeafe is the *Scurvey*, which this Golden Elixir hath had fuch admirable Succefs far beyond any thing Extant for the *Scurvey*, and that it cures moft Diftempers, for there are few Difeafes , but has a fpice of the *Scurvey*, which corrupts the Blood.

The Symptoms and Nature of the Scurvey.

THe Scurvy is the Original of moft violent Diftempers, which this Golden *Elixir* preventeth , as Stoppages, Obftructions, raifing Vapours that caufes Swimming and Fumes in the Head, Dimnefs of Sight, Deafnefs, an. Drowfinefs which makes the Body dull and heavy, and alters the Complexi-

A   on :

"No one has ever seen one." After 1926, though, all this changed. Two Dutch scientists, B. C. P. Jansen and W. F. Donath, finally extracted pure crystals of vitamin B-1 from rice polishings. Only a hundredth of a milligram of the crystalline substance cured a deficient pigeon, a finding that was confirmed later. In 1929, the Nobel committee finally awarded a joint prize to Dutch scientist Christiaan Eijkman and English biochemist Gowland Hopkins, both of them for work on the role of vitamins in disease, health, and metabolism.

THE ROLE OF HORMONES

As the list of known vitamins grew, researchers turned their attention to another class of mysterious substances: the bodily secretions that also seemed to have an effect on metabolism, growth, and health in general. Secreted by the endocrine glands—such as the thyroid, pituitary, and adrenal—these substances flowed directly into the bloodstream. In 1905, they were named hormones, from the Greek word for "excite." Clearly they seemed to act as messengers, stimulating responses in various organs and even affecting emotions. Medical researchers already had some understanding of the thyroid gland, a two-lobed organ in the neck, in front of the trachea, that seemed to produce various hormones. Oversecretion of some thyroid hormones produced weight loss and nervousness. The gland could enlarge, due to an iodine deficiency, and form a goiter, a visible swelling in the front of the neck.

In the late 1800s, neurologists and neurosurgeons, sometimes playing hunches, began tinkering with the thyroid gland. Their efforts paid off: The Austrian Nobelist Julius Wagner-Jauregg discovered that treatment with iodized salt, the kind commonly sold today, prevented goiter.

Another notable Austrian, Anton Freiherr von Eiselsberg, produced experimental tetany, a disorder characterized by painful muscle spasms and tremors, by excising the thyroid and parathyroids of a cat. His surgery proved that tetany was caused by faulty calcium metabolism, associated with diminished function of the glands. It was also discovered that people suffering from a condition called myxedema could be successfully treated with extracts of the thyroid gland. Today the condition is simply called hypothyroidism and is usually treated using natural or synthetic thyroid hormones.

By 1901, Japanese chemist Jokichi Takamine had discovered adrenaline, which is produced by the adrenal glands, located over the kidney. Adrenaline floods the bloodstream in times of stress, raising blood pressure, inhibiting stomach juices, expanding the pupils of the eyes, and tensing muscles—all because of the presence of a particular protein. Experiments with other hormones followed, including several that traded on the isolation of the first potent testicular extract containing the male sex hormone, testosterone.

As might be expected where sex and the possibility of improving it

RECEPTORS AND MEMBRANES

Cells have thousands of duty-bound internal structures, virtually all in motion, but the membrane that encases them like a skin is particularly remarkable, studded with thousands of receptors and other structures that control the passage in and out by various kinds of molecules.

There are two ways of looking at receptors. They can be considered molecular structures or sites on or in a cell capable of binding with substances such as antigens, drugs, neurotransmitters, or hormones. Or they can be considered specialized cells or groups of nerve endings that respond to some sensory stimuli. Membrane receptors on intestinal cells admit various products of digestion, for example, and relay those molecules to the bloodstream. The outer membranes of heart muscle cells have receptors for the stimulant hormone adrenalin, the fight-or-flight hormone produced by the body in times of stress. Receptors on disease-fighting B-cells bind with sites on a particular antigen.

When hormones are released into the bloodstream by the endocrine glands, they come into contact with every cell. But only certain cells, called target cells, will respond to any given hormone. Once the hormone molecules bind to receptor proteins in the target cells, the hormones set off a cascade of reactions, causing specific chemical reactions to speed up or slow down.

Some hormones enter the cell and bind to a receptor protein in the cytoplasm. Together, the hormone and receptor move to the nucleus, bind to the chromosome, and cause the cell to synthesize certain proteins. Other hormones never enter the cell at all but simply bind to receptor proteins on the cell's surface and touch off the release of a second messenger in the cytoplasm, initiating the cell's response to the hormone.

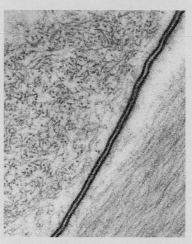

This color-enhanced transmission electron micrograph shows the cell membrane between two cells.

The lock-and-key mechanism essential for molecular recognition has helped in designing pharmaceuticals. In the past, creating a new drug meant testing many compounds, but now computers can simulate, for instance, protein receptor sites on a virus or a disease-associated enzyme, then generate a model of a potentially useful drug molecule calculated to fit the receptor.

Researchers recently discovered a whole new family of taste receptors (called T2Rs), perhaps as many as 80 different members, which help detect bitterness, a complex set of flavors often associated with poisons. Since the tongue is replete with taste buds, which contain the cells that allow us to detect and distinguish salty, sour, sweet, and bitter sensations, it was no surprise that the T2R receptors were found only in the cells that were present in the confines of taste buds. When receptor genes were introduced into experimental cells, the cells reacted only with bitter compounds. Moreover, individual receptor molecules appeared very discriminating in their taste for bitter. A receptor that reacted with one form of bitter essentially ignored compounds that looked different. This explained why there are some 80 different bitter receptors, and why no single receptor could possibly recognize the many versions of bitter.

were concerned, a number of male scientists of both legitimate and dubious credentials became preoccupied with the vivifying powers supposed to be lurking in the testes. Remedies to enhance performance flowed like wine, spurred on perhaps by the recall of a little-known experiment done in 1848.

German physiologist Arnold Adolphe Berthold, a credible scientist who had discovered an antidote for arsenic poisoning, tried something that would not in the long run enhance his reputation: He grafted the testicles of a cockerel into the abdominal cavity of a capon—a castrated cock—and watched in awe and delight as the rooster began chasing hens again. He reasoned that what was causing this sudden change was some "internal secretion," as he put it, he didn't know, though, that he was on the threshold of developing modern hormone therapy.

The work of a French neurologist, Charles-Édouard Brown-Séquard, stimulated the notion that sexual vigor and rejuvenation were closely linked. In 1889, when he was 72, Brown-Séquard suggested that seminal fluid contained secretions that get into the bloodstream and thus strengthen the body's systems. He injected himself ten times with the blood and semen of dogs and guinea pigs, thinned down with water. If one can believe this account, the results were extraordinary. He regained all the strength he possessed when he was young, he reported, and was no longer impotent. Laboratory work no longer fatigued him, and he was able to write on difficult subjects even after hours of exhausting lab work. To prove his point, he stopped the injections—and he returned to a state of weakness. A few other scientists claimed to have duplicated his results.

Critics galore emerged, and his claims were not taken seriously. He may have given himself some trace hormones, but on the other hand, perhaps the injections acted as a placebo, just right for an aged male longing for youthful vim and vigor.

There was nothing specious about the lifesaving impact of insulin, the hormone that regulates sugar levels in the blood. Until the 1920s, diabetes mellitus was, in effect, a death sentence. Described as far back as the Ebers Papyrus in ca 1550 B.C., it was first associated with the pancreas, the gland that secretes insulin, in the late 1700s. Scientists tried feeding ground-up pancreas tissue to diabetics, to alleviate their condition, but that did not work. Something in the pancreas's own digestive enzymes was destroying the hormone.

Canadian physiologist Frederick Banting thought it possible to obtain the unaltered pancreatic secretions by tying off the ducts that connected the organ with the intestines. If the substance could be isolated, Banting reasoned, it might be used to treat diabetes. He could induce diabetes artificially in a dog by removing its pancreas and test the hypothesis. He and his University of Toronto assistant, Charles Best, began experimenting.

In 1921, they reached conclusive results. A dog named Marjorie,

See pages 75-76 for more information on the Ebers Papyrus.

127

STEROID DISCOVERY

The discovery of hormones gave physicians new insights into how the body's organs function. E. C. Brown, an American chemist, identified the adrenal gland's steroids, among them cortisone, capable of reducing inflammation.

whose pancreas had been removed, developed a classic diabetic syndrome. Banting and Best injected her with extracted pancreatic secretion, and the diabetes vanished. Later, colleagues purified and further investigated the hormone, which was called insulin, from the Latin for "island," because the body produces it in pancreatic sections called the islets of Langerhans.

The next year, 1922, researchers administered the first dose of insulin to a human being, a 14-year-old boy who was dying of diabetes. His symptoms disappeared, the first signal that a scourge that had been fatal was now coming under medical control. Banting shared the 1923 Nobel Prize with John R. R. Macleod, in whose lab the work had been done. But in an unhappy twist, Best was not recognized with a share of the prize, a snub that long annoyed Banting.

In 1936, American chemist and physiologist Edward Calvin Kendall isolated other important hormones from adrenal glands. Together with eight other steroid hormones, he separated out a substance known at first as Compound E and later given the name cortisone. Like adrenaline, it is hormone secreted by the body in response to stress.

Cortisone is still widely used to reduce inflammation. In the late 1940s American chemist Percy Lavon Julian developed a synthetic cortisone, which is often prescribed as a treatment for connective-tissue disorders, rheumatic conditions, and acute allergic reactions.

CANCER

Isolating hormones—which means separating them out of a combined mixture in a culture—is a relatively easy job compared with what early scientists confronted when they attempted to comprehend cancer and get at its core. They may not have understood the mechanism, but at least they knew it wasn't normal.

The idea of cancer is at least as old as Hippocrates, who gave it its name, and perhaps even older. Tumors have been found in Egyptian mummies, but whether the ancients knew what they were is debatable. A 16th-century English physician, Andrew Boorde, called attention to cancer in language that flirts between truth and error. "Carcinoma is the greke worde," he wrote. "In englyshe it is named the sickenes of the prison. And some auctours doth say that it is a Canker, the whiche doth corode and eate the superial partes of the body, but I do take it for the sickenes of the prison."

What is clear is that cancerous growths were widely feared, considered undoubtedly to lead to the grave. Futile efforts to understand the disease ranged from attempts to transmit it by injecting material from human cancers into dogs, to experimenting with substances like coal tar applied to the skin.

In the 19th century, when the theory of cells and tissues was developed, researchers made more progress. Rudolf Virchow, as we have seen, believed disease was caused by cells run wild, and that

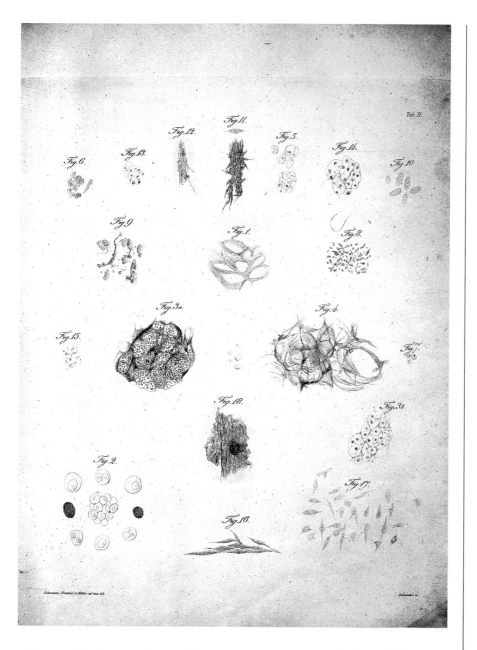

cells amid abnormal conditions generate abnormal offspring. Scientists learned to transplant, and even retransplant, cancers in mice and rats, and a few noted that various chemicals and irritants could cause skin cancer.

It would not become clear until the 20th century, however, that cancer was wholly cellular, an intricate combination of elements and mechanisms that turned cells savage as they divided. Researchers observed that chemical, physical, or viral agents could sabotage and rearrange the genes that regulate cell growth and differentiation. In this scenario, a single cell could divide uncontrollably, multiplying and joining with others to create a colony of mutant cells—for example, a malignant tumor.

The cause of this sort of cellular misdirection was unclear, but that simply spurred on research. As the great American medical educator Abraham Flexner said, "The fact that disease is only in part accurately known does not invalidate the scientific method in practice. In the twilight region probabilities are substituted for certainties. There the physician may indeed only surmise, but—most important of all—he knows that he surmises. His procedure is tentative, observant, heedful, responsive."

Several theories began to surface about how cancer arose. Viruses were at the core of most. This was

not surprising given the history of viruses in cancer: Rous's chicken sarcoma virus; the Epstein-Barr virus, linked to nose and throat cancer; Burkitt's lymphoma, a facial cancer found in African children; and a herpes simplex virus, associated with cervical cancer. But a viral connection to the majority of human cancers had not been established. Still, the hunt went on.

If there were cancer-causing viruses in most cancers, some reasoned, they took up residence somewhere in our bodies, perhaps in a cell nucleus, possibly hiding for generations until something freed them and made them develop malignancies. But how?

Cellular instructions, it seemed logical, had to have a hand in the process. Imagine, theorists held,

BREAST CANCER

One of eight women will develop breast cancer in their lifetimes. It is treated by several methods—from removal of mass to partial, total, or radical mastectomy, which is often followed by chemo- or radiation therapy.

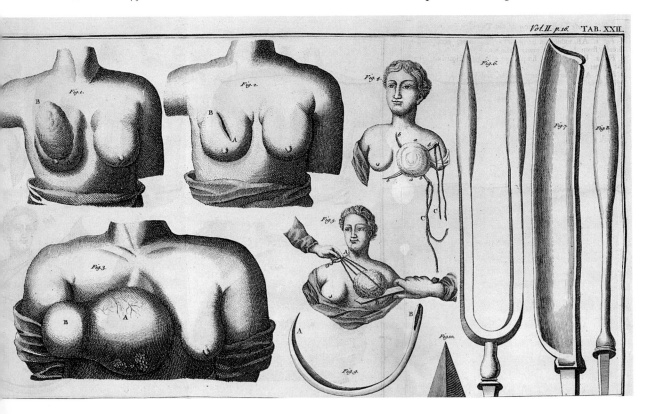

that viro-genes—genes capable of specifying the synthesis of a virus in a cell—originate inside viruses. When those viro-genes get into a cell nucleus, the theory went, and into its DNA, the blueprint for cancer reproduction is drawn. This insidious system could be handed down through generations. What would cause the viral gene fragments to burst into cancer? The suggestion was that various carcinogens—chemicals and drugs, radiation, perhaps other viruses—did that.

Then researchers made a discovery that raised questions about how viral genes worked their will. They began by closely examining animal cancer viruses and the genes they carried. Ultimately, they discovered that in animal cells there were genes with counterparts in the viruses that cause cancer. Could this mean that these genes, which had a high similarity to the viral genes, might cause cancer themselves, without a virus's assistance? The suspicious genes were named proto-oncogenes: a normal gene with the potential ("proto-") to transform itself into a cancer-causing ("onco-") gene. With this discovery, a new molecular theory, a unique basis for cancer, was uncovered.

Teams of scientists were now hot on trail of the mechanism that makes these proto-oncogenes. The genes could be found in animals and humans. Ordinarily and benignly, they control cell division and growth, and then they turn deadly. Key among the researchers on these questions were Harold Varmus, who later became the director of the National Institutes of Health, and J. Michael Bishop, both at the University of California at San Francisco.

In the 1970s, experimenting with the Rous chicken sarcoma virus, Varmus and Bishop found something unusual: The so-called src gene (also known as "sark") that was found in the sarcoma chicken virus was part of the fowl's routine genome. In other words, this meant that the gene started out as a normal gene, with a cellular origin, but could mutate to cause cancer.

This momentous discovery led to the isolation of many normal, growth-regulating cellular genes that spelled trouble—genes with counterparts in the viruses that cause cancer. Varmus, Bishop, and others pointed to about a dozen such genes belonging to almost all vertebrate species, from fish to monkeys, but not in humans. That sort of information would come later, as evidence mounted that cancer was truly a genetic disease.

Instrumental in this phase of the work, Dr. Robert Weinberg, a professor of biology at the Whitehead Institute in Cambridge, Massachusetts, pursued genes with direct correspondence to cancer potential. Through his pioneering work, and that of others, the actual genes responsible for human cancers of the bladder, colon, breast, lung, and lymph system were identified.

In 1982, Weinberg confirmed that the human cancer genes he was studying were virtually identical to those in animal cancer viruses.

X-RAYS
X-rays are electromagnetic radiation of very short wavelengths generated by deceleration in charged particles or the movement of electrons in atoms. Wilhelm Conrad Röntgen discovered x-rays in 1895 in Würzburg, Germany.

At about the same time, researchers with the National Cancer Institute connected an animal cancer virus to a human bladder cancer gene. In a dramatic addition to the work, Weinberg isolated an oncogene from transformed cells. He showed that by introducing the oncogene into a normal cell, the normal cell could be converted into a cancerous cell.

The mysterious relationship between viral genes implicated in cancer and cellular oncogenes was becoming better understood. Oncogenes of a virus and those in a cell were now accepted as close relatives. The same miscreant gene, whether introduced by a virus or created by alteration of a normal cellular gene, can instigate a malignancy when specific, definable lengths of DNA are transformed by some damaging exposure such as radiation or pollutants. It cannot occur everywhere in the chromosomes, as was earlier believed. In recognition of his work, Weinberg was awarded the National Medal of Science in 1997. Varmus and Bishop shared a Nobel Prize in 1989.

With a new understanding of the relevance of oncogenes and a firmer grasp on the ways that genetic information can be adversely affected, researchers began turning their attention to what would become one of the most intensively studied topics in modern biology: the concept of apoptosis and its important role in cellular death.

First suggested in 1972, apoptosis is an intriguing organic event that can best be defined as programmed cell death or, as some have called it, the process of "deliberate suicide" undertaken by an unwanted cell in a multicellular organism. Unlike necrosis, the death of cells or tissues through injury or disease, apoptosis is an ordered event, a quick and easy process by which a cell shrinks and is speedily digested by neighboring cells. The sequence of events can have advantages. One example often cited occurs in the fingers of a developing embryo: Apoptosis is the process that loosens and eliminates the cells between the tiny fingers, so that they separate and become distinctive structures.

It is estimated that the average human adult loses up to 70 billion cells each day due to apoptosis, a normal and important part of the biological process that assures the removal of superfluous or damaged cells. A number of other events, events that are not necessarily normal events, can incite apoptosis as well, among them radiation or drugs used to treat cancer, viral infection, and some hormones like corticosteroids. Through laboratory investigations that carried on well into the 1990s, scientists confirmed that apoptosis helps developing organisms shape their neural and immune systems, and it is essential in molding tissues. They also showed that the process directs the natural balance between cell death and cell renewal.

One concern of scientists was that if a cell is damaged in some way and loses its capacity to kill itself off, that damage could go on

CANCER AND APOPTOSIS

Cancers often give no hint of their existence until they are revealed through chemical and other laboratory tests or imaged by one of today's powerful, all-seeing scanning devices. Their fleeting invisibility, however, still cannot hide their modus operandi—coercing cells into dividing uncontrollably to form a colony of mutant cells, a malignant tumor. In many cases, cancerous cells enter the bloodstream or the lymphatic system, carrying their deformed counterparts to the body's far reaches, where they organize secondary communities, called metastases.

When a cell becomes cancerous, its membrane may change slightly so that it bears markers somewhat different from the body's own. Ordinarily, the immune system recognizes and reacts to the new markers, eliminating the mutant cells. Our bodies are built to resist metabolic damage by destroying and replacing cells or components that have been damaged, a process that goes on all the time. Indeed cells contain specialized structures called lysosomes and peroxisomes, which destroy cellular materials no longer necessary. Such structures are essentially chemical waste-disposal units, and their importance is underscored by noting that a mutation in the gene that codes for these enzymes causes Tay-Sachs disease, an inherited malady characterized by seizures and blindness that usually kills its victims before age four.

As the waste-disposers obliterate damaged cell components, those components are replaced when the genes that construct them are turned on. If the genes themselves are injured, cells have the capacity to repair the DNA. DNA consists of two complementary strands, and if one strand is incapacitated,

Surgeons perform a lobechtomy, removing part of a cancerous lung.

the other can act as a template for its flawless repair. If unrepaired, though, DNA generally leads to the cell's self-destruction and replacement through the division of neighboring cells (assuming the cell is in a tissue capable of continued cell division).

Cell suicide is known scientifically as apoptosis, a word derived from the Greek for "falling." As apoptotic cells die, they shrink, break into small fragments, and are absorbed by their neighbors. Cell suicide, a lifelong process, occurs continually. As an example, a layer of skin regularly manufactures new cells; as they migrate to the skin surface, they kill themselves off, then are sloughed off and replaced by new cells from below. In this regard, apoptosis is not a bad thing.

Apoptosis is also beneficial when it thwarts cancer. There are genes called tumor-suppressors that govern cell suicide; they kill damaged cells that may be more likely to replicate uncontrollably and grow into tumors. But other genes, called brake genes, can enter the picture. These promote tumor growth by producing products that block apoptosis, thus avoiding programmed death. Runaway cell division is the result of the anti-apoptosis factor, and so is cancer. Indeed, evidence suggests that the acquired ability to resist apoptosis is a hallmark of most, perhaps all, kinds of cancer.

Scientists are searching for ways to trigger apoptosis in the battle against cancer. Clinical trials have been under way for some time to test the efficacy of new apoptosis-inducing drugs. Perhaps some could be found to block the brake genes' protein production, leaving the cancer cells more vulnerable to apoptosis-inducing chemotherapies.

to be replicated, possibly developing into cancer. Indeed, evidence mounted that the ability to resist apoptosis is commonly shared among most, maybe even all, cancers. And even though the body has ways to eliminate malignant cells, mutations in cancer cells can interfere with that.

Scientists and pharmaceutical manufacturers began focusing on ways to harness apoptosis, to goad it into destroying cancer cells. But encouraging selective cell death is no easy job. There were, and still are, challenges. Scientists need to determine, for example, why some tumors resist cell suicide even when exposed to radiation and chemotherapy. They must know more about what regulates apoptosis, and, if they do come up with a way to induce suicide in cancer cells, they must uncover ways to

EDUCATION AND CONTROL

A campaign on cancer awareness begun in 1935 by women's clubs pressed thousands of volunteers into service. At the time the campaign began, only 15,000 people were involved with cancer control. By 1938, the number was 150,000.

ensure that it doesn't produce a remedy too strong for the disease, as Sophocles once said, and end up killing healthy cells.

GENETICS AND THE DISCOVERY OF DNA

None of the knowledge that fed scientific theories about oncogenes and apoptosis and a panoply of other biochemical happenings would have been possible without one of science's most extraordinary achievements: the cracking of the genetic code, the template for heredity and the diseases associated with it. The pathfinder in solving what had puzzled generations of scientists was an Austrian botanist and monk, Gregor Mendel, who experimented with a common vegetable in an unlikely laboratory, a tranquil monastery garden.

Before DNA was even imagined, even before the structure of the cell was outlined, Mendel demonstrated the phenomenon we now know as genetic inheritance. To do so, he grew many generations of pea plants, using the seeds of each generation to procreate the next and keeping careful records of all the features that revealed themselves. Purebred plants, grown from a recognized strain of seed and not mixed with any others, always produced plants with similar traits, one generation after another. Purebred red-flowered plants, for instance, always brought forth more red-flowered plants.

Mendel then hybridized, or crossed the strains of, his plants. He bred dwarf varieties with tall ones, red-flowered varieties with white-flowered ones, and so on. As the hybrids ripened, he collected their seeds and replanted them, spring after spring, observing the characteristics of the resulting offspring.

There were several surprises. For example, mixing the pollen of a tall plant with that of a dwarf did not produce a plant of average height. Nor did a plant with pink flowers result from the union of a plant with red flowers and a plant with white ones. What did happen was that each new plant inherited certain traits as complete units, and that these units—now known to be genes—were passed along in pure form to subsequent generations.

Thus, crossbreeding tall plants with short ones produced plants that were tall or short, with the plants of the first generation all more likely to be tall. Likewise, crossing red- and white-flowered plants produced plants with flowers of one or the other color, but the first generation of crossbred plants produced only red flowers.

Mendel also discovered that when he crossbred first-generation hybrids with each other, the result could be the alternative: white-flowering plants, say, or dwarfs. That meant that the ingredients for short and tall, or for red and white flowers, were always present and could show up at any time in future generations.

Mendel soon saw that these hereditary units occur in pairs, one from the mother, one from the father, for each trait. One gene may predominate over the other—

See pages 280-85 for more information on Gregor Mendel.

135

DOUBLE HELIX-HEROES

British biologist Francis Crick, left, and American geneticist James Watson set out to discover the structure of DNA in 1951. In 1953 they proposed the double helix, for which the two were awarded the Nobel Prize in 1962.

in a human being, this might mean that a person inherits her mother's brown eyes rather than her father's blue. Genes can be dominant or recessive, but every one of the inherited genes remains part of the offspring's genetic makeup, potentially expressing itself in generations to come. Like so much of the work done by scientists, past and current, Mendel's ideas were not fully appreciated until years after his death. Scientists digging through biology literature from 1900 rediscovered the monk's experimental data in an obscure journal. Other researchers confirmed his findings, not only in plants but in animals, and the laws of heredity became a fixture of modern biology. Being a chip off the old block was a proverb now based on valid experimentation.

Jump ahead to 1944, to New York's Rockefeller Institute, where three researchers—Oswald T. Avery, Colin M. MacLeod, and Maclyn McCarty—demonstrated for the first time that DNA, deoxyribonucleic acid, was the bearer of hereditary information. They did so by extracting some of it in pure form from a bacterium and then using it to replace a defective gene in another related bacterium.

Ten years later James Watson, a young Harvard biochemist, and Francis Crick, an English physicist, described the intricate molecular structure of DNA. But before they could do so, they had to consider the essential components of DNA.

The stage had been set three years earlier when a Czech-born biochemist, Erwin Chargaff, was studying the distribution of four bases—small chemical units called cytosine (C), guanine (G), thymine (T), and adenine (A)—that are essential parts of DNA. Chargaff determined that in any living thing, these bases do not occur in equal numbers. There is always the same amount of T as A, and the same amount of G as C, but not necessarily the same amount of T as G, T as C, and so on.

Watson and Crick interpreted this to mean that T always binds to A, and G always binds to C. No other combinations occur. This would explain why the complicated DNA molecule almost never errs when it replicates itself during mitosis: Bases connect only to each other in those specific pairings. So, presumably, when a long DNA strand unravels into a pair during reproduction, breaking its C-G and T-A bonds, each half is a perfect template, automatically making an exact duplicate of itself by picking up more of its matching bases from the surrounding cellular material. If one half has an exposed A, it finds a T. If the open base is a C, it binds to a G.

But how was all this arranged? What was the shape of DNA? Earlier, two other English researchers, Maurice Wilkins and Rosalind Franklin, had been studying DNA by means of x-ray crystallography, an arcane method of shooting x-rays through crystalline materials in order to analyze their chemical structure.

Based largely on an x-ray crystallography plate taken by Franklin, plus their own fertile imaginations and hard work, Watson and Crick eventually teased out the structure of DNA: the famous double helix, or twisted

GREGOR MENDEL

Father of genetics

1822
Born Johann Mendel on July 20 in Heinzendorf, Austria-Hungary (now Hynice in the Czech Republic).

1843
Enters the Augustinian monastery at Brünn, Moravia (later Brno, Czech Republic), and takes the name Gregor.

1847
Ordained to the priesthood at the St. Thomas Monastery of the Augustinian Order in Brünn.

1851-1853
Studies science and mathematics at the University of Vienna. His coursework includes experimental physics and plant physiology.

1856
Begins experiments on pea plants that lead to the discovery of the principle of heredity; also begins cultivation and testing of almost 28,000 other plants.

1863
Publishes the first of his meteorological observations, which continue through 1882.

1865
Describes the results of his experiments in plant hybridization to the Brünn Society for the Study of Natural Science.

1866
Publishes his article "Experiments with Plant Hybrids," which sets forth concepts later known as Mendel's laws of heredity.

1868
Elected abbot of the St. Thomas Monastery in Brünn.

1872
Awarded the Cross of the Royal and Imperial Order of Franz Joseph I.

1884
Dies on January 6 in Brünn.

1900
Ignored during his life, Mendel's conclusions are rediscovered.

See pages 292-95 for more information about DNA.

ladder, a spiral staircase capable of unhinging itself as it brings about the two most important activities in a cell's life: reproducing itself exactly by dividing in two, the process known as mitosis; and manufacturing protein. Among its various parts, the nucleotides, a chemist would find no unfamiliar substances. The spiral sides of the ladder are made of phosphates, combinations of the mineral phosphorus, oxygen, and sugars. The rungs are the four chemical bases, and each rung, as noted by Chargaff, consists of two of the chemicals, joined in the middle.

The helix's rungs determine the form and function of life, and the number of possible arrangements for them is almost endless. As a mental exercise, choosing combinations would keep one occupied forever. For example, a set of rungs might look like this: CG, GC, AT, TA, TA, AT, CG, CG, GC, GC, AT, GC, A. . . .

A virus might contain some 200,000 DNA rungs arranged in different sequences; a germ might have five million or six million in its chromosomes. A single human cell, the top of the line, contains billions. But whatever the form of life—microbe, mouse, or man—it's all composed of the same chemicals; it's the *order* in which the four-letter chemical alphabet is arranged that spells out what form life will take and gives each gene its special code to direct the manufacture of the protein for which it is responsible.

Once DNA's structure had been initially unveiled, the next step was for researchers to find out how the double helix tells the cell what to do, and how the cell uses that information. It soon became apparent that each gene in DNA contains the coded instructions for constructing one special protein out of various amino acids—organic chemicals, popularly called the building blocks of life, that are present in the cell's fluid cytoplasm. But how did the information get outside the nucleus to start building protein? Crick speculated that protein creation had to involve some sort of template molecule.

Confirmation of this hypothesis was found by two American

1967 – 2003

1967
South African surgeon Christiaan Barnard performs the first successful human heart transplant.

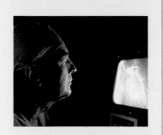

1978
The first test-tube baby, Louise Joy Brown, is born in Manchester, England, through the now-common procedure of in vitro fertilization.

1980
The World Health Organization announces that smallpox has been eradicated worldwide.

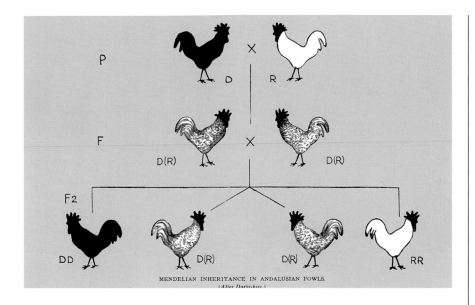

P

D R

F

D(R) D(R)

F2

DD D(R) D(R) RR

MENDELIAN INHERITANCE IN ANDALUSIAN FOWLS.
(After Darbishire.)

HEREDITY
Austrian botanist
Gregor Mendel
demonstrated that
inherited characteris-
tics can be dominant
(D) or recessive (R).
When dominance is
incomplete, a blending
may occur, as in the
color of these birds.
When the gray birds
mate, the original
color genes will
reexpress themselves.

biochemists, Mahlon Hoagland and Paul Berg, who worked independently. Both Hoagland and Berg succeeded in isolating bits of RNA in the cytoplasm, showing that each bit was configured to capture a different amino acid. Different sequences of these short RNA strands (called transfer RNA, or tRNA) would determine the assembly pattern for different proteins.

But that raised another question: What determines the tRNA sequence? How do the individual strands know where to go and when to turn off? The answer came from two French scientists, Jacques Monod and François Jacob, who had been studying how genes in the nucleus are able to regulate chemical synthesis in the human body. They suggested that special units of genetic code, called "operons," controlled the activity of other genes.

Some ten years after the advances made by Watson and Crick, Monod and Jacob finally identified the molecular courier system that reads instructions from a DNA sequence

1983
HIV, the virus that causes AIDS, is identified by Luc Montagnier in France and Robert Gallo in the United States.

1986
The first genetically engineered vaccine, which protects against hepatitis B infection, is developed.

1998
The first human stem cells are isolated by scientists at the University of Wisconsin and Johns Hopkins University in Maryland.

2003
The Human Genome project is completed, identifying and mapping the sequence of human DNA, which reveals between 20,000 and 25,000 genes.

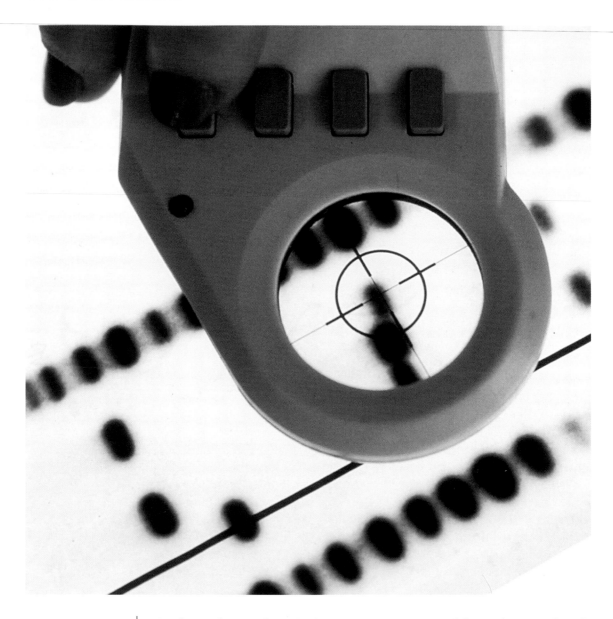

DISTINGUISHING TRAITS

The distinctiveness of each living thing's inheritance can be seen in its DNA. Such genetic evidence is now used to identify criminals with more accuracy than fingerprints.

in the nucleus and carries it out to protein factories in the cell body. What happens is this: A section of DNA, a gene, unzips itself and makes another nucleic acid, this time yet another type of RNA called messenger RNA, or mRNA.

The gene hands over to the messenger the entire coded blueprint for one protein. This done, it zips itself up once more. The messenger now moves out of the nucleus into the cellular cytoplasm, carrying those instructions to one of the dense granules, or ribosomes, that lie scattered about in the cell. The ribosomes are, in effect, the workshops where the proteins are assembled. The whole process is akin to an architect passing blueprints to a construction engineer, only the plans aren't on paper but coded in genes, and the building materials aren't bricks and mortar but amino acids. Simply put, genetic information stored in DNA is transcribed into the RNA molecule and then translated into the molecular structure of proteins by means of the genetic code. The process is over when the instructions are embodied in the structure, hence the function, of the protein. Protein itself doesn't carry data that will make RNA, DNA, or other proteins.

With so much emphasis on DNA's role in manufacturing life-sustaining protein, one might tend to forget that DNA has a dark side, as when lengths of it are damaged in some way so that they cause cancer. One single error in the genetic code—a "word" misspelled or a "paragraph" misplaced—can induce diseases involving many organs. Important chemicals may not be made if the production line breaks down, or they can accumulate in dangerous amounts, clogging the brain and arteries. A coding mistake in DNA can also lead to its making the wrong kind of protein. Errors in the code may even occur as part of the aging process, resulting in flawed protein and body slowdown.

In some chromosomal abnormalities, like Down syndrome, more genes than nature intended may be present. In others, some may be missing, producing multiple inherited defects. A disease called phenylketonuria, or PKU, is an example of a gene gone amiss, which in turn adversely affects its specific enzyme workhorse. Many such inherited metabolic diseases lead to mental retardation.

Scientists have been searching for ways to repress injurious gene expression and to stimulate underactive genes. Learning how to right what are essentially serious biochemical wrongs became, years after Watson and Crick and others, one of the goals of a recent milestone in scientific history: the compilation of the human genome—all the genes of all human beings, the very blueprint for the construction and functioning of the human body.

FRANCIS CRICK

Codiscoverer of the structure of DNA

1916
Born June 8 near Northampton, England.

1934
Begins the study of physics at University College, London.

1937
Graduates from University College with honors; embarks on research toward a Ph.D. degree.

1949
Joins the Medical Research Council Unit at Cavendish Laboratories, Cambridge, England.

1951
James Watson arrives at Cavendish Laboratories and begins working together with Crick.

1953
Publishes article, "Molecular Structure of Nucleic Acids," with James Watson, first one discussing their findings on the structure and function of DNA.

1954
Obtains a Ph.D. from Caius College, Cambridge, his thesis entitled "X-ray Diffraction: Polypeptides and Proteins."

1958
Proposes the sequence hypothesis and central dogma, both accepted today as central tenets of molecular biology.

1961
Awarded the Prix Charles Leopold Meyer of the French Academy of Sciences.

1962
Shares the Nobel Prize for physiology or medicine with James Watson and Maurice Wilkins.

1976
Moves to the Salk Institute for Biological Studies, where he changes his field of study to consciousness and the brain.

2004
Dies on July 28 in San Diego, California.

MAPPING THE HUMAN GENOME

Completed in 2003, the Human Genome Project was a monumental 13-year effort that created the field of genomics, the understanding of genetic material on a large scale.

The science behind the project turned up enough numbers to satisfy all participants. They now know that the total number of human genes is around 30,000; and that the human genome contains 3,164.7 million chemical nucleo-tide bases (A, C, T, and G); that the average gene consists of 3,000 bases, but that sizes vary greatly. The largest known human gene, with 2.4 million bases, is dystrophin, a structural protein found in small amounts in normal muscle but absent in

Eric S. Lander of the Broad Institute, a leader in the study of the human genome, was named the first author of the published genome in 2001.

people with muscular dystrophy. We now also know that the order of nearly all nucleotide bases—99.9 percent—is exactly the same in all people.

With all that information, there are still gaps. For instance, functions are unknown for over 50 percent of discovered genes. The exact number of genes remains debatable. And while genes associated with disease have been found—more than 30 connected to breast cancer and muscle disease, among others—challenges lie ahead in finding the DNA sequences underlying cardiovascular disease, diabetes, arthritis, and many cancers.

There are challenges, too, regarding the ethical, legal, and social issues that the project has raised.

For instance, the project determined that there needs to be a better understanding that cloning, one of the activities associated with the results coming from the genome project, is an umbrella term. Traditionally used by scientists to describe different ways of duplicating biological material, many understand the term cloning as creating living creatures, like the celebrated sheep Dolly, or like imagined human replicants. Concerns over such research are understandable, given not only technical difficulties but also lack of information about how cloning could affect physical and mental development of human beings.

On the other hand, information from the genome project can be used for other types of cloning technologies and purposes besides producing genetic twins. Recombinant DNA technology or gene cloning has potential for treating certain genetic conditions; and therapeutic cloning, also called embryo cloning, is aimed at producing human embryos for the purpose of harvesting stem cells that can be used to study human development and to treat a number of diseases.

As the genome project managers observed, "A basic understanding of the different types of cloning is key to taking an informed stance on current public policy issues and making the best possible personal decisions."

THE HUMAN GENOME

The time was right, now that scientists had the ability to read DNA sequences in a given cell, thus unraveling one of cell biology's least understood events. But the task was of enormous scope, seemingly next to impossible: to identify all the genes in human DNA, determining the sequences of the three billion base pairs that make up that DNA, sorting and filing the information in logically accessible databases, and addressing the ethical, legal, and social issues that would inevitably arise regarding the completion and impact of such a project.

The genes were there, to be sure, a complete genome in every cell except the mature red blood cell. But to catalog every single one in a human being? It was nearly incomprehensible. Some genes are too small to be detected easily; one gene can code for several different protein products; some code only for RNA; pairs of genes can overlap. All added up to a daunting task.

But if it could be achieved, science would have a much clearer understanding of human genetics on a grand scale—of how and why a person looks the way he or she does, of genetic contributions to human health and resilience, of how faulty genes can cause disease. It would give credence to a remark once made by Frederick the Great of Prussia in the year 1777, before the terms "genes" or "DNA" had ever been mentioned: "Men are born with an indelible character."

The Human Genome Project got under way in 1990, a projected 13-year effort coordinated by the U.S. Department of Energy and the National Institutes of Health. One of its important features was the federal government's dedication to the transfer of technology to the private sector. By licensing technologies to private companies and awarding grants for innovative research, managers of the project sought to catalyze the multibillion-dollar U.S. biotechnology industry and foster the development of new medical applications.

The work, to say the least, was intensive. To an untrained eye, the code of life was gibberish. But to the scientists deciphering it, it was often more clear than murky. Mapping it all, they knew, was the key to curing disease by actually manipulating genes themselves.

Chromosomes, the threadlike strands of DNA in the cell nucleus that carry the genes, had to be broken up into shorter pieces—a demanding job, given that they could contain from 50 million to 250 million bases. Fragments from each short piece had to be separated by a process known as gel electrophoresis, and then dyed so that their component bases could be identified. Automatic sequencers helped to scan and record the actual information from short sequences of genes, after which computers assembled the short sequences (blocks of about 500 bases each) into long continuous stretches. Each of those was analyzed for errors, gene-coding regions, and other characteristics.

GENETIC LINKAGES
Reginald Punnett, an English geneticist born in 1875, worked with English biologist William Bateson and discovered genetic linkage, sex linkage, sex determination, and autosomal linkage. Punnett developed the Punnett Square, which illustrates the number and range of genetic combinations. He died in England in 1967.

The project included studies of the genetic makeup of several organisms other than the human, including the bacterium *E. coli,* the fruit fly, and the lab mouse.

It was like separating wheat from chaff, given that only a small percentage of the genome codes for proteins, the useful information that scientists sought; the vast majority of it contains repeated sequences without any important protein-building information, often called "junk DNA."

The project was essentially completed in 2003, ahead of schedule, and while the exact number of genes encoded by the genome is still under investigation, it was somewhere between 20,000 to 25,000, perhaps more, but surely a much smaller number than early estimates of around 100,000. This came as a surprise to scientists, since it is only a few thousand more than that of the simple roundworm.

It may be years before an accurate count is reached. Scientists can look forward to much more labor-intensive experimentation. But what is certain is that, aside from practical applications like gene therapy, the results of the Human Genome Project present scientists with an understanding of biological systems that will define research for many years to come. And not only human research: The techniques created by the project scientists, and the information they have collected, will also help unravel the genomes of many other organisms, notably those used for biological research such as mice, fruit flies, and flatworms. Impor-

tantly, most living organisms share many homologous, or similar, genes, so identifying the sequence or function of a gene in a model organism—the roundworm, for example—can potentially explain a homologous gene in humans or any other organism.

Francis Collins, director of the National Human Genome Research Institute, compared the genome project results to a book with many uses. "It's a history book," he said, "a narrative of the journey of our species through time. It's a shop manual, with an incredibly detailed blueprint for building every human cell. And it's a transformative textbook of medicine, with insights that will give health care providers immense new powers to treat, prevent, and cure disease."

But there is still more to celebrate. In 2005, a group called the International HapMap Consortium published a comprehensive catalog of human genetic variation. Built on the foundation of the human genome sequence, the catalog is a landmark achievement that has accelerated the search for genes involved in common diseases such as asthma, diabetes, heart disease, and cancer.

More than 200 researchers from the United States, Canada, China, Japan, Nigeria, and the United Kingdom used blood samples drawn from 269 volunteers from widely distributed geographic regions. Thus far, the results have provided overwhelming evidence that variation in the human genome is organized into local

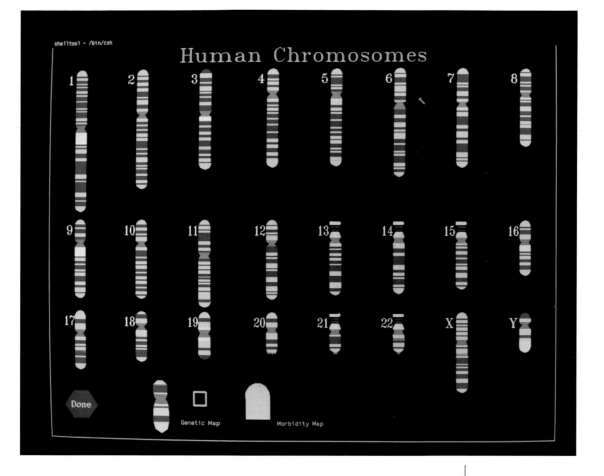

shelltool - /bin/csh

Human Chromosomes

1 2 3 4 5 6 7 8

9 10 11 12 13 14 15 16

17 18 19 20 21 22 X Y

Done   Genetic Map   Morbidity Map

neighborhoods, called haplotypes, that usually are inherited as intact blocks of information.

THE GENOME IN GENERATIONS TO COME

The HapMap catalog will help doctors prescribe the right drug in the right dose for individual patients; it will alert them to prevention strategies that take into account the varying responses of individuals to environmental factors. It may also help re-searchers identify the genetic factors that contribute to people's good health, protect against infectious diseases, or promote healthy longevity.

"It's a phenomenal tool that is making possible research that was impractical, if not unimaginable, only a few years ago," said Yusuke Nakamura, director of the Human Genome Center at the University of Tokyo. "It offers the scientific community an enormous savings, reducing the expense of searching the genome for hereditary factors in common disease by a factor of 10 to 20."

From Hippocrates to HapMap, from germ theory to the human genome, the human body continues to amaze, fascinate, and perplex medical scientists—as well as all of us humans who inhabit it.

TELLTALE STAINS

DNA fragments can be analyzed by staining them following their separation by exposure to an electric field. The revealed patterns will be unique to the individual from whom the DNA has been extracted.

Matter & Energy

3

THE SEARCH TO UNRAVEL THE mysteries of matter and energy has been going on for over two millennia. While we have uncovered a vast store of knowledge, that search is being pushed ever further by scientists in our own day. One thing we have learned clearly is that mathematics is crucial for understanding many aspects of the natural world. But even the simplest parts of mathematics—those parts taken easily for granted today—were developed gradually by our ancestors, in response to their own needs and desires. Our story must begin with numbers.

That written language and mathematics developed at the same period in human history is no coincidence. Both are ways to describe the physical world, and both require the ability to put information regarding the physical world into a set of symbols. But the symbols are the final step in a process that took humans a million years. When it began, humans, like many animals, most likely could recognize fewer from greater, more from less. They could count intuitively—like a bird that senses the number of eggs in its nest or the wasp that senses how many caterpillars it feeds its young—and could recognize that a pile

GNOMON

Dating from as early as the 35th century B.C., the gnomon—primitive version of a sundial—was the world's first timekeeping device. More accurate devices had come into use by the eighth century B.C.

of four stones was different from a pile of ten stones or that a distance of four steps was different from a distance of ten. What is hard for us to comprehend, however, is that although there were stones and steps, there was no "four," no "ten."

If there were any numerical truths recognized at all, they might have come out of self-recognition: an understanding of the number one, for instance, through recognition of one body, one head, one mouth; or the truth of two, since as bilaterally symmetrical beings, we have two of most appendages. One indicated singularity; two might have indicated comparison or opposition: male and female, day and night, sun and moon, Earth and sky, water and land, hot and cold. In ritual and religious practice even today, some numbers are believed to speak potent and primal truths.

TOOLS FOR COUNTING AND MEASURING

When did the human mind begin to enlarge its store of such truths? Experience and tradition told pre-literate migratory herders or hunters how to shape and size their tools and weapons, how close they needed to be to their prey, or how long their next journey would take. Did our ancient ancestors more than a million years ago count the number of times they struck a stone to turn it into a blade? Before they went off to hunt, did they count the number of stones they carried with them? Did they tally up their prey? Did they mark how many strides they had taken in their day's journey? If they did not do so a million years ago, when human brains were 37 cubic inches smaller than they are today, then when did such acts of outright counting begin?

Did the complexities of life in changing environments 50,000 years ago create a need to make superior calculations? Did making such calculations require our larger brains? Does the understanding of numbers—both those that denote quantity, called cardinal numbers, and those that denote order, ordinal numbers—signify the start of human culture?

Little evidence exists of when people developed the first forms of counting and arithmetic, or when

ca 600 – 50 B.C.

ca 600 B.C.
Thales of Miletus concludes that the fundamental element of life and Earth is water.

ca 500 B.C.
The Pythagoreans study mathematics and greatly advance the study of geometry.

ca 420 B.C.
Greek philosopher Democritus argues that all matter is made of tiny, indivisible constituents that he calls atoms.

SUNDIAL
Elaborate or simple, the sundial signifies how the human sense of time connects intimately with the natural world.

they began to measure the regular movements of the sun, moon, stars, and planets. If they didn't wander aimlessly in search of food and shelter, did they take bearings of some kind to mark their journeys? Surely prehistoric humans noticed that shadows shifted over the course of the day and that a circle could be drawn around a stick placed in the ground and marked off at intervals to measure the day's progress. Such devices, called gnomons (Greek for "the one that knows"), are still used by tribes such as Africa's Bushmen.

ca 320-260 B.C.
Euclid collects all geometric knowledge and extends it in his famous work, *Elements.*

ca 300 B.C.
Mathematicians in India make first use of zero as a numeric placeholder.

287-212 B.C.
Archimedes determines that the buoyant force on a floating object is equal to the weight of the fluid it displaces.

ca 50 B.C.
The base-ten numeral system is developed in India.

And the fact that some of the earliest systems of measurement known were based on parts of the human body—the span of a hand, the length of an arm, foot, or stride—indicates that these methods have long been in use.

Counting is a different matter. It is a great leap to go from looking at two trees, for instance, to putting two sticks on the ground to represent those trees, and a greater leap still to add groups of sticks together.

Anthropologists and archaeologists surmise that the advent of agriculture and domestication of animals in the Middle East some 10,000 years ago moved this process along. Counting on fingers or toes or counting a few notches in a piece of wood worked for limited numbers. But once hunters and nomads settled in fertile lands to raise grain or cattle, they had to manipulate larger quantities of goods. Even in early settlements they had to account for grain, which they stored in communal silos. Such new quantities required a more advanced and streamlined counting methodology.

By 7500 B.C. in the land that was called Sumeria, now southern Iraq, small clay tokens in various shapes were used to keep track of farmers' stores. Imagine the kind of tokens used in children's board games. A small clay marble would stand for a bushel of grain, a cylinder might represent an animal, and a little egg-shaped token was a jar of oil. Such counters have been found in the shape of spheres, disks, and little pyramids.

These artifacts come from before the Bronze Age, a time when clay was fired at temperatures high enough to give it some lasting hardness, a time when artful pottery was being produced. Each token represented a single unit, and they could be counted up to assess one's holdings.

As more goods were manufactured—cloth, perfumes, tools—counting tokens became more elaborate and, as archaeologist Denise Schmandt-Besserat theorized, could be used for a purpose new to civilization: tax collection. The tokens themselves were stored in clay globes, marked on the outside to indicate the shape of tokens being kept inside. Soon the marks that illustrated the tokens began to replace the tokens themselves, and the clay globes were flattened into more readily inscribed tablets. Instead of 50 egg-shaped tokens, 50 egg-shaped marks would be carved with a stylus on a clay tablet.

According to Schmandt-Besserat, a great advance came around 3100 B.C., Instead of recording 50 bushels of grain with 50 images of grain tokens, a system was devised by which the symbol for a bushel of grain would be preceded by a special sign or combination of signs that represented the number 50. The number was still not completely abstract, in that it referred to some specific item. Two, for instance, still meant nothing on its own, only when used to denote two of something. But the fact that the same symbols could be used for quantities of different things was a giant step beyond simple counting. And although only two number symbols came into use to begin with, they still served to create a simple base-ten system—intuitive, perhaps, because of the number of fingers on the human hand. A wedge came to stand for one; a circle came to stand for ten.

By 3000 B.C. clay tokens were obsolete, replaced by durable clay accounting tablets and a new system of pictographic data storage that would be used and refined in the Middle East for the next 3,000 years. This period of history also saw the beginning of written language, using a new collection of inscribed symbols that became known as cuneiform, meaning "wedge-shaped." This seemingly simple development happened over more than 4,000 years, yet it led to extraordinary advances in knowledge about the world, as human beings came to use numbers to measure and describe their new observations and ideas.

CUNEIFORM
The ancient Middle East's most important and widespread writing system was cuneiform, said to be the equivalent of the Latin alphabet in the ancient Middle East. The earliest known people to use cuneiform were the Sumerians.

EARTH, AIR, FIRE, WATER

What is the world made of? The human senses appear to have provided diverse ancient cultures with the same answer to this basic question, first, in China, around 2,000 B.C., then in ancient India, and finally in Greece, in the fifth century B.C.: All concluded that all matter was composed of a few basic elements. For the Chinese, the elements were water, metal, wood, fire, and earth; for the Greeks and Indians, they were earth, air, fire, and water. For the ancients, physics and metaphysics were rarely far apart, and these elements were imbued with conceptual as well as actual attributes.

In Greece, in the early fifth century B.C., Empedocles first articulated the idea of the four elements. Poet, philosopher, politician, and follower of Pythagoras, Empedocles concluded that earth, air, fire, and water form the rhizomata, or roots, of all life and matter. In opposition to atomists such as Democritus, who believed everything was composed of either atoms or void, and to Parmenides, who believed that matter could be neither created nor destroyed, Empedocles asserted that the elements were in constant flux and stress, acted upon by the two great forces of the cosmos, attraction and repulsion—or, as he called, them, love and strife. These forces created the world's recurrent cycle of creation and destruction.

Empedocles's idea that matter could be created then destroyed ran counter to Aristotle's view that all things were created with a purpose. Earth, air, water, and fire were combined within all matter, Aristotle agreed, but they combined in ways that advanced the perfection of all things along a chain of being from the low and inanimate to the human and divine. Aristotle worked out in intricate detail just

Earth, air, fire, water—the four elements—link in this Italian woodcut dating from 1496.

how the four elements, paired in opposites—earth to air, water to fire—changed one into the other:

"Air, for example, will result from Fire if a single quality changes," he wrote, "for Fire, as we saw, is hot and dry, while Air is hot and moist, so that there will be Air if the dry be overcome by the moist. . . . The transformation of Fire into Water and of Air into Earth, and again of Water and Earth into Fire and Air, respectively, though possible, is more difficult, because it involves the change of more qualities."

The physician Hippocrates, in the fifth century B.C., believed that health resulted from a balance of four bodily humors—blood, phlegm, and two kinds of bile—which were analogous to four major organs, the four seasons, the four ages of man, and the four elements. Throughout the Middle Ages, this system of symbolic qualities was as important as the elements themselves. The balance of wetness and dryness, heat and cold, signified spiritual and physical health.

Like so many of Aristotle's ideas, the theory of four elements and four corresponding bodily humors long went unchallenged. When alchemists in the Middle Ages began discovering the actual physical properties of materials, the theory of the Aristotelian elements came into question.

English chemist Robert Boyle disputed the nature of the four elements in 1661. True elements, he argued, can neither be decomposed into nor formed from other materials. By the time of the Renaissance, the interpretation of the elements was recognized as metaphorical, not scientific. In the late 18th century French chemist Antoine Lavoisier published a list of elements based on Boyle's criteria, marking the starting point for today's periodic table.

The Babylonians, a part of the greater Mesopotamian cultures of the Fertile Crescent, began refining the advances of the Sumerians. They developed more number signs and created systems within which one unit could be converted into another, in the same way we convert ounces into pounds and pounds into tons. For instance, ten cones equaled one small circle. Six small circles equaled one big cone. Ten big cones equaled a big cone with a circle inside, and six of these were represented by a large circle. The Babylonians worked on a base

RIGHT TRIANAGLES

Pythagoras is now chiefly known to the general public as the man who explained the mathematical relationship among the sides of a right triangle. Whether he was the first to do so is unclear, but the concept spread far and wide. This document is a 13th-century Arabic rendition of Euclid's proof of the Pythagorean theorem.

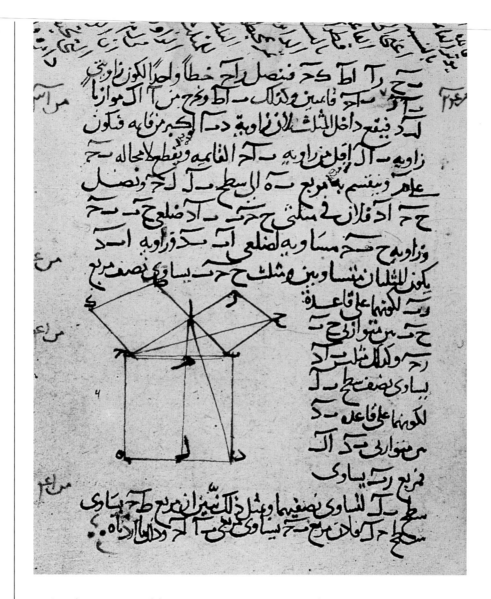

unit of 60, comparable to our units of angles and time. A large circle with a small circle inside equaled ten large circles: 10 x 6 x 10 x 6 x 10, or 36,000 base units.

Different counting systems were applied to different things—the system used for counting up grain stores was not the same as the system used for counting cattle—and yet the symbols in each system could be identical.

Over the next thousand years, the complexities of this transitional period were streamlined into a system that used only two symbols: A wedge shape standing on its point represented numbers less than ten; a wedge pointing left represented the number 10. Addition, subtraction, multiplication, and division were done the same way we do them now, except that numbers were carried at 60 rather than 10.

(Think, for example, of 53 minutes plus 20 minutes. The addition of 7 minutes makes one hour, and the 13 minutes are carried over.) To make things easier, the Babylonians created extensive multiplication and division tables, so that large calculations could be broken down into smaller ones that could then be added together. With this system, the Babylonians could accomplish sophisticated calculations.

The Babylonian penchant for creating mathematical tables did not seem to carry over to creating general mathematical formulas. They were able to accomplish algebraic calculations—such as finding the base and height of a rectangle when their product and sum were known—but they did this by a series of steps and not by working with what we would recognize as an equation.

The Greeks claimed that their early knowledge came from the Egyptians. Although Egypt may have seemed the more accomplished civilization at the time, when it came to mathematics it never extended its base-ten system much beyond practical arithmetic. Still, the Greeks had established trade with Egypt by the seventh century B.C., and by the third century B.C., Egypt was part of the Greek empire.

Wherever mathematics developed in the ancient world—and it developed independently in China and India, as well as among the Inca in the Western Hemisphere—it gave cultures a new way to express their increased wealth, productivity, and knowledge. Written

language that developed at the same time served much the same purpose. Just as writing isn't necessarily philosophy, so measurement does not become science until it is used to investigate natural phenomena. Parlaying the language of mathematics into scientific discoveries required yet one more step: the conviction that nature itself was subject to mathematical laws.

How did this understanding come about? The earliest evidence points to Greece in the seventh century B.C., then a confederation of freethinking, politically capricious, and independent states stretching from the Greek mainland across the Aegean to the coast of Turkey.

In the middle of a trade network that brought goods and ideas from Africa, the Middle East, India, and China, this Ionian civilization arose quickly, inspired from the beginning with intellectual curiosity. Schools of philosophy sprang up on small islands or in the midst of growing cities and made their founders household names. In the late seventh and early sixth centuries, natural philosophers from the Ionian city of Miletus on the Turkish coast—including Thales, his student Anaximander, and his student Anaximenes—developed intricate cosmogonies. Their studies led them to the conclusion that simple mathematical ratios could in fact describe the universe.

The Pythagoreans in Italy took this idea to its extreme. Their work had a great impact on the course of Greek—and, later, all scientific—thought. Nothing of the actual

WORLD-RENOWNED

The Pythagorean theorem is used and honored the world around. A coin from Uganda shows a right triangle, the formula for the theorem, and an image of Pythagoras himself.

See pages 239-240 for more information about Plato's theory of forms.

teachings of Pythagoras remains, but his influence on mathematics, science, and all Western thought is undeniable.

Born in 560 B.C. on the island of Samos, just off the Turkish coast, Pythagoras traveled as a young man to Egypt and Babylonia. When he returned to Samos, he established a cultlike order of men and women devoted to asceticism, vegetarianism, temperance, politics, philosophy, astronomy, reincarnation, music, and mathematics. Pythagoras and his followers discovered the numerical ratios that determine the intervals between notes in a musical scale. From music, they extended their search for mathematical relationships to geometric forms and number progressions, always in search of harmonies and symmetries.

For us, the importance of these developments lies in the recognition that something as natural as sound was liable to mathematical law. The Pythagoreans made it a theoretical discipline: mathematical statements required rigorous proofs. For the Pythagoreans, "all things are number." In the regular movements of the stars and planets the Pythagoreans sought the "music of the spheres." It was their contention that geometry might be the way for humans to comprehend the universe and bring life itself into a state of harmony.

The Pythagoreans were awed by a strange discovery: They recognized that there was a constant ratio between the lengths of the hypotenuse and the two sides of any right triangle, but they could not find a way to express it as a fraction made with the numbers they knew.

What kind of a number was this that could not be expressed exactly? They were on the verge of discovering what we today call irrational numbers. Their investigation eventually led to the formula that we now call the Pythagorean theorem.

The theorem is expressed mathematically as $a^2 + b^2 = c^2$, where a and b are the lengths of the sides and c is the length of the hypotenuse. If the triangle's sides are one unit long, then using the theorem shows that c, the length of the hypotenuse, would be the square root of two. The Pythagoreans were right: There is no way to represent this value as a ratio of two other numbers. In our modern decimal notation, the numbers coming after the decimal point (1.414213. . . .) neither repeat in a pattern nor end. The ratio of the diameter to the circumference of a circle, called pi, was similarly a mathematical entity that could not be expressed in known numbers.

After Pythagoras, Greek thinkers found a spiritual allure in geometric forms as well. Plato argued that all things we observe or encounter in daily life are flawed reflections of timeless, ideal forms that exist outside the realm of earthly human experience. The Platonists, following the lead of the Pythagoreans, asserted that nature's forms and phenomena possessed inherent mathematical symmetries—new truths—just awaiting discovery.

The idea that mathematics could describe nature represents a huge

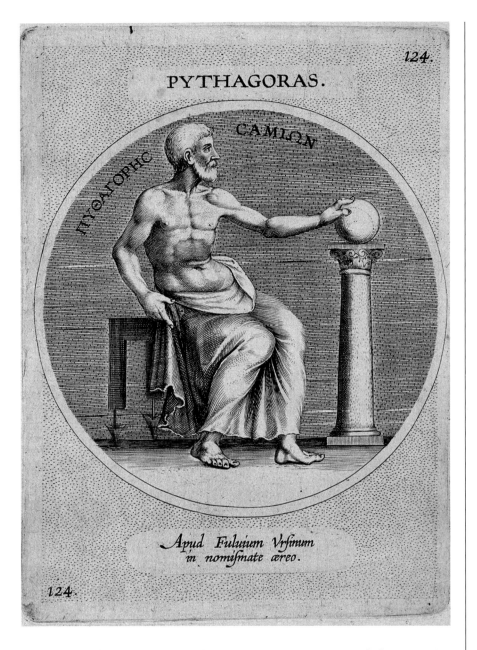

PYTHAGORAS.

124.

ΠΥΘΑΓΟΡΗC CAMIΩN

Apud Fuluium Vrsinum
in nomismate æreo.

124.

MATHEMATICS EVERYWHERE

Pythagoras and his followers believed that reality was mathematical in nature. With intense study, the hidden harmonies and mathematical order of the cosmos could be discerned.

conceptual advance. For example, it is generally believed that Plato set mathematical astronomy into motion by urging his students to uncover the regular, harmonious, mathematically perfect movements of the planets hidden behind their seemingly erratic heavenly paths. The Platonic view is summarized in a motto, repeated for centuries thereafter: "God alway geometrizes."

Almost two millennia later, Galileo would say essentially the same thing, declaring that the universe is a "great book . . . written in the language of mathematics; its characters are triangles, circles and other geometric figures."

159

The Greek mathematician Euclid is widely regarded as the greatest teacher of geometry, past and present.

The search for geometrical truths inspired Euclid, who lived around 300 B.C., to record all the geometric knowledge up to his day, from ancient Babylon up to the work of Eudoxus, around 400 B.C.

In the resulting book, *Elements,* Euclid states that all of geometry derives from four basic postulates: that a straight line can be drawn between any two points; that any straight line can be extended indefinitely in a straight line; that given any straight line segment, a circle can be drawn with that line as its radius and one endpoint at its center; and, finally, that all right angles are congruent. Euclid's careful step-by-step mathematical reasoning in *Elements* became the standard for mathematical proofs.

Euclid's book has served as a primary geometry text for more than 2,000 years. "Almost from the time of its writing and lasting almost to the present, the Elements has exerted a continuous and major influence on human affairs," wrote Dutch mathematician B. L. van der Waerden. "It was the primary source of geometric reasoning, theorems, and methods at least until the advent of non-Euclidean geometry in the 19th century."

THE GREEKS: MIND AND MATTER

Alongside Greek advancements in geometry, mathematics, and astronomy, the study of nature called physics likewise draws its origins from the Greeks. These early natural philosophers questioned the world of matter. How did it come into being? What was the primary substance of the cosmos? Was it air, water, fire, or some combination of them all? Could matter come from nothing? Was there a creator? Did life have a purpose, or did things come into being by chance? Was the universe of matter always the same, or was it always changing? For many, these were metaphysical questions, not liable to mathematical solutions.

Some early philosophers of the seventh and sixth centuries B.C. developed their concepts of the cosmos around a primary element or combination of elements. That the forms of matter were so diverse and various—from nonliving to living things—meant that these elements must be in constant flux, at some point finding a balance between coming into being and passing out of being, over and over. These concepts governed the main stream of debate until the fifth

HEAVENLY ORDER

Euclid's teachings in geometry prompted attempts to locate the Earth in relationship to the stars, sun, moon, and planets. Ptolemy placed the Earth at the center of the cosmos, a mistake that proved difficult to correct.

century B.C., when the conversation diverged into two paths.

Parmenides of Elea, born around 515 B.C., argued that matter coming and going would mean that at a certain point, nonbeing must exist, and that this was not possible since being is, and, if it is, it remains as it is. As Parmenides wrote in his poem "The Way of Truth," "Never

THE LAUGHING PHILOSOPHER

Greek philosopher Democritus believed that both space and matter were made up of an infinite number of indivisible and vanishingly small units called atoms. Atoms remained in constant motion, he believed, and could combine into seemingly solid form.

shall this prevail, that what is not, is: Keep your thoughts from following that path!"

Empedocles, a contemporary and perhaps a pupil of Parmenides, agreed that an immutable cosmos, once established, remains unchanged, but argued that change in the world in which we live was possible through the intricate interactions of the four "roots" of all matter: earth, water, air, and fire. These roots were alternately pulled apart and drawn together by love and strife—the names he gave to the forces of attraction and repulsion. Each root had its own characteristics, and all matter was made up of different combinations of these roots, soon called elements.

Democritus of Abdera took a very different stand in the debate.

Born circa 460 B.C., he came to be known as the laughing philosopher, for the attitude of amusement he maintained toward the human condition. He is rumored to have lived to be a hundred.

Democritus saw no reason why being and nonbeing could not coexist. "No less aught is there than naught," he chided Parmenides's adherents. He envisioned the world as a great void in which there is a constant rain of imperceptibly tiny and impenetrable atoms (a word from the Greek, *atomos,* meaning unable to be cut or divided) of all different shapes and sizes. Random collisions of atoms form objects; those objects decompose when the atoms come apart.

While Plato directed his students to seek the eternal realities lurking behind the imperfect appearances of the world, his most famous student, Aristotle, greatly valued the direct observation of nature. Aristotle studied not only the exalted celestial motions celebrated by the Platonists and the Pythagoreans, but also the mundane particulars of the natural world, from worms to the creatures of the sea.

On logical grounds, Aristotle rejected the atomic theory and instead formulated a very detailed theory of matter using Empedocles's four elements of fire, water, earth, and air. These, in Aristotle's view, formed living and nonliving matter. He differed from Empedocles, though, in his belief that the elements could change. They could give up or take on wetness or dryness, heat or cold, and they could transform one into another.

Aristotle's observations of the natural world—how fish are designed to swim, how cows are designed to chew—told him that everything in nature had a design or purpose. In fact, life was organized on an ascending order of purpose, he believed, starting with inanimate things and going up to plants, which found perfection in growing; then to animals, which found

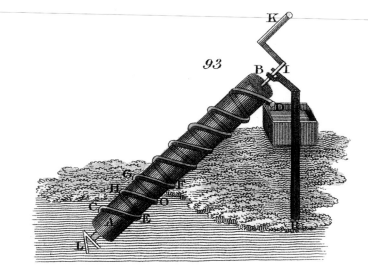

93

perfection in finding food; and finally to humans. who found perfection in thought and happiness.

Aristotle's world is dynamic. Change and motion are its chief characteristics. He identified four causes, as he called them, that lie behind every object; once these are known, the object itself is understood. The first cause is the matter out of which the object is made. The second is the form taken on by this matter. The third, called the efficient cause, is the thing that makes the object. The fourth and last cause is the most important in Aristotle's worldview. Called the final cause, it expresses what a thing is for, what its purpose is, *why* it exists.

All natural things—unlike the artificial works of human hands—have within themselves a driving principle that pushes them on toward their goal or final cause.

An acorn, for example, needs no external impetus to drive it onward toward fulfilling its purpose, namely sprouting and growing into a mature oak tree. Thus, for Aristotle, material substances were always in flux, moving from one state to another, driven either by their internal principle of change toward their proper ends or diverted to other ends by the external hand of human artificers.

More than a century after Democritus, Epicurus returned to his atomic theory and contemplated a materialistic world made of atoms moving within a void without benefit of soul, gods, or creator. The atoms of Epicurus, unlike those of Democritus, had weight; they might suddenly be diverted and collide; and, when endowed with certain shapes, they

1600 – 1704

1600
English physician William Gilbert publishes his *De magnete (On the Magnet)*, greatly advancing the understanding of magnetism.

1604, 1609
Italian astronomer Galileo Galilei performs experiments relating to gravity, acceleration, and velocity.

1621
Dutch astronomer Willebrord Snell discovers the law that determines the path of a refracted ray, eventually called Snell's law.

1654
French mathematician and philosopher Blaise Pascal states that force is transmitted through a fluid equally in all directions.

1662
English philosopher Robert Boyle determines that a gas held at constant temperature has a volume inversely proportional to its pressure, eventually called Boyle's law.

1668
English physicist Isaac Newton determines that the linear momentum of an object is equal to its mass multiplied by its velocity.

1687
Newton publishes *Philosophiae Naturalis Principia Mathematica* (or simply *Principia)*, presenting his laws of motion and the law of universal gravitation.

1704
Newton publishes *Opticks*, his work on light and the spectrum.

BATHTUB INSIGHT
Legend has it that Archimedes's eureka moment came when he noticed how the displacement of water could help him determine whether the king's new crown was gold or alloy.

could evoke sensations, such as smell or taste. For Epicurus, natural events had no purpose; all was due to the chance actions of atoms. Even the mind was not any different from the body in being a structure of atoms. When death came, the atoms of both mind and body dispersed into the air.

The Greeks left behind basic physical concepts: Elements, atomic or otherwise, are the basic building blocks of all matter; matter is something that undergoes creation and growth, decay and destruction; since matter undergoes transformation, its forms are often impermanent. These are all ideas—and in some cases, questions—that still excite scientists and philosophers some 2,500 years later.

"EUREKA!"

Thanks to astonishing conquests by young Alexander the Great—tutored by Aristotle himself—in Africa and Asia, Greek knowledge and culture spread far and wide through the ancient world starting in the fourth century B.C. After the premature death of Alexander in 323, his empire was divided among his generals, but Hellenistic culture remained a unifying force.

Probably the most Hellenized, and certainly the most productive, area in terms of science and mathematics, was Egypt. There the city of Alexandria (one of over a dozen cities founded and named after the Macedonian general, and the only one to retain the name) became the ancient world's most cosmopolitan city. Merchants and scholars from various nations flocked to this teeming center.

The geometer Euclid worked out of Alexandria, and so, too, most likely, did the ancient world's prolific mathematician Archimedes. Born in Syracuse, Sicily, around 287 B.C., he is known by legend more than by fact. Most famously, he jumped out of his bath and ran naked through the streets crying *"Eureka!*—I have found it!" when he discovered that a submerged body displaces an amount of water equal to its volume. He was a thinker who could put his science to work alongside his practical genius, a thinker who wanted to know how processes occurred and to figure out which mathematical principles lay behind them.

His eureka moment was exemplary. The king of Syracuse had asked Archimedes to determine whether a certain crown was made of pure gold or of an alloy. The story goes that when he lowered himself into his bath, Archimedes noticed that the amount of water that overflowed the tub must be equal to his own volume. Therefore, he had found a way to measure the exact volume of the gold crown. Since gold is the densest metal, all Archimedes had to do was to make a brick of pure gold that displaced the same amount of water as did the crown, then compare the weights of the crown and the brick. If the crown weighed less than the brick, then it must be made of a metal alloyed with a lighter metal. As it turned out, the weights were unequal, proving that the crown was not pure gold.

In his studies in geometry Archimedes advanced the work of Eudoxus and, by painstaking labor, calculated with great accuracy the ratio of the circumference of a circle to its diameter, pi. He also discovered formulas for the surface area and volume of spheres. (He took such pride in the latter that he asked for it to be inscribed on his gravestone.) He also developed a formula to determine an object's center of mass.

Archimedes's earliest mechanical invention appears to have been a device to move water uphill. Known as the Archimedean screw, it was a spiral-shaped pipe that, when rotated, raised water from a stream up onto land.

LORD KELVIN

Discoverer of absolute zero

1824
Born as William Thomson on June 26 in Belfast, Ireland.

1834
Enters University of Glasgow.

1841
Enters Peterhouse College, University of Cambridge.

1845
Graduates with honors in mathematics, elected a fellow of Peterhouse College, Cambridge.

1846
Becomes professor of natural philosophy at University of Glasgow; a member of the Royal Philosophical Society.

1848
Publishes work *On an Absolute Thermometric Scale;* the proposed scale is later named the Kelvin scale.

1851
Elected as fellow of the Royal Society.

1852
In collaboration with James Prescott Joule, discovers that gas temperatures change as gas containment changes; the discovery is later named the Joule-Thomson effect.

1854
Produces his first patent, with brothers James and William Rankine, for improvements in telegraphic communication equipment.

1857
Embarks on venture to lay Atlantic telegraph cable from on board H.M.S. *Agamemnon* and U.S.S. *Niagara.*

1860
Publishes important papers on the thermoelectric, thermomagnetic, and pyroelectric properties of materials.

1907
Dies on December 17 near Ayrshire, Scotland.

MECHANICAL KNOWHOW

Armed with the knowledge of his law of levers, Archimedes reputedly boasted: "Give me a place to stand on, and I will move the Earth."

He detailed the principle of the lever, namely that things balance at distances from the fulcrum in inverse ratio to their weights, as well as those of the pulley, the wedge, and the windlass.

The lever was not a new invention, but once Archimedes formulated the mathematics that made it work, he could calculate for any weight the length of lever needed to lift it. In a legendary demonstration, he set up a series of pulleys to show the king of Syracuse that he could move an enormous ship with no more than the strength of his hand.

Archimedes experimented with mirrors and reflected light, although the story that he used an array of burning mirrors to set fire to the Roman fleet is most likely apocryphal. In fact, the Romans sacked Syracuse, and Archimedes was killed in the melee. Even so, the Romans celebrated Archimedes for his brilliance and mechanical inge-

Europe. Archimedes's devices, as well as his theoretical investigations of such things as buoyancy, floating bodies, and hydraulics, continued to inspire analytical pursuits and inventiveness in the 16th and 17th centuries. French mathematical prodigy Blaise Pascal, for instance, drew upon Archimedes's work when he discovered in the mid-1600s that pressure applied to a confined liquid is transferred equally throughout the liquid. His experiments led to his invention of the syringe and the hydraulic press, still essential in hydraulic braking systems today.

Archimedes and Pascal studied hydrostatics, the science of fluids at rest. But fluids are often in motion, and in the 18th century the study of hydrodynamics emerged: the physics of flowing water, of water running through pipes, of sea currents and waves, and even of raindrops on windowpanes.

Daniel Bernoulli was to hydrodynamics what Archimedes was to hydrostatics. Bernoulli, born in Groningen, Netherlands in 1700, was the son of Swiss mathematician Johann Bernoulli, one of three brothers, all mathematicians. The father taught the son mathematics, but the son's work would soon exceed that of the father. The younger Bernoulli studied mathematics, medicine, and physics and in 1738 published his groundbreaking *Hydrodynamica*. In it, Daniel Bernoulli established the principle that bears his name, which says that pressure in a fluid decreases as its velocity increases— and that became the basis of the

nuity, and his fame survived well beyond the age of antiquity. Archimedes's mathematical achievements were widely appreciated by Arab mathematicians, who rediscovered his work in the eighth century A.D. Archimedes enjoyed another surge of popularity in the Italian Renaissance and became the model for a new and enormously productive generation of Italian engineers in northern Italy, and from there across wider swaths of

BAROMETER
A barometer's measures the level of atmospheric pressure. A barometer can also determine altitude, since air pressure corresponds to distance from sea level. When the barometer falls rapidly, a storm is usually expected; when it rises rapidly, fair weather is usually in the forecast.

AERODYNAMIC PRINCIPLE

Archimedes and Pascal described fluids at rest, but mathematician Daniel Bernoulli found that fluids in motion had different physical properties. He explained his findings in *Hydrodynamica*, from the Greek for moving water.

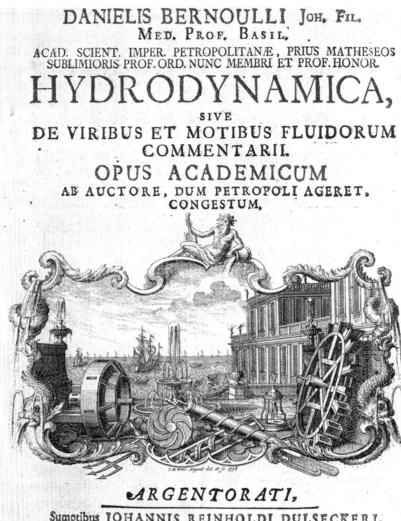

DANIELIS BERNOULLI Joh. Fil.

Med. Prof. Basil.

ACAD. SCIENT. IMPER. PETROPOLITANÆ, PRIUS MATHESEOS SUBLIMIORIS PROF. ORD. NUNC MEMBRI ET PROF. HONOR.

HYDRODYNAMICA,

SIVE

DE VIRIBUS ET MOTIBUS FLUIDORUM COMMENTARII.

OPUS ACADEMICUM

AB AUCTORE, DUM PETROPOLI AGERET, CONGESTUM.

ARGENTORATI,

Sumptibus JOHANNIS REINHOLDI DULSECKERI, Anno M D CC XXXVIII.

Typis Joh. Henr. Deckeri, Typographi Basiliensis.

1738 – 1827

1738
Swiss mathematician Daniel Bernoulli determines that the faster a fluid moves, the lower its pressure, a principle that describes wings and makes human flight possible.

1785
French physicist Charles-Augustin de Coulomb discovers the force between electrical charges, later named Coulomb's law.

1798
American-born British physicist Benjamin Thompson studies heat and argues that it results from friction, not from any substance residing in material.

1800
Italian physicist Alessandro Volta invents the electric battery.

science of fluid dynamics. It explains the movement of water through pipes as well as water moving through rivers. It begins to explain how bird and airplane wings work. Air is a fluid, too, and wings are shaped to reduce the air pressure above and create lift from below.

In 1734 Daniel Bernoulli and his father were declared joint winners of a grand prize in astronomy given by the Paris Academy of Sciences. The elder Bernoulli was furious at having to share the prize with his son, and he threw Daniel out of the house. Johann Bernoulli even later tried to claim that his son's path-breaking *Hydrodynamica* was copied from his own work, and went so far as to publish a similarly entitled book (based on Daniel's) with a false printing date to support his spurious claims.

THE ISLAMIC CONTRIBUTIONS

After the collapse of the Roman Empire and the disruption caused by barbarian invasions of Europe, the next great flourishing of scientific thought occurred in the newly ascendant Muslim world, particu-larly in the capitals of Baghdad and Cordoba from about A.D. 800 to 1300. Sponsored in part by the caliphs, a great translation project turned hundreds of Greek texts into Arabic. The scholars of the Islamic world built extensively upon these Hellenistic foundations.

An exemplar of the golden age of Islamic science was Abu 'Ali al-Hasan ibn al-Haytham (Alhazen is the Latinized version), born in Basra (in today's Iraq) in about A.D. 965. As a young man, Alhazen gave up a minor government post to study science. Especially interested in the work of Aristotle, he soon developed a reputation as a mathematician and natural philosopher. He eventually moved to Cairo at a time when Egypt was ruled by the Fatimids, an Islamic dynasty named for the prophet Muhammad's daughter, Fatimah. The Fatimids ruled part of North Africa and Sicily, and they made Cairo the capital of their empire. The Fatimid caliph, al-Hakim, had a great interest in science, and he had built a center of learning in Cairo that rivaled the House of Wisdom, Baghdad's library, archives, and record office.

1803
English chemist John Dalton concludes that each element is made up of atoms and that these atoms combine to make compounds.

1811
Italian physicist Amedeo Avogadro shows that equal volumes of gases at the same temperature contain an equal number of molecules.

1821-1825
French physicist André-Marie Ampère discovers that moving electrical charges create a magnetic field.

1827
German physicist Georg Simon Ohm publishes his law, which states that voltage is equal to the current multiplied by resistance.

ARAB INFLUENCE

Middle Eastern thinkers made substantial contributions to mathematics. An image from 1508 commemorates the triumph of arithmetical algorithms over the conventional abacus for calculation. The figure on the left is employing Arabic numerals, which Muslims transmitted to the West from India.

After his arrival in Egypt, Alhazen considered the possibility of controlling the annual Nile floods. At some point he either sought al-Hakim's patronage or was summoned by the caliph for the project. In either case, Alhazen found himself heading up the Nile with a team of engineers and a commission to construct controls to the great river's flow.

Once upstream, Alhazen realized that his plan wouldn't work. He returned to a displeased caliph, and although he was given a nonscience post in the government, Alhazen worried that the caliph was not done with him. Al-Hakim was a man used to having his way, and, as enlightened as he was, he could also be a dangerous eccentric. After the conquest of an enemy city, he had all the dogs killed because their barking annoyed him. Alhazen, a man of unquestionable scientific genius, decided to protect himself by pretending to go mad. He continued to do science but posed outwardly as a madman until al-Hakim died in 1021.

Alhazen, by then in his 50s, was able to accomplish major innovations in the science of optics, involving light, vision, color, and refraction. He rejected the Greek idea that vision emanated from the eye as a visual ray. He used mathematical models and experiments to argue that illuminated objects emit light in every direction. He posited that light travels in straight lines, which he called "rays." The lens of the eye, he believed, received these rays, thus allowing us to see our surroundings. He even delved into anatomy, considering how the eye connected to the optic nerve.

Islamic scientists of the Middle Ages made original discoveries and crucial contributions in the fields of astronomy, medicine, early chemistry, and mechanics. One of the most wide-ranging and important fields of Islamic scholarship was mathematics, both simple and complex. One key figure to whom we owe a great deal (even though the original Arabic versions of his most important works are now lost) is Muhammad ibn Musa al-Khwarizmi.

Al-Khwarizmi was born in Baghdad around 780. He became a scholar and translator of Greek manuscripts in the Baghdad House of Wisdom, built by caliph al-Mamun after he came to power in Baghdad in the year 813. What al-Khwarizmi eventually wrote, however, became at least as important as any of the texts he translated. His intention was to explicate "what is easiest and most useful in arithmetic, such as men constantly require in cases of inheritance, legacies, partition, lawsuits, and trade, and in all their dealings with one another, or where the measuring of lands, the digging of canals, geometrical computations, and other objects of various sorts and kinds are concerned." He would write about the practical applications of mathematics, in other words.

To do this he offered the reader a way to state the terms of a problem so that all the functions are coordinated into statements that can be placed into an equation that can

See pages 252, 255, 259 for more information about microscopes.

ARABIC NUMERALS

The numerals 1, 2, 3, 4, 5, 6, 7, 8, 9, and 0 are commonly known as "Arabic" numerals, but their proper name is "Hindu-Arabic." Indian Hindus developed most of this system in the third century B.C. It was not until the ninth century A.D. that the zero became known—to al-Khwarizmi, an Arabic scholar. Although most of these numerals originated in India, the Arabs introduced them to Europe, and the Europeans misidentified them as "Arabic" numerals.

be solved. He called the first part of the process—removing the negative terms from the equation—*al-jabr,* and the balancing of the equation *al-muqabala.* From the former term we get our word algebra, and from a Latin corruption of al-Khwarizmi's name we get the word algorithm.

Had this been al-Khwarizmi's only accomplishment, it would have been sufficient, but his next book, on the *Hindu Art of Reckoning,* began the standardization of Arabic numerals and, just as important, introduced zero to mark a place in a written number. Although al-Khwarizmi's work contributed to advanced mathematics, it also, as he intended, brought mathematics into everyday use. For the next 700 years Arab mathematicians, astronomers, and makers of scientific instruments dominated the Western world, thanks to their mathematical and analytical proficiencies.

As often happens, science awaits a technological advance before it can move forward. Alhazen's work on optics had been precocious. Glass lenses were not yet well enough refined to demonstrate his theories. Galileo had worked to improve the telescope, trying to develop lenses that didn't present a view with color distortions at the edges of the image—what's known as chromatic aberration. He finally gave up. Meanwhile, in the Middle Ages, Robert Grosseteste and Roger Bacon had both predicted that magnifying lenses would help researchers see things not only far away but also smaller than what could be seen through ordinary human vision. It took centuries to

develop better grinding techniques and suitably transparent glass.

The earliest microscopes used only a single lens mounted between two pieces of metal, with a screw device that could be used to bring an object into focus. In the 1590s the Dutch lensmaker Hans Jansen found that a compound microscope, with two lenses, would magnify things even more, but only once the lenses were painstakingly matched and properly aligned. In the late 17th century Antoni van Leeuwenhoek achieved magnifications of more than 250-fold and astonished the scientific world by revealing the structure of many previously invisible objects.

In the 17th and 18th centuries advances in optics also inspired investigators to consider the very nature of light. They observed clearly that a ray of light bent as it passed through a lens or fluid, and in 1621 Willebrord Snel of Leiden developed a mathematical formula for the angle. Why light bent was another problem altogether. The search for a solution to that question would eventually come to alter the world's understanding of all forms of energy.

In the 17th century, though, light was considered to move at an infinite speed. In 1676 Ole Rømer, a Danish astronomer, found that when Jupiter and the Earth were farthest apart, the regular eclipses of the Jovian moons occurred later than the calculations predicted, but when Jupiter and the Earth were close in space, this discrepancy did not occur. Rømer proposed that the delay was due to the speed of light:

NEWTON'S TELESCOPE

Isaac Newton developed his reflecting telescope in 1668. Using mirrors rather than lenses to gather an object's light, he avoided the haze caused by the prism effects of light as it passes through glass.

The light took more time to cross over to us from the other side of the solar system. Rømer calculated that light moved at a speed of 140,000 miles per second. He was wrong by about 25 percent but close enough to make the point.

At about the same time, Dutch mathematician Christiaan Huygens made another assertion about light.

In 1659, he discovered the rings of Saturn, using a telescope with lenses that he and his brother had ground and polished. He believed that light traveled in waves that moved through the invisible but ubiquitous ether. The waves of light traveled outward like a circle of ripples from a rock dropped into a pond. When they met other objects,

See page 37 for more information about Huygens.

STATIC ELECTRICITY
English physician William Gilbert investigated the properties of static electricity and contrasted them to magnetic effects. In this 19th-century painting, Gilbert (standing, in black) demonstrates an electrical experiment before Queen Elizabeth I and various onlookers.

like ripples in a pond, they rebounded—or, in the case of light, reflected—and created what Huygens called "secondary wavelets."

Huygens's ideas did not go unquestioned. Light waves seemed to slow down when they entered a denser medium; how was it that they speeded up when they came out again? Isaac Newton, who was then a professor at Cambridge, England, asked why light waves did not simply bend around obstructions.

At about this time, Newton was beginning to lay out the broad outlines of his theory of gravity and his three laws of motion. He had become a professor at Cambridge at the age of 26, but outside of Cambridge, he was generally unknown—until 1668, that is, when he designed a reflecting telescope that used a mirror as its main light-gathering device.

Despite the acclaim he won for his telescope design, he remained determined to tackle the problem

of chromatic aberrations in lenses, too. Where did the colors come from? At the time it was widely believed that pure light—sunlight, for example —contained no colors. Many people had seen that prisms, oil on water, and lenses could create a beam of light with a rainbow of hues, but the belief was that those colors came from the object that the light struck. Newton sought to prove that, far from being colorless, white light in fact contained a spectrum of many colors. He used a

prism to break a ray of light into a spectrum, then used a second prism to combine the colors back into a single white beam. Going further, he passed a colored beam of light through the prism. The beam was not altered, proving that the individual colors of the spectrum were not further divisible. He also found that different colors are refracted— their beams bent by passing through a prism—to different angles.

Newton soon offered a view of light, different from that of

**NAVIGATIONAL
NECESSITY**

A woodcut of a
compass illustrated
William Gilbert's *De
Magnete* very well,
since the magnetic
forces of which he
wrote were essential
to the operation of
this navigational tool.

Huygens and Robert Hooke, who also believed that light traveled in waves. Light, Newton proposed, was made up of particles. The different refractions of different colors, Newton said, would make it impossible to create lenses that had no chromatic aberrations. He published his *Opticks* in 1704. It was a remarkable work, and he was knighted by England's Queen Anne in 1705.

But on lenses, at least, Newton was soon proved wrong. An English lawyer, Chester Moor Hall, found that in a telescope made with two kinds of glass, one glass could cancel out the chromatic aberrations of the other. But the question still remained: what was light? Particles or waves?

THE ATTRACTION OF MAGNETISM

The groundwork for exploring this question was set in place in 1600, when an English physician, William Gilbert—Queen Elizabeth's personal physician—published *De magnete,*

Magneticisque Corporibus et de Magno Magnete Tellure (On the Magnet, Magnetic Bodies, and the Great Magnet of the Earth). Gilbert based his work solely on his own observations and measurements, studying a force that had been known since ancient times but that had never been so pains-takingly investigated.

The ancient world knew the magnetic properties of naturally occurring lodestone, a form of iron oxide also known as magnetite, but to them, the forces involved seemed utterly inexplicable. The Greeks knew about lodestones, and in fact the very word "magnetism" comes from the name for lodestones found near Magnesia in Asia Minor.

According to science historian Colin Ronan, ancient Chinese fortune-tellers used a divining board of two disks, a lower one that represented the Earth, and an upper, rotating one that represented the heavens. Both boards were marked with compass points. Symbolic objects would be tossed onto the board and the future divined by where they landed.

Sometime in the first century A.D. a rotating spoon, symbolic of the Big Dipper, replaced the upper board. Sometime later, diviners began making the board and spoon out of lodestone. When they did, they realized that the spoon's handle always pointed in the same direction. It seemed like magic. This "south-pointing spoon" as it came to be called, according to Ronan, evolved into something more like a pointer. Eventually it was put to uses other than on the divining board.

Later, it was discovered that iron needles could be magnetized if stroked on a lodestone or if heated in a fire and allowed to cool while held in a south-north direction. This important practical knowledge led to the use of compasses in determining the alignment of building sites and, by the tenth century, as a tool for navigation. Chinese scientists also discovered, 700 years before Western scientists, that magnetic north and south—that is, the directions to which compasses point—are not the same as geographic north and south.

By the 13th century, the Chinese magnetic compass had come west. In 1269 Pierre Pèlerin de Maricourt (latinized to Perigrinus), a French crusader, scholar, and military engineer, wrote *Epistola de magnete* (*A Letter on Magnets*), the first treatise of Western science on the properties of magnets. Peregrinus was the first to call the opposite ends of a magnet

ELECTRICITY AND MAGNETS

In 1820, Hans Christian Ørsted observed that a magnetic needle, when brought near an electric current, turned at a right angle to the current. He noted the phenomenon but had no explanation for it.

poles, the first to study how like poles repel each other, and the first to begin to consider the practical applications for magnets. He made a good start at the science of magnetism, especially considering that at the time he was a soldier serving in the army of Charles I of Anjou, besieging the Italian city of Lucera.

William Gilbert's *De magnete,* published in 1600, represented a new concept in science writing— "Baconian science, based on experiment and observation rather than hearsay, being practised twenty years before the publication of Bacon's *Novum organum,*" as historians Stuart Malin and David Barraclough put it. Gilbert's text, written in Latin, came out nine years before Kepler's *Astronomia nova* and ten years before Galileo set down his first astronomical observations in *Sidereus nuncius.*

For all the previous centuries of using and describing magnets, no one came as close as Gilbert to understanding how they worked. In the first of the six parts of *De magnete,* Gilbert concludes that the Earth itself is a great magnet. He then draws an important distinction (a controversial one, eventually proving to be an important similarity) between the attractive properties of magnets and what Gilbert called the "electric force" produced when certain materials, such as amber, rub lightly against cloth or fur and then attract light objects. Gilbert used a spherical lodestone that he called a *terrella,* a miniature Earth, to study the effects of geomagnetism.

Two hundred years later, Hans Christian Ørsted, a professor of science at the University of Copenhagen, demonstrated that when a

See pages 250-51 for more information about Francis Bacon.

TO MEASURE GASES

The eudiometer (from the Greek for measuring pure air) was an instrument invented by Italian physicist Allessandro Volta to measure gases after combustion. This model was developed by English chemist Henry Cavendish, who first identified hydrogen gas in 1766.

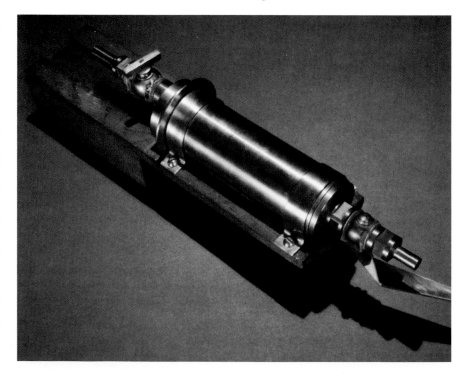

wire carrying an electric current was held over a compass needle, the needle turned to stand at right angles to the wire. Why? Ørsted published his results with no conclusion offered.

THE NEW ELEMENTS

Henry Cavendish was rich. With both the Duke of Devonshire and the Duke of Kent as grandfathers, he had an impeccable aristocratic pedigree. When he came into all his inheritances at age 52, in 1783, he held the largest individual account at the Bank of England. Although he was the man who discovered hydrogen and was first to analyze the composition of the atmosphere, he was ill-dressed in a faded violet suit with frilled sleeves and a tricornered hat that had long gone out of fashion. He was so painfully shy that he had a special staircase built in his house so that he would never have to encounter the servants in person; he communicated with them by writing notes. He spent nothing on himself, and when asked to give to charity, found out who had given the most and matched that amount to the penny. He never sat for a portrait and had to be persuaded to report his important discoveries in chemistry and physics.

Yet for all his peculiarities, Cavendish was a tireless experimenter. In the front of his house, he built a scaffold to allow him to climb into the trees to make astronomical observations. On his roof he installed a huge thermometer. He was eager to learn of the nature and composition of gases, a subject that drew in some of the best scientific minds of the time, from Scottish chemist Joseph Black, who first isolated carbon dioxide, to Joseph Priestley and Antoine Lavoisier, an equally wealthy Frenchman whose life was cut short, despite his scientific achievements, at the guillotine.

Cavendish created meticulous experiments to analyze the gases produced by reactions of solids and liquids. These "factitious" gases, as he called them—isolable in the laboratory, but not found in nature—could be isolated, contained, and weighed. He discovered and finally reported to the Royal Society in 1766 one particular factitious gas that had no name. When it burned in a flask, water remained on the glass. Cavendish's first explanation was that all gases contained water. But when news of the discovery reached Lavoisier, he ran experiments that produced not only water but also "inflammable air" when acids acted on metals. He finally was able to prove that there were two components of water: a gas he called oxygen and the gas identified by Cavendish. Lavoisier called the latter hydrogen—watermaker in Greek. After 3,000 years of considering it one of the four basic elements, water became known as a compound of two gases.

Cavendish went on to conduct experiments in which he passed an electric spark through air, forcing it to combine to form nitrogen oxides. He then dissolved the oxides in water to produce nitrous acid. Working like a medieval alchemist, holed up in the laborato-

See page 322 for more information about Henry Cavendish.

ry of his great London villa, the ascetic Cavendish found that air was no element either, but a mixture of nitrogen and oxygen in a ratio he figured to be four to one, surprisingly close to the actual five-to-one ratio. He even found that, no matter how hard he tried to get all the nitrogen and oxygen in the air to combine, a tiny amount of something was left over that resisted any chemical reaction. This inert substance, as he called it, was in fact, argon—an element whose existence would not be confirmed for another century.

By the end of the 18th century, chemistry was science's cutting edge. Lavoisier's and Cavendish's work led to a reorganization of chemical nomenclature based on a substance's composition. In the first years of the 19th century French chemist Joseph Louis Gay-Lussac found that equal volumes of all gases expand equally with the same increase in temperature. Gay-Lussac was a daredevil chemist who, in 1804, made hydrogen balloon ascents to an altitude of 22,000 feet, to measure the atmosphere. His more down-to-earth finding about expanding gases came to be called Charles's law, in honor of Jacques Charles, who had arrived at nearly the same conclusion 15 years earlier but had not published it. In 1808, Gay-Lussac determined that different gases always seemed to combine in certain specific, whole-number ratios by volume: two-to-one or five-to-three, for example. Why? And why, as Gay-Lussac also found, when gases combined, did they seem to occupy less space?

See pages 162-163 for more information about Democritus.

The first answer would come from a Quaker teacher from Manchester, England, John Dalton, a man who had taught himself science and who, up to the age of 30, kept a daily record of the weather. He also performed a systematic study of color blindness, from which he suffered.

Dalton's considerations of the atmosphere led him to think further about Gay-Lussac's problem in light of the compound nature of air, composed of two gases of different weight, as Cavendish had discovered. Why, for instance, didn't the heavier gas separate from the lighter one? Why did different gases dissolve in different amounts? The gases must not be combining chemically at all, he realized, but rather must be a mix of gas particles held together by heat. In deference to the ancient Greek Democritus, Dalton called these gas particles atoms. Democritus's atoms were all the same, though, adding up to a simple unified view of the natural elements. Dalton's atoms were all different.

The existence of atoms of different types, Dalton reasoned, would explain why compounds always combined in the same proportions by weight. Each gas, each element, had its own distinct atoms and distinct properties—heavy gases had heavy atoms, for example. Atoms, he argued, could combine in different proportions by weight to produce different compounds. This law of multiple proportions, as he called it, meant that depending upon the proportions, a mixture of carbon and oxygen, for example,

THE PERIODIC TABLE

It is the ubiquitous chart on the wall of the science lab, a colorful chart of squares, each bearing letters and numbers. For students, the periodic table of the elements is an imposing challenge. For scientists, it is an expression of the structure and behavior of all matter.

Dmitry Mendeleyev, a Russian chemist, first charted the elements in 1869. He organized them in order of their atomic weights. As he plotted out the 50 elements that had by then been identified and analyzed, he recognized that each element resembled ithe eighth element that followed it on his chart. For example, lithium resembled sodium, and both resembled potassium.

As an explanation for this, Mendeleyev proposed what he called the periodic law: "The elements arranged according to the magnitude of atomic weights show a periodic change of properties."

Once he had distributed all the known elements according to their characteristics, Mendeleyev noticed that there were still empty holes in his table. So confident was he in his theory and the orderliness of nature, he predicted that there were yet undiscovered elements and that, when these were found and analyzed, their properties would qualify them to fit into those empty spaces.

Remarkably, Mendeleyev proved to be right. As more elements were discovered, studied, and added, they fit the table and matched the pattern he had conceptualized.

In 1871, Dmitry Mendeleyev faced skepticism over his periodic table.

Over the next 50 years, the table was refined. When it was realized, in 1911, that an element's atomic number—the number of positive charges, or protons, in its nucleus—distinguished its properties, that number replaced atomic weight in the chart. The periodic table demonstrates that atoms are constructed in an orderly fashion—the identity of the elements changes as successive protons are added to each nucleus.

The modern periodic table arranges elements by increasing order of atomic number from left to right. The seven horizontal rows are called periods, and the eight vertical rows are called groups. The elements in each period begin with metals and progress to nonmetals, with noble gases at the farthest right in each row. The periodic table now contains 92 natural elements and 20 man-made elements (those that occur in nuclear reactions).

Mendeleyev's law still provides insight into the relationships of the elements to one another. It provides a physical representation of groupings of atoms with similar hardnesses, melting points, and densities, and helps express how, and how readily, elements bond with one another. With a thorough understanding of the periodic table one can tell at a glance how stable an element's atomic structure is and how well a given element will conduct electricity and heat. Mendeleyev's insight gave scientists a new way to view and construct information regarding natural phenomena.

could create either carbon monoxide or carbon dioxide. Moreover, chemical reactions either combined or separated elementary particles; no new atoms were created, and none were destroyed.

Dalton delivered his first paper in 1803 to the Manchester Literary and Philosophical Society, but its repercussions reached very far. Assuming that a given volume of a given substance always contained the same number of atoms, weighing the substances in a chemical reaction would provide the relative weight of the atoms involved. Dalton created a table of relative atomic weights, giving hydrogen a weight of one unit and using it as the standard. We now use a similar system based on the atomic weight of carbon, 12.

As to why combined gases took up less space than the volumes of the gases separately, the answer came just a few years later, when Amedeo Avogadro of Turin hypothesized that when gases combined, they created groups of atoms that Avogadro called molecules, from the Latin, *molecula*, meaning small pile or heap.

Dalton was elected a fellow of the Royal Societies of both London and Edinburgh, elected to the French Academy of Sciences, and awarded an honorary degree from Oxford (which would never have admitted him as a student because he was not an Anglican). Eventually, he was summoned to an audience with the king. None of this seemed to change Dalton's habits. He continued to record the daily weather of his native Lake District, as he had since 1787. His last weather record was made on July 27, 1844, the day he died.

In 1800, the list of known elements numbered 30. By Dalton's death in 1844, it had nearly doubled. Soon chemists began asking whether the list was anything more than a checklist. In 1864 British chemist John Newlands wondered aloud why some elements showed similar chemical properties. His question implied some sort of classification among the elements. The idea might have gone no further were it not for the recreational habits of an eccentric Siberian professor named Dmitry Mendeleyev, thrown out of

EARLY TABLE OF ELEMENTS

John Dalton, a science teacher in Manchester, England, formulated the modern atomic theory and published this table of elements with their atomic weights in 1808.

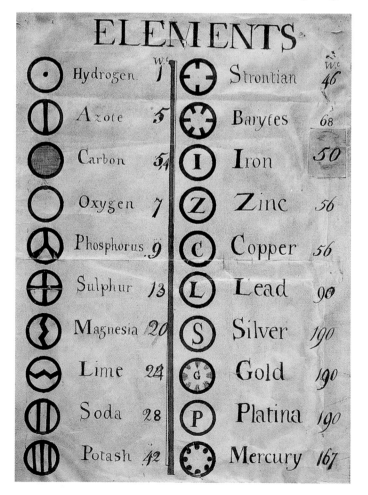

St. Petersburg University for unconventional behavior, including supporting student protests.

At work on a new chemistry text, Mendeleyev made a set of about 60 cards on which he wrote the names and properties of the known elements. An avid solitaire player, he began to place them into patterns by order of weight and chemical properties. He found that one arrangement placed all the elements that behaved similarly in the same vertical rows. It was a visual display of the concept at which Newlands had hinted: that chemical properties recurred periodically. In 1869 Mendeleyev published his so-called periodic table, noting that the scheme seemed to suggest that there were still several elements yet unknown. He left blank spaces in the table but predicted the properties those elements would have based on their position.

In 1860 two scientists in Heidelberg, Germany, Gustav Kirchhoff and Robert Bunsen, had taken to improving on an idea first tried in 1814 by German optician Joseph von Fraunhofer. In the course of his experiments, Fraunhofer had found that the sun's spectrum was not a continuous array of colors but was shot through with hundreds of black lines of various widths. By the early 1820s he had determined that these lines were present, though in slightly different patterns, in light from bright stars, and that they also showed up when beams were split by a grating rather than a lens. Although he didn't know what they meant, he used the letters A through K to name the divisions of lines.

Kirchhoff and Bunsen, working with an instrument with better resolution than Fraunhofer's, repeated the work and found what by then were known as Fraun-hofer's lines. Even more fascinating, they discovered that each element absorbed and emitted its own unique combination of wavelengths, a line pattern that served as a kind of spectral fingerprint.

Spectral analysis replaced long and tedious chemical analysis as a method for determining the components of any material. Once the spectra of the known elements were described, scientists began searching for new line patterns among substances in the laboratory, in the field, or even in light from space. They soon began to find new elements. And once they had analyzed the properties of those new elements, they found that they filled the very spaces that Dmitry Mendeleyev had reserved for them. His solitaire-like table of elements, expanded to include more than 100 elements, hangs today in science classrooms around the world.

ELECTRICITY EVERYWHERE
William Gilbert's introduction of the word "electric" in association with the magnetic effects of a rubbed piece of amber would prove prophetic. One of the first to take a keen interest in furthering Gilbert's work was a German, Otto von Guericke, an ingenious scientific dabbler, born in Magdeburg in 1602, two years after Gilbert published his *De magnete*.

WHAT IS AIR?
Astute 18th-century scientists realized that although invisible, air had distinct gaseous components. We now know that it is approximately 78 percent nitrogen, 21 percent oxygen, and 1 percent argon and carbon dioxide, with tiny amounts of many other elements mixed in.

JOHN DALTON AND COLOR

To test his own color blindness—and understand the phenomenon scientifically as well—English atomic theorist John Dalton created this booklet of colored threads.

Von Guericke had little formal education, but he was popular enough in his hometown that at the age of 24 he was elected alderman, a post that he would hold for the next 50 years.

Von Guericke was deeply interested in the nature of space. He questioned whether a vacuum, a space containing no matter, could actually exist. Aristotle and Descartes had both denied it.

Two related questions were how the planets move in their orbits and how they interact with one another. Kepler and Gilbert had proposed a magnetic cause, and von Guericke set out to investigate

the possibility. He devised a means of creating a partial vacuum, and by 1650 he had invented an efficient pump by which he could evacuate large volumes of air from vessels. He thereby showed the elasticity of air and the possibility of producing a vacuum. He explored the properties of a vacuum as well. Combustion could not take place in a vacuum, he determined, but magnets in a vacuum still attracted metal.

In a famous experiment conducted at Madgeburg in 1657, von Guericke made a sphere of two copper hemispheres and demonstrated that by pumping the air out

ELECTROMAGNETISM

Electromagnetism is a branch of physics that considers the relationship between electricity and magnetism, long sought but not demonstrated until 1819, when it was shown that an electric current or a changing electric field produces a magnetic field and, conversely, a changing magnetic field produces an electric field.

One of the first useful devices to come out of this discovery was the electromagnet. A coil of wire, usually wound around an iron core, produces magnetism in the iron core as long as an electric current flows through the wire. The basic device still works in doorbells, circuit breakers, telephone receivers, and other devices today.

The force of magnetism can also produce an electric current, through the process called electromagnetic induction. A changing magnetic field sets up an electric field within a conductor. In early experiments, a bar magnet moved through a coil of wire, changing the magnetic field, which in turn caused an electric current to flow along the wire. Today a coil of wire rotates between the poles of a strong magnet. The coil is wired as part of a closed circuit, and as the wire coil rotates, electricity can be drawn off from it.

Scottish physicist James Maxwell concluded that light is a form of electromagnetic radiation.

Electromagnetic induction is the basic process behind the electric generator, one of the most important inventions in history. Without generators all our lights would go out, all our electrical and electronic equipment would shut down, and all our industries would stop.

In the case of the electric motor, another device of major importance in our technological lives, the procedure is reversed. With the same basic equipment as described for the generator, a current is sent through the conductor, which lies in a magnetic field; this makes the wire coil move—and turns electrical energy into mechanical energy.

Starting around 1864, the Scottish mathematician and physicist James Clerk Maxwell considered much of the existing research on the relationship between electricity and magnetism. Maxwell proposed that not only are electricity and magnetism interrelated, but they act together to produce electromagnetic waves that propagate outward as radiant energy. He argued that visible light makes up only a small portion of a spectrum of electromagnetic wavelengths. Later experimental findings showed him to be quite correct.

THE VOLTA PISTOL

Italian physicist Alessandro Volta's batteries found a host of uses, some of them less than entirely serious. This one, called a "Volta Pistol," consists of a cylindrical chamber into which explosive gases such as hydrogen or oxygen were placed. The barrel was plugged with a cork. When an electrical charge was applied, a spark ignited the mixture and the cork popped off.

of the sphere, the two halves were sealed shut by the force of the surrounding air pressure. To prove the strength of the air pressure, two teams of eight horses each tried unsuccessfully to pull the spheres apart. Von Guericke took his dramatic experiment to the courts in Vienna and Berlin.

Having shown that magnetism traveled in a vacuum, von Guericke set out to see whether the same force might affect celestial bodies. Working from Gilbert's experiments with a lodestone terrella, von Guericke created a larger sphere composed of earthen materials including sulfur.

Gilbert found that by rotating the sphere and rubbing it with his hand, he could make it exhibit the effects that Gilbert had deemed electric. The sphere acquired attractive properties and gave off sparks, and the effects lasted even after the ball was no longer being rotated. Intrigued, von Guericke created a machine by which he could turn the ball with a crank; then he designed a belt-driven machine that turned the sphere even faster. He was able to cause the sulfur sphere to glow. He had conducted the first experiment to demonstrate electroluminescence. Replicas of von Guericke's machine proved as popular for entertainment as for serious scientific study. During the first half of the 18th century, static electricity machines became ubiquitous, with variations made of glass spheres and disks and even of beer bottles.

In England, Stephen Gray discovered two things about static electricity: first, that the effluvium, or outpouring, of static electricity could be transmitted along a silk thread; and second, that objects brought near to the electrified source were themselves electrified.

1827 – 1864

1827
Scottish botanist Robert Brown discovers motion within small particles suspended in water, later named Brownian motion.

1835
French physicist Gaspard de Coriolis shows that in a rotating frame of reference, objects appear to move in a curved path due to the rotation; it is named the Coriolis effect.

1842
Austrian physicist Christian Johann Doppler predicts the shift in frequency of a wave dependent on the velocity of the source, later called the Doppler effect.

Volta demonstrates his battery—a "pile" of alternating layers of silver and zinc—to Napoleon Bonaparte (seated) and other scientists in 1800. Napoleon was so impressed that he awarded Volta the medal of the Legion of Honor and made him a count.

1848
Scottish physicist William Thomson (Lord Kelvin) discovers the absolute zero point of temperature.

1850s
First and second laws of thermodynamics developed by physicists William Rankine, Rudolf Clausius, and William Thomson (Lord Kelvin).

1859
Physicists Robert Bunsen and Gustav Kirchhoff discover that elements emit unique wavelengths of light with certain absorption lines missing from their spectra.

1864
Scottish physicist James Clerk Maxwell describes his four equations associated with electricity and magnetism.

FRANKLIN'S KITE

Benjamin Franklin's famous kite-flying experiment not only demonstrated the electrical properties of lightning but also became an iconic image of the eccentric American printer, writer, statesman, and inventor.

In France, Charles François de Cisternay Du Fay found that electrified bodies could attract or repel one another, which made him think that there were two kinds of electrical effluvia, which he called vitreous and resinous.

As these machines became more efficient, they produced greater amounts of static electricity. The only problem in continuing to increase the electrification was that it could not be stored. This problem was solved when two men—a German inventor, Ewald G. von Kleist, in 1745, and a Dutch scientist, Pieter van Musschenbroek of the University of Leiden, in 1746—

independently developed devices to store electricity and invented the first capacitors.

A jar half filled with water was closed with a cork stopper. A wire was passed through the cork into the jar, so that it reached the water. The wire was then charged by bringing it near a static electricity generator. When the jar was taken away from the generator, it held the charge—as anyone who touched the wire would find out. A letter published in the *Philosophical Transactions of the Royal Society* dated February 4, 1745, described someone who had: "He lost the use of his breath for a few moments;

and then he felt so intense a pain all along his right arm that he at first apprehended ill consequences."

Von Kleist improved the system by coating the glass with metal, so that its charge would pass through the glass into the water. In what was an early battle of technological one-upmanship, Musschenbroek coated both the inside and outside of the glass with metal, so that the metal from outside would charge the metal on the inside. In doing so he discovered that the thinner the glass between the layers of metal, the greater the spark emitted from the jar. What this seemed to indicate was that the electricity was a single flow, not two: a hypothesis that would be proved by American inventor Benjamin Franklin. Musschenbroek's device was named the Leyden jar, and some versions of it are still in use today.

By this time, the mid-1700s, electricity was becoming the fashionable science. People invented an array of devices with armatures that rotated toward the charge and, once charged, were repelled. "Far from being an arcane preoccupation reserved for privileged intellectuals, electricity rapidly became a topic of conversation throughout society," writes science historian Patricia Fara. "Many wealthy families bought their own apparatuses, and aristocratic women produced miniature lightning flashes from their fingers and their whale-bone petticoats, or titillated their admirers with a sensational—if rather painful—electric kiss." Benjamin Franklin invented a bell that rang when exposed to static electricity. Charlatans promoted electrostatic charges as cures for everything from headaches to disease.

The dangerous possibilities of electricity became apparent as greater charges were built up in Leyden jars and when arrays of Leyden jars were connected to store large amounts of electricity for study. In 1750 Franklin was able to show that he could

BENJAMIN FRANKLIN

Father of American science

1706
Born on January 17 in Boston, Massachusetts.

1718-1723
Apprenticed as a printer to his brother James.

1729
Begins publishing the *Pennsylvania Gazette*.

1730
Elected the official printer for Pennsylvania.

1732
Publishes the first edition of his *Poor Richard's Almanac*.

1737
Elected postmaster of Philadelphia.

1744
Creates the Franklin stove, a modified fireplace that more efficiently warms the home.

1746
Begins investigations into electrical phenomena.

1751
Publishes *Experiments and Observations on Electricity*.

1753
Awarded the Copley Medal by the Royal Society of London. Becomes deputy postmaster general for the northern colonies.

1756
Elected a fellow of the Royal Society.

1770
Begins inquiries into meteorology; charts the Gulf Stream.

1776
Signs the Declaration of Independence.

1790
Dies on April 17, in Philadelphia, Pennsylvania, a hero to both the Americans and the French.

See page 93 for more information on Joseph Priestly.

charge a Leyden jar by flying a kite outfitted with a metal tip and a silk string in a thunderstorm. Lightning, Franklin proved, was static electricity. Another person who tried charging his battery with lightning was killed, leaving him, as the coroner's report put it, with "a small hole in his forehead, a burnt left shoe and a blue spot at his foot": a harsh demonstration that electricity on Earth and from the skies was clearly one effluvium.

Joseph Priestley met Benjamin Franklin in 1765, and along with their discussions on politics—both were liberal men of the Enlightenment—they compared notes on their studies of electricity. Franklin encouraged Priestley to publish his work, and in 1767 Priestley published *The History and Present State of Electricity, with Original Experiments*. He suggested, among other things, that the force of attraction or repulsion between electric charges varied according to the inverse square of the distance between them. This was exactly Newton's finding for gravitational attraction as well.

In 1785, French physicist Charles de Coulomb invented a sensitive mechanical apparatus that proved Priestley's hypothesis. Coulomb's law, as it later became known, states that the force between two electrical charges is proportional to the product of the charges and inversely proportional to the square of the distance between them. Coulomb also found that his law applied to the force of magnetic attraction.

But what was electricity? Each Leyden jar was capable of only one discharge, making any investigations difficult. These conditions changed, however, at the beginning of the 19th century, though, with the work of Italian physicist Alessandro Volta.

Volta had been skeptical of the mysterious force, dubbed animal electricity, whose discovery had been announced by his friend and countryman Luigi Galvani. Galvani had probed frogs' legs with metal implements and found that the leg muscles twitched when touched. Galvani hypothesized that the metal liberated some sort of electrical

THERMODYNAMIC LAWS

Energy does not come and go at random. It follows the laws of thermodynamics, first set out by scientists in the middle of the 19th century.

The first law of thermodynamics—also called the law of the conservation of energy— states that the energy created is equal to the energy used. The amount of heat you get from two sticks will be equal to the energy stored in the wood and the energy applied in rubbing them together. The amount of energy from a steam engine can't be greater than that of the coal burned to make it.

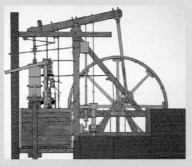

This schematic drawing shows the interior construction of James Watt's steam engine of 1788.

Thermodynamic law also observes the tendency toward equilibrium in a system. If you put hot coffee in a cold cup, the heat energy will flow from the coffee to the cup, and soon they'll both be the same temperature. But why doesn't the heat go from the coffee to the cup and back again? Now the second law of thermodynamics comes into play: Energy can flow in only one direction. The calories your body burns to run a mile will not return back to your body when you stop running, any more than the energy you've dissipated in running will return. An engine needs more fuel; you need more food.

There is a second part of the second law, which states that in this irreversible process, some of the energy is not available for work. In the process of running, some of the energy from the calories you're burning will not be available for use. The calories represent potential energy, sitting in ordered equilibrium. When you transform that energy into kinetic energy when you're running, it's being moved about, and in the disorder, some of it will dissipate. This dissipation of energy is called entropy, from the Greek word *entrope*, meaning change.

Heat is caused by the motion of molecules, so if that motion is stopped, no heat can be transferred, and there will be no entropy. The third law of thermodynamics states that at absolute zero, entropy is zero. If there's no energy, there can be no loss of energy, in other words. But beyond this frozen state, in the world —and the universe—irreversible processes abound. If the laws of thermodynamics are correct, the longer these processes go on, the more entropy is introduced into every system. Eventually, collapse may be unavoidable.

MICHAEL FARADAY

In a rendering by
John Eyre of 1886,
Michael Faraday is
depicted here in one
of a series of tiles
celebrating famous
scientists from
the Cafe Royal in
Edinburgh, Scotland.

B MICHAEL FARADAY, DISCOVERER of D

flow. Duplicating Galvani's experiments, Volta became convinced that the electricity was being generated not by the frogs' muscle tissue but by moist conditions and by the use of dissimilar metals in the probes.

To find out, Volta undertook a fairly direct experiment: He placed various combinations of metals, such as silver and tin, brass and iron, on his tongue. They produced bitter sensations, which

Volta speculated might be caused by a current flowing from metal to metal by way of the tongue's saliva. Different combinations of metals produced various intensities of bitterness, which Volta carefully charted. He then created an artificial version of his experiment, stacking up silver and zinc disks, separated from one another with paper soaked in saltwater. The result was a continuous flow of electricity. He had invented the device that would come to be called the voltaic pile—the first battery. It produced a current large enough to study, and it suddenly added chemistry as an essential factor in the investigation of the still imponderable force of electricity.

One of the first to exploit Volta's work was the British chemist Humphrey Davy. Known for his inventive experimentation with gases, Davy became intrigued by the implications of the voltaic pile. If chemical reactions produced electricity, he wondered if electricity could react with substances to separate them into their constituent elements.

Davy built an enormous voltaic pile and applied electrical current to compounds such as potash, the material that results when ashes are soaked in a pot of water. He found that from a lump of potash, to which he had attached a wire from a battery, shiny metallic droplets began to form and explode into the air. He had discovered a new element: potassium. Davy also isolated other elements: sodium, calcium, strontium, barium, magnesium, boron, and silicon. He was now certain that, as he put it in his 18th-century language, "chemical and electrical attractions are produced by the same cause."

Among Humphrey Davy's many legacies were his belief that atoms were bound together in compounds by some arrangement of electrical forces and his championing of a young man named Faraday, whom he hired as an assistant after one of his experiments literally blew up in his face and temporarily blinded him.

Born in 1791, Michael Faraday was the son of a blacksmith. He was frequently ill and left school at 13 to become an apprentice to a bookbinder. He read many of the science books that he helped to produce, nurturing a hidden talent, and attended a series of lectures on chemistry, delivered by Humphrey Davy. Faraday sat rapt through the talks and made extensive notes.

When Davy suffered his accident and needed an assistant, Faraday was recommended. Based on the notes he had taken, which revealed his astuteness, Davy hired him for the job. Davy—by then an internationally celebrated lecturer—was just leaving for an 18-month tour of the Continent, and he brought the 22-year-old Faraday along. Davy's wife treated the young man as a sort of valet. Faraday was happy just to attend Davy's lectures, observe his experiments, and meet many of the greatest scientific minds of Europe.

Faraday began conducting his own research, especially on the possible relationship between electricity and magnetism. In 1820, Hans Christian Ørsted had just published his paper on how an electrical current near a magnet sets the magnet at right angles to the flow of the current.

French physicist André-Marie Ampère had followed up Ørsted's work, and in studies conducted between 1821 and 1825 found a basic relationship between electricity and magnetism. He found that two wires with electricity running

TRANSFORMER

Faraday suspected that, just as an electric current could produce magnetism, a magnetic field must be able to produce a current. He proved that effect in 1831 with this apparatus, the first transformer.

through them in the same direction were magnetically attracted, while wires with the electricity running in opposite directions repelled one another. By making coils of wires and running an electric current through them, Ampère found he could create an electromagnet whose strength increased with each added coil. Wrapping the coils around a piece of iron made the magnet all the stronger. Ampère suggested that the magnetic force came from the electricity lining up all the atoms in the wire and iron.

With Ørsted's and Ampère's work in mind (and having already created a little electric motor, based on Ørsted's spinning compass), Faraday posed this question: If electricity could generate a magnetic effect, could magnetism generate electricity? Taking an iron rod wrapped with a coil of wire—Ampère's electric circuit without the electricity—he moved a pair of strong magnets along it. A galvanometer, a device used to detect electricity, showed that a current had been induced in the wire coil. Then Faraday improved the model by keeping the magnets stationary and placing a copper disk between them. Rotating the disk between the magnets created electricity that was conducted to a wire, one end set close to the rim of the spinning disk, the other end connected to the spindle on which the disk rotated.

By doing this, Faraday had created the first electromagnetic dynamo. Over the course of the 19th century, this principle of electromagnetic induction would create a new world of engines and machines, altering the fields of transportation and communication in revolutionary ways.

How did the dynamo work? Faraday worked on this question for many years, but he had no knowledge of electrons, the particles whose movement constitutes electrical current. That was still more than a generation away. Nonetheless, Faraday hypothesized that when an electric current passed through a substance, it loaded up these atomic force fields with tension; and that the tension was relieved when the atoms passed it on to the next cluster. Electricity ran along lines of tension through a conducting substance just as a wave maintains its peak as it moves through the water: It's not the water moving toward the shore, but the energy. This, Faraday suggested, might also be the way lightning occurs, the way static electricity is created, the way current runs through a voltaic pile. He still had no clear sense of what electricity was—but the answer seemed very close at hand.

A FULL SPECTRUM

The 19th century witnessed a spectacular revival of the long-standing debate of the nature of light. Was it made up of particles—corpuscles, as Newton had called them—or waves, as continental theorists such as Huygens had urged? The battle was revived as early as 1800, when British physician and physicist Thomas Young, interested

ATOMIC FORCES

As physicist Ernest Rutherford discovered, a single atom—the basic unit of all matter—is made up of mostly empty space. A positively charged nucleus, composed of protons and neutrons, occupies about one billionth part of that space. Surrounding the nucleus are negatively charged electrons, the lightest charged particles in nature. They are held in place by electrical force, but they are readily attracted to passing positive charges as well. A unique arrangement of electrons around the nucleus gives each element its distinctive chemical and physical properties. The atomic configuration determines how well it conducts heat or electricity, how quickly it melts, and how readily it will form compounds with other elements.

Rutherford modeled the atom as a central nucleus with electrons spinning around it, like central sun around which planets orbit. Although that is still the most popular depiction of an atom, in fact it is nearly a hundred years out of date. When scientists now describe the movements of electrons around a nucleus, they picture a kind of stationary wave-pattern cloud, within which the actual location of any single electron is only one probability among every other possible location. Protons and neutrons within the nucleus also create wave patterns.

With the discovery of radioactive materials, it appeared as if there must be more to an atom than its protons, neutrons, and electrons. In 1932 the positron was found: a particle with the mass of an

A uranium atom, with 92 electrons and 143 protons, can be readily split, releasing substantial energy.

electron but with an opposite charge. Beginning in the 1960s, new particles were discovered within the nucleus itself and given the name quarks.

The basic force of electromagnetism helped scientists understand how the an atom was held together, because it shed light on the relationships between charged particles. But it did not fully explain the forces at work within the fantastic subatomic world, because in that invisible yet discernible realm, the terms "mass" and "particle" have little substance or meaning.

Then investigators discovered two new basic forces. One, called the strong force, holds together the protons and neutrons in the nucleus. The other, called the weak force, alters the composition of the nucleus—in radioactive decay, for instance—and influences the comings and goings and interactions of subatomic entities.

Of these four forces. the strongest is the strong force, which holds together the nuclei of all matter. Its effects, however, can be sustained only over an extremely short distance. Gravity, on the other hand, can act over great distances, as shown by the gravitational effects of the moon on Earth's tides. Electromagnetic force is strong as well, although not as strong as the strong force, and it has a range of distances over which it can be effective. The weak force, as its name indicates, is very weak . Like the strong force, it has a very limited range. Scientists are confident that one day they will discover how these four fundamental forces are unified. They already have a name for the discovery: the Grand Unified Theory.

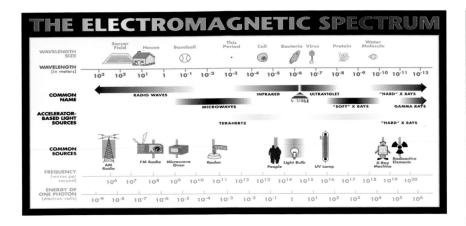

THE ELECTROMAGNETIC SPECTRUM

VISIBLE AND BEYOND

Visible light and the colors we see make up only a small part of the electro-magnetic spectrum. Beyond the range of human vision are short wavelength gamma rays and long wavelength radio waves.

in the physiology of vision, began his experiments.

Young shined a light through a tiny hole in a barrier. Beyond that barrier was a second one with two pinholes in it, beyond that a screen. The light that reached the screen was arranged in alternating bands of dark and bright areas, indicating that at some points, light waves were canceling each other out, creating dark bands; at others, the waves were reinforcing each other, producing bright bands.

The image clearly suggested wave-like interference patterns, not particle behavior. Newton's partisans in England didn't buy Young's revelations, but they were accepted on the Continent, where French physicist Augustin-Jean Fresnel confirmed Young's work.

In the 1850s, Scottish physicist James Clerk Maxwell (who had formed a friendship with Faraday through correspondence) sought ways of explaining Faraday's electric and magnetic fields. He found that an electric charge that moved back and forth would generate a pattern of connected, oscillating electrical and magnetic waves.

Over six years of intensive mathematical labors, Maxwell worked to accurately describe Faraday's and his own findings and to formulate a theory that would unify the forces of electricity and magnetism. Finally, in 1864, he presented his astonishing results: The equations describing a magnetic field created by an electric current were nearly identical to the equations used to describe the propagation of light waves. The results also showed that magnetic waves moved at 186,000 miles per second—exactly the speed of light. Maxwell concluded that electricity and magnetism were one and the same, and that light was a form, but by no means the only form, of electromagnetic radiation. His equations suggested an invisible world of forces much larger than anyone had thought, and also predicted that there would be wavelengths both longer and shorter than visible light.

Maxwell's theory electrified the scientific community, especially a young German physicist, Heinrich Hertz, who set out to test Maxwell's prediction that there were many different kinds of electromagnetic

FEARLESS CURIE
French physicist Marie Curie experimented with uranium, radium, and polonium to understand more about radioactive emissions. Curie did not know how toxic exposure to radio-activity could be.

radiation. By 1888, Hertz had collected the equipment he needed: an electrical circuit with a small gap in it and a metal device (now known as an antenna) designed to respond to electromagnetic waves. Closing the circuit would cause a spark to jump across the gap. That spark, Hertz reasoned, should generate waves that, although they could not be seen, would be detected by his antenna yards away—and it happened just as he had predicted. Hertz then determined that these electromagnetic waves had a length of about a foot and that, as Maxwell predicted, they could—like light and heat waves—be reflected off walls, refracted by various substances, and even polarized (that is, made to vibrate in one plane). In addition, these waves, then called

Hertzian but now called radio waves, seemed to move at the speed of light.

Maxwell had died ten years before, but Hertz's work confirmed his field theory. It also sparked the inventive genius of an Italian physicist, Guglielmo Marconi, who improved Hertz's apparatus piece by piece, controlling the spark by means of telegraph keys, enlarging the antenna, and using a device called a coherer to detect the Hertzian waves. Very quickly, Marconi was able to send and receive waves over a distance of a mile and a half. By 1901, he was successfully transmitting radio waves across the Atlantic.

But a major mystery remained. Water waves moved through water, sound waves moved by fluctuations in air pressure. What was the medium that was carrying all these electromagnetic waves—especially those that brought starlight from space?

Since the time of Aristotle it had been pretty well considered universal knowledge that surrounding all things was an invisible medium, the fathomless ether through which all things moved. In 1887 two American physicists, Albert Michelson and Edward Morley, set out to measure the effects of this presumed ether. Michelson and Morley used an ingenious L-shaped invention called an interferometer. The two arms of the instrument were perpendicular to one another. At the end of each arm was a mirror. In the center, where the two arms joined, was a light source and a device that could split a light beam in two, sending half to each mirror, and then recombine the two halves when they bounced back from the mirrors. They placed the interferometer with one arm pointing in the direction that the Earth was moving through space.

In theory, as the Earth sailed through the motionless ether, the beam moving in the direction of Earth's orbit would move faster, receiving a slight boost from the Earth's motion. The beam moving at a right angle

MARIE CURIE

Pioneer of radioactivity

1867
Born Maria Sklodowska on November 7, in Warsaw, Poland.

1893
Receives a degree in physics from the University of Paris.

1895
Marries Pierre Curie. Becomes a research scientist, studying magnetic properties of tempered steel.

1896
Discovers that radiation is not a property of chemical reactions but of the atom.

1898
Along with husband, Pierre, discovers polonium and radium.

1903
Wins the Nobel Prize in physics, sharing it with Pierre Curie and Henri Becquerel.

1904
Receives her doctorate.

1906
Takes over as professor of physics at the University of Paris.

1910
Publishes *Treatise on Radioactivity*.

1911
Awarded the Nobel Prize in chemistry, becoming the only person to win two scientific Nobel Prizes.

1914-19
Directs the Red Cross Radiology Service, organizing mobile x-ray units for the French Army during World War I.

1918
Becomes director of her own laboratory in the Radium Institute at the University of Paris.

1934
Dies on July 4 near Sallanches, France.

would travel only at the speed of light. Each beam, therefore, would arrive back to the center at a slightly different time, and the light waves, thus out of phase, would be seen to interfere with one another. Yet every time the physicists measured, they found no difference at all. Science was finally forced to face the possibility that there was no ether—or at least none that could be detected. Light and electromagnetic waves, it seemed, didn't need a medium through which to move.

By the end of the 19th century, many of the questions about electromagnetic radiation seemed to be solved—all except the mystery of what it was. Then came a series of sudden, serendipitous discoveries that deepened both the mystery of radiation and science's knowledge of the nature of atoms.

In 1895, German physicist Wilhelm Röntgen, like many of his colleagues, was investigating the puzzling phenomenon of cathode rays. Scientists had been observing the properties of a cathode, or a negative electrode, the piece through which the current leaves a battery or other electricity storage device. A cathode placed in a vacuum tube would give off a strange sort of emission, detectable only when it struck certain chemicals.

Röntgen set up his cathode ray device in a darkened room, covering its tube in black cardboard. Then, by chance, he noticed something very odd. An object several feet away began to glow. When he turned off the cathode tube, the glowing stopped. Some beam was radiating from the tube.

This made no sense, because Röntgen knew that cathode rays—whatever they were—couldn't travel more than a few inches in air. He realized he must have discovered something different. He soon found that the beams would travel through his hand, casting a shadow with the outline of his bones on a screen. After weeks of meticulous experiments, he announced the existence of electromagnetic waves so peculiar that he called them simply "X."

Almost immediately, these x-rays were being used in medicine. Still, scientists did not really know what they were or why they did what they did. Cambridge University physics professor Joseph John Thomson found that when the rays were beamed through a gas, it could conduct electricity. French physicist Antoine Henri Becquerel thought that the Röntgen rays might be involved in fluorescence, or the glow of certain compounds after being exposed to sunlight.

Becquerel placed a photographic plate wrapped in heavy black paper beneath a compound and planned to expose it to sunlight, surmising that if the compound, in this case uranium, gave off x-rays while fluorescing, their emission would fog the plate.

But the weather turned cloudy, and Becquerel stuck the uranium and photographic plate in a drawer to await the sun. When he took them back out, he developed the plate anyway and, to his amazement, found that it was highly exposed. The uranium alone was generating some sort of radiation. But what was that? Becquerel found that the uranium rays, like Röntgen's x-rays, allowed a gas to conduct an electrical current.

Polish-born French physicist Marie Curie soon discovered that the property that she called radio-activity was common to uranium and another element, thorium. Testing other substances, she discovered that pitchblende, a uranium ore, had a higher level of radioactivity than pure uranium.

To figure out why, she and her husband, Pierre, who was also a physicist, labored in a dismal laboratory in Paris, working through tons of the ore until, in 1898, they made the announcement that they had discovered two new substances: polonium and radium. Radium was the most radioactive substance known, and its strong emissions gave the surrounding air an electric charge.

THE SECRET LIFE OF HEAT

While studies and discoveries in electromagnetic radiation were stealing the scientific headlines, studies of another kind of energy were moving along at a quieter pace. That energy was heat, and perhaps so familiar that its study wasn't deemed newsworthy. After all, everyone knew that fire was hot, that it took heat to boil water and cook food, and that heat was needed to create the steam that, by the middle of the 18th century, ran engines and soon trains, boats, and machines.

For scientists, though, heat was as much a mystery as electricity. Based on the fact that materials expand as they get warmer, Galileo had devised a thermometer. He trapped a volume of air in a sort of upside-down flask partly filled with liquid. As the temperature changed, the air expanded or contracted, moving the level of the liquid down or up. Without a scale against which to measure the movement of the fluid, the device showed only relative temperature changes.

That next step—creating a scale with fixed points—finally took place in the beginning of the 18th century, when Danish astronomer Ole Rømer, who in 1675 had been first to measure the speed of light, developed a thermometer using alcohol as the liquid. He arbitrarily set 0° as the point where water froze and 60° as the point where water boiled.

In 1708, Polish-born Dutch instrument maker Daniel Gabriel Fahrenheit visited Rømer. He returned to the Netherlands and produced his own version of an alcohol thermometer, setting 0° as the temperature at which beer freezes and 100° as the temperature of the human body. By this scale, water freezes at 32° and boils at 212°, quite different from the numbers set for those temperature points by Rømer. Swedish astronomer Anders Celsius

PRECURSOR TO TELEGRAPH

William Thomson's sensitive mirror galvanometer, which he patented in 1858, made the long-distance telegraph cable possible.

created a thermometer with exactly 100 degrees between the freezing and the boiling points of water. While Celsius originally set 0° as the boiling point and 100° as the freezing point, after Celsius's death in 1744, the Swedish biologist Carolus Linnaeus turned the scale around, resulting in the Celsius scale of temperatures that we use today. But what exactly were these thermometers measuring? Some thought heat came from vibrations set off in a substance. Others thought it was a weightless fluid—they called it caloric—that was contained in matter and flowed from place to place. At the end of the 18th century, Benjamin Thompson, an American living in England, stepped into the debate.

Born near Boston, Thompson had escaped his native country in 1776. He sided with the British during the early days of the American Revolution and served as a British military commander and a spy. Accusations of adultery and sodomy were leveled against him as well. Leaving his wife (some 20 years his elder) and daughter behind, Thompson expatriated to England and took up a scientific career. By 1779 he had been named to the Royal Society.

Thompson received an invitation to Bavaria from Prince Maximilian while traveling in France. Made major-general of cavalry and privy councilor of state, he worked on improving the lot of the army and constructing English gardens outside of Munich. Eventually he earned the title of count and chose the name Count Rumford, after the town in New Hampshire where he had left his wife and child.

While at the Munich munitions works, Thompson noticed that the metal of the cannons became quite hot when they were being drilled out. He deduced that the amount of heat being produced was greater than the heat within the metal itself. Otherwise, the heat in the metal would have melted away on its own. This proved that the idea of heat as caloric, a fluid contained within the metal, was not possible. Friction, he realized, was causing the heat. Motion was the key. Thompson even made estimates of how much heat a certain amount of motion would produce. He presented his *Enquiry Concerning the Source of the Heat Which Is Excited by Friction* to the Royal Society in 1798.

Thompson was a colorful character. When France and England were at war, each side considered him a spy—and both may have been right. He chartered the Royal Institution in England and hired Humphry Davy as a lecturer. He pursued a career as an inventor—redesigning fireplaces and stoves to conserve heat; developing central heating, a smokeless chimney, and an oven roaster; and experimenting with silk and the manufacture of thermal underwear. He made and lost fortunes and finally married the wealthy widow of the great French chemist Antoine Lavoisier. In a final act of irony, he established the Rumford Prize of the American Academy of Arts and Sciences and a Rumford Professorship at Harvard University, a center of pro-British sentiment during the Revolutionary War.

FAHRENHEIT AND CELSIUS
Fahrenheit and Celsius each invented a scale for measuring temperature. A steady ratio exists between the scales. The formula to convert Celsius to Fahrenheit is 9/5 x (°C) + 32. To convert Fahrenheit to Celsius, it is 5/9 x (°F) – 32.

TRANSITION POINTS

A melting point is the temperature at which a solid becomes a liquid. A freezing point is the temperature at which a liquid becomes a solid. In theory, the two are equal. A boiling point is the temperature at which a liquid becomes a gas.

Thompson's work was eventually taken up by James Prescott Joule, the son of a Manchester brewer. Of a conservative theological temperament, Joule believed that all forms of energy were one and the same and could be converted one into the other. It was a difficult proposition for a brewmaster to prove, even one who had studied under John Dalton, but Joule persisted.

He began with electricity. In 1840, Joule discovered that the rate of generation of heat by an electric circuit was proportional to the square of the current multiplied by the resistance. He then sought to determine whether both electrical current and mechanical motion could produce heat in predictable quantities, which Thompson had conceived but had only been able to estimate. For Joule, as for Thompson, the conversion of energy from one form into another could be explained without referring to hypothetical caloric fluids.

With so little mathematical training, Joule had trouble getting his ideas recognized. But other researchers were able to duplicate his careful experiments, notably his 1847 discovery of exactly how much mechanical force on a set of paddle blades it took to raise the temperature of water by one degree, using the Fahrenheit scale. Joule established that the amount of work done by a heat engine was proportional to the amount of heat lost in converting energy to work. To this day, a standard unit of work is called a joule.

Joule worked with William Thomson (later Lord Kelvin), who was also convinced that the study of heat and electromagnetism was leading toward a unified energy theory. He and Joule shared research findings, and eventually Thomson reconsidered his belief in the caloric heat theory. A generous scientific collaborator, Thomson produced a great body of work on the mathematics of heat, electricity, and magnetism.

While Joule was conducting his experiments, a German physiologist and later physicist, Hermann von Helmholtz, was formulating one of the most profound and useful ideas in physics, the law of the conservation of energy. It states that nature contains a fixed amount of energy that can be neither increased nor diminished. (The word energy comes from the Greek *energia*, meaning "in work.") This law applies even as energy is converted from one kind to another—from heat energy to mechanical energy, chemical to electrical, kinetic to potential. The rule applies to the energy produced by a windmill or by flowing water as well as by burning fuel. It applies to the energy produced by the body, and would eventually be found true for gravitational, radiant, and nuclear energies as well. Measure the total energy at any point in a process, and it will always be the same.

Joule and German physician and physicist Julius Mayer had already expressed related notions, but the law found its most valuable expression in Helmholtz's 1847 book, *On the Conservation of Force*. His concept of the conservation of

LIGHT FANTASTIC

Einstein may not have invented the laser, but he certainly helped. As early as 1916, he predicted that there were two ways for atoms to emit photons, or individual units of light.

One was spontaneous emission, which produces the familiar glow of a lightbulb. When atoms get excited—for example, by an electric current running through a tungsten filament in the bulb—their electrons jump to higher energy orbits. But nature always favors the lowest energy configuration (which is why water runs downhill). so the electrons almost immediately fall back to their original positions, shedding a photon to get rid of the extra energy. Those shed photons appear as light.

But if an atom was already excited, Einstein said, whacking it with a photon of precisely the right energy would cause the electron to emit two photons—the original one that hit it plus a second one identical to the original. In theory, that could produce a very powerful beam of light, with all its photons of the same wavelength and direction, precisely in phase, so that none cancel the others out.

In 1954 American physicist Charles Townes actually built a device in an effort to produce Einstein's effect. He called it a maser. Townes excited a cloud of ammonia atoms and then bombarded it with microwave radiation. The cloud

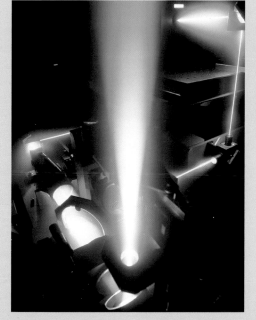

When manufacturing mirrors and lenses that must be perfect, laser beams are used to detect defects.

emitted more microwaves than had gone into it, thus demonstrating Einstein's second concept of atomic emissions.

Six years later another American, Theodore Maiman, constructed a device that could do the same thing for visible light. He took a cylinder of ruby and excited it with a xenon flash tube, causing light to emit and thus producing the first laser. (The name for the device is actually an acronym for "light amplification by stimulated emission of radiation.") In 1960 it was a good idea with no apparent good use.

It did not take physicists long to figure out reasons for lasers. They made them in various strengths and wavelengths, finding uses in surgery, surveying, cutting materials, and printing, to name just a few. Laser probes have measured the distance to the moon; they sit at the center of every bar code reader in the grocery store.

The invention of fiber-optic strands presented a new set of uses for the laser. Photons will move along a fiber-optic cable considerably faster than a wave of electrons can shuffle down a wire. Now flashes of laser light carry signals essential to the operations of the telephone, television, computer modem, and many other information and communication devices, with greater speed and capacity than electric signals in copper wires ever could.

energy proved key to the emerging science of thermodynamics and served as its first law. With the realization that energy could be transformed from one sort to another, many unexplained observations began to make sense.

French physicist Nicolas Sadi Carnot had found that the efficiency of a steam engine was related to the difference between the highest and lowest temperatures in the machine. In other words, the amount of work that you can get out of a heat engine depends on the temperature difference between the heat source, such as the steam from the boiler, and the temperature of the heat sink, the region of the engine into which heat was finally transferred. The relationship was known and accepted, but no one actually knew why. Carnot, using the caloric theory, had assumed that all the heat passed through the engine unchanged. If that were so, argued German physicist Rudolf Clausius, the heat could be recycled and run the engine forever.

What Clausius concluded was that in nature, heat always flows spontaneously only in one direction—from hot to cold. The path is not reversible. If it were, a cup of coffee would stay hot all day, pulling heat out of the surrounding air. Moreover, Clausius observed, as time passes, some fraction of energy in a system always dissipates and is therefore unavailable for work. This disorder

COOLING DOWN HYDROGEN

To cool hydrogen sufficiently to turn it to a liquid, engineers John Wood and A. J. Schwemin built a bubble chamber in 1954. Cooled under pressure to –423°F (–252°C), hydrogen gas becomes liquid.

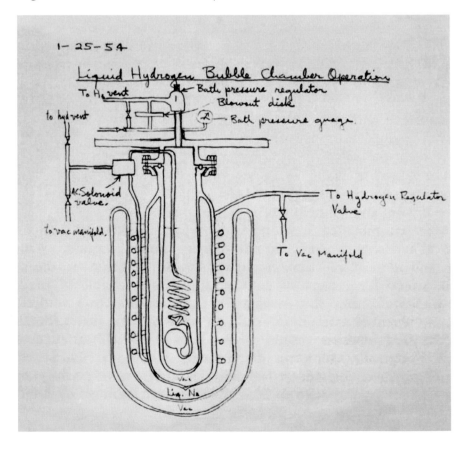

in the system accumulates; it came to be called entropy. Together these axioms constitute the second law of thermodynamics and were developed independently in England by William Thomson, Lord Kelvin.

(In a neat twist, Lord Kelvin turned the second law inside out, noting that if a hot gas could cause mechanical force and dissipation of heat, then the reverse would also work: Using mechanical force to compress a gas could transfer heat from low- to high-temperature areas. The proof of the idea spurred the growth of the early refrigeration industry in the 19th century.)

Following up on this second law, Viennese physicist Ludwig Eduard Boltzmann posited that if energy is based on the motions of atoms, thermodynamics could be analyzed mathematically. Boltzmann created equations for both the distribution of energy among molecules and for the effects of entropy.

The disorder in a system, he said, can be measured, if not exactly then at least on probabilities. By establishing statistical relationships between the atomic structure of substances and all forms of energy that might affect them, Boltzmann became, with Maxwell, the key figure in articulating the relationships of matter and energy and synthesizing their studies in late 19th century. Those times also saw a reaction against the atomic theory of matter, and Boltzmann, the theory's most energetic proponent, found himself entangled in academic battles. Exhausted and depressed, in 1906 he hanged himself.

THE STRANGE WORLD OF ABSOLUTE ZERO

With the nature of heat explained and brought into the fold with electrical and chemical energy, questions arose regarding the state of matter when it was cold. Lord Kelvin had established absolute zero—some −470°F or −273°C—as the point at which nothing could become any colder, and he predicted that as they neared such low temperatures, substances would increase in electrical resistance, becoming oblivious of energy.

The emerging studies in heat and thermodynamics brought Kelvin's prediction into question. Motion seemed not only to produce heat but also to affect liquids and gases similarly. Dutch physicist Johannes Diderik van der Waals established that the molecular state of liquids and gases depends not only on temperature but also on pressure and volume. As temperatures drop, the random motion of molecules that produces heat slows.

In 1877 physicists managed to cool oxygen to 90K (kelvins, a unit defined as equal to the number of degrees, Celsius scale, above absolute zero). At that point, the gas liquefied. Just before the turn of the century, hydrogen was also liquefied, at around 20K; in 1908 Dutch physicist Heike Kamerlingh Onnes liquefied helium at 4.2K. Kamerlingh Onnes also found that, contrary to Kelvin's prediction, substances at such temperatures lost all resistance, becoming what are today called superconductors. Others lost all viscosity, becoming what we call superfluids. At 2.19K,

for instance, helium liquid will flow up the side of a glass, over the top, and through the tiniest cracks.

What was this state called superconductivity? In the late 1950s, three American physicists—John Bardeen, John Schrieffer, and Leon Cooper—argued that in the supercold state, when atoms are arranged in distinct geometrical arrays, electrons (essential components of atoms) form into pairs that emit and absorb energy equally, so there's nothing to impair their movements. The atoms, for instance, in the 2.19K state all have the same momentum. Like runners tied together, if one moves, they all move. Heat is conducted so fast that it forms a wave through the material. If a magnetic field approaches a superconductor, it causes swirling electric currents in the outermost layers of the material that shove the field away. Superconducting materials will actually levitate above a magnetic field, a property now used to support trains above a track and allow them to move without the friction of wheels on rails. Superconductivity has inspired another technological race, for materials that will become superconducting at temperatures high enough that they can be used in everyday appliances and machines.

INSIDE THE ATOM

British physicist Joseph John Thomson, in studying cathode rays, found that there seemed to be negatively charged particles that could be deflected by electric and magnetic fields. He believed they were about one thousandth the mass of the hydrogen atom. He called them corpuscles, but the name they came to be known by was coined by Irish physicist George Stoney, who called them electrons.

Scientists knew that atoms are electrically neutral. If they contain a negatively charged particle, they must also contain a positively charged particle. The leading theory was that electrons were embedded in surrounding, positively charged atomic matter, like raisins in a pudding. That notion was swiftly shattered by the New Zealand-born physicist named Ernest Rutherford, who, along with others, had determined by 1900 that there were three kinds of radioactive emissions, which he called alpha, beta, and gamma, and that in the course of giving off such emanations, some elements transmuted into others.

The heavy alpha particles, decided Rutherford, were likely helium atoms stripped of their electrons. He designed an experiment to see what happened when he aimed alpha particles at metallic foils and measured how they scattered. Most of them bent only slightly. But one day in 1911, Rutherford's assistants reported amazing results: One out of about 8,000 alpha particles hit the foil and bounced back in nearly the same direction from which it had come. It was, recalled Ruther-ford, "quite the most incredible event that has ever happened to me in my life. It was almost as incredible as if you had fired a 15-inch shell at a piece of tissue paper and it came back and hit you."

HELMHOTLZ

One of the great figures in thermodynamics was Hermann von Helmholtz, pictured here in 1881. In addition to formulating the law of the conservation of energy, he made substantial contributions to medicine, including the invention of the opthalmascope for examining the inner eye.

The reflected particles, Rutherford concluded, had struck the tiny nucleus of the atom. He believed that the nucleus contained nearly all of an atom's mass but took up a minuscule fraction of its volume. There was no escaping the logic: Atoms were almost entirely empty space. Moreover, he and others determined in 1919 that bombarding atoms with the right kind of radiation could knock key particles out of the nucleus, transmuting the target substance from one element to another. The ancient goal of the alchemists, to transmute matter, had been achieved. We now call those key particles protons.

Cracking the atom and examining its constituent parts posed a formidable challenge. Scientists knew that it was possible to accelerate particles such as protons and electrons by exposing them to electrical charges. But getting particles to move fast enough to smash a nucleus or do other interesting tricks required voltages that seemed unattainably high.

Nature provided a few sources of high-energy particles in the form of so-called cosmic rays, which are not really rays at all but charged particles that come streaming through space from various sources and strike Earth. Because they strike with enough energy to tear the electrons off the atoms they hit, their effects can be observed by filling a jar with a gas (the cloud chamber) or liquid (the bubble chamber), in which the incoming particles leave distinctive tracks.

But controlled study of particle collisions required artificial means of acceleration. In 1932 in England, physicists John Cockcroft and Ernest Walton created an accelerator so mighty that it was able to blast protons into lithium atoms with such force that they could split the lithium into two helium nuclei. American physicist Robert Van de Graaff devised a generator that was capable of even higher voltages. Its design is still used today in many state-of-the-art facilities today. Soon scientists needed even more power.

American physicist Ernest Lawrence saw a way to get it. Instead of accelerating particles in one quick blast, he reasoned, it should be possible to keep them

ACCELERATED PARTICLES

A particle accelerator generates and shoots a beam of very fast charged particles, either atomic or subatomic. Today this complex machine is used for radiocarbon dating, cancer treatments, radioisotope production, and research into the nature of atomic nuclei.

1868 – 1905

1868
English physicist Joseph Norman Lockyer discovers helium on the sun by analyzing spectral absorption lines in sunlight.

1869
Russian chemist Dmitry Ivanovich Mendeleyev presents the organization of the elements in his periodic table.

1877
Austrian physicist Ludwig Boltzmann finds that the temperature and energy of atoms can be correlated.

1886
Radio waves are discovered by German physicist Heinrich Hertz.

POWER-PACKED URANIUM
Well-protected hands display a button of uranium-235, the highly radioactive form of the element, which is used as a fuel inside nuclear reactors and as an explosive in nuclear weapons.

1897
English physicist Joseph John Thomson discovers the component of the atom that is eventually named the electron.

1900
German physicist Max Planck determines that black bodies emit radiation at all wavelengths.

1905
German physicist Albert Einstein publishes his special theory of relativity.

1905
Third law of thermodynamics is developed.

**TRACKING
COSMIC RAYS**

Three electrons and
three positrons from
a cosmic ray leave
tracks on the wall
of a cloud chamber.

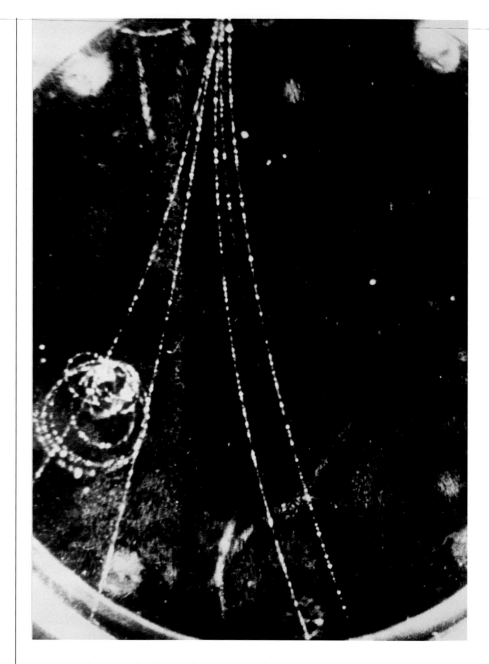

moving in a circle, by exploiting a convenient physical law: Charged particles in a magnetic field tend to move sideways. Lawrence figured that if he could cause a particle to circle a magnet, he could give it an extra kick of electric charge once or twice on every lap, eventually boosting it to tremendous levels of energy.

Lawrence's first cyclotron, as he called the machine he invented, was only five inches across, but it still did the job. Soon larger models were raising each particle to millions of volts.

In 1930, electrons and protons were the only two known atomic components. Scientists knew how many electrons surrounded the atoms of each element and knew that there must be an exactly corresponding number of protons. But if that were true, then atoms would be far too light.

Carbon, for example, has six electrons. So it must also have six protons. But it has a well-established atomic weight equivalent to 12 protons. Where were the rest? Either there were six more proton-electron pairs lurking in the nucleus, or atoms contained a nuclear particle with the same mass as the proton but with no electric charge. In 1932 British physicist James Chadwick determined that a mysterious form of nuclear emission that had been observed for decades but that fit none of the three categories of radiation was actually the long-sought neutron.

A similar puzzle surrounded the neutrino, a nearly massless product of nuclear reactions. Its existence was suggested when the energy products of radioactivity didn't add up. In Italy, physicist Enrico Fermi named and described the particle in 1934, but it would take more than 20 years to detect one. Similarly, in 1930 British physicist Paul Dirac had predicted the existence of antimatter, a particle with the mass of an electron but with the opposite charge. Two years later such a thing was found, and it was named the positron.

By the late 1930s, the basic constituents of the atomic nucleus had been identified, and researchers were busily bombarding nuclei with protons to see what would happen. Fermi became interested in using neutrons instead. Protons were electrically repulsed by the other protons in the nucleus; but neutrons could slip in and produce radioactivity. Most likely, he thought, they would create new isotopes, variant atoms with a different number of neutrons. Before fleeing fascist Italy for the

ENRICO FERMI

Atomic physicist

1901
Born on September 29 in Rome, Italy.

1922
Awarded a fellowship, receives doctorate degree in physics from the University of Pisa.

1924-26
Lectures in mathematical physics and mechanics at the University of Florence.

1926
Discovers the statistical laws governing subatomic particles, now known as Fermi statistics.

1927
Elected professor of theoretical physics at the University of Rome.

1929
Elected to the Royal Academy of Italy.

1935-36
Discovers slow neutrons, which leads to the discovery of nuclear fission.

1938
Awarded the Nobel Prize for his work in nuclear physics; leaves Italy and settles in the United States.

1939
Becomes a professor of physics at Columbia University.

1942
In charge of the Manhattan Project at the University of Chicago, works on devloping nuclear energy and the atomic bomb.

1945
Present in New Mexico at the first testing of the newly developed atomic bomb.

1954
Dies on November 28 in Chicago.

QUANTUM MECHANICS

Named for packets of energy, called quanta, that move in an electromagnetic wave, quantum mechanics is the study of matter and energy on the atomic and subatomic level. It is a study made difficult by the seemingly weird ways that energy and matter interact at this scale, and made even more difficult by the fact that within the quantum world exact measurements are impossible since the very act of measurement affects that which is being measured. Observation requires light, light is energy, and light quanta will affect what you are trying to observe.

The amount of matter inside the atom is tiny in comparison with the amount of space. Shine a light on a solid brick of matter, and at the subatomic scale there's every probability that some of the light energy will get through. In quantum mechanics this process is called tunneling. Matter at this level can be

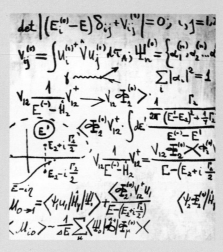

Physicists working to comprehend the forces of atomic particles use high-level mathematics to express their findings.

imagined as an extra-fine mesh, and quanta can be imagined as tiny blind fleas jumping toward it. Some fleas won't have the energy to reach the mesh. Most of the fleas will get caught up in it. A few fleas will pass through the mesh altogether. The configuration of fleas left stuck to the mesh is comparable to the light's wave pattern.

Most people know matter and energy only on a macro scale, and therefore they will consider many of these ideas in quantum mechanics arcane if not downright bizarre. But just as studies of energy showed that electricity and magnetism were related, so quantum mechanics has made it clear that at the subatomic level, the distinctions between matter and energy vanish. Both, it appears, have the properties of particles—quanta—and waves, and both bear the same burdens of indeterminacy.

1913 – 1970

1913
Danish physicist Niels Bohr presents his quantum model of the atom.

1916
Albert Einstein publishes his general theory of relativity.

1924
Austrian-born American physicist Wolfgang Pauli states that no two electrons can occupy the same state at the same time, now called the Pauli exclusion principle.

1925
Atomic theory of dispersion articulated, stating that light travels at different speeds through different materials depending on the materials' properties.

United States in 1938, he had discovered that he could slow down neutrons enough so that they were readily captured by some nuclei.

That same year, German researchers Otto Hahn and Fritz Strassmann were using slow neutrons to blast uranium, the heaviest naturally occurring element. The results surprised them: The uranium seemed to have been changed into elements of lower atomic weight. That seemed impossible. Uranium was such a huge atom that it was simply assumed that nothing could split it.

Austrian-born physicists Otto Frisch and Lise Meitner (who had worked with Hahn but as a Jew had fled Germany) heard of these results. They concluded that the uranium nucleus had fissioned, or split, into smaller nuclei, throwing off two neutrons in the process. The total fission products were slightly less massive than the original uranium atom. The missing mass, Meitner calculated, had converted to energy—a lot of energy.

With war imminent, the fact that Germany had achieved atomic fission was worrisome, and the United States embarked on a high-intensity, supersecret research program called the Manhattan Project to exploit and control nuclear fission. Fermi built the first nuclear reactor under the stadium walls of the University of Chicago. He wanted to confirm that neutrons emitted by fission would go on to cause other nuclei to split in a chain reaction. His reactor was packed with neutron-absorbing carbon and cadmium, so the chain reaction took place in slow motion. Even then, it got intensely hot. If uncontrolled, a fission chain reaction would explode.

At Los Alamos, New Mexico, the secret team created the first atomic bomb, setting it off in the summer of 1945. A few weeks later, atomic bombs were moved to the Pacific and dropped on Japan. The war was over in days.

The bombs that obliterated Hiroshima and Nagasaki left the world in no doubt that the release of energy by nuclear fission was a stupendous source of power. By 1957, fission energy was being used to generate electricity in commercial power plants; it is still used for that purpose around the world.

1932
English physicist James Chadwick discovers the neutron.

1932
American physicist Carl Anderson uses a cloud chamber to detect the existence of antiparticles.

1968
Gabriele Veneziano publishes his dual resonance model of the strong interactions, inspiring modern string theory.

1970
Stephen Hawking shows that black holes can emit radiation, later named Hawking radiation.

STRING THEORY

In explaining the way the world works, physicists seem always to be driven by a sense that all of the matter, energy, and forces in the universe ought to be related at all scales. Electromagnetism provided the means to unify the theories of electricity, magnetism, and light. Quantum theory unified the electro-magnetic world with the sub-atomic world of matter. Einstein's theory related light and gravity, time and energy. Then he spent the last 20 years of his life trying to connect his theory of general relativity, which elaborated the nature of gravity, to quantum theory, which described the atomic world of electromagnetic force. All his attempts at what was called a unified field theory failed, and physicists were left with different sets of formulas describing things on a very small scale and things on a large scale. Gravity, shown to be the result of curvatures of space surrounding mass, seemed to be on its own.

Is it now possible to unify all of these theories into one that describes all of matter and the forces of the subatomic and macrocosm? And if one created such a theory, how could it be proved? These questions face the proponents of a theory proposing that at the heart of all matter and energy are vibrating strings: infinitesimal filaments of energy. Each string has distinctive vibrations that relate it to a particular particle, just as the vibrations of a violin string relate to a single note.

These strings are small—about 10^{33} centimeters: a point followed by 32 zeros and then a 1,

British physicist Stephen Hawking shared the exhilaration of modern cosmology.

or a millionth of a billionth of a billionth of a billionth of a centimeter. As described by American physicist Brian Greene, one of the developers of string theory, "If an atom were magnified to the size of the solar system, a string would be the size of a tree."

String theory had its beginnings in the 1960s. Researchers were studying the strong force that holds protons and neutrons together in the atom's nucleus, and they found that the mathematical analysis resulting from their work seemed to describe energy as vibrating filaments.

According to string theory, the relationships between all the fundamental forces—gravity, electromagnetic radiation, the strong and weak forces—take place by the resonance of these strings in many dimensions. They hypothesize as many as 11, all of them but the three dimensions we experience so small that they can't be seen. The passage of vibrations through these dimensions, from one string to another, particle to particle, force to force, would unite them all. Gravity relates to these subatomic forces through the notion of gravitons, which, as University of Maryland physicist Sylvester James Gates puts it, are "waves of gravitational energy in space/time that are responsible for communicating the gravitational force."

Is this Einstein's unified theory? Many have their doubts, but string theorists continue to work on the idea, using complex mathematics. Empirical proof may not come until particle accelerators can find evidence of strings in action.

The atom had still more secrets to impart. One notion, propounded in the 1960s by American physicist Murray Gell-Mann, was that protons and neutrons were made up of even smaller things, whimsically called quarks. Theory predicted six kinds, and the last of those six was finally detected in 1995.

Yet there may be more. Today's accelerators have circular particle tracks that are miles long and accelerate their contents very close to the speed of light. With such devices, researchers have detected exotic particles that don't occur at the energy concentrations anywhere near those of our planet. The next generation of colliders may reveal particles that will help explain two of the deepest mysteries: why the big bang created a preponderance of matter over antimatter, and why nearly dimensionless, pointlike electrons and quarks have mass.

EINSTEIN'S ENERGY

Isaac Newton had proposed that light emanated in particles he called corpuscles. Thomas Young's experiments at the beginning of the 19th century seemed to clearly demonstrate that light must be waves. This remained the thinking all through the century, and it served well enough to solve many problems and help generate experimental and statistical evidence of the relationships between light, magnetism, and heat.

The first signs that there might be more to light than had met all these experimental eyes came after cathode and penetrating x-rays provided evidence for the electron. Setting up another experiment to visualize the energizing of electrons, German physicist Philipp Lenard focused a beam of single-frequency light onto a metal surface and found that the light ejected electrons from the metal plate. Another plate, connected to a sensitive current-measuring device, collected the ejected electrons. An electrified grid was set up that could vary the voltage of

ALBERT EINSTEIN

Father of the theory of relativity

1879
Born on March 14 in Ulm, Germany.

1896-1900
Studies at the Zurich Polytechnic Institute.

1905
Publishes paper on special relativity, Brownian motion, and the interactions of the quantum of light and the photoelectric effect.

1911
Becomes professor at Karl-Ferdinand University, Prague; predicts the bending of light.

1914-33
Becomes professor of physics and director of theoretical physics at Germany's Kaiser Wilhelm Physical Institute.

1915
Publishes work on the general theory of relativity.

1921
Awarded Nobel Prize in physics for the photoelectric effect.

1930
Produces model of the expanding universe.

1933
After Nazis gain power, leaves Germany and takes position at Institute for Advanced Studies, Princeton, New Jersey.

1946
Serves as chairman of Emergency Committee of Atomic Scientists.

1952
Offered presidency of Israel; declines.

1953
Publishes *The Meaning of Relativity.*

1955
Dies on April 15 in Princeton.

KEY TO IT ALL
Twice a Nobel
winner, American
chemist Linus Pauling
displays the complex-
ities of a protein
molecule, using a
wooden model.

*See pages 57-60 for
more information
on Einstein.*

the light beam as it passed through
the grid to the first plate and affect
the charge of the electrons that
jumped toward the collecting plate.
Lenard found that when he
increased the voltage of the grid, the
current measuring the electrons that
hit the collecting plate—the photoelectric effect—decreased sharply.
(The collecting plate now had a negative charge and repelled many of
the negatively charged electrons.) At
a certain point, the current disappeared altogether. When the light
intensity was increased, to give the
electrons more energy, however, it
made no difference in the outcome
of the experiment.

In 1905, Austrian physicist Albert
Einstein found an explanation. He
knew that in 1900, German physicist Max Planck, working on the
problem of why hot objects did not
radiate with the predicted mix of

infrared, visible, and ultraviolet light, had hit upon a mathematical formula based on Boltzmann's second law of thermodynamics that seemed to prove that energy was not released in a continuous stream of all magnitudes, but only in discrete bits, each of which was called a "quantum." Einstein assumed that Lenard's light beam was made up of particles or photons, and that each of these transferred its energy to the electron on the first plate. As the electrons emitted from that plate worked their way toward the collecting plate through the charged grid, they used up energy. Some made it; some didn't: Most likely the ones closest to the surface, with less distance to travel, made it. Intensifying the light, then, wouldn't give the photons or the electrons any more energy; it would simply add more photons, allowing more electrons to escape. When the interfering voltage got high enough, no electrons would make it to the collecting plate.

So was light then made up of particles?

Based on the discovery of the electron and his conclusion that atoms were mostly empty space, in 1911 Rutherford conceived of a model atom that resembled a tiny solar system. A positively charged nucleus sat in the center—occupying one billionth of the entire space but containing most of the mass of the atom. Negatively charged electrons orbited like planets around the nucleus.

In 1912, Danish physicist Niels Bohr suggested that if electrons worked this way, they would quickly dissipate their energy. With Planck and Einstein's work in mind, he proposed a way to revise the models' concept of electrons. The model needed to show that when electrons received heat or electromagnetic radiation, they responded in distinctive wavelengths, those spectral fingerprints that identify one substance from another. Electrons orbit the nucleus, but the orbits in which they can travel are fixed, different for each atom. When the atom receives light

LINUS PAULING

Leader in biochemistry and physics

1901
Born February 28 in Portland, Oregon.

1925
Graduates from the California Institute of Technology with a Ph.D. in chemistry. Remains at Caltech for the next 38 years.

1933
Elected, youngest member ever, to the National Academy of Sciences.

1937
Appointed director of the Gates Laboratory and chairman of the Division of Chemistry and Chemical Engineering, Caltech.

1939
Publishes *The Nature of the Chemical Bond*, classic of chemistry and biochemistry.

1942
With Dan Campbell and David Pressman, announces successful formation of artificial antibodies.

1954
Receives Nobel Prize in chemistry for research on the chemical bond.

1955
With more than 50 other Nobel laureates, issues the Mainau Declaration, calling for an end to the use of nuclear weapons.

1958
Publishes *No More War;* leaves Caltech owing to antagonism from Caltech administrators.

1963
Receives Nobel Peace Prize.

1973
Founds the Institute of Orthomolecular Medicine, which later becomes The Linus Pauling Institute of Science & Medicine.

1994
Dies on August 19 at his California ranch.

FUSION VISIONS

FUSION VISIONS

Particle Beam Fusion Accelerator II, operating in Albuquerque, New Mexico, was used in the 1990s to investigate what happens in the core of a nuclear explosion, on Earth or in space.

energy, it is distributed among the electrons, which then jump from one fixed orbit to another. When the electron jumps back to its original orbit, it releases light photons at the atom's distinctive wavelength.

These ideas suggested that light was both particle and wave. Soon a host of European theorists—including Werner Heisenberg from Germany, Erwin Schrödinger from Austria, and Louis de Broglie from France—took Bohr's quantum theory to its logical conclusion: Particles actually behaved like waves, which explained their quantum nature; but waves of light also had particlelike properties, such as momentum. In fact, matter was so wavelike that it was, in principle, impossible to tell where an electron was at any given instant. It

didn't actually exist in any particular place until it was measured, and there was no way to measure it. Instead, it was everywhere at once and had only a probability of having a certain position or speed. Even Einstein found it difficult to conceive of this idea. "God does not play dice" with the universe, he declared. As mind-boggling as it was, though, quantum mechanics would soon prove an accurate physical theory.

EINSTEIN'S SPACE-TIME

The September 1905 issue of the German physics journal *Annalen der Physik* proved to be, according to physicist Max Born, "one of the most remarkable volumes in the whole scientific literature." In it, 26-year-old Albert Einstein, then an examiner at the Swiss Patent Office in Bern, published three papers that together pulled back the curtains on the long-established Galilean/Newtonian world view, revealing a universe hidden until then, in which time, space, matter, energy, and gravity performed seemingly impossible feats.

How does one begin to appreciate Einstein's groundbreaking theories? First, it's best to recognize that the world of relativity is not the world with which we are familiar, in which time, speed, space, place, and matter are concrete realities. We mark time by the clock, travel our fastest in a car or plane, recognize our place by a set of basic coordinates, and know that matter is solid. As Einstein himself put it, in our daily lives, "All our thoughts and concepts are called up by sense-experiences and have a meaning only in reference to sense-experiences." Einstein's theories seem difficult because they take us outside our sense experiences. When he published them in 1905, his theories seemed outside the experience of most physicists as well.

Although by the turn of the 20th century much had been learned about the nature of light, physicists puzzled over why the speed of light remained the same even when beamed from a moving object. If you're swimming along at a mile an hour in a current that's moving two miles an hour, your total speed will be three miles an hour. If you swim across the current, your speed will be back to one mile an hour.

In the 19th century, scientists believed that, analogously, the Earth moved through invisible but fluidlike ether. Einstein argued that there was no ether, and that the speed of light was constant whether or not the object from which it was beamed was at rest or in motion. For light, at least, this view argued against Newtonian physics, in which velocities were simply added together. Einstein imagined what would happen if one actually traveled at the speed of light.

RICHARD FEYNMAN

Theoretical physicist

1918
Born May 11 in Queens, New York.

1939
Graduates with bachelor of science degree from the Massachusetts Institute of Technology.

1941
Begins work on the atomic bomb project at Princeton University; continues later at Los Alamos, New Mexico.

1945
Observes detonation of atomic bomb in New Mexico; appointed professor of theoretical physics at Cornell University, where he studies the fundamentals of quantum electrodynamics.

1950
Accepts position as professor of theoretical physics at the California Institute of Technology.

1950s
Provides quantum mechanics explanation for theory of superfluidity; develops theory to account for the weak force associated with radioactive decay.

1959
Appointed Richard Chace Tolman Professor of Theoretical Physics at Caltech.

1961
Publishes *Quantum Electrodynamics* and *Theory of Fundamental Processes*.

1965
Awarded the Nobel Prize for fundamental work in quantum thermodynamics; elected fellow of the Royal Society.

1986
Serves on the commission investigating the *Challenger* space shuttle accident.

1988
Dies on February 15 in Los Angeles, California.

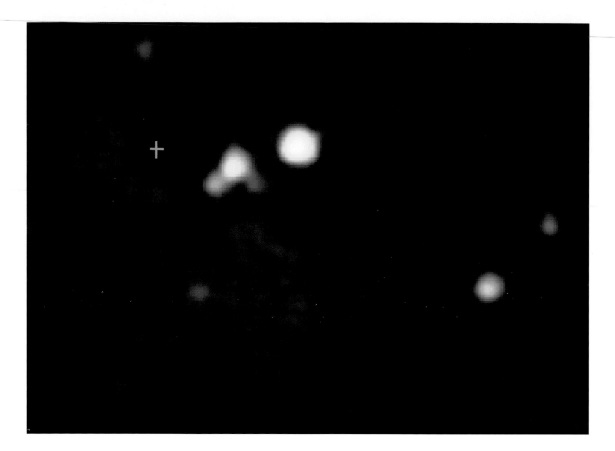

BLACK HOLE

This x-ray image of the starburst galaxy M82, taken by the Chandra X-ray Observatory, is the first confirmed case of a black hole outside the nucleus of a galaxy—possibly a new type of black hole.

Our sense-experience tells us that time everywhere moves at the same rate. If we're standing on the street and a plane flies overhead, we have no doubt that the passenger's watches are moving at the same speed as our own. Further, if we see lightning strike the ground in front of the plane and behind the plane at the same time, we assume that anyone in the plane would have seen the same thing, since time is the same for both of us. Einstein realized that all these things depend on where we are and how fast we, or another person seeing the same thing, are moving.

If I'm driving at ten miles per hour, the light from my headlights still moves at 186,000 miles per second. If someone else is driving at 20 miles per hour, the light from her headlights is still moving at 186,00 miles per second. If neither could move faster than the speed of light, and speed is distance divided by time (miles per hour), then the only way to account for the constant speed of light from cars moving at different speeds is that distance and time must change.

Einstein's theory says just this: The faster an object travels, the more slowly time passes for that object. Neil Tyson, director of the Hayden Planetarium at the American Museum of Natural History, created a chart showing that at 25 percent of the speed of light—

47,000 miles per second—a second will lengthen by 0.03 seconds. At 50 percent of the speed of light, a second will lengthen by 0.15 second; and at 99 percent of the speed of light, one second will be 7.09 times as long as a second experienced on Earth. At 99.99999999 percent of the speed of light, a second will be 19.6 hours long relative to a second on Earth.

This is not just a concept—evidence of Einstein's theory can be measured in a fast plane, and it becomes an important reality to factor into the consideration of objects, such as atomic particles, whose velocity does approach the speed of light. In an atomic accelerator, the mass of such particles appears to increase as well, to the point that at the speed of light, an object's mass would be infinite. Such technology wasn't available for Einstein, yet his thoughts did turn to mass and its relationship with energy.

A few months after he published his special theory of relativity—in the very next volume of *Annalen der Physik*, in fact—Einstein published the beginnings of his general theory of relativity. "Does the Inertia of a Body Depend on Its Energy Content?" was a very subtle title for his groundbreaking paper, which went up against the well-established theory that neither matter nor energy could be created or destroyed. Magnetic energy might become electrical energy, liquid might become a gas, but the laws of the conservation of matter and energy seemed inviolable.

Einstein thought otherwise. Matter and energy, he stated, were two sides of the same coin. Energy could be created out of matter, and matter out of energy. He even gave an equation that described the transaction: $E = mc^2$, in which E is energy, m is mass, and c is the speed of light. Since the speed of light squared is such a huge number—something close to 448,900,000,000,000,000 in miles per hour squared—a great amount of

STEPHEN HAWKING

Theorist of black holes

1942
Born January 8 in Oxford, England.

1962
Graduates with honors from Oxford University; enrolls at Cambridge University to pursue a Ph.D. in cosmology.

1963
Diagnosed with amyotrophic lateral sclerosis, also known as motor neuron or Lou Gehrig's disease.

1966
Completes doctorate; awarded fellowship at Gonville and Caius College, Cambridge.

1970
Shows that black holes can emit radiation, a phenomenon later named Hawking radiation.

1974
Elected one of youngest fellows ever of the Royal Society.

1979
Appointed Lucasian Professor of Mathematics at Cambridge, chair held by Isaac Newton in 1669.

1985
Contracts pneumonia, undergoes tracheotomy, and is left entirely without speech. Begins communicating by computer, which allows him to write and synthesize speech.

1988
Publishes *A Brief History of Time*.

1998
Publishes *Stephen Hawking's Universe: The Cosmos Explained*.

2004
Announces solution to black hole paradox; presents findings at international conference on general relativity and gravitation in Dublin, Ireland.

2005
Awarded the Smithson Bicentennial Medal.

energy can be produced from a small bit of mass.

Einstein realized that part of the radium that Marie Curie studied, was in fact being transformed to energy. What we now call radioactivity is mass being converted to energy, and Einstein's theory measures it exactly. Knowledge of this equation led to the development of nuclear fission, a process by which atoms are split in order to release energy from their mass. This technology, much to Einstein's regret, led to the atom bomb.

Even greater amounts of energy could be produced by nuclear fusion—the combining of atoms. In the sun, intense heat tears apart hydrogen atoms, separating positively charged nuclei and negatively charged electrons. These particles collide and create helium atoms, four hydrogen atoms making one helium. The mass of the resulting helium, however, is less than the combined mass of the hydrogen. The differential changes into smaller nuclear particles—and energy. Scientists began trying to replicate this process, which powers the sun and stars.

Einstein's special theory raised another question. If the sun's gravity, for instance, were acting on the Earth, it would mean that gravity would have to be traveling at 93 million miles in an instant—faster than the speed of light. Since Einstein had concluded that nothing could move faster than the speed of light, either something besides gravity was keeping Earth in orbit or gravity was not what Newton thought it was.

Einstein calculated that what causes the force called gravity is the distortion of space around a mass. Newton's law states that the force of gravity depends on the distance between two bodies; Einstein's general relativity theory states that such distances are along curves caused by the matter's distortion of space.

When large masses are involved, space bends so that gravity pulls light beams along its curve. The mass of the sun can bend light rays, but it is hardly noticeable compared with the bending of space when a star collapses and its mass is squeezed into a small volume. The warp in space becomes so great and the gravity so intense that even light cannot escape. Such a whirlpool of acceleration is known as a black hole.

Einstein's special and general theories of relativity altered the way physicists understand the universe, but it also changed the way all thinking humans imagine our place in it. Einstein was aware of the philosophical impact of his theories. He wrote: "The non-mathematician is seized by a mysterious shuddering when he hears of 'four-dimensional' things, by a feeling not unlike that awakened by thoughts of the occult. And yet there is no more commonplace statement than that the world in which we live is a four-dimensional space-time continuum."

QUANTUM MECHANICS

Researchers began using the theories of quantum mechanics to analyze how atoms worked in the real, although unseen, world.

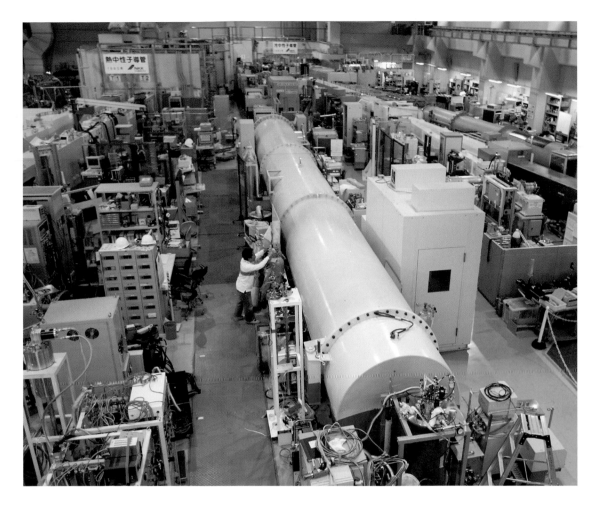

Among the many question posed by quantum theory was how, within the new understanding of atomic structure, chemical bonds could form.

In the 1920s, American chemist Linus Pauling had found that, just as the atom has no fixed structure, combinations of atoms in chemical compounds exist in intermediate states between one structural form and another, a phenomenon called resonance. In 1929 Pauling was able to set down rules by which relationships among electrons in such bonds could be discovered. Through those, he was able to understand more of the properties of the compounds that they form.

Pauling's work was distinguished by his ability to combine theoretical and practical chemistry, as well as by his understanding that chemical bonds could be both stable and variable. This led him to investigate sickle-cell anemia, and he discovered that the disease resulted from a variation in the structure of hemoglobin molecules. His paper, "Sickle Cell Haemoglobin: A Molecular Disease," contributed significantly to interest in the genetic causes of

NUCLEAR FISSION

At the Tokai Research and Development Center in Japan, neutrons generated by nuclear fission assist researchers exploring materials and life sciences.

RICHARD FEYNMAN
Nobel Prize–winning
American physicist
Richard Feynman
stands in front of a
blackboard strewn
with his own nota-
tions in Los Angeles,
California, in
March 1983.

disease, not only sickle-cell anemia but many others as well.

Pauling had also been attempting to model the structure of a DNA molecule. In 1953, with crystallographer Robert Corey as co-author, he published images and a discussion of his proposed three-dimensional version of DNA, with three twisted strands. In 1954, Pauling received a Nobel Prize for his work on chemical bonds. In 1963, he won a second Nobel, this time the Nobel Peace Prize for his work on behalf of nuclear disarmament. Had he envisioned one fewer strand in his DNA molecule, he might have won a third Nobel—but in the end that went to Francis Crick and James Watson, who ultimately discovered the double, not triple, helix as the structural backbone of the DNA molecule.

Another researcher inspired by quantum physics was American physicist Richard Feynman. The indeterminism of quantum physics seemed to inspire his innate sense of independence. Working with the difficult mathematics of quantum mechanics, Feynman was able to picture the relationships of subatomic forces at work in electromagnetic radiation—how, within the indefinite structure of the atom, photons interact with electrons and their positively charged opposite particles, positrons. Moreover, Feynman was able to illustrate the exchange of force and the collisions of particles, using drawings that came to be known as Feynman diagrams. Feynman was awarded a Nobel Prize for his groundbreaking work in quantum electrodynamics.

Working with physicist Murray Gell-Mann, Richard Feynman also succeeded in describing the forces at work in the process of radioactive decay. Called the weak force, it provided a glimpse into the smallest particles now theorized to exist within the atom—fermions, bosons, W particles, and Z particles. Because they are often slow to react, these particles can, under extreme heat and pressure, trigger larger reactions. These particles have been found to lie at the heart of nuclear fusion. Charismatic and genial, Feynman became a great popularizer of science. He made use of his prodigious talents as a storyteller, and he managed to fascinate scientists and nonscientists alike with his descriptions of the logic and the implications of advanced work in physics.

In the 21st century, there are students of energy and matter who return to the ancient study of cosmology. English physicist Stephen Hawking works to unify quantum physics with Einstein's general theory of relativity. Hawking combines these two concepts—the first dealing with subatomic realms and the second dealing with large masses—and uses the intellectual synthesis as a way to understand such unfathomables as the beginning of the universe and black holes, where gravity is so strong it keeps light from escaping. Hawking describes black holes as billions of tons of mass, compressed into a volume the size of a single proton. In such a state, the particle would act according to quantum theory: It would emit radiation and then gradually dissipate and disappear.

In a later formulation Hawking, along with Thomas Hertog of the European Organization for Nuclear Research, made a bold suggestion. We cannot know the exact momentum or location of any particle at any moment, but if the particle that was the early universe complied with quantum theory, the universe itself is a quantum event. If that is the case, then, as Hertog put it: "The universe doesn't have a single history, but every possible history, each with its own probability."

The ancients began by gazing up into the skies and wondering about matter and energy. Today, given the elegance of general relativity and the inexplicable truths of quantum mechanics, we still find ourselves in a similar state of wonder.

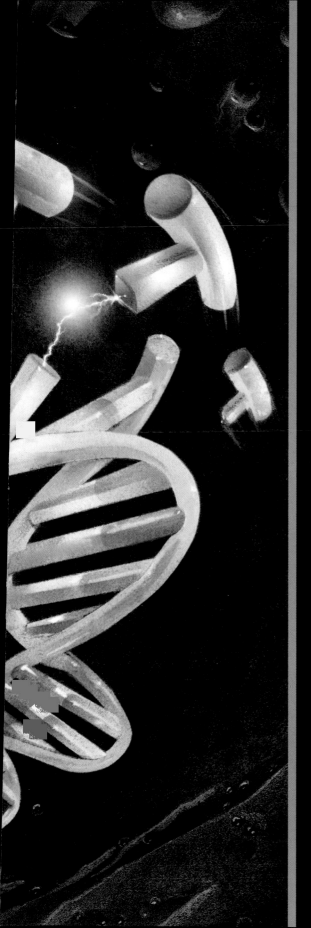

Life Itself

4

IN THEIR ABILITY TO OBSERVE THE natural world and use their knowledge of it for survival, the earliest humans were anything but primitive. For all our scientific wisdom, left out in the wild, we would be no match for the preliterate people who began moving out of Africa some 150,000 years ago and who, over the next 100,000 years, populated most of the rest of the world.

Nomadic life is complex. It requires fitness and adaptability, but more important, it requires very detailed intelligence about how the natural world functions. Familiarity with one place won't do. You must know the nature of every environment through which you pass, camp, hunt, forage, or graze your herds. The key to this existence is to be in the right place at the right time: to be there when the water flows, when the grasses grow, when the trees are fruiting, when the plants are going to seed, when the herds you hunt are ready to migrate. This study of the timing of natural events is now known as phenology, and although not formally recognized as a science until the 18th century, it was perhaps the earliest natural science practiced. Unfortunately, without writing, phenological data went unrecorded for tens of thousands of years, passed on only orally from generation to generation.

Not that we lack evidence of early human cultures and their knowledge of the natural world. Archaeologists have found traces of early humans' tools and encampments and, most dramatic of all, the images these people left on cliff or cave walls—images of animals, hunts, even of themselves. We also learn some things from the nomadic tribes that still exist, although these are few and vanishing, and we are only belatedly beginning to appreciate the breadth of their knowledge.

For instance, humans have inhabited Australia for at least 50,000 years. Just getting there from Indonesia required building boats capable of sailing open seas. Once there, these people had to adapt to an entirely different climate. Evidence from the surviving aboriginal cultures (and how many cultures have survived 50,000 years?) shows that they developed complex calendars based on neither the sun nor the moon but on seasonal changes that they marked by the growth of specific plants and changes in prevailing winds. Native people of the Americas knew when salmon or caribou would be migrating by recognizing which plants were in bloom and which birds they saw.

THE PRECURSORS OF SCIENCE

With all this intimacy with the natural world, did these early humans wonder how life, the world, and they themselves came to be? Once again, without written accounts we have only slim archaeological evidence and the beliefs of present nomadic tribes to go on. Some anthropologists have proposed that ritual burial practices suggest the earliest attitudes of the self-conscious regard for human life. They point to burial sites that date back 20,000 years as demonstrations that at least some tribes treated their dead with respect and buried them with what appear to be personal possessions for use in the afterlife.

When anthropologists look at present tribes, such as the nomadic fishing people of the Andaman Sea off the west coast of Thailand, they conclude that

ca 15,000 B.C. – A.D. 70

ca 15,000 B.C.
The earliest cave paintings in France depict animals: the first evidence of human curiosity about the natural world.

ca 570 B.C.
Greek philosopher Anaximander believes that the earliest creatures lived in water and later developed into land animals.

ca 560 B.C.
Greek philosopher Xenophanes examines fossils and speculates on the evolution of life.

early humans most likely compared their own lives with those of the living things around them, and everywhere they found resemblances. Like humans, animals and plants are born, live, and die. They have mothers and fathers; they find mates, reproduce, and protect and care for their young. Without food and water, living things, whether plant or animal, wither and die. So it was not too great a stretch for people to imagine that all living things also experienced infancy, growth, sexual maturity,

PREHISTORIC HONEY

In the sparse lands of central Australia, aboriginal tribesmen prized the honey of wild stingless bees, now called sugarbags.

ca 380 B.C.
Greek philosopher Plato describes the effects of soil erosion, overgrazing, and deforestation in his native Greece.

ca 350 B.C.
Greek philosopher Aristotle works on a comprehensive classification of animals; writes *The History of Animals* and *The Parts of Animals*.

ca 320 B.C.
Greek scientist Theophrastus begins the systematic study of botany. He writes influential books: *History of Plants* and *On the Causes of Plants*.

ca A.D. 50-70
Historia Naturalis by Roman scholar Pliny the Elder (Gaius Plinius Secundus) is published.

HUNTER-GATHERERS

San or *Khoisan* is a general term for the indigenous hunter-gatherers who have inhabited the Kalahari Basin in southern Africa for the last 11,000 years. Those not forced into farming still retain much of their Paleolithic ways of life.

sickness, and aging. And if all of these things were true, then it followed that, like humans, all living things had emotions, desires, and even dreams. They suffered pain and pleasure. They could express themselves. For example, in the fall, frozen lakes made loud cracking noises, and some might have said that they were asking for snow to cover them up and protect them from the cold. If living things were so much like humans, then they must also be imbued with the same kind of spiritual essence, a sense of being alive.

This interpretation of the natural world is called animism, a word that comes from the Latin *animus,* meaning breath or soul. Animistic peoples treat the natural world as they would one another: They pay respect to those plants and animals that provide them with food, clothing, or shelter. They give thanks to propitious winds or seas, and they fear those things that they perceive might bring them harm. When they feel it necessary, they make offerings to assure continued good relationships with the natural world, for they believe that the beings in the world around them will thank and reward them for those offerings.

Animism is not the same as nature worship. Animistic people feel that they share a common bond with the natural world, not a position of subservience. Nature speaks to them. Is this—was this—science? At least it can sometimes amount to wisdom.

The Moken of the Andaman survived the great tsunami of December 2004, which killed tens of thousands across the Indian Ocean basin. Scientists predicted it too late to get out warnings, yet when the Moken saw the sea recede from the shores of their islands, they took it as a sign to move to high ground—despite the fact that no such tsunami has occurred in the Andaman for at least 500 years.

Some 10,000 years ago, great changes took place on Earth. Glacial ice thousands of feet thick had pushed its way down from the Arctic across half the Northern Hemisphere, but now it began to recede. Human life in northern climes became easier, and people migrated into territories never before explored. There—an seemingly around the world during that period—people began practicing agriculture.

Many had already domesticated animals that traveled along with them on their migrations. By 5000 B.C. people had a basic understanding of biological inheritance, at least enough to selectively breed crops as well as animals. By intelligence or chance, they came to understand the benefits of crop rotation, irrigation, and cultivation.

The ability to produce food rather than chase it forever changed the relationship between humans and nature. It also changed human thinking about the origins of life. Perhaps humans no longer felt akin to the spirits of plants and animals, since they could now manipulate both to their own ends. Perhaps new ideas arose out of the demands of new social structures as people settled in communities, towns, and cities. Whatever the cause, people began to devise larger schemes to make sense of nature and its forces.

In the Middle East, gods arose who set the cosmos in motion and gave humans, animals, and plants their places in it. In the Far East, the world was made up of patterns and cycles whose rules and relationships human beings needed to comprehend. Speculation ranged as far as the cultures themselves did. The persistence of such speculation—combined with the demands of agriculture and trade and the development of written language and mathematics—gave way, in the final centuries B.C., to the first scientific investigations of the nature of life.

THE ROOTS OF SCIENCE

Greece and the land now called Turkey lay on a crossroads of trade and travel. Port cities hosted arrivals from centers of culture all around the Mediterranean. The Greeks were active seafaring traders. Commerce moved ideas as well as goods, and the world of the sixth century B.C. seemed to be full of new ideas.

In northern India at this same time, Siddhartha Gautama gave up his wealth to seek his spiritual fortune instead. This wandering philosopher, full of questions about the nature of life in what he considered an impermanent world, would become known after his enlightenment as the Buddha.

In sixth-century B.C. China, technology flourished alongside six schools of classical thought, ranging from the rigorous morality of Confucianism to the abstract and opposable truths of Daoism. While any of these might give Greek moral philosophy a run for its money, the Chinese had less curiosity about the actual workings of nature. In this, the Greek natural philosophers from the sixth to the fourth centuries B.C. had no peer in the ancient world.

In schools of learning that sometimes bore more resemblance to cults than academies, Greek philosophers began to expand upon the idea of *physis,* or nature. This concept became key to the development of Western science.

Although most often translated as "nature," the Greek root of the word physis means "to grow" or "to become." It implied that despite its orderly arrangement, the cosmos was a system in flux, subject to its own laws and not to external forces. Combined with the notion of a comprehensible universe, the first of the natural philosophers hypothesized that all of nature was made up of some basic, irreducible substance, some element that could be acted upon by all of nature's forces yet could still retain its identity and come to constitute all matter.

The first to tackle this problem and solve it—at least to his own satisfaction—was Thales, a Greek astronomer, mathematician, and philosopher who lived between 624 and 547 B.C. and came from the Ionian city of Miletus on the coast of Asia Minor. He also gained fame by predicting a solar eclipse at a time when few knew how.

Thales believed that the fundamental element of life was water. What other substance, he theorized, is so capable of coming to be, passing away, yet remaining the same? Water flows like a liquid, freezes into a solid, and even evaporates into the air.

Later philosophers, including Aristotle, disagreed with Thales, but they still considered him to have founded the study of nature. He had formulated a view of the natural world that had physical as well as philosophical integrity

See page 25 for more information about Thales of Miletus.

and that did not depend on gods or myths to explain the way life and nature worked.

Thales was followed by Anaximander, who argued that water could not possibly be the universal element. Instead, he proposed that the primary element was not a material substance at all but rather something he called the *apeiron,* which had no characteristics of its own but was boundless, indefinite, divine, and capable of remaining itself no matter how nature's forces of generation and destruction acted upon it.

Anaximander's student, Anaximenes of Miletus, rejected the apeiron in favor of air or vapor as the primal substance. It, like water, could retain its essential nature despite being turned into fire, wind, cloud, water, earth, and stone.

Heracleitus rejected air and built his cosmos out of fire. The smoke from fire rises into the air and returns as rain, he believed; rain creates the oceans, and oceans give way to earth. More important, however, Heracleitus expanded on the evolving concept that all of nature is in a constant state of change. As his most notable saying puts it, "You can't step into the same river twice."

Heracleitus saw the world as full of opposing internal forces, an ebb and flow of creation and decay, a push and pull that kept it in a state of continual tension like, as he put it, the string of a taut bow. Despite this, or rather because of it, nature is ultimately in a state of dynamic equilibrium. Change maintains the cosmic order. But these forces conform to certain laws, so the cosmos has an underlying order known as the *logos.* Even the cosmic fire is "kindled in measures and quenched in measures," Heracleitus wrote in one of his surviving aphorisms.

"Nature loves to hide," he also wrote, but added, "An unapparent harmony is stronger than an apparent one." Nature, like the harmonics of a string, is susceptible to understanding, even measurement.

ARISTOTLE

Father of science

384 B.C.
Born in Stagira, Greece.

367 B.C.
At the age of 17, joins Plato's Academy in Athens, where he stays for the next 20 years.

348 or 347 B.C.
On Plato's death, Aristotle leaves Athens for Assos in Mysia (in Asia Minor).

345-342 B.C.
Studies natural history on the island of Lesbos.

342 B.C.
Returns to Macedonia to become tutor to Alexander, son of King Philip II.

336 B.C.
Begins gathering material in preparation for writing an encyclopedia of all knowledge.

335 or 334 B.C.
Returns to Athens, where he leads his own school in the Lyceum.

322 B.C.
Dies in Chalcis, Greece

Prominent scientific works

Physica (Physics)

De caelo (On the Heavens)

Meteorologica (Meteorology)

Historia animalium (The History of Animals)

De generatione animalium (On the Generation of Animals)

De partibus animalium (The Parts of Animals)

De incessu animalium (The Progression of Animals)

Heracleitus was convinced of the importance of logos, the rule or proportion of things, not only as a way to understand the cosmos but also as a prerequisite to a vital life. He could not abide people's ignorance of it. "Even though all things occur according to the Logos, men seem to have no experience whatsoever, even when they experience the words and deeds which I use to explain physis, of how the Logos applies to each thing, and what it is," he complained. "The rest of mankind is just as unconscious of what they do while awake as they are of what they do while they sleep."

Heracleitus's tendency toward despair and his pessimistic view of human nature earned him the sobriquet of "the Weeping Philosopher." By one account, probably mocking, he eventually became

PLATO'S ACADEMY

"Philosophers of the Academy," a Roman mosaic, pictures Greek philosopher Plato and his students at the Athenian Acropolis.

a hermit, lived in the mountains eating grass and plants, and died when he tried to cure himself of dropsy by shutting himself in a stall and warming himself up by the heat of the manure.

His own supposed idiosyncrasies notwithstanding, Heracleitus along with his contemporaries, not only delineated the Greek view of the cosmos, but also set Western thought—especially scientific thought—on the path it would follow to the present day. He was not alone in applying his understanding of the cosmos to his understanding of human existence. Neither he nor other Greek philosophers of the time distinguished between their investigations into the nature of the universe and their investigations of human nature and morality. Democritus of Abdera, whose life bridged the fifth and fourth centuries B.C., wrote, simply enough, that "man is a little cosmos."

For the philosopher Plato, the world that we experience through our senses was full of change and uncertainty. As a way to understand the workings of the universe, sensory experience and observation were unreliable at best. Reason and contemplation were Plato's favored methods of investigation. From this premise, Plato derived the famous idea that beyond the world of our senses lay a world of eternal forms— unchanging, ideal realities.

For instance, the tree we see with our eyes and touch with our fingers can be measured, cut down, chopped up, and burned. For the purposes of investigation, the particular tree may be of some interest, but in the larger scheme of truth, the tree we perceive is simply an appearance, far less important than the idea of the tree that we recognize within our higher mind. The idea of the tree is not subject to change or destruction. It presents an ideal form, the permanent reality of what a tree is, what all trees are. Investigation of the realm of unchangeable forms requires contemplation and reason instead of empirical observation.

When we read Plato and the philosophers who came before him, it's important to know that they were theorizing about the natural world with very little understanding about how it actually worked. Experimentation was limited, especially when philosophical speculation came so much to the fore.

Aristotle looked to change these circumstances. Although a student of Plato's for 20 years, upon Plato's death in 347 B.C. Aristotle left the academy to pursue his own broadening range of interests. On the island of Lesbos he and a student, Theophrastus, began observing plants and animals, making detailed notations. This alone would have distanced him from his mentor: Plato held such pursuits in low regard, but they marked Aristotle and Theophrastus as innovative scientific minds of their times.

But Aristotle also believed that his observations of the physical world told him more than Plato's ideal forms ever could. How could

TELEOLOGY

Philosophers from Aristotle to Emmanuel Kant, in the 18th century, have taken a teleological approach to science, assuming that all change in the universe and among living things leads to perfection and follows a design found immanent, or secretly influential, in their current state.

239

ARISTOTLE THE TEACHER

From the 7th to the 13th centuries, Arab and Jewish scholars translated, analyzed, and built upon the works of Greek philosopher Aristotle, whom this 13th-century Turkish manuscript depicts as he teaches a group of students.

the ideal and unchangeable form of, say, a plant exist without there being an actual plant as well? Forms could give no information about nature, for they exist outside of it. For Aristotle, facts came from observation, theories from facts, and then those theories must be confirmed through observation.

Aristotle concluded that all things have, first, a substance out of which they are created; second, a means of creation; third, a set of properties; and finally, an end or purpose. He called these properties of things "causes." Everything in the material world has a purpose that it realizes in its final perfection, stated Aristotle: That condition is simply part of the internal nature of things.

This belief that nature proceeds with a purpose and toward perfection is known as teleology, from the Greek *telos,* meaning end or goal. Aristotle was convinced by his

1551 – 1735

1551-1558
Swiss naturalist Conrad Gesner publishes *Historia animalium,* an important early work of zoology.

1590-1608
Dutch inventors Hans and Zacharias Janssen make a compound microscope.

1665
Looking through a microscope, Robert Hooke discovers cells in cork.

1665
Hooke publishes *Micrographia,* in which he describes his biological observations with the microscope.

observations of nature that everything he saw displayed rationality in its design and purpose in its function. In Aristotle's universe, matter, space, time, and motion all had teleological functions.

Motion is the enabler of the physical world. Without motion there would be no change in the universe. Without change there would be no time. And time could have no effect if there were no mind to observe and measure change and motion. So all things contain the ability to move toward their full realization, which Aristotle called entelechy.

Looking for the ultimate stuff of life, Aristotle didn't agree with any one of his predecessors' choices: water, apeiron, fire, atoms, or air. Rather, he believed in a foursome of ultimate elements—fire, air, earth, and water. According to Aristotle, each was able to transform into another, and thus matter, like all things Aristotelian, had an immanent teleology. It attained form along a continuum, a scale of being that ascended from lower forms to higher ones. The higher up the scale, the more advanced and organized the form, the more complex the soul, from inanimate matter up to humans.

Aristotle even suggested that the soul, which other philosophers thought separable and different from the body, might be an organic part of the body. "Being the actuality or entelechy of the body, the soul is at the same time form, principle of movement, and end." Plants possessed what Aristotle called a nutritive soul, which allowed them to assimilate nutrients and reproduce. Animals possessed a nutritive soul but with added sensations and motion, which enabled them to find food. The human soul had, in addition to these, the possibility of rational thought. The one thing common to all was that the body and soul of each had a purpose: the realization of their own natures.

What use did Aristotle make of this grand design? For one, it enabled him to begin to analyze the differences, rather than only the similarities, among the vast array of bodily forms that he observed in nature. No natural

1668	**1669**	**1674**	**1735**
Italian physician Francesco Redi disproves the theory of spontaneous generation by observing flies and maggots in putrefying matter.	Dutch naturalist Jan Swammerdam publishes *The Natural History of Insects*, in which he describes and classifies insects and scorpions.	Antoni van Leeuwenhoek observes protozoa and calls them animalcules.	Swedish taxonomist Carolus Linnaeus publishes *Systema naturae*, describing a classification system for plants, animals, and minerals.

philosopher before him had made so many or such detailed field observations. Fully a third of the writings by Aristotle that survived to modern times—a large body of work which ranges in topic from logic and physics to ethics and politics—are on nature. No equal to the classification of living things that he undertook emerged for more than a thousand years.

With only his accumulated observations to go on, Aristotle realized that it would be futile to classify species only by their outward physical appearances. He was well aware of the story about Plato who, after classifying humans as "featherless bipeds," was presented with a plucked chicken called "Plato's man."

So Aristotle devised a simple system: He divided up the animal kingdom between those with red blood and those without. The first group (akin to vertebrates) included mammals, birds, reptiles and amphibians, fishes, and whales. The bloodless animal groups (akin to invertebrates) were cephalopods, crustaceans, insects andspiders, shelled animals, and animals that resembled plants, such as corals. Overall were broad categories he called genera, within which he named species.

Aristotle distinguished another division between those animals that bear live young and those that produce eggs. He then divided the egg layers into those with birdlike eggs and those with fish-like eggs. By this method Aristotle was able to conclude that because dolphins bear live young, they must be more closely related to mammals than to fish.

In his *On the Generation of Animals,* Aristotle investigated reproduction. He discovered by dissecting chicken eggs that embryos are not tiny adults that grow in the eggs or womb. He recognized some of the workings of inheritance. He discerned that ruminants such as cattle had complex stomachs and broad, blunt teeth. These characteristics, he reasoned, might be complementary: The dietary limitations imposed by the teeth might be compensated by the compound stomach. "Nature," he wrote, "invariably gives to one part what she subtracts from another." At a time when actual experimental work was rare, Aristotle continued to pore over his data, using it to formulate problems and looking to the data for answers.

The range of Aristotle's thought may have been exceeded only by his capacity to systematize all that he observed and cataloged, and yet at the same time stay faithful to his original conception that all things have a purpose and proceed toward the perfection of that purpose. He applied these criteria to motion, matter, form, and function; to things organic or inorganic; to plants, animals, and humans.

What is the purpose of human life, many of the ancient philosophers asked? To be happy, Aristotle answered. What marks the progress toward happiness? Moral and intellectual virtue. And what constitutes the realization of human nature? The perfection of the faculty of reason. All these philosophical tenets

VIVISECTIONISTS

A vivisectionist is a person who dissects live animals or humans. Alcmaeon, a sixth century B.C. physiologist and philosopher in Italy, is believed to be the first person to perform a vivisection. Herophilus, a Greek physician from the fourth and third centuries B.C., is known to have vivisected over 600 human prisoners. Nazi physician Josef Mengele and Japanese physician Fukujiro Ishiyama both performed vivisections on humans during World War II.

VITALISM

Many have considered Aristotle's writings on cause, soul, and form responsible for the concept of vitalism, the idea that what distinguishes animate from inanimate life is an unspecified vital force. Although the idea persists even today, vitalism had its greatest influence from the 16th to the 18th century, when it stood in opposition to the mechanistic view that organisms are like highly complex machines. As advances in physiology during the Renaissance and after increased the knowledge of how muscles, nerves, and organs functioned, a more mechanistic view of the body became prevalent, but to the vitalists, anatomical physics could explain only so much. Some vital force had to power the organism, give it perception and understanding, direct reproduction, and perhaps even maintain order in the system.

Marie-Francois-Xavier Bichat identified 21 kinds of tissues in the human body.

This idea of a vital force was not a religious, spiritual, or philosophical concept—although it was one that religion, spiritualism, and philosophy would latch on to. It was a scientific concept, presuming a physiological reality yet to be identified. The vital force was elemental. It was neither the Western soul nor the Chinese *Chi* or *Tao*. Louis Pasteur, a rigorous experimental scientist, still believed that nothing other than a vital force could explain certain cellular phenomena. Just as things fall as a result of the invisible force of gravity, so the vitalists believed that certain cellular functions, and therefore those of organisms, are caused by the invisible vital force.

René Descartes, the French mathematician and philosopher, was the primary advocate of the mechanistic view. French anatomist Marie-François-Xavier Bichat took exception, not from any religious objection to Descartes's thinking but because of his extensive examinations of human organs and tissues. Bichat believed tissues to be the basic units of life, and he thought that a vital force must exist that enabled them to resist disease, decay, and death.

The microscope revealed the intricacies of the cell, chemistry revealed its complex molecular functions, and those mysteries that had been explained by the vital force became fewer. Eventually vitalism faded, although to some it still seemed a worthwhile philosophical notion. Some still believed that something like it must direct an organism's basic chemistry and must have inspired the evolution from inanimate chemicals to complex life forms.

Did Aristotle have this sort of scientific vitalism in mind? Vitalism proposes that some unknowable force exists and can explain things when experiment and observation fail. As more is explained by theory and experiment, though, vitalism's rationale fails.

Aristotle proposed no unknowable forces. He regarded observation and reason as the heart of every science. Those phenomena that cannot yet be explained—soul, imagination, evolution, the grandeur of the universe—demand continued observation, in the faith that human perception and reason can ultimately grasp all.

SPECIES AND TAXONOMY

Aristotle worked out a system for organizing animals, but explorations in the 16th and 17th centuries and the discoveries through the microscope, revealed new life forms that demanded new ways to categorize and classify.

One task was to determine which characteristics genuinely separated one kind of plant or animal from another and which were, on the other hand, incidental variations within a single kind. English scientist and Anglican priest John Ray proposed the simple rule that if a male and female can reproduce and the resulting organism looks like its parents, they are all members of the same species, despite differences in color, size, or other external characteristics.

Linnaeus, father of taxonomy, dressed sportily to go botanizing.

The Swedish naturalist known as Carolus Linnaeus, born Carl von Linné in 1707, began distinguishing plants by the design of their sex organs. He devised a classification system that required two Latin names for each organism, genus first and species second. A dog and a wolf, for instance, both belong to the genus *Canis*. To distinguish between the two, he named the species of the common domestic dog *familiaris;* the wolf *lupus.*

Genus and species fit into a larger hierarchical system that began with the "empire," which was everything on Earth. From here each organism belonged to a "kingdom"—animal, plant, or mineral—then a "class"—animals could be fish, bird, mammal, insect, amphibian, or worm in Linnaeus's system—then, dividing further, "order," "genus," "species," and sometimes "variety" within species.

Linnaeus published his first proposal for this system in 1735. With just one change—"kingdom" to "phylum"—it remains in use today. The scientific names of all species are cataloged in an official International Code of Nomenclature. The criteria by which species are distinguished, however, have been clarified and honed since Linnaeus's time.

Linnaeus chose basic attributes of species to separate one from another—birds' beaks, mammals' teeth, fishes' fins, and insects' wings. Even at the time, not all scientists agreed. Some argued that the system assumed that these attributes stayed constant over time, but new fossil findings suggested otherwise. Not until nearly 200 years later did the science of taxonomy truly coordinate with current findings in paleontology and evolutionary biology.

In 1950 Willi Hennig, a German entomologist, devised a system of classification that took into account the common evolutionary ancestry of organisms. Evolution results in modifications of characteristics over time. The new science of phylogenetic taxonomy—or cladism, as it is more commonly known—focuses on the features that an organism shares with its ancestors.

Cladistics brings to light previously unrecognized relationships among organisms. For instance, by recognizing similar features derived and modified over time, cladists were able to demonstrate (although not to every scientist's satisfaction) that birds and dinosaurs shared a common ancestry. Like Linnaeus's system, the cladistic system is only as good as the decisions made concerning what characteristics are singled out in order to make the classification. Recently new systems have been proposed, in the search for the best blend of classification logic and evolutionary theory.

THE HEAVENS BURST FORTH

An illuminated medieval manuscript of Dominican friar Albertus Magnus's *De natura* portrays lightning over the sea in shapes and colors strikingly modern.

barnacles and goose necks—and therefore concluded that gooselike barnacles developed into barnacle-like geese.

Christian scholars debated whether these geese should be classified as fish or fowl and, if the latter, whether they could be eaten on Friday or during Lent, when meat was forbidden but fish was allowed. Jewish philosophers debated whether this goose was a shellfish, hence food forbidden to Jews, and, if it was not, whether it had to be butchered according to ritual practice. Some saw a convenient compromise: Since both barnacle and goose fell from a tree, they were neither fish nor fowl, but fruit.

Within the theological matrix, there was a growing conviction that ancient authorities, even those as apparently incontestable as Aristotle, Ptolemy, and Galen, may simply have been wrong

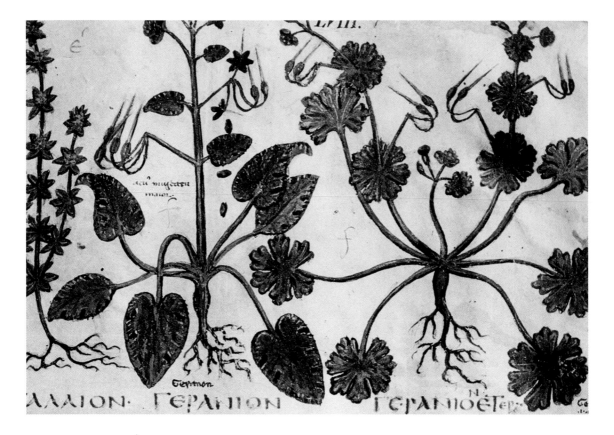

MEDICINAL TOME

De materia medica, written in A.D. 77 by Greek physician, pharmacologist, and botanist Dioscorides, was the primary reference for herbal and animal decoctions until the 16th century. This page is from a seventh-century manuscript about herbs.

about many things. Scientific evidence and rational argument could be used to challenge these intellects, it began to seem, yielding new views that explained nature more logically.

At the same time, a parallel trend in thinking was under way: the gradual retreat of God from the day-to-day events of the world. Not that those who came up with new ways of thinking were in any way atheists. Most were pious; many were ordained priests. But they viewed divine intervention with the cosmos rather differently than their predecessors did. For centuries, most had assumed the living hand of God in all natural and human existence. Now it began to appear as if the creator

had wound nature up like a clock and then set it aside to tick through time according to invariable principles—principles that might be understood through reason and experimentation.

INKLINGS OF SCIENCE

A 13th-century English bishop named Robert Grosseteste was inspired to pursue science by his studies of Aristotle, whose works had been preserved by Islamic scholars, translated from Arabic into Latin, but were now reappearing in Europe. Whereas Aristotle believed that to know a thing was to know its causes, Grosseteste established a more scientific method: to observe, analyze, and discover the causal principles; to hypothesize;

See pages 86-87 for more information about da Vinci.

and then to test the hypothesis. Grosseteste's associate, Roger Bacon, 50 years his junior, was no less enthusiastic about experimental science. Bacon believed that the greater the understanding of the world, the greater the knowledge of the creator. Bacon's ideal of scientific wisdom organized by theology inspired Copernicus, Kepler, Boyle, and Newton.

Albertus Magnus, born in Swabia (present-day southwestern Germany) around 1200, was also stimulated by Aristotle. Albertus made close observations of insects, dissecting them and examining their genitalia. He followed up on Aristotle's examinations of chicken eggs and fish development. He also began a simple systematic classification of plants, distinguishing them by the forms of their flowers.

Organized scientific inquiry was sweeping Europe. In the second half of the 13th century, Thomas Aquinas argued that the new Aristotelians could study and experiment all they wanted, because in the end what they were doing was revealing more of the creator's world.

Over the next 300 years, new technologies—paper and printing from China, metal engraving from Italy, and, finally, moveable type—promoted new ideas and learning. Voyages of exploration and the discovery of the New World enlarged civilization's frame of reference. Artists in 15th-century Italy explored a new realism, depicting the world as it was instead of as it might be imagined. Even when painting allegorical subject matter, monochromatic backgrounds gave way to detailed perspective and carefully observed light. Art—engraved illustration, in particular—would serve as one of the catalysts to the Renaissance study of natural history. Although the full extent of the work of Leonardo da Vinci, the greatest of these "scientific" artists, would not be known until after his death, other artists were delving into a new empiricism.

German Renaissance painter and engraver Albrecht Dürer, born in Nuremberg, Germany, in 1471, advocated for a science-based art. He drew precise botanical and zoological depictions and wrote treatises on perspective. Botanical encyclopedias flourished in the next century. In the 1530s Otto Brunfels of Mainz, Germany, published his three-volume *Living Illustrations of Plants,* depicting 238 species. Many herbals, collections of medicinal plants, had been produced before Brunfels's collection, but, like medieval bestiaries, they were rarely accurate. Hans Weiditz, the woodcut artist who illustrated Brunfels's books, showed not only precise structures of the plants but also how they appeared in the wild.

The *Neu Kreüterbuch (Book of Herbs)* by Hieronymus Bock (Tragus) appeared in 1539. In it, the German Lutheran physician described each plant's life history. But not until its illustrated edition came out in 1546 did it receive proper attention, even then having to compete with Leonhard Fuchs's *Notable Commentaries on the*

ST. ALBERT THE GREAT
Albertus Magnus was the most notable botanist in medieval times. His classification system for plants recognized our modern concepts of vascular and nonvascular plants as well as monocots and dicots. Teacher of Thomas Aquinas, he was declared a saint by the Vatican in the 20th century.

History of Plants, which appeared in 1542. (The plant fuchsia is named after him.) Lavishly illustrated and engraved, Fuchs's book described some 400 species native to Germany and 100 from other countries. The first New World herbal appeared in 1552, based on Aztec plant drawings.

Conrad Gesner—a Swiss prodigy who had compiled a Greek-Latin dictionary, received his medical degree, compiled an annotated bibliography of 1,100 authors, and produced a 19-volume encyclopedia—published *Opera Botanica (Botanical Works),* containing 1,500 woodcuts and classifying plants according to structure. All of this didn't leave him sufficient time

to finish his five-volume, 4,500-page compendium of animal life, which was finally completed in 1587, 22 years after Gesner's death. It was one of a number of encyclopedic zoological reference books that the age produced.

A vital step in the transition to a new view of science was made by a man who was more politician than scientist. Francis Bacon was born in London in 1561, the son of the Lord Keeper of the Great Seal of Queen Elizabeth. Entering Parliament at 23, Bacon had a political career that rose and fell like that of many others during this turbulent time in England. When Queen Elizabeth died, Bacon served James I, who named him Keeper of the Seal in 1617, and Viscount St. Albans in 1620. Throughout his political career Bacon was writing books of philosophy, including a work destined to alter the course of scientific thinking: *The Novum Organum (New Organon)*, the second installment of his *Instauratio Magna (The Great Instauration)*, the first part of which had appeared in 1605.

Bacon set out to redirect the course of science. "We must begin anew," he wrote, "from the very foundations." Science is neither philosophy nor humanism, he argued, but a process of discovery that leads to an accumulation of knowledge. Like Roger Bacon—no relation—before him, Francis Bacon believed that the pursuit of knowledge was blocked by conventional ways of thinking and weaknesses in human nature and perception: "the idols and false notions which are now in possession of the human understanding." Among these idols he included wishful thinking; the tendency to look for proof of what we already believe or to find results that please us; and too great a reliance on the senses instead of instruments of measurement. None of these prejudices, Bacon argued, has a place in the pursuit of scientific knowledge.

He also stated that one cannot begin to investigate nature with an overarching concept of nature already in place. Rather, one has to begin with the particular and progress "regularly and gradually from one axiom to another, so that the most general are not reached till the last." This mental discipline Bacon called "true and Perfect Induction," and it was to become an essential methodology of science. "If a man will begin with certainties, he shall end in doubts," wrote Bacon, "but if he will be content to begin with doubts, he shall end in certainties."

In 1628, William Harvey announced to England's Royal College of Physicians that he had discovered that blood circulates through

FRANCIS BACON

Founder of the scientific method

1561
Born January 22 in London.

1573
Enters Trinity College, Cambridge, en route to Gray's Inn for a legal education.

1582
Admitted to the bar as a barrister; first involvement in English politics.

1584
Takes a seat in the House of Commons.

1603
Knighted Sir Francis Bacon by King James I.

1605
Publishes *The Advancement of Learning*, in which he describes the "idols of the mind" and other obstacles that stand in the way of clearheaded knowledge.

1613
Appointed Attorney General by King James I.

1618
Becomes Lord Chancellor, receives title of Baron Verulam.

1620
In his *Novum Organon*, lays out a plan for the reorganization of knowledge into categories.

1621
Becomes Viscount St. Alban; later convicted of bribery and dismissed from chancellorship.

1626
Dies on April 9 at Highgate, London.

1627
New Atlantis, published posthumously, describes Bacon's ideal of scientific research, including details on laboratories, instruments, and the roles of scientists, researchers, and interpreters.

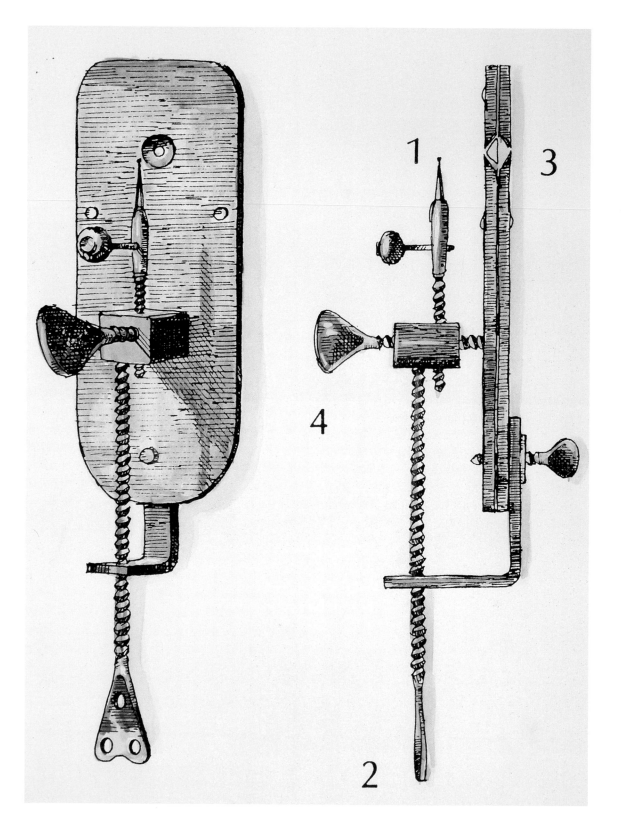

the body. As self-evident as it seems to us today, the concept of a circulatory system in which blood circulates not only from heart to lungs but, pumped by the heart, through a system of veins, arteries, and capillaries was unknown at the time. Harvey made the discovery, as he describes it, through gradual steps of observation and understanding.

Harvey's book *Exercitatio de motu cordis et sanguinis in animalibus* exemplifies Francis Bacon's inductive process. He reports all previous theories—beginning with those of the ancient Greek physician Galen—and questions each, comparing them with his own observations. He conducts his own investigation, building one fact onto the next until the entire system comes into view. He concluded that the circulation of blood is a system that reflects the nature of life itself, the very image of the Earth's circulatory system as well as the cosmic circulations of sun and planets. The heart, he wrote, is "the sun of the microcosm. . . . It is the household divinity which, discharging its function, nourishes, cherishes, quickens the whole body, and is indeed the foundation of life."

Scientists tried to place their discoveries within the context of established religious and philosophical systems. Meanwhile, philosophers found it necessary to catch up with the revolution in science.

René Descartes, a French mathematician and philosopher, took Bacon's cautions against old ideas to the extreme. He believed that the human mind could reach an understanding of the universe by reasoning from intuition. He considered the senses themselves unreliable and posed to himself the question, What, if anything, is free of doubt?

For Descartes, the primary certainty was that he existed: "I think, therefore I am," he stated as the fundamental principle of all human knowledge. Only humans have such thoughts, and because humans conceived of God, God must exist, too. The natural world

RENÉ DESCARTES

Enlightenment philosopher

1596
Born on March 31 at La Haye, France.

1616
Takes a license in law at University of Poitiers, France.

1629
Completes *Rules for the Direction of Mind*, not published until 1701.

1633
Abandons plans to publish his work *The World*, because of the church's condemnation of Galileo.

1637
Publishes *Discourse on Method*, which includes essays explaining the law of refraction, the origin of rainbows, and analytic geometry.

1641
Publishes *Meditations on First Philosophy*, along with six sets of objections and replies.

1642
Publishes second edition of the *Meditations*.

1643
Begins a long correspondence with Princess Elisabeth of Bohemia; is condemned by officials at the University of Utrecht for his philosophy.

1644
Publishes *The Principles of Philosophy*.

1647
Awarded a pension by the King of France; publishes *Comments on a Certain Broadsheet* and begins work on *The Description of the Human Body*.

1649
Publishes *Passions of the Soul*.

1650
Dies in Stockholm on February 11.

PAGE 252

One of the nearly 500 microscopes constructed by Antonie van Leeuwenhoek after 1674, with labeled parts: 1) point to hold object; 2) and 4) adjustment screws; and 3) lens, some of which could go up to 200x magnification.

COMPLEX CREATURE

Dutch microscopist Jan Swammerdam's studies of insect anatomy changed the perception of them as simple creatures without the complexity of higher animals.

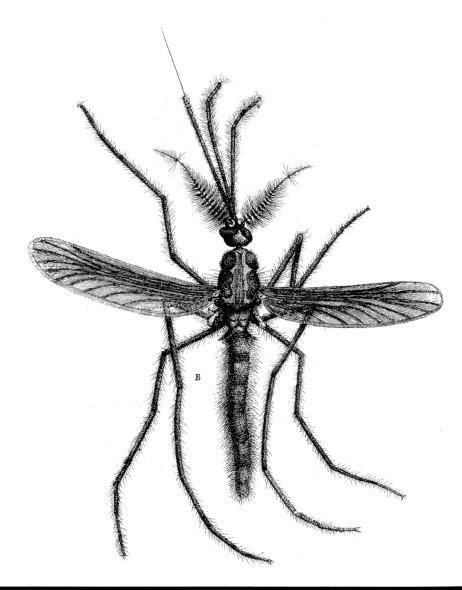

1749 – 1828

1749
French naturalist Georges-Louis Leclerc, the Comte de Buffon, publishes his great work *Histoire naturelle, générale et particulière*.

1771
English scientist Joseph Priestley discovers that plants convert carbon dioxide into oxygen.

1794-1796
English physician Erasmus Darwin publishes *Zoonomia, or the Laws of Inorganic Life*, which contains early ideas on the theory of evolution.

1798
In *An Essay on the Principle of Population*, economist Thomas Malthus envisions the possibility of human overpopulation.

was discoverable and, he believed, made up of a limited number of basic mechanisms and motions.

NEW WAYS OF SEEING AND BELIEVING

While the voyagers of the 15th and 16th centuries had discovered new horizons of terrestrial geog-raphy, and while the invention of the tel-escope brought the heavens into focus, life's processes were still a far-reaching sea that had been observed and considered only from the shore. With the invention of the microscope, 17th-century scientists, and eventually laymen as well, embarked on another new realm of exploration. From the first look, the microscope revealed unimagined depths of new knowl-edge. The only question seemed to be what to look at first.

Marcello Malpighi, a 17th-century Italian biologist, began by examin-ing the skin, then went on to other tissues of the body. (The inner, or Malpighian, layer of skin was named for him.) He identified tastebuds; he studied blood cells and plant structures. He investi-gated the structures of the liver, kidneys, brain, and spleen, and saw that plants and animals share certain organizational features.

Malpighi discovered the small threadlike vessels in lung tissue that join arteries to veins—capillaries, which, he concluded rightly, proved William Harvey's theory of a closed circulatory sys-tem. Authorities at the University in Bologna questioned his work, but by the end of his career, he had been appointed personal physician to Pope Innocent XII.

Working in London, Robert Hooke observed and, with his extraordinary skill at draftsman-ship, recorded his observations of a wide variety of natural things, from fly feet and bee stingers to mollusk tongues and cork, the material that led him to propose the existence of living cells. Hooke's *Micrographia,* published in 1665, gave the public its first remarkable glimpses of the worlds teeming within living nature. Samuel Pepys, the 17th-century diarist, called it "the most ingenious book that I ever read in my life."

Dutchman Jan Swammerdam took up his microscope to study

See pages 92-93 for more information on Malpighi.

1801
French biologist Jean-Baptiste de Lamarck publishes his study of invertebrate taxonomy, leading toward an early version of the theory of evolution.

1804
French zoologist Georges Cuvier proposes his theory of the extinction of species.

1809
Lamarck bases his theory of evolution on the concept of inherited traits.

1828
Friedrich Wöhler synthesizes urea, the first time an organic compound has been synthesized from inorganic materials.

insects. He discovered, among other things, that in bee colonies a fertile female rules over sexless female workers and male drones. In 1669 Swammerdam published *The Natural History of Insects*, extraordinary even by today's standards. For it, he dissected and categorized more than 3,000 insect species as well as spiders and scorpions. His evidence was overwhelming: Contrary to

THE STRUCTURE OF CELLS

The essential tenet of science is that as each discovery or theory is replicated and verified by others, it becomes a foundation upon which further work can stand. The cellular theory is a perfect example.

Like all scientific theories, it emerged through a long history of observations—in this case, some 2,000 years of evidence. Once observation and theory coalesced to provide some certainty as to the existence and nature of cells in living things, it opened the door for discoveries that have brought science very close to the origins of life.

Essentially, all scientists now take as a principle that cells are the fundamental units of all living organisms, the simplest units to possess the functional characteristic of life. All cells have universal characteristics, but they also have unique distinct identities, often shaped by form and function. They share a lot of traits with the living beings made up of them.

The theory of cells has enabled progress in the understanding of heredity and genetics. In early development, a cell prepares a copy of its chromosomal DNA. When a cell divides, the two matching sets of chromosomes line up in the middle of the cell

This drawing illustrates German hematologist Paul Ehrlich's theory of how blood cells produce antibodies.

nucleus. As the cell divides, the two sets separate, like interlocked fingers pulling apart. Each set moves into a new cell nucleus. Enzymes and proteins participate in the micro-mechanical division at the molecular and cellular levels.

Cells hold within their lipid membranes a dynamic molecular industrial complex. Pumps and transporters move molecules in and out. Chemical reactions occur. In protein scaffoldings, or internal structures, enzymes are synthesized. Every process is precisely regulated and quality-controlled. If any part of the process gets out of order or moves too fast, the cell will attempt to bring it to a halt.

There is still much to be learned about the cell's ability to control dynamic chemical reactions. But in healthy cells, the processes of division are always the same, ensuring the precise replication and transfer of genetic material. This realization came thanks to a theory of cells—and it helps to confirm that theory, too.

"Because cell reproduction is the basis for all biological reproduction," wrote cell biologist Sir Paul Nurse, "it follows that these same cellular properties are the basis of the evolution of all living organisms."

Aristotle's opinion, insects did have an internal body structure and could reproduce on their own.

British doctor Nehemiah Grew found that plants, too, had reproductive organs. Flowers were not just objects of beauty but they contained sexual organs. The male sexual organ, or stamen, produced pollen, and the female sexual organ, or pistil, received pollen and bore the seeds.

At the same time, a countryman of Swammerdam's, Antonie van Leeuwenhoek, a cloth merchant with no formal education, had become intrigued—and then, to the detriment of his cloth business, obsessed—with the perfection of lenses. He achieved magnifications of 40 to 270 diameters. He, too, saw the capillaries that connected arteries and veins. He looked at muscle tissue, the lens of the eye, the tartar on his teeth, and red blood cells. He saw things 25 times smaller than red blood cells—the first look at bacteria.

Leeuwenhoek's discovery of spermatozoa in male seminal fluid provoked continuing debate over a prevailing theory of conception called preformation. Harvey, Swammerdam, Malpighi, and others believed that the unborn animal existed as a miniature individual inside the mother. Leeuwenhoek and another Dutch microscopist, Nicolaas Hartsoeker, posited that the individual existed within the sperm. Hartsoeker claimed to have seen these entities, which he called homunculi, or little men.

Leeuwenhoek made his second extraordinary finding in a drop of water. Under his microscope, he saw the water brimming with tiny, lively, swimming creatures. He called them animalcules—we know them now as protozoa. Their discovery incited a debate over the long-held theory of spontaneous generation, predating Aristotle—the belief that lower animals such as these, along with flies, bees, and even amphibians, had no parentage but arose spontaneously in streambed mud or rotting flesh. For many,

ROBERT HOOKE

Discoverer of cells

1635
Born on July 18 at Freshwater, Isle of Wight, England.

1655
Employed as assistant to Robert Boyle, physicist and chemist, at Oxford.

1660
Discovers the scientific law of elasticity, later named Hooke's law. This discovery is not made public until 1678.

1662
Elected curator of experiments for the Royal Society; soon thereafter, elected a fellow of the Royal Society.

1664
Infers that Jupiter rotates on its axis.

1665
Becomes professor of geometry at Gresham College, London.

1665
Publishes his most famous work, *Micrographia*, in which he describes his observations with the microscope, including his discovery of plant cells, which he first finds in cork.

1666
In a lecture to the Royal Society, proposes that gravity could be measured by using a pendulum.

1672
Discovers the phenomenon of diffraction; puts forth the wave theory of light.

1674
Builds a Gregorian reflecting telescope, first ever to do so, and with it makes important astonomical observations.

1678
Describes the motion of the planets mathematically. Newton later elaborates in his studies of planetary motion.

1703
Dies on March 3 in London, England.

NATURAL SELECTION

Philosopher Herbert Spencer coined the term "evolution" to refer to Darwin's theory, but the word did not appear in Charles Darwin's famous book, *The Origin of the Species*, until the sixth edition, 1872. The concept of progress of teleological evolution—development toward some perfect Lamarckian state, some divinely ordained endpoint, or some Aristotelian purpose—was not what Darwin had in mind. He was, as his title makes clear, interested in origins, and how particular species came into existence.

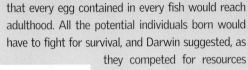

"Mr. G-g-g-o-o-o-rilla," reads the caption of this 19th-century cartoon mocking the theory of evolution.

Darwin was no natural philosopher. He was a 19th-century English scientist who knew that theories could be proved only by persistent questioning, observation, and experimentation. For instance, writes Richard Milner in his *Encyclopedia of Evolution*, "Darwin doesn't merely speculate that certain plants might have reached far-flung oceanic islands as floating seeds; he soaks many kinds of seeds in barrels of salt water for months, then plants them to see which species will sprout." Darwin didn't just assume the great diversity of species; he spent eight years describing and classifying the thousands of barnacles he'd brought back from his journey. He had collected specimens and observed geological formations all over the world.

Darwin built the arguments in his book from the ground up, in such deliberate steps, that by its conclusion, the theory that changed the world seems almost self-evident. With Malthus in mind, Darwin posited that organisms produce far more offspring than will survive. It was obviously impossible that every seed released by every tree would take root, or that every egg contained in every fish would reach adulthood. All the potential individuals born would have to fight for survival, and Darwin suggested, as they competed for resources over time, chance variations would appear.

Linnaeus, Lamarck, and Cuvier had already shown that while individuals in a species might look alike, they could still have a wide range of structural and organic variations. Darwin recognized that a single chance variation would allow the "surviving one of ten thousand trials" to pass that superlative trait on to its offspring. Those born out of those who had survived such trials would, in most cases, be more resilient and able to withstand trials in the future.

What Darwin couldn't know then about either artificial or natural selection was that the variations occur within the animal's or plant's genetic makeup. Such genetic changes can be caused by mutations over several generations, by interbreeding between populations, or purely by chance. They are all random, meaning that they do not happen to increase or decrease an individual's fitness. Some may be advantageous, but just as many may not. The random genetic changes that provide an individual with a competitive advantage will most likely survive.

Evolution of a species might occur from natural selection, but not necessarily. Other variables such as predation or environmental change might impede evolution, too. Like Lyell's geological history, Darwin's evolution works slowly, with neither clear direction nor ultimate end.

the sheer number of these minute creatures glimpsed by Leeuwenhoek through the microscope could be explained only by the theory of spontaneous generation. Nothing else they could imagine would account either for such numbers and for the origin of such tiny creatures.

Spontaneous generation seemed borne out by simple observation. In the winter, frogs and salamanders, for instance, were nowhere to be seen. Come spring they seemed to appear wherever there was water. A pile of hay would suddenly be full of mice. Exposed garbage and sewage seemed to generate maggots, flies, and fleas. One recipe for generating bees was to kill a young bull and bury it; in a month a swarm of bees would fly out of it.

In 1668 an Italian physician, Francesco Redi, set up jars containing meat. Some he sealed, others he covered with gauze, and the rest he left open. Flies entered the open jars, and soon maggots and flies appeared on that meat. While the jars whose mouths were covered with gauze attracted flies on the outside, only a few maggots appeared on the meat inside. The meat in the sealed jars remained free of either maggots or flies, he concluded, since flies could not reach the meat to lay their eggs.

Redi had proved that flies are born and not made. But even those who followed his experiment still believed that smaller organisms, such as those that Leeuwenhoek found in water and that others found in spoiled broth,

arose spontaneously. A theory of spontaneous generation, however limited, would prevail for another 150 years.

THE ORGANIZATION OF LIFE

Voyagers and explorers bestowed an embarrassment of biological riches on early modern scientists at the same time that those scientists were discovering new life forms through the lenses of their microscopes. Add to this the realization, reached through the study of structural distinctions, that what seemed to be one kind of plant or animal might actually be two or three or more different ones—and the result was a world in need of some sort of biological filing system.

Not that earlier scientists hadn't tried to systematize the world of living things. Aristotle used the Greek words *genos* and *eidos,* genus and species, to make distinctions among large groups of plants or animals and among the individuals in those groups. His student Theophrastus had begun separating the plant world into groups, and that work was continued in the 13th century by Albertus Magnus and in the 16th century by Conrad Gesner. In the 17th century, efforts to categorize all living species were complicated even more by the discovery of impressions made in rock formations by leaves, stems, and skeletons of plants or animals that no one had ever seen before. Where did these petrified remains— named fossils, from the Latin for "dug up"—fit into the scheme?

MICRO-ORGANISMS
Belief in spontaneous generation paled by the early 1800s, but not until later in the century was the origin of microorganisms understood, when Louis Pasteur discovered how they reproduce.

DIVERSITY OF SPECIES

In his *Histoire naturelle*, Georges-Louis Leclerc attempted to catalog all of the natural world known to the 18th century. Nature's diversity, he argued, showed that the world was much older than the 6,000 years the Bible reported.

John Ray, an English naturalist and botanist, created a system of classification by concentrating on structural differences and similarities among species. Close examination revealed, in his view, that some characteristics genuinely separated one kind of plant or animal from another, while others, such as size and color, only demonstrated accidental variations within a single kind. Ray came up with a simple rule: If a male and female can reproduce, creating an organism that looks like its parents, then those individuals belong to the same species.

The Swedish botanist Carolus Linnaeus found Ray's emphasis on species rather than genus instructive. So rather than start by defining large groups and fitting species into them, Linnaeus gathered similarly structured species into groupings of genera (the plural of "genus") and worked up, grouping genera into families, families into orders and classes. This path of reasoning followed Bacon's scientific ideal of induction, moving from the specific to the general.

For Linnaeus, an avid plant collector, this path of reasoning also seemed to parallel the way he identified plants in the field. In recognition of Grew's research, he classified plants according to their method of reproduction, those with flowers and seeds separated from those without flowers and seeds. He distinguished mammal species by their toes and teeth, birds by their beaks.

When Georges-Louis Leclerc, Comte de Buffon, a French mathematician, was charged with cataloging France's natural history collection, he divided the world of science into geology, natural history, and anthropology. The first volumes of his encyclopedic dissertation on all human knowledge, *Histoire naturelle, générale et particulière,* appeared in 1749, but, despite Buffon's intense daily writing schedule, the work's 50 volumes were not completed until 1804.

This historical suite of important efforts at taxonomy (from the Greek *taxis,* arrangement, and *nomos,* law) inspired and to some degree forced scientists to consider the comparison of species' structural similarities and differences part of their responsibility. How was it, for example, that vertebrates shared so many of the same anatomical features? Or that a frog's heart functioned the same as a human's? They asked why the bones of a bird's wing looked and functioned much like a lizard's foot—and why the ape, inside and out, bore resemblances to the human being.

This last question lies in among the mass of Buffon's writings. He had the sense that organisms changed through time, and that living where and when they did established distinguishing characteristics. Buffon's assistant and eventual successor at France's National Museum of Natural History, Jean-Baptiste de Lamarck, pursued his mentor's line of thinking.

Trained as a physician and botanist, Lamarck was nevertheless put in charge of the museum's collection of invertebrates—a term he himself coined—and soon became fascinated by invertebrate diversity. "Relative to the animal kingdom, we should chiefly devote our attention to the invertebrate animals," Lamarck told students in 1803, "because their enormous multiplicity in nature, the singular diversity of their systems of organization, and of their means of multiplication . . . show us, much better than the higher animals, the true course of nature."

Lamarck recognized that "time and favorable conditions are the two principal means which nature has employed in giving existence to all her productions. We know that

Inventor of scientific nomenclature

1707
Born Carl von Linné on May 23 at Råshult, Småland, in southern Sweden.

1727
Enters the University of Lund to study medicine.

1730
Appointed lecturer in botany at the Uppsala Academy of Sciences.

1732
Travels on a scientific expedition to explore Lapland. Results of this journey published in 1737 as the *Flora Lapponica.*

1735
Travels to the Netherlands and finishes his medical degree at the University of Harderwijk.

1735
Publishes *Systema Naturae,* in which he describes a new classification system for plants, animals, and minerals.

1741
Appointed professor at Uppsala; begins restoring the university's botanical garden, arranging the plants according to his system of classification.

1744
Appointed secretary of the Royal Swedish Society of Sciences in Uppsala.

1753
Publishes *Species Plantarum,* his greatest botanical work, which organizes 5,900 plant species using new scientific nomenclature, the Latin binomial system.

1761
Granted nobility by Swedish king Adolf Fredrik.

1778
Dies on January 10 in Uppsala, Sweden, after a series of mild strokes.

for her time has no limit, and that consequently she always has it at her disposal." He saw it as a process: As natural surroundings change over time, so will a species living in them adapt new behaviors. These may in turn mean a greater or lesser use of some of the species' anatomical structures or organs. Eventually, useful structures would increase in size while unused structures would wither. These changes happened over long periods of time, and the changes were passed from one generation to another.

The giraffe, for example, developed a long neck because it was forced to reach high for the leaves it ate, as Lamarck perceived it. Over succeeding generations, the characteristic of long-neckedness was passed on, until finally the perfect neck length was achieved. Like Aristotle millennia before him, Lamarck held a teleological view of changes in the world. The evolution of species was not haphazard, he believed: It led toward the ultimate complexity and perfection of a species. Lamarck may have gotten a lot of things wrong, but what he did get right was that species change over a long period of time—and that scientists had a lot to learn from the invertebrates.

DARWIN'S REVOLUTION

If a single discovery could be said to mark the advance of science at the end of the 18th century, it was a new understanding of time. Despite the imprecision of his conclusions, Lamarck realized that for things to become the living things that they are today, it must have taken more time than the 6,000 years the Bible allowed. Georges Cuvier, Lamarck's countryman and nemesis, doubted many of Lamarck's theories but did believe, based on his precocious studies of fossils and anatomy, that the Earth was far more ancient than anyone had ever imagined.

"Why has not anyone seen that fossils alone gave birth to a theory about the formation of the earth?" asked Cuvier. "Without

JEAN-BAPTISTE DE LAMARCK

Early theorist of evolution

1744
Born on August 1 in Picardy, France.

1756
Enters the Jesuit seminary at Amiens.

1760
Leaves school at the Jesuit College, joins the French Army in its campaign in Germany during the Seven Years' War.

1769
Begins studying medicine in Paris; soon turns instead to the study of botany.

1778
Publishes his first botanical work, *Flora Française*, classifying the plants of France.

1781
Becomes conservator of the herbarium of the Royal Gardens.

1794
Appointed professor of invertebrates—a subject he has little knowledge of—at the French Museum of Natural History.

1801
Publishes *System of Invertebrate Animals, or General Table of Classes*, in which he describes a new classification of the lower invertebrates.

1802
Publishes *Hydrogeology*, which includes a history of the Earth, stating that it has periodically been inundated by a global sea.

1809
Publishes *Zoological Philosophy*, including theory on evolution of species through inheritance of acquired characteristics.

1815, 1822
Publishes *Natural History of Invertebrate Animals*.

1829
Dies on December 18 in Paris, France.

PRECEDING PAGE

Lamarck regarded the giraffe as an excellent illustration of his theory that acquired characteristics could be inherited—in other words, the efforts an animal makes in the course of interacting with its environment during life, such as stretching to eat leaves from a tree, would affect the shape of its offspring.

them, no one would have ever dreamed that there were successive epochs in the formation of the globe." Others had come to similar conclusions already: Danish scientist Nicolas Steno had identified fossilized shark teeth in the late 1600s, and the Comte de Buffon had called fossils "monuments taken from the bosom of the Earth," granting that "some of the fish and plants that these materials contain do not belong to species currently existing."

To Cuvier, the shared structures and organs among organisms reflected shared functions, not ancestral connections. An altered organism would be unfit to survive, and there was no such thing as an organism that went extinct by being unfit. To explain the lost species that the fossil record showed, Cuvier hypothesized natural "revolutions," periodic events so catastrophic that they could drive a species to extinction.

What caused these revolutions and extinctions? Cuvier did not specify. Those who held tight to their Bibles believed that Noah's flood might have been such an event. Other occurrences of reported history qualified just as well: eruptions of Mounts Etna and Vesuvius, as well as reported volcanoes and earthquakes in South America. A massive earthquake and tsunami destroyed the city of Lisbon in 1755, killing tens of thousands and casting doubt on the faith in God's ever-present hand in events occurring in the natural world. More doubts were soon to develop.

In 1794 Erasmus Darwin—physician, philosopher, botanist, sometime poet, and grandfather of the better known scientist named Charles Darwin—published a theory of evolution titled *Zoonomia; or, the Laws of Organic Life*. In it, Darwin considered the possibility of a common ancestry to all living things, a "living filament" from which all life descended. His theory suggested that one species could develop into another.

Erasmus Darwin also suggested other intriguing hypotheses: that competition due to overpopulation may have prompted species to evolve, that man was closely related to monkeys and apes, and that sexual selection might play a role in shaping species. "The final course of this contest among males seems to be," he wrote, "that the strongest and most active animal should propagate the species which should thus be improved."

Early on, Erasmus Darwin's grandson—born in 1809, seven years after his grandfather died—showed little interest in such matters. His student record was dismal, and he seemed interested only in leading a wealthy squire's life, collecting beetles, and shooting birds. He was about to enter divinity school (at his father's urging) when he received a letter recommending him to serve as captain's assistant aboard the H.M.S. *Beagle* on its surveying journey around the world. Against his father's wishes, Charles Darwin took up the offer.

He set sail December 27, 1831, bound for South America, well supplied with notebooks and reading material, including Sir Charles Lyell's recently published *Principles of Geology*.

Lyell was a British lawyer turned geologist who, after much travel and investigation, concluded that change on Earth had not happened as revolutions, as Cuvier and many geologists now known as catastrophists believed. Lyell suggested that the most important changes had come gradually, imperceptibly, over very long periods of time, through the action of constant forces such as wind and water. Lyell, along with Scottish farmer and geologist James Hutton, developed the theory of uniformitarianism: The Earth was old; change was slow; what was built up would be eroded away. The process was continual.

Strong stuff for a 22-year-old, but Darwin apparently absorbed it all. "My ideas," he would write later, "come half out of Lyell's brain." Darwin's voyage gave him not only the impetus for serious study but also an opportunity to observe the diversity of life firsthand. The trip also set him considering new ideas about the transformation of species over time.

For the next 20 years, Charles Darwin allowed what he called the "species question" to linger in his mind. He married, fathered ten children, spent eight years describing and classifying the thousands of barnacles he had collected during his travels. He wrote papers but discussed his "development hypothesis" with only a few colleagues, primarily Charles Lyell and Joseph Hooker, a botanist. Darwin hoped that by establishing a secure reputation by publishing unarguable theses, he could secure more ready acceptance for his emerging new theory. Meanwhile another Englishman, 14 years his junior, was developing ideas along the same line as his.

Alfred Russel Wallace had dropped out of school at age of 14. Fascinated by the voyages of explorers, including Darwin, he and a colleague took to sea. Wallace had hoped to

CHARLES DARWIN

Father of evolutionary theory

1809
Born on February 12 in Shrewsbury, Shropshire, England.

1827
Admitted to Christ's College, Cambridge University, preparing for a career in the church.

1829
On an entomological tour of North Wales with F. W. Hope, his interest in insects and biology begins.

1831
Receives an invitation to serve as an unpaid naturalist on the survey ship H.M.S. *Beagle*.

1835
Studies geology, fauna, and flora of Galápagos Islands; makes detailed observations of finches and tortoises.

1839
Elected a fellow of the Royal Society.

1840-46
Publishes works on geology and zoology, based on his experiences aboard the *Beagle*.

1858
Learns about Alfred Russel Wallace's theory of evolution through natural selection, with key concepts closely reflecting his own, as yet unpublished.

1858
Along with Wallace, gives public reading of paper on theory of evolution through natural selection to Linnaean Society of London.

1859
Publishes *On the Origin of Species by Natural Selection*, which is revised six times in Darwin's lifetime.

1882
Dies on April 19 at Downe House, Downe, Kent, England. He is later buried in Westminster Abbey in London.

EVOLUTIONARY THEORY

"If we look into the future," read the London *Times's* obituary for Charles Darwin, "we would see that the debate started by Darwin goes on and on." This American magazine cartoon following Darwin's death shows how some felt about the debate that would not end.

collect specimens in South America and sell them to finance more travel. He was doing well until the ship with all his collections burned. Undeterred, he sailed to the Malay Archipelago and started over. Along the way, he kept thinking about the way species transformed over time.

Like Darwin, Wallace had been influenced by the works of Thomas Malthus, a British clergyman and political economist whose 1798 *Essay on the Principle of Population as it affects the Future Improvement of Society* theorized that in all species, unchecked population growth will eventually outdistance the resources needed for survival. For Malthus, not only was this a mathematical reality—populations grew geometrically; food resources grew arithmetically—it was a reality he could clearly see in the streets of London, where, amid a growing population, the poor went hungry. Without some control on population growth, Malthus warned, the poor would grow poorer and hungrier. Catastrophic epidemics were all that stood in the way of eventual worldwide famine.

What Wallace and Darwin each found intriguing in Malthus's theory was that an increasing population meant competition for survival. "It at once struck me that under these circumstances, favorable variations would tend to be preserved, and unfavorable ones to be destroyed," wrote Darwin of Malthus's ideas. "The results of this would be the formation of new species. Here, then, I had at last got a theory by which to work."

CAUSES OF DISEASE

A lifetime spent practicing medicine and performing post-mortems showed Italian anatomist Giovanni Battista Morgagni that diseases had specific etiologies and pathologies— a concept new to the 18th century.

But Wallace was at work as well, and he sent his completed paper, "On the Tendency of Varieties to Depart Indefinitely from the Original Type," to Darwin. Perhaps, wrote Wallace, if Darwin thought it worthy, he would pass it on to Sir Charles Lyell for publication."

Darwin panicked. Lyell had warned him that Wallace was on the same track. "Your words," he wrote Lyell, "have come true with a vengeance."

Now, when he published his ideas, he would risk being accused of stealing from Wallace. Hooker and Lyell proposed that Darwin write his book anyway, but that both his and Wallace's theories be presented at the same 1858 meeting of the Linnaean Society. Both Darwin and Wallace agreed. Within

1831 – 1865

1831
Scottish botanist Robert Brown discovers the cell nucleus.

1837
Purkinje cells—large neurons with many branching fibers, located in the cerebellum—are discovered.

1857
Louis Pasteur announces that microorganisms cause fermentation.

1858
Charles Darwin and Alfred Wallace independently propose a theory of evolution by natural selection. Darwin publishes his seminal *On the Origin of Species* in 1859.

the year Darwin's *On the Origin of Species by Means of Natural Selection, or the Preser-vation of Favoured Races in the Struggle for Life* was published—and it became a best-seller.

THE CHEMISTRY OF THE BODY

Just as Darwin's understanding of life's origins drew on the scientific work that came before him—Lyell's geology, Malthus's economics, and even Lamarck's Lamarckism—so the eventual understanding of animal physiology—the chemical, physical, and anatomical functions of living creatures—was a result of work in a number of seemingly unrelated scientific disciplines.

The first of these was anatomy (from *ana temnein*, Greek for cut up), which is the name Theophrastus gave to the practice of dissection. Herophilus did history's first human dissections at the Alexandrian medical school around 300 B.C. Erasistratus continued the work. He concluded that air entered the lungs, but he also assumed that air, and not blood, circulated through the heart and arteries. He did figure out how heart valves function, but blood, he presumed, ran only through the veins.

Giovanni Battista Morgagni in Italy developed more useful conclusions based on his anatomical studies, establishing the science of pathology by using his knowledge of anatomy to establish the causes and treatments of diseases. His book *The Seats and Causes of Diseases Investigated by Anatomy,* published in 1761, is a catalog of morbidities, from blood clots to gallstones, but through his careful analyses, Morgagni began to develop new ideas for the diagnosis of disease. His book also provides an overview of the varieties of illness possible in that era—and their poor prognoses.

The microscope provided new clues as to anatomical function. Malpighi recognized the capillary system, which completed Harvey's theory of circulation. Hooke recognized that tissue was made of cells. Swammerdam's dissections of insects proved that even these creatures had intricate working parts

See page 81 for more information about Erasistratus.

1858
German pathologist Rudolf Virchow proposes that cells can arise only from preexisting cells.

1861
Pasteur evolves the germ theory of disease.

1862
Pasteur disproves spontaneous generation of cellular life.

1865
Austrian botanist Gregor Mendel completes his experiments on the crossbreeding of pea plants.

and reproductive systems. Cuvier reported that an organism was of a piece, with anatomical parts to serve each function. The body, as Harvey had exclaimed, was a system like every other system on Earth or in the heavens.

If this was so, did bodily functions comply with the same physical principles that scientists were finding ruled every other system? Were the pumping heart, expanding lungs, contracting muscles, and twitching nerves nothing more than working levers, springs, and fulcrums possibly run by some kind of heat engine?

Complex mechanisms were not unfamiliar to the 17th- and 18th-century mind. In fact, the more bizarre, complex, weird, and wonderful, the better. It was the age of the automaton. People could awaken to the singing of tiny mechanical birds, mechanical fingers in magic boxes answered questions, and robotic human forms played games of chess. Figures moved through framed three-dimensional "paintings" called *tableaux mécaniques,* and automatons performed entire theater productions. Visitors to the gardens of Hellbrunn, near Salzburg, Austria, in 1752 could see some hundred hydraulically operated figures.

Giovanni Borelli, an Italian mathematics professor, was one of many who attempted to see if the human body had a similar mechanical aptitude. Borelli, a friend of Malpighi's, began to analyze the body's mechanics as one would the workings of a machine. He analyzed bird wings and fish muscles, and he accurately described the mechanical forces needed for flying and swimming.

He examined the way the human body adjusts and maintains its center of gravity directly over the feet as if it were a system of weights and pulleys. He measured how much force arm and leg muscles exert and then compared their output with that of similarly proportioned levers. He modeled the movements of walking, running, jumping,

ANTOINE-LAURENT LAVOISIER

Father of modern chemistry

1743
Born on August 26 in Paris.

1764
Receives a degree in law from College Mazarin.

1768
Elected member of the Royal Academy of Sciences, Paris.

1769
Works on the first geologic map of France.

1770
His paper showing that water cannot be transmuted into earth is read at the Royal Society.

1775
Proves that burning metals absorb a vital principle in the air—namely, oxygen.

1775-1792
Becomes commissioner of French Gunpowder and Saltpeter Administration; applies chemical expertise to military projects.

1776
Argues that acids contain oxygen.

1783
Obtains water by combining hydrogen and oxygen.

1787
With three colleagues, publishes *Method of Chemical Nomenclature*, in which he introduces a system of names describing chemical compounds.

1788
Elected member of the Royal Society of London.

1789
Publishes *ElementaryTreatise of Chemistry.*

1794
Dies on May 8 in Paris, executed by guillotine during the French Revolution.

PAGE 270

Just 14 when she married French chemist Antoine Lavoisier, Marie-Anne Pierette Paulze served as his translator and laboratory assistant. Both are shown here in Jacques-Louis David's painting.

See pages 90-91 for more information on the mechanistic theories of the body.

and weight lifting, and then he analyzed the forces and counter-forces involved.

Could the internal organs also have mechanistic analogues? The heart, for Borelli, worked like a piston in a pump cylinder, and he calculated the pressure necessary to move the blood around the body. The stomach, he thought, worked like a grinding machine, the lungs like a set of bellows. To Julian Offroy de la Mettrie, the body was nothing but mechanics. His 1748 book *L'homme machine (Man, a Machine)* presented his extreme and, for the time, shockingly atheistic thesis that human life was basically a set of reactive responses to stimuli. For him, as the liver produced bile, so the brain secreted thought.

The same year that la Mettrie's book came out, Albrecht von Haller, working at the University of Göttingen, Germany, published the first manual of human physiology. A tireless polymath, Haller was a physician, a biologist, a botanist, an anatomist, and an experimental physiologist. He demonstrated the mechanisms connecting the heart and human respiration. His experimentation with muscles and nerves demonstrated that sensation causes little change in the nerves but rather is transferred to the muscles, which then respond.

Haller's work brought him fame and a secure chair at the university, but in 1753 he returned to his native Bern, Switzerland, to complete his eight-volume work *Physiological Elements of the Human Body,* and to write poetry and novels, all of which were well received.

Haller's success with experimentation inspired other researchers. In France, François Magendie became widely known both for his analytic rigor and for his inhumane methodologies. Trained as a chemist, Magendie's early work involved studies of digestion and how ingested chemicals affect the body. He extracted the active ingredients in strychnine, morphine, codeine, and quinine and introduced each of them into use in medicine. Following up on the experiments of Scottish anatomist Charles Bell, who had studied the nerves of the spinal cord, Magendie was able to trace the separate paths taken by the nerves that carry sensations to the brain and those that send signals from the brain to the muscles.

Although Magendie's pioneering work earned him the reputation of being the father of experimental physiology, such a distinction came at a cost. His work often involved cruel experiments on animals. On an 1824 lecture tour in England, Magendie used live dogs to demonstrate the effects of cutting nerves. The demonsration provoked broad revulsion and inspired England's heated antivivisectionist movement.

Magendie's student Claude Bernard nevertheless continued his mentor's vivisectionist methodologies, but he focused on how the body regulated its internal environment. For Bernard, in order for physiology to be correct, it must be correct for all living things. If the body is actually a self-regulating living system, rather than a machine, blood and fluids must be responsible for homeostasis—an internal state of equilibrium in which cells can carry out their activities, such as the exchange of oxygen and carbon dioxide or the absorption of nutrients.

Bernard found that, contrary to the orthodox view, most of the breakdown and absorption of food takes place in the intestines, not the stomach. He identified the sugar-storing substance glycogen in the liver. He determined the role of enzymes in digestion and the method by which carbohydrates are broken down into simple sugars. The body might be an elegant network of circulating fluids inside a biomechanical system of bone and muscle, but it was also becoming clear that life and the body could be understood by reference to the principles of chemistry as well.

Much of this work depended on discoveries made nearly a century earlier when the mystery of phlogiston was finally solved. Although derived from the Greek for inflammable, the word "phlogiston" was put into use by the German physician and chemist George Ernst Stahl. He needed it to identify the substance that he hypothesized was present in all flammable materials, the essential ingredient that enabled them to burn. But what was phlogiston? For Stahl phlogiston was not so much a real substance as it was a hypothetical construct to help him explain combustion. It seemed to him, as it did to many scientists at the time, that the processes of rusting, burning, and respiration were all somehow related.

After Stahl, however, scientists began to consider phlogiston as if it were a real substance. If it was, though, it had some very strange properties. Wood ashes weighed less than the wood, presumably because all the phlogiston had been used up. But sulfur and

JOSEPH PRIESTLEY

Discoverer of oxygen

1733
Born on March 13 near Leeds, England.

1752
Enters the Dissenting Academy in Daventry, Northamptonshire.

1755
Begins working as a minister in Suffolk and Cheshire, England.

1767
Discovers that charcoal can conduct electricity.

1767
Based on his experiments with electricity, elected a fellow of the Royal Society of London.

1767
Encouraged by Benjamin Franklin, publishes *The History and Present State of Electricity, With Original Experiments.*

1771
Discovers that plants release a gas, which he calls dephlogisticated air.

1772
Succeeds in dissolving carbon dioxide in water; publishes the first of his treatises, *Experiments and Observations on Different Kinds of Air.*

1773
Is awarded the Royal Society's Copley Medal for his work on the properties of gases.

1774
Heats red mercuric oxide and, obtaining a colorless gas, identifies it as oxygen.

1794
Emigrates to the United States.

1804
Dies on February 6 in Northumberland, Pennsylvania.

phosphorus, after being burned in air, weighed more than they had before combustion. Antoine Lavoisier, a French chemist, decided that during combustion, the sulfur and phosphorus must be absorbing some part of the air.

Earlier in the century chemists had devised means of trapping gases. The heir to both his father's and mother's fortunes and a capable businessman himself, Lavoisier

had the means to build and equip a laboratory for the study of gases, where he set to work attempting to understand what happens during combustion. Extremely patient, he took painstaking care in his experimentation. When an effort failed to produce results, Lavoisier would stubbornly begin all over again.

In England in 1774, Joseph Priestley had been experimenting with gases as well. He knew that

after a candle burned in a glass chamber, the remaining air would not keep a mouse alive. He found, however, that a small plant placed inside the chamber would make the air breathable again and allow the mouse to keep breathing.

Heating certain compounds of mercury and lead—compounds that we now call oxides—also replenished the unidentified lost gas. A candle exposed to the gas

burned more brightly. Priestley gave the life-giving gas a name: "dephlogisticated air."

Lavoisier's own experiments bore out Priestley's findings, and he began experimenting with the newly discovered gas. He found that it was responsible for the weight gains that occurred when sulfur and phosphorus were burned, as well as for the formation of oxides when metals rusted. Lavoisier called the gas "oxygen," meaning acid-generating. The newfound gas helped him explain the process of combustion, which resulted, he concluded, from a chemical combination between atmospheric oxygen and combustible matter. Since the new gas was the same substance that kept the mouse in the glass chamber alive, Lavoisier felt certain that combustion was in some way related to respiration.

Lavoisier's work took place at a combustible place and time. The French Revolution brought brief jubilation, then sheer chaos to the nation. Lavoisier supported the cause of liberty, but he remained in France too long, for his wealth and financial connections with the monarchy doomed him when the Reign of Terror began. In 1794 he and other wealthy financiers were rounded up and sent to the guillotine.

Hearing of Lavoisier's fate, French mathematician Joseph-Louis Lagrange commented, "It took them only an instant to cut off that head—and a hundred years may not produce another one like it."

PHOTOSYNTHESIS

Photosynthesis is the process by which plants convert inorganic matter such as carbon dioxide and water into organic substances for growth and repair of their own tissue. Although a function mainly of green plants, photosynthesis also occurs in algae and even in a limited number of bacteria. Since most animals are herbivorous (that is, plant eaters), photosynthesis is therefore the basic food supply manufacturing process for just about all living things. It is a process that is driven by sunlight (or artificial light) and that also releases oxygen into the air, which gives it a doubly important role for the animal world and for the environment on Earth.

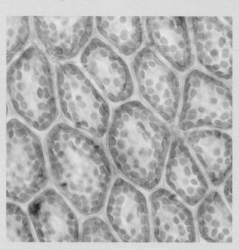

The average leaf of a green plant contains five billion chloroplasts, seen here as tiny dots in cells.

There are two stages in the process of photosynthesis: first, capture and use of the sun's light; and second, carbon fixation.

In green plants, which make up the most important case, photosynthesis takes place mainly in the leaves. Water, an important factor in the process, is absorbed by the roots of the plant and then transported to the leaves. At the same time, carbon dioxide diffuses from the air into the leaves through small holes in the leaves called stomata. The water goes into solution on the moist walls of chloroplasts, tiny lens-shaped bodies that contain the all-important pigment, chlorophyll. The chloroplasts are the multiple arenas where the actual photochemical process takes place.

In the second stage, the chlorophyll acts as a catalyst, helping the light energy split the water molecules into oxygen and hydrogen. A complicated series of chemical reactions—the second stage—begins when some of the hydrogen molecules combine with the carbon from the carbon dioxide to make sugar.

The sugar then becomes the basis for further conversion to the starch, fat, protein, vitamins, and other substances that the plant needs to grow and reproduce. These substance also provide the basis for the food chain of the animal world.

A small portion of the oxygen may remain unused in food production, but it gets used in the plant's respiration process. At night, for example, when there is no energy available from the sun, the plant may produce any energy it still needs by oxidation of its own food. The balance of the oxygen produced in the photosynthetic process is emitted through the stomata, and it goes back out into the atmosphere.

It is no coincidence that chlorophyll—and hence the great majority of our plant world—is green. As it turns out, the red and blue parts of the sunlight spectrum supply all the energy needed by plants. Chlorophyll absorbs most efficiently in these regions. Very little of the green region (between 500 and 600 nanometers) is absorbed; it is therefore reflected, which is why plants appear green.

ALL CELLS COME FROM CELLS

Despite the limited capabilities of early microscopes, scientists energetically advanced their understanding of cells. In the 18th century, anatomists and physiologists began to consider the body as a composite collection of smaller working parts. Anatomists, for instance, believed that the cause of a disease could be found in one of the internal organs. During the brief span of his research, the French anatomist Xavier Bichat identified 21 types of human body tissue. At the same time it was thought possible, analogously, that living tissue might be made up of even smaller units, perhaps similar to the atoms proposed by Greek natural philosophers as early as fifth century B.C. Were they simply smaller organs, and did they represent an atomic structure of the body?

In 1805, a German natural philosopher, Lorenz Oken, suggested that cells were themselves living things, similar to the creatures Leeuwenhoek saw swimming in a magnified drop of water. In 1830 Oken asserted that assemblages of these living units made up the tissue of all plants and animals. His proposition had little impact with the scientific establishment, since Oken had never looked through a microscope.

His assertion seemed less strange, though, when British botanist Robert Brown observed that plant cells contained an inner component, like Leeuwenhoek's animalcules, which Brown called a nucleus. Czech physiologist Jan Evangelista Purkinje, known primarily for his work on vision, observed that the cells of animal tissue were not hollow, but filled with what he called protoplasm. Purkinje also reported that he had witnessed cells dividing.

Although philosophy was insufficient to provide proof of cell structure and function, observational science was stymied by the lack of better technology. Microscope lenses were good, but not good enough until the refractive haze that affected compound lenses could be lifted. By the 1830s, much of the problem had been solved, and the structures of cells, along with the similarities between plant and animal cells, became much clearer—clear enough for an obstreperous German lawyer turned botanist to declare, in 1837, that the mystery of cells had been solved.

Matthias Jakob Schleiden, by 1837 no longer practicing law but teaching botany at Jena, Germany, had little patience for the painstaking practice of classifying plants, the work that occupied most botanists. In a paper on plant origins, Schleiden brazenly held the theory that cells formed the essential units of all living organisms.

His claim was backed up by the work of his friend, physiologist Theodor Schwann. Schwann, who had a less abrasive personality than Schleiden, was investigating digestion and fermentation, or the conversion of sugar into carbon dioxide and alcohol.

The phenomenon had been well known since antiquity, if not since

> **FERMENTATION**
> Once Louis Pasteur recognized that fermentation is due to microorganisms, different types of fermentation, generated by different organisms, were identified. Sour milk involves homolactic fermentation, the holes in Swiss cheese propionic acid fermentation.

See pages 103-106 for more information on early studies of cells.

See pages 104-105 for more information on Schleiden and Schwann.

INHERITED TRAITS

According to studies in the 1860s by Austrian botanist Gregor Mendel, sweet pea generations follow after the crossbreeding of plants with round and wrinkled seeds. The cross produces all round seeds in the first generation, but three round to one wrinkled seed in the third generation.

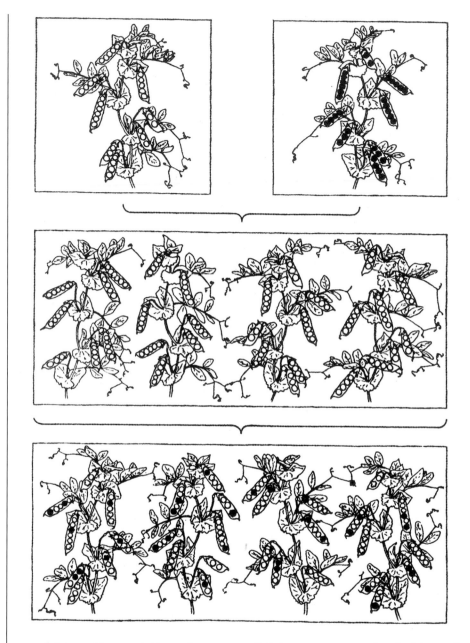

prehistory: Fermentation of sugars in grapes makes wine, and fermentation of sugars in grains produces beer or spirits. But Schwann's assertion that fermentation was part of the normal life processes of living cells—in his studies, yeast—appeared absurd to scientists. Schwann eventually fled to Belgium to escape the derision of his German colleagues. He had been right, however: Living cells obtain their energy by breaking down sugar molecules.

To Schwann, understanding the individual cell was the key to understanding physiology. "Each of the elementary parts possesses a force of its own, a life of its own," he wrote in his 1839 volume, *Microscopical Researches into the Accordance in the Structure and Growth of Animals and Plants.* "The whole organism exists only through the reciprocal action of the single elementary parts."

Although Schwann and Schleiden wrongly believed cells were born of a chemical process akin to the formation of crystals, and that some vital force inspirited cells to work for the organism's common good, they had together succeeded in demarcating the basic parameters of cell theory.

Polish-born pathologist Rudolf Virchow advanced the work of the two Germans. In 1858, in his *Cellular Pathology,* Virchow asserted that vital force had no role in cell theory. Basing his work on discoveries made by fellow Pole Robert Remak, who worked with animal cells, and French botanist Barthélemy Dumortier, who worked with plant cells, Virchow ultimately adopted the motto *Omnis cellula e cellula* ("All cells originate from cells"). No central life force shaped each organism. Cells, he wrote, "are the last link in the great chain of subordinated formations that make up tissues, organs, systems and the individual."

From Virchow's point of view as a pathologist, illness resulted from cells' responses to abnormal conditions. Virchow likened cells to autonomous citizens, all members of a living society in which each individual should act for the well-being of its neighbors and the organism as a whole. Sometimes that did not happen, though, and the result was disease. Any living organism was the sum of its cells, and each one of those cells was a unit unto itself, "vital" and "full of the characteristics of life."

MENDEL

Gregor Mendel, through crossbreeding some 10,000 plants, did not seek fame or acknowledgment of his work on genetics.

ANTISEPSIS

Surgical practice changed dramatically in the years following the discoveries of physicians Ignaz Philipp Semmelweis, Joseph Lister, and Robert Koch. In this photograph, pathologist Rudolf Virchow observes a brain operation in 1900.

See pages 135-36 for more information on Gregor Mendel.

THE LAWS OF INHERITANCE

Although the theories of the cell and of evolution engaged much of the scientific world at the end of the 19th century, neither explained how species passed on their traits or modifications from one generation to the next.

As microscopes continued to improve, it became apparent that cells were wondrously complex, complex enough to bear out Virchow's assertion that cells contained within them all of an organism's characteristics. If that were true, and cells could originate only from other cells, how did the cells transfer all that information from one to another? How did organisms inherit the characteristics of their parents? The theory that would begin to resolve this question came out of the garden of a Bohemian monk.

Johann Mendel's youth, by his own account, had been a poor and unhappy one, and over the course of his life he would apparently suffer several nervous breakdowns. The church seemed his best option to live a secure existence.

He entered the Augustinian monastery at Brünn, Moravia (later Brno, in the Czech Republic) in 1843, at the age of 21, and adopted the name of Gregor. Although he studied science, especially physics, his aptitude didn't seem great. He even failed his teaching certificate exams. He studied physics, mathematics, biology, and botany for two years at the University of Vienna, and then he returned to the monastery in 1854

to teach natural science in a technical high school.

Over the next dozen years, with obsessive precision, Mendel carried out a carefully planned series of experiments. The subjects were pea plants that he grew in the monastery garden. Under ordinary

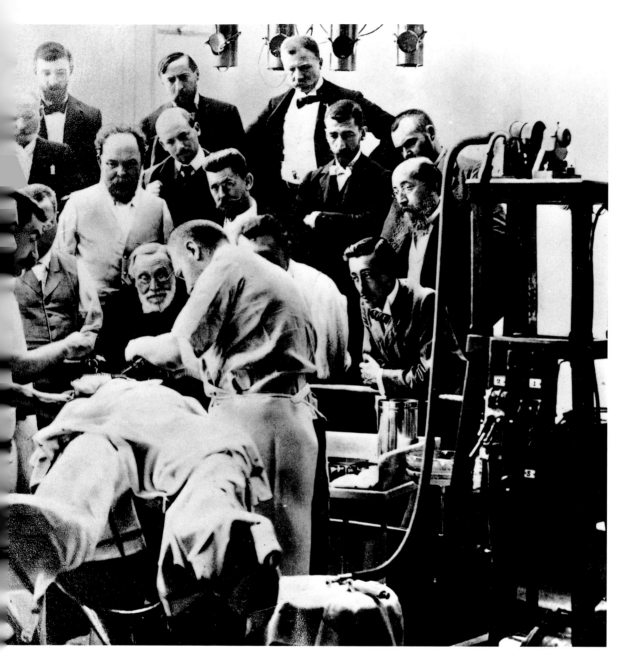

circumstances, these plants would fertilize themselves and produce short and tall plants, plants with differently colored flowers, and plants with differently shaped seeds. Mendel's experiment, to see if there was a system in all of these variations, was to cross-fertilize the plants: tall to tall, short to short, tall to short.

The procedure itself was not new. Artificial crossbreeding to improve varieties of crop plants or lines of domesticated animals had been done since prehistory. Mendel intended to establish a science that explained these age-old breeding practices.

So he proceeded with experimental meticulousness, repeating and rechecking his results, eventually rearing some 10,000 plants. What he found contradicted the prevailing notion at the time, which was that combining two strains of a species simply resulted in offspring with a blend of the characteristics of each.

Crossing tall with tall produced tall. Crossing short with short produced short. But when he crossed tall plants with short plants and grew the seeds that resulted, he didn't end up with all medium-height plants. He didn't end up with a few short and a few tall. He ended up with all tall plants. Surprised by the result, he planted the seeds that these tall plants produced. Those seeds grew into plants of two different sizes, tall and short, with a ratio of three tall plants to every short one. Repeated trials gave the same results. What was happening?

Mendel reasoned that each plant must have two hereditary factors that controlled its height—one from the male parent and one from the female. When he crossed a tall plant with a short one, four combinations of the two factors were logically possible: tall-tall, short-short, tall-short, and short-tall. Because three out of four plants turned out tall, he reasoned, the tall factor must be dominant and the short factor recessive.

When the same ratios described results from experiments on six other traits, Mendel concluded that every trait must be represented by two hereditary factors. Moreover, a sperm or egg cell will have one hereditary factor or the other—say, either a tall or a short—but not both. Finally, he realized that hereditary factors are not passed on as a set. Height and seed shape, for instance, don't necessarily get passed on together. Rather, each germ cell gets a random collection of factors from each parent.

"The striking phenomenon, that hybrids are able to produce, in addition to the two parental types, progeny that resemble themselves is thus explained," wrote Mendel. Short-tall, for instance, will give the same result as tall-short. Or,

1876 – 1916

1876
German embryologists Oskar Hertwig and Hermann Fol show that fertilized eggs possess both male and female nuclei.

1882
German anatomist Walther Flemming investigates cell division and calls the process mitosis.

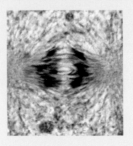

1892
Russian microbiologist Dmitry Ivanovsky discovers that agents smaller than bacteria are linked to disease: the earliest concept of viruses.

in Mendel's words, "it makes no difference to the consequence of fertilization which of the two traits belongs to the pollen and which to the germinal cell."

Mendel published his results in 1866 in the journal of the Brünn Natural Science Society. And although the paper is now recognized as a model of experimental design and reporting, innovative in its use of probability theory and statistical analysis, it was hardly known and rarely cited by botanists or biologists for decades. Mendel sent a copy to Darwin, but there is no evidence that Darwin ever read it. Mendel himself never wrote anything else resulting from his scientific research. Elected abbot of the monastery, he served in that capacity until he died, in 1884.

In 1900, an odd confluence of events conspired to bring Mendel's work to light among those working in the mainstream of science. In fact, soon enough, Mendel's work would define the mainstream of science.

Three researchers, each working independently, reported that they had discovered the process of heredity. Each also declared that in the final stages of their work, or shortly thereafter, they had found the work of an obscure monk who, to the researchers' astonishment, not only had already discovered the basic laws of heredity but had surpassed the work being done by these later researchers.

As geneticists Daniel L. Hartl and Vitezslav Orel put it in a 1992 paper, Mendel, though essentially doing the work of a hybridist, had the remarkable insight to see that "hereditary traits are determined by cellular elements . . . that exist in pairs, undergo segregation and independent assortment, and persist unchanged through successive generations of hereditary transmission." Thirty-five years later, there was not much that the researchers could add.

Just when these researchers discovered the work of Mendel, and how much influence that work then had on their work, has been debated ever since. But scientists granted Mendel all the credit. The burgeoning study of heredity came to be known as Mendelism, and his theories regarding the formation and

BACTERIA EATERS

Bacteriophages (from the Greek for bacteria eater) are viruses that infect bacteria. Discovered in the 1940s, they seemed promising as treatments for diseases such as cholera and bubonic plague. Trials failed, though, and the practice was abandoned with the advent of antibiotics. The viruses are still under research, given the emergence in the 1990s of drug-resistant bacteria.

1902
American geneticist Walter Sutton states that chromosomes are paired and may be the carriers of heredity.

1905
American zoologist Clarence McClung shows that female mammals have two X chromosomes and males have one X and one Y.

1911
American geneticist Thomas Morgan suggests that Mendelian factors—the active elements of heredity proposed by Mendel—are arranged in a line on chromosomes.

1916
Canadian microbiologist Félix d'Hérelle discovers bacteriophages.

**VACCINE
RESEARCH**
Scientists at a London laboratory in February 1946 inject the influenza virus into a sedated ferret in hopes of discovering a cure for the deadly virus. The influenza pandemic of 1918-19 had been the cause of an estimated 25 million deaths worldwide.

development of hybrids and the transfer of heritable factors became known as Mendel's laws. The terms dominant and recessive, which he coined, became common terms used in the science of heredity, and are still essential language in the field today.

Not long after Mendel's work was recognized, researchers began to sense the importance of the threadlike formations known as chromosomes that form and split longitudinally as cells divide. These forms had been seen under microscopes a century earlier, but only with the principles in place, thanks to Mendel and his followers, could scientists begin to understand that their function was to carry the hereditary factors, as Mendel had called them—the bits of life-shaping information that would soon be called genes.

STRANGE NEW FORMS

As early as the 1880s, it was known that certain kinds of bacteria produced certain diseases. Still, diseases such as smallpox and influenza persisted, and no one had been able to find the pathogens that caused them. Indecipherable diseases also struck plants, and of special concern was the unknown pathogen that spread disease among tobacco plants. In 1898, Dutch botanist Martinus Beijerinck found that juice from tobacco plants disfigured by disease could pass the disease on to other tobacco plants. Some investigators suspected the juice contained a toxin, but when even highly diluted juice still passed on the disease, they conceded that an organism of some kind must be responsible.

Whatever pathogen this was, it seemed to defy detection. Since it readily passed through the minute pores of ceramic filters designed to trap bacteria, it had to be smaller than any bacteria. It was invisible under the best microscope of the time, it could not be killed by alcohol, and it could not be grown on an artificial medium. Beijerinck called it *contagium vivum fluidum,* a virus.

Over the next decades methods found to isolate viruses only increased the mystery surrounding them. The largest barely approached visibility under a microscope.

JAMES WATSON

Codiscoverer of DNA's double helix

1928
Born on April 6 in Chicago, Illinois.

1943
At age 15, enters the University of Chicago on a scholarship.

1947
Receives a B.Sc. degree in zoology.

1950
Earns Ph.D. degree in zoology from Indiana University, presenting a thesis on effect of x-rays on bacteriophages.

1950
Spends postdoctoral year in Copenhagen as a Merck Fellow of the National Research Council.

1951
Begins work on structure of DNA with Francis Crick at the Cavendish Laboratories, Cambridge, England.

1953
With Crick, publishes "Molecular Structure of Nucleic Acids," announcing discovery of the structure and function of DNA.

1961
Appointed professor of biology at Harvard.

1962
Receives Nobel Prize for physiology or medicine, sharing it with Francis Crick and Maurice Wilkins.

1968
Publishes his account of the DNA discovery, called *The Double Helix.*

1988
Becomes associate director of Human Genome Project undertaken by National Institutes of Health.

1989
Becomes director of Human Genome Project.

KINGDOMS AND DOMAINS

"Kings play chess on fairly green spaces." That sentence, or others like it, has served for at least a hundred years as a mnemonic by which students remember the taxonomic hierarchy of living organisms developed by Linnaeus in the 18th century: kingdom, phylum, class, order, family, genus, species. That this system has survived three centuries of scientific advance and the discovery of thousands of new species proves Linnaeus's insight into the characters of living things. He wasn't just constructing a convenient filing system. His taxonomy was designed to enable scientists to compare species' anatomical characteristics and, through intelligent comparison, come to understand more about each individual and its relations.

Lepidopterists often pin their specimens to help with identification and categorization.

Much has changed over time, though, especially the criteria used by scientists as they decide where an individual organism belongs in the hierarchy. Before the invention of microscopes, an organism might be categorized according to its size, colorations, type of claw, number of toes, or shape of eyes—not arbitrary criteria, but limited by what could be observed about an organism. The more characteristics compared, the better. That birds and bats both have wings would not mean they belonged to the same species, any more than, as Aristotle realized, fish and dolphins belonged together.

As simple as this sounds, disagreements on taxonomic placement take place over the hierarchy's higher rungs as well. In fact, over the past 50 years the greatest changes have come at the top of the hierarchy. As scientists looked first into the cells and then into the molecular structures of living things, the number of kingdoms has grown from two—animals and plants—to five.

As Linnaeus intended, taxonomy is based upon how closely or distantly organisms are related. With the development of cell theory, it became clear that while the cells of humans and other animals have a nucleus, there was an entire group of animals—bacteria—whose cells had no nucleus. Neither plant nor animal, they were assigned their own kingdom, Monera. Soon the fungi were split from the plant kingdom, and then single-celled organisms assigned their own kingdom: Protista. Then there were five: Animalia, Plantae, Monera, Fungi, and Protista. Viruses were left out, but were viruses living things?

Then molecular studies of DNA began to suggest a different set of distinctions. Taxonomists shifted species from one genus to another, added in species that had been called varieties, and subtracted species, considering them varieties. Then Carl Woese of the University of Illinois found that archaea, an entire group in the Kingdom Monera, were genetically as unlike bacteria as humans are.

So the kingdoms were placed into larger domains, reflecting evolutionary origins. The Eukaryota all had nucleated cells and included the Plantae, Animalia, Fungi, and Protista. The Prokaryota included the Monera: bacteria and blue-green algae. Molecular taxonomists pulled archaea from Prokaryota, increasing the domains to three: Eukaryota, Bacteria, and Archaea.

Since every organism known, every cell known, contai-ned molecules of genetic material as well as a means of respiration and metabolism, how could a virus be a living organism? Could it, in fact, be a living chemical molecule instead?

In 1932, American biochemist Wendell Stanley, in studies for which he would be awarded the 1946 Nobel Prize in chemistry, found that treating concentrated cultures of tobacco virus resulted in crystalline formations that contained the chemicals of proteins and nucleic acids. Stanley found that even if these crystals were broken down and re-formed, the virus was still able to pass on the infection.

Not long after Stanley performed this work, it became clear that although viruses contain the chemistry of life, they are the quintessential parasites. Without a host cell that they can inhabit and whose contents they can hijack to provide them with the means to conduct metabolism, store energy, and reproduce, they remain inert. They have astonishingly sophisticated strategies for penetrating and entering cells, and once inside a living cell, they can reproduce very quickly, creating new generations of encapsulated virus particles called virions, which are exact copies of themselves and which join the brigade, attacking and infecting other cells.

Fortunately, most viruses do not cause disease. Furthermore, one exposure to a virus grants immunity to it and some of its close relatives. The Chinese realized this a thousand years ago and put that knowledge to practical use, controlling outbreaks of smallpox by preparing a powder made from skin already infected by the disease. People as yet unaffected inhaled small amounts of the powder—and they gained immunity to smallpox. Modern vaccinations against viruses such as mumps and measles do the same thing. When the actual disease intrudes on the body, the immune system recognizes the virus and can produce antibodies against it.

Unfortunately, some viruses, such as those for the common cold and the flu viruses, mutate and evolve very quickly. Therefore the vaccination against one flu virus will not be effective against a new strain of the same virus. Unlike bacteria, which can be killed by antibiotics, viruses inhabit the body's cells and can't be killed without killing the cell itself. That is why, despite recognizing the virus that causes AIDS, researchers have not been able to develop a cure for it. HIV, the human immunodeficiency virus, in fact, kills off the cells of the immune system, so antibodies to new infections—even those that can usually be readily fought off—can be fatal.

With all that's known regarding viruses, the question of their evolutionary origins remains uncertain. Since their existence depends on taking over the machinery of host cells, it is likely that they evolved from cells, not the other way around.

But if viruses remain a mystery, the very existence of a pathogen that has no genetic material whatsoever

See pages 106-15 for more information on vaccinations.

See pages 118-20 for more information about viruses.

See pages 120-21 for more information about prions.

CELLULAR RESPIRATION

Cellular respiration is the process by which an organism breaks down food molecules to produce energy. There are two types: aerobic respiration, which occurs in the presence of oxygen, and anaerobic respiration, which occurs in the absence of oxygen.

seemed—and to some still does seem—impossible. A deadly pathogen fitting this description was discovered in the 1980s by American neurologist Stanley B. Prusiner. He identified it as a proteinaceous infectious particle, or prion for short.

Found first in association with the neurological condition in sheep called scrapie and in the ailment called mad cow disease in cattle, prions seemed to be bizarre forms of normal proteins—the large, complex molecules that provide nutrition—in the brain. But somehow the presence of a mutated protein induces normal proteins nearby to copy its mutation. The number of mutated proteins grows, and as it does, the nerve or brain cells inhabited by those proteins die off. The brain becomes riddled with dead cells, giving it a spongelike appearance.

The diseases caused by prions are often the most incurable. They include Creutzfeldt-Jakob disease, Gerstmann-Straussler-Scheinker disease, fatal familial insomnia, and kuru in humans; scrapie, bovine spongiform encephalopathy (mad cow disease); and chronic wasting disease of mule deer and elk.

We are constantly learning more about these prion-based diseases, but the ultimate questions about the formation and persistence of prions remain unsolved.

THE BREATH OF LIFE

In 1779 a British physician, born in Holland, named Jan Ingenhousz published a paper with a portentous title: "Experiments upon Vegetables, Discovering Their great Power of purifying the Common Air in the Sunshine, and of Injur-ing it in the Shade and at Night. To Which is Joined, A new Method of examining the accurate Degree of Salubrity of the Atmosphere."

Through a series of experiments, Ingenhousz observed the release of gases from plants exposed to light and in water. He discovered that plants survive on light, carbon dioxide, and water; and that they produce oxygen, or, as he called it, dephlogistated air. Jan Ingenhousz was observing the process of photosynthesis.

"Plants have a power to correct bad air," he wrote, and he cited Joseph Priestley's earlier discovery that a mouse in a sealed container with a lit candle will die, but when a plant is set into the container as well, the mouse will stay alive.

Since plants release dephlosticated air (or oxygen), and animals need it to survive, Ingenhousz surmised, then the atmosphere in which humans live benefits similarly from the exhalations of the Earth's plant life. It was a great but important leap that would take nearly two centuries to be understood: Two basic chemical reactions, mirror images of one another, are key not only to the processes of living things but also to the creation and maintenance of the Earth's atmosphere.

In photosynthesis, plants take energy from the sun, combine it with water and carbon dioxide, and produce carbohydrates (sugars and starches) and oxygen. Animals take in carbohydrates and oxygen and, from these substances, produce carbon dioxide and energy. By the end of the 19th century, scientists had established that these very processes took place inside the cells of living things. But their actual workings remained obscure until scientists in the 20th century began to understand the cell's astonishing biochemical facility.

In the 1940s British biochemist Robert Hill discovered that during photosynthesis, oxygen is produced by green particles inside the plant cell. These particles are called chloroplasts. Isolated from the cell, chloroplasts could still absorb light and complete photosynthesis. The oxygen required for the chemical reaction came from water molecules, broken apart. American biochemist Melvin Calvin then investigated the path of carbon atoms inside plant cells as they are building carbohydrates. Finally, in the 1980s, the process was discovered: A photon of light initiates a sequence of electron exchanges among molecules that begins photosynthesis.

Energy production in animals' cells proved no easier to understand. In the 19th century French physiologist Claude Bernard had shown that the body could store sugar by turning it into glycogen, a carbohydrate in the liver. It was not until 1935, though, that two Czech-American biochemists, Carl Cori and Gerty Cori, showed how cells break down glycogen to fuel their activities. A few years

later, German-American biochemist Fritz Albert Lipmann confirmed that phosphate molecules called ATP (adenosine triphosphate) take the energy from the breakdown of food molecules and convey it to the rest of the cell. Hans Krebs, a German-born biochemist working in England, figured out the cycle, complex yet elegant, whereby citric acid is metabolized, yielding energy

GREEN WORLD

When photosynthesis developed some 3.5 million years ago, life as we know it began. Using sunlight, CO_2, and water, green plants produce the carbohydrates that feed the world's animal life.

INFLUENCE OF ENVIRONMENT

Russian agricultural scientist Trofim Lysenko asserted that environment alone altered hereditary characteristics—a theory that during the 1930s found more acceptance among the Soviet hierarchy than among scientists.

for cells and releasing carbon dioxide and water. How did these systems evolve?

By the end of the 20th century, molecular biologists had made a convincing case that until 1.75 billion years ago, life on the Earth contained only two categories of cells: prokaryotes, which have no nuclei, and archaea, which lack a nucleus. These two cell forms had been distinguished from one another in the 1970s, by Amer-ican biologist Carl Woese. The archaea were killed by oxygen. Many produced methane, and they lived in some of the most extreme environments on Earth, such as highly saline water, deep muds, and waters at temperatures near boiling. Woese found that although these microbes were distinct from bacteria, their genetic material appeared closer to the cellular chemistry of the higher plants. Both groups may have contributed some of their characteristics to form the third large category: eukaryotes, or cells with true nuclei, the category to which both plants and humans belong.

DECODING LIFE

Just as the technology of microscopes led to the discovery of cells, new technology in the 20th century led to the discovery and understanding of more of the complex structures within the cell.

In 1912 British physicists William Bragg and Lawrence Bragg, father and son, found that when they took an x-ray of a crystal, the beam was scattered by the atoms of the crystal, resulting in images that reflected the three-dimensional arrangements of the molecules in the crystal. They had discovered what would come to be known as x-ray crystallography.

Cell scientists began investigating the individual molecules within the cell. Knowing a molecule's structure gives clues as to its function, and such knowledge could be critical to understanding how cells worked. Proteins, for instance, were found to be constructed like long chains, linked amino acid molecules coiled into a variety of complex shapes.

But although biochemists were solving the complex chemistry of cells, how these molecule-filled envelopes managed to pass on their own—and ultimately the organism's—complete inheritance of biological traits remained a mystery. In fact, approaching the middle of the 20th century, not much more was known about heredity than had been outlined by Gregor Mendel in the 1860s. Better microscopes provided clearer views and made it evident that those long filaments called chromosomes found in the cell's nucleus must play a key role in inheritance. It could plainly be observed that they stretched, duplicated, and separated during cell division.

Mendel had realized that there had to be two factors, as he called them, for each of the inherited traits he studied. But his experiments had focused on only a few traits, and living organisms obviously had many, many more. Could chromosomes account for them all? Many scientists had their doubts, and they continued seeking other explanations for hereditary patterns.

Famously, Russian agricultural scientist Trofim Lysenko mixed Marxism with Lamarckism to declare that environmental factors such as nutrients were responsible for altering hereditary characteristics. His idea became the official Soviet theory for genetics in the 1930s, and once that happened, disagreeing with the science could be dangerous; Russian geneticist Nikolay Vavilov, who doubted Lysenko's ideas and instead advocated gene theory, died in a Soviet prison. Up to World War II, science suffered greatly in the name of national ideology. Many scientists had

FRANKLIN AND RNA

At the crystallography laboratory at Birkbeck College, London, Rosalind Franklin investigated the molecular structure of the tobacco mosaic virus. She discovered that ribonucleic acid (RNA) was a single strand rather than the double helix found in the nucleus of other organisms.

See page 137 for more information on base elements of DNA.

appeared to be a spiral of repeating layers, like a twisting stack of coins, with a constant width. Crystallographer William Astbury had imagined just such a structure, with equal spaces between the base layers, in 1938, but he thought the genetic material must be protein rather than nucleic acid. In 1950, biochemist Erwin Chargaff, studying the distribution of DNA's four base elements, had determined that every living cell contained the same number of thymine (T) as adenine (A) bases, and the same number of guanine (G) as cytosine (C) bases.

Building on their own observations and Astbury's findings, Watson and Crick decided that T always connects with A, and G with C, a solution that could explain why the complicated DNA molecule rarely makes a mistake in replicating itself during cell division. During reproduction, a long DNA strand unravels into two halves. Each base pair separates. Then, in forming a new molecule, a base bonds only with its complement: A finds T, C finds G, and the pairs form up into a new molecule of DNA.

Next it was a matter of conceptualizing these bonded base pairs interlarded with sugars and nucleic acids. Watson and Crick seemed stymied. Pauling in California appeared to be gaining ground, returning to his helix. In a lab not far from Crick and Watson in England, Franklin was getting very close to observing DNA's structure in her increasingly explicit diffraction images. Crick and Watson had consulted with Franklin, but their relationship was far from a collaboration. Female primary investigators were rare in science laboratories in those days, and in fact they were often not even allowed to eat in university dining rooms with their male counterparts. Personality conflicts had estranged Franklin and Wilkins, so she was working very much on her own.

Although the stories differ as to how it happened, at some point Wilkins gave Crick and Watson copies of Franklin's images. They realized—as she already had—that the molecule's shape was a spiral or a helix. The model came into focus: DNA was made of two long, helix-shaped sugar-acid strands, wound around each other like spiral staircases, each step another paired chemical group of atoms. For their work, Crick, Watson, and Wilkins shared the 1962 Nobel Prize for Physiology or Medicine. None of them acknowledged the part played by Franklin, who had died of ovarian cancer in 1958 at the age of 37.

The new model of DNA made it apparent that each gene in the molecule carries the instructions for building one particular protein out of the various amino acids in the cell. Those amino acids, however, are in the cell fluid, or cytoplasm, not in the nucleus, where the DNA resides. American biochemists Mahlon Hoagland and Paul Berg, working independently, found that strands of RNA in the cytoplasm are responsible for capturing amino acids. Different sequences of these short RNA strands, called transfer RNA, or tRNA, determine the assembly patterns of different proteins. They receive information from a kind of molecular courier, another type of RNA called messenger RNA, or mRNA, that "reads" the DNA. When tRNA strands connect to the mRNA, they can determine which amino acids to put together to form which protein. Once the genetic instructions are embodied in the protein, the code, and the organism's inheritance, is set.

DEPTHS AND EXTREMES

When Carl Woese concluded that the archaea were living things, no one realized just how different they were, nor how many different kinds existed, nor how many different places they inhabited. Not only did these creatures have no cell nucleus; they lived at deep-sea rift vents, where temperatures reach over 100°C; in Dead Sea salt ponds; in Yellowstone's hot springs; in the guts of both cows and termites; and deep below Earth's surface, up to 3 kilometers underground, where some may have been secluded for a hundred million years, surviving temperatures of 75°C on diets of water, hydrogen, and carbon dioxide. Considering its living conditions, one such organism recently discovered earned the name *Bacillus infernus*. Thomas Gold of Cornell University calculated that the weight of all subterranean microbes could equal that of all organisms

ROSALIND FRANKLIN

Pioneer of x-ray crystallography

1920
Born on July 25 in London, England.

1938
Enters Newnham College, Cambridge, studying natural science.

1941
Graduates, but remains at Cambridge to investigate gas-phase chromatography under Ronald Norrish.

1942
Studes the physical and chemical structure of coal for the British Coal Utilisation Research Association.

1945
Earns a Ph.D. degree in physical chemistry from Cambridge, studying carbon and graphite microstructures.

1947
Begins working with x-ray crystallography at Laboratoire Central des Services Chimiques de L'Etat in Paris.

1951
Joins the Biophysical Laboratory at Kings College, London; begins work with Maurice Wilkins.

1952
Using x-ray crystallography, captures Photograph 51, best display of the helical structure of the DNA molecule.

1953
Begins working in the Crystallography Laboratory at Birkbeck College, London, investigating the molecular structure of the tobacco mosaic virus.

1958
Dies of ovarian cancer on April 16 in London.

1962
James Watson, Francis Crick, and Maurice Wilkins share the Nobel prize for discovering the structure and function of DNA—work dependent on Franklin's Photograph 51.

DEEP DIVES

Exploration of deep seas awaited the invention of vessels that could tolerate the cold and the pressure. The bathysphere, invented by William Beebe and engineer Otis Barton (at left), was suspended from a surface ship.

above the surface. Explorers were not yet done finding new species. In 2002 geneticist J. Craig Venter set out on a project to explore the diversity of the world's oceans. Setting sail from Nova Scotia on his specially equipped vessel, Venter sailed toward the Sargasso Sea in the Atlantic Ocean, taking 200-liter samples of seawater every 200 miles. Venter found that each milliliter of seawater contained about a million bacteria and ten million viruses. In three years of sailing, he doubled the number of all genes known to science. The oceans were bursting with life, and with life forms never before observed. Venter went on to a similar atmospheric sampling effort.

1935 – 1996

1935
American biochemist Wendell Stanley achieves the crystallization of viruses.

1937
Ukrainian-American geneticist Theodosius Dobzhansky links evolution and genetic mutation in *Genetics and the Origin of Species*.

1937
German-born British biochemist Hans Adolf Krebs discovers the citric acid cycle, central to cellular respiration. It is later renamed the Krebs cycle.

1967
British biologist John Gurden uses nuclear transplantation to clone a clawed frog, the first cloning of a vertebrate.

In the meantime, scientists were still trying to grapple with the new diversity discovered on the deep seabed and even below. A microbe known as Strain 121, an exemplary archaean, was discovered in 2003 by University of Massachusetts microbiologist Derek Lovley. Strain 121 lives in hydrothermal vents at fissures in the ocean floor. Their environment can be as deep as four kilometers beneath the surface, along the mid-oceanic ridges where the Earth's tectonic plates are spreading and where magma erupts at temperatures over 1,000°C, forming new crust for the ocean floor.

The microbe that Lovley found presented what he called "a novel form of respiration": It used iron to digest its food and generate life energy, as animals use oxygen. It had no trouble thriving at 121°C, a temperature at which no previously known microbe could survive. The extreme temperature gave the microbe its name.

The temperature was important for other reasons: First, since the time of Louis Pasteur, 121°C had been the temperature at which surgical instruments were sterilized. Second, a debate raged over whether life had its origins in environments like hydrothermal vents, and the argument hinged on whether life could survive at such high temperatures.

If such unearthly "extremophiles" do exist here on Earth, might it not be possible for such life to exist beneath the surface of other planets? As we come closer to understanding life's origins, the definition of life becomes broader. Strain 121 just "opens that window where life can exist a little bit wider," said Derek Lovley.

Do these deep-ocean vents hold the keys to life's origins? Little is known of microbial life in the oceans, compared with terrestrial ecosystems, which make up 70 percent of the Earth's surface and average two and a half miles deep. The mid-ocean ridge stretches for some 43,500 miles around the planet. The sun's energy penetrates only some thousand feet below the surface. With cold water sinking to the seafloor, the depths are frigid places where whatever is capable of surviving lives in utter

BATHYSPHERE
William Beebe and Otis Barton first descended in the bathysphere in 1930, to a depth of about 1,300 feet. Because of the significant risks associated with exploring in this steel vessel, the bathysphere was replaced with the safer bathyscaphe and mesoscaphe.

1974
Fossils of the hominid ancestor named Lucy are found in Africa, providing more information about the origins of man.

1977
Chemosynthetically based animal communities are discovered around submarine hydrothermal vents on the Galápagos Rift.

1996
Dolly the sheep is born in England: the first clone created from cells of an adult mammal.

GOING UNDER
Alvin, a deep-sea research submarine, made its first dive in 1974 and has since traveled the world's oceans, descending 15,000 feet and discovering hydro-thermal vents and deep-ocean ridges.

darkness and under pressures a thousand times greater than on the surface.

The ocean depths had been presumed an uninhabitable dead zone until 1884, when a French biologist, A. Certes, discovered microbes in the sea at a depth of nearly 17,000 feet. Further proof of the ocean's vitality came during the voyage of the British ship *Challenger*, which sailed between 1872 and 1876 and sampled more than 68,000 nautical miles of ocean, a trip that resulted in 50 volumes of scientific reporting.

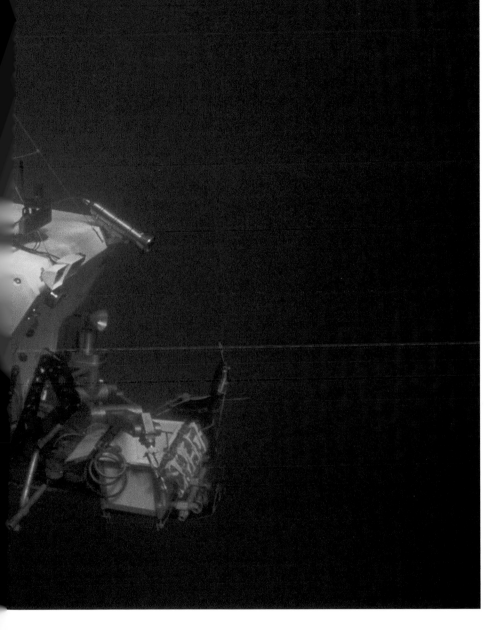

Human exploration of the deep sea began in 1934, when American zoologist William Beebe and engineer Otis Barton descended to 3,000 feet inside the bathysphere, a spherical steel vessel suspended by cable from a ship on the ocean's surface. Maneuvering the tethered craft was difficult and dangerous. If the cable was cut, the bathysphere would have sunk like a cannonball. Beebe, a stylish writer, gazed all the while through the craft's porthole, taking notes and making dramatic observations of the creatures he observed.

In 1953, Swiss-born Belgian physicist Auguste Piccard, after a lifetime of work exploring the atmosphere in hot-air balloons of his own design, descended 10,000 feet below the surface of the sea in his bathyscaphe, a word taken from the Greek *bathos* (deep) and *skaphos* (vessel). A small submarine-shaped diving vessel, powered by propeller, hung suspended from a liquid-filled surface float. In 1960, two years before his death, Piccard watched with pride as a second version of the bathyscaphe, manned by his son, Jacques, descended more than 35,000 feet into the Marianas Trench near Guam, the deepest spot on Earth.

In 1977, two geologists on a joint French-American research submarine named *Alvin*, a highly maneuverable, 25-foot long, submersible vessel, dove into the Galápagos Rift off the coast of Ecuador. They discovered hot springs, one and a half miles down, and found the area teeming with weird sea life. While scientists had assumed that deep-ocean ridges might hold geothermal vents—hot springs spouting superheated water up through fissures in the seafloor—they did not expect to find any life in these sulfurous environments, bubbling at around 300°C. But, much to their surprise, there they were: exotic clams, crabs, giant mussels, tubeworms two meters long, sea anemones, and even large fish.

How did they live? John Corliss, one of the geologists aboard *Alvin* when the first of these communities was discovered, proposed in 1981 that, in the absence of sunlight, the heat plus dissolved hydrogen sulfide and methane in the fluids erupting from the seabed might provide ample energy to support life.

If his hypothesis is true, these seabed ecosystems demonstrate a unique set of adaptations, where chemical energy and chemosynthesis replace light energy and photosynthesis. Heat-resistant microbes such as Strain 121 form the base of this food chain, drawing their energy from the oxidation of sulfides in the hot water and creating biological compounds for the whole system. These chemosynthetic microbes could either be free-living organisms that are food for vent-living mollusks, or they could live in symbiotic relationships with animals further up the food chain.

Some corals survive on the oxygen and waste materials provided by the microscopic zooxanthellae that live within them. Similarly, the fantastictubeworms that thrive around hydrothermal vents depend upon their symbiotic microbes.

Without a mouth, stomach, or intestines, the tubeworm would starve if it weren't for the bristly, red, hemoglobin-rich filaments on its gills, which absorb oxygen, carbon dioxide, and hydrogen sulfide from the surrounding water. The tubeworm's heart pumps these dissolved gases down to an internal sac that fills much of the worm's body, swelling with cells that are packed with bacteria,

some 285 billion to every ounce of tissue. In exchange for the oxygen and hydrogen sulfide they use for their own survival, these worm-dwelling bacteria synthesize organic carbon and with it feed both host worms and themselves.

Although none of these eco-systems has the diversity of species found in a terrestrial ecosystem, the way in which this underwater community makes use of its virtually limitless supply of sulfide-carrying minerals makes

**THE GREAT
RED SPOT**

As the Voyager 1 spacecraft flew by Jupiter in 1977, it captured this photograph of the Great Red Spot, a high-pressure storm that has been observed from Earth for hundreds of years—but still no signs of life. Scientists are searching for life in other, less extreme environments.

these chemosynthetic ecosystems as productive as any coral reef. More than 300 species, most of them previously unknown, have been identified among some 200 vent fields discovered since the late 1970s. Lying in the Pacific, Indian, and Atlantic Oceans, the fields range from the smokers of Galápagos to the huge Lost City in the mid-Atlantic. Other chemosynthetic communities have been found away from the vents, wherever the seabed yields sulfides.

Are these communities completely disconnected from the light-inspired life that goes on at the Earth's surface? Perhaps not totally. The carbon dioxide in the seawater comes from life on the surface, and it appears that the larvae of these hydrothermal creatures may drift up into shallower waters and feed on what drifts down from above. Still, the discovery of chemosynthetic life has moved scientists to reconsider the range of conditions at which life is possible and to reconstruct their theories of the origin of life. These vent habitats create life out of the most basic elements. Did life first evolve in such places or under such conditions?

The vents are no doubt very ancient formations that have survived through various extinctions of life on Earth's surface. Did the temperature gradient between the hot vents and the cold ocean waters around them provide a nursery zone for organic molecules? There is no question that these heat-loving bacteria and archaea are the most ancient living things; it is likely as well that they are the most adaptable.

New communities are being found to exist beneath the surface of the sea bottom and deep in solid rock, where bacteria were found to generate energy from the reaction of hydrogen with carbon dioxide, producing methane and water.

Stephen Giovannoni of Oregon State University has recently discovered a community of bacteria living a thousand feet beneath the floor of the Pacific Ocean. Every microbe he has found there belongs to a completely new species, and this deep-sea community has almost nothing in common with other deep-sea bacterial communities.

The most abundant species is a bacterium that makes its energy through the interaction of hydrogen and nitrate, reacting together to form ammonium. This discovery gives only a glimpse of what may be a vast ecosystem independent of the sun's energy.

All these kinds of new and unusual findings have launched the science of astrobiology—the study of extraterrestrial organic life. Astrobiologists aren't seeking to make contact with humanlike Martians or Venusians, but they are seeking places in the solarsystem or the Milky Way galaxy where chemosynthesis, if not photosynthesis, may have once supported life—places that were thought too hot, cold, or dry to support life, but that now are being reconsidered as living environments, given the new discovery of extremophilic life on Earth.

As of this writing, no such life has been found beyond the planet Earth, but the clues—unearthed as spacecraft make closer observations of Mars and the moons of Jupiter and Saturn—are tantalizing. Could the geysers of water vapor seen on Saturn's tiny moon Enceladus indicate the possibility of life, for example? Certainly these are terribly harsh environments, but not long ago we would have considered the extreme habitats on Earth incapable of supporting life as well.

The universe is full of organic molecules—powerful space telescopes have discovered them in clouds surrounding young stars hundreds of millions of light-years away. Perhaps those molecules ride comets through the galaxies. Our understanding of life's possibilities may be just beginning.

5

EARTH & MOON

ON DECEMBER 21, 1968, THREE MEN— Frank Borman, James Lovell, and William Anders—boarded Apollo 8, their command module atop a Saturn V rocket that launched them toward the moon. The crew circled Earth's satellite ten times, then returned to Earth on December 27. It was humankind's first journey to another world, yet the most profound image captured on this historic mission was a photograph of our home planet.

As their tiny craft orbited through the dark shadow, around the far side of the moon, the crew watched Earth as it appeared to rise steadily above the lunar horizon. The famous image that resulted— called "Earthrise"—revealed a blue, cloud-covered world that seemed suspended above the barren moon. Surrounded by the stark blackness of space and in contrast to the desolate black and white landscape of the moon, this first image of Earth from deep space revealed the planet's beauty, grace, and fragility. It provided an entirely new perspective of this pale blue dot that we call home.

The earliest notions of our world can be found in the observations and myths of ancient times. The endless clockwork motion of celestial objects, rising and

PRECEDING PAGES

An allegorical representation of the universe reveals Adam (the sun) and Eve (the moon) on either side of God in the Garden of Eden. Each figure is associated with a symbolic constellation. Beyond the stars is heaven.

See page 176-78 for more information about Isaac Newton.

setting, led early humans to picture Earth at the center of the universe.

FROM MYTH TO SCIENCE

Stories about the origins of Earth have been told and retold in myths around the world. Creation myths from cultures ranging from Navajo to Buddhist describe Earth taking form in the mind of a supreme being who existed before existence itself. The Judeo-Christian God is sometimes depicted as an architect, methodically designing, building Earth from nothing. Icelandic, Norse, Greek, Japanese, Chinese, and Babylonian mythologies tell of creation emerging out of chaos.

In short, it is a quintessentially human impulse to picture how the Earth looks and to explain how it was made. Science requires that such images and explanations match quantitative evidence, though, and not until the 18th century, though, did the theories, equipment, and strong foundation of empirical records and principles of observation exist to help decipher the mysterious workings and origins of our solar system.

With the publication of Isaac Newton's *Principia* in 1687, the basic concepts of celestial mechanics began to be understood and accepted. By the mid-1700s, solar, lunar, and planetary tables had appeared, with rational explanations for small deviations in the motions of the sun, the moon, and the planets. Although these tables were far more accurate than earlier

ca 1800 B.C. – A.D. 132

ca 1800 B.C.
Chinese keep records of earthquakes.

ca 1150 B.C.
The Turin Papyrus, the oldest existing map, is created in Egypt during the reign of Ramses II.

ca 540 B.C.
Greek philosopher Xenophanes suggests that seashell fossils resulted from a great flood, which buried them—an observation corroborated by Giovanni Boccaccio in the 1300s.

ones, but unexplained anomalies in solar system mechanics remained. For example, observation suggested that Jupiter and the moon were speeding up in their orbits while Saturn was slowing down. If these trends continued, Jupiter's orbit would shrink while Saturn's gradually expanded. Eventually Jupiter would meet its end by spiraling into the sun. Saturn would drift away toward the outer reaches of the solar system. And the moon would spiral into Earth. Based on these early observations, the solar system appeared to be doomed.

Three prominent mathematicians—Leonhard Euler, Joseph-Louis Lagrange, and Pierre-Simon de Laplace—studied the problem. Their work revealed two types of variations in the motions of the

ca 530 B.C.
Pythagoras of Samos reasons that the Earth may be spherical, based on the shadow it casts on the moon during eclipses.

ca 450 B.C.
Greek historian Herodotus suggests that earthquakes could significantly alter the shape of the landscape.

ca 235 B.C.
Greek philosopher Eratosthenes performs his experiment to measure Earth's circumference. His estimate is only 15 percent larger than the actual number.

A.D. 132
Chinese engineer Chang Heng develops the first known earthquake recording device, capable of detecting movements too small to be felt by humans.

planets. The first, called periodic variations, subsided relatively quickly, while the second, called secular variations, represented enduring changes. Euler even believed them irreversible. They could go so far as to alter the shape of a planet's orbit. The apparent acceleration and deceleration of Jupiter and Saturn, which we understand in other ways now, were to the 18th century examples of these secular variations.

By 1772, Laplace had proved that the gravitational forces between two planets could not permanently change a planet's orbital period. Building on work done by Lagrange, he later proved that apparent secular variations in the orbits of Jupiter, Saturn, and the moon were really periodic variations across very long time intervals. For Jupiter and Saturn, his calculations revealed that changes in their orbits occurred over a period of roughly 900 years, making them look permanent.

In 1796 Laplace published his *Exposition du système du monde (Demonstration of the World System),* which introduced Newton's celestial mechanics to a wide audience. His later work *Traité de mécanique céleste (Treatise of Celestial Mechanics)* also offered British and American astronomers detailed outlines of the methods he and his colleagues had developed. The work became invaluable to researchers. Laplace's work on orbital variations also led him to develop a stable model of the solar system as well as a model of how the solar system might have looked during the first few moments of its existence. Laplace believed that a giant

gas cloud or nebula was slowly spinning around the sun, and that the planets and their moons condensed out of this cloud.

Today astronomers believe that the solar system formed through the condensation of a slowly rotating, roughly spherical cloud of interstellar gas and dust. The cloud's density may have been enough for it to begin contracting under its own gravity, but it is far more likely that a pressure wave from a nearby event (such as the death of a star in a supernova explosion) started the initial collapse.

As the nebula started to collapse, it began to heat up and spin faster in a rotation that would gradually flatten the cloud to a disk. Matter whirling toward the center of this disk would pick up speed as it fell. Atoms would collide with each other, converting kinetic energy into heat. As more matter accumulated at the center of the disk, the disk spun faster and shrank further and its temperatures and pressures climbed. Meanwhile, gas in the disk began collecting at regular intervals going out from the center, and that material eventually formed into the planets.

Eventually enough matter collected at the center of the disk to form a protostar. The primordial sun achieved the temperature and pressure needed to begin fusing hydrogen into helium, igniting the sun's nuclear furnace. The intense heat of the young sun vaporized nearby grains of water ice and frozen carbon dioxide. These substances could survive only in the outer reaches of the developing

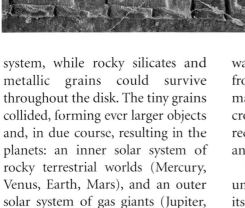

MEASUREMENTTS
When Assyrian ruler
Ashurbanipal traveled
in his chariot, as por-
trayed in this relief,
how did he know how
far he had gone?
Many different and
often inexact units
of distance were
employed in the clas-
sical era. Nowadays,
international coopera-
tion sets rigorous
standards for time,
length, weight, and
other measurements.

system, while rocky silicates and metallic grains could survive throughout the disk. The tiny grains collided, forming ever larger objects and, in due course, resulting in the planets: an inner solar system of rocky terrestrial worlds (Mercury, Venus, Earth, Mars), and an outer solar system of gas giants (Jupiter, Saturn, Uranus, Neptune).

In some ways, the vision is yet another story of the creation and the workings of this world. In other ways, it is extraordinarily different from any myth, for it is mathematically verifiable and carefully cross-referenced with the detailed records of generations of observers and theorists.

The human understanding of the universe, especially our planet and its moon, has evolved from myth to science in these few thousands years. How those concepts, and the beliefs that underpin them, have changed is the story that we tell here.

MEASURING EARTH

Early concepts of Earth's shape and size vary tremendously. The earliest Greeks assumed that the Earth was flat. They questioned what supported the planet; they wondered what held it steady. The earliest known records of Earth's shape come in the poetry of Homer, where Earth is decribed as a flat disk surrounded by an ocean.

The astronomer Thales of Miletus claimed that Earth was flat and that it rested on water. Anaximander, a student of Thales, considered Earth a flat, unsupported cylinder whose depth was one-third its breadth. He proposed that Earth was suspended in emptiness, but that it remained in its place because it was equidistant from all other objects in the universe. He also believed that Earth was supported not by water or any other elemental material but by a spiritual force, the cause of all things, an infinity from which all things rise and into which all things pass away.

Anaximenes of Miletus believed that the Earth was broad, flat, and supported by air. Xenophanes of Colophon asserted that the upper limit of the world was at our feet, where Earth's surface meets the air, and that the lower portion extended downward endlessly.

The first suggestion of a spherical Earth is attributed to Pythagoras, the famous Greek philosopher and mathematician of the sixth century B.C. An advanced thinker for his time, Pythagoras viewed the world as a series of shapes, patterns, and rhythmic cycles. He noted that other celestial bodies such as the moon and the sun are round and that the shadows cast on the moon and sun during an eclipse are round. He also watched ships sailing on the horizon. All phenomena led him to the conclusion that Earth was a sphere.

The idea of a spherical Earth has been attributed to several other ancient Greek philosophers, going back as far as the eighth century B.C. Diogenes Laertius, a biographer of ancient Greek philosophers who wrote in the fifth century, cited both Parmenides and Pythagoras as knowing the world was a sphere. Aristotle's *On the Heavens*, dating from the fourth century B.C., is the earliest known surviving work that

WATER CLOCK

The passage of time could be marked by several ways. One was the dripping of water. The Tower of the Winds, built in Athens around 50 B.C., is thought to have contained an intricate water clock that may have looked like the representation here.

not only declares Earth a sphere but offers proof of the statement.

To explain Earth's spherical shape, along with its stationary position at the center of the universe, Aristotle posited that heavier elements tend to move toward the center. Like Pythagoras, he used the shadow cast by Earth on the moon during a lunar eclipse as proof of Earth's roundness. These shadows were consistently round, and different from the variety of straight-edged, concave, and convex shapes that characterize the moon as it goes through its monthly phases.

Aristotle knew that the stars in the night sky seem to change their position as you move north or south on Earth. As you travel north, stars in the southern part of the sky appear closer to the horizon, or even disappear below it, while stars in the northern part of the sky seem to climb higher above the horizon. The opposite holds true as you travel south. Aristotle used these observations to reason that Earth was a sphere—in fact, a rather small sphere, because moving a relatively short distance caused the stars to shift position noticeably.

A century after Aristotle, Eratosthenes calculated Earth's circumference. Born around 276 B.C. in Cyrene (modern-day Libya), Eratosthenes was an astronomer, geographer, athlete, philosopher, poet, and mathematician. He was also a champion of the pentathlon. He had two nicknames, Pentathlos—for his athletic prowess—and Beta—for the second letter of the Greek alphabet, because he seemed to be second best at so many different things.

Eratosthenes studied many years in Athens. He was a good friend of the mathematician and physicist Archimedes. At roughly the age of 40, Eratosthenes accepted the directorship of the great library in Alexandria, Egypt. This scientific institution was the most advanced learning center of its time, housing exhibition rooms, lecture halls, reading rooms, and quarters for resident and

JOHN HARRISON

Inventor of marine timepieces

1693
Born March 24 in Foulby, Yorkshire, England.

1713-17
Builds three clocks entirely of wood.

1730
Travels to London to present his findings to Edmund Halley, astronomer royal. Hopes to win Longitude Prize by building an accurate maritime clock.

1735
Completes H1, his first attempt at a marine chronometer.

1736
Tests H1 on a sea voyage of some 1,700 nautical miles from London to Lisbon and back.

1737
Begins work on H2, designed to be sturdier than H1.

1740
Realizing flaws in the design of H2, begins work on H3.

1753
Commissions John Jefferys to make H4 more like a large pocket watch, following his design.

1759
H3 fails to reach the level of accuracy required by the Board of Longitude. H4 is completed.

1761-64
His son takes H4 on transatlantic passages, proving it highly reliable. The Board of Longitude doubts the clock's accuracy, though, begrudging Harrison the prize.

1773
Championed by King George III, finally receives a substantial monetary prize from the Board of Longitude.

1776
Dies at his home in Red Lion Square in London on March 24, his 83rd birthday.

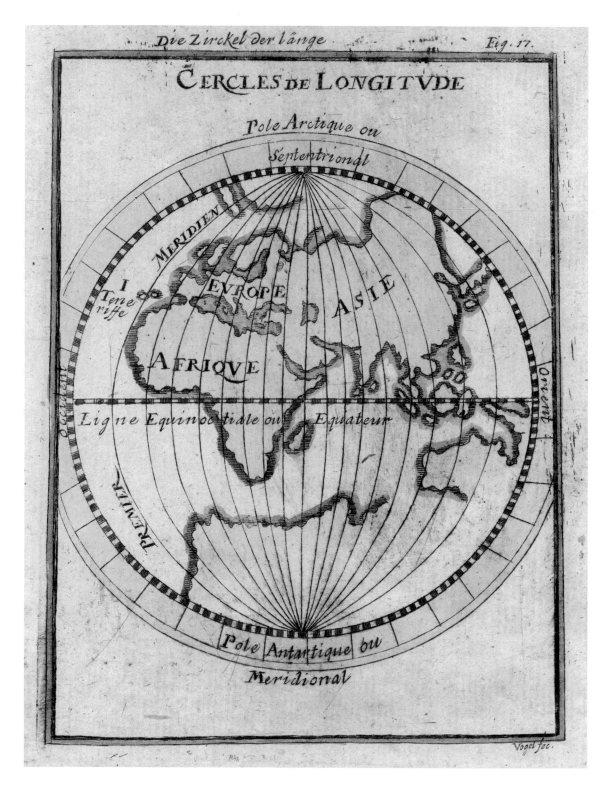

visiting scholars. At its peak, the library held more than 700,000 scrolls of papyrus. As director of the library, Eratosthenes had access to the greatest scientific and literary works of his day.

He learned of an observation that had been in the southern town of Syene, Egypt (now Aswan). On June 21, as the sun reached its highest point in the sky, shadows cast by temple columns disappeared, and the sun completely illuminated the bottom of a well. The account piqued his interest, and Eratosthenes decided to see if the same effect could be observed in Alexandria.

He found that the shadows at midday on June 21 in Alexandria did not grow shorter and shorter, then disappear, as they had in Syene. When the sun reached its highest point in the sky, distinct shadows were still visible. If Earth were flat, he reasoned, objects of the same height would cast shadows of the same length in both cities. But the shadow lengths were different. Because of that, he deduced, Earth's surface must be curved. With this knowledge at hand, Eratosthenes set out to calculate Earth's size.

The details of the procedure that Eratosthenes followed are not known. His original work, *On the Measurement of the Earth,* was lost. We do, however, know that he had access to the work of Euclid, circa 300 B.C., and to other mathematical and scientific works of his day. Eratosthenes must have reasoned that at midday on June 21, for shadows to disappear and for the

bottom of a well to be illuminated, the midday sun must be directly over Syene, or 90° exactly above the horizon. On that same date and time in Alexandria, Eratosthenes measured the sun's highest point above the southern horizon. He found the difference between the sun's position in Alexandria and Syene to be just over 7°—roughly one-fiftieth of the 360° needed to form the full circumference of a circle.

To calculate Earth's circumference using the procedures of geometry, Eratosthenes needed the distance between Alexandria and Syene as well. Caravans traveling between the cities offered an estimate of roughly 5,000 stadia, or approximately 500 miles. Multiplying this distance by 50, the angular difference he had measured, yields a value for Earth's circumference of 250,000 stadia (or about 28,738 miles). Remark-ably, Eratosthenes's calculations were about 15 percent too large: The actual measurement of Earth's circumference is 24,902 miles. By using simple Euclidian geometry and astute observation, Eratosthenes was able to calculate Earth's size more than two millennia ago.

Another astronomer of the third century B.C., Aristarchus of Samos, was the first to suggest that the sun was at the center of the universe. Aristarchus observed the moon moving through Earth's shadow during a lunar eclipse. These observations led him to estimate the moon size as three times smaller than Earth. Using Eratosthenes's calculations, he estimated the moon to be roughly 83,333 stadia (8,285 miles). We now know that the

CIRCLES OF LONGITUDE
This 1690 map of Earth depicts lines of longitude that radiate out from the poles. Lines of longitude are also called meridians.

EARTH'S CIRCUMFERENCES
Earth's equatorial circumference is 24,902.44 miles; Earth's polar circumference is 24,860.535 miles.

See pages 26-27 for more information about early Greek concepts of the Earth's place in the universe.

moon's circumference is 6,785 miles.

Aristarchus used geometry and the phases of the moon to calculate the distances from Earth to the sun and moon. His calculations suggested that the sun was roughly 19 times farther away and 19 times larger than the moon. In fact, the sun is about 389 times farther away from Earth than the moon. Although way off, Aristarchus's calculations did demonstrate that the sun was much larger than Earth, a major step toward the suncentered model of the solar system.

FINDING OUR WAY

Mediterraneans are seafaring people. Homer's epic tales and Egyptian hieroglyphics testify to their early journeys, all of which contributed to understanding the shape and nature of the Earth.

The Phoenicians had circumnavigated Africa 400 years before Eratosthenes calculated Earth's size. To find their way, early sailors hugged coastlines, looking for familiar landmarks to guide them. They also used sounding—measurements of the depth of the ocean—and dead reckoning—positional calculations based on star and planet positions—to steer to their destinations.

In the fourth century B.C., the Greek historian Herodotus wrote a description of how to determine one's distance from Alexandria. In effect, when a lead-weighted line touches the ocean bottom, showing a depth of 11 fathoms, you are roughly a day's journey from Alexandria.

The sun and stars also played a role in helping them find their way. The Phoenicians used Asu (sunrise) and Ereb (sunset) to locate two of the four cardinal points, east and west. At night they looked to the stars, particularly Polaris, the North Star. Earth's geographic North Pole points almost directly toward Polaris, which acts as a beacon, pointing out the third cardinal point.

In the Northern Hemisphere, not only does Polaris point out due north, but its position relative to the horizon indicates latitude. To see Polaris directly overhead at the zenith (90° above the horizon), you must be at the North Pole. When Polaris is halfway between the zenith and the horizon (45° above

EARTH'S CORE IN OLDEN DAYS

In this 1664 vision of Earth's interior, subterranean lakes and rivers surround a central fiery core.

1546 – 1785

1546
German humanist Georgius Agricola writes *On the Nature of Fossils*, a comprehensive classification system of minerals.

1568
Flemish cartographer Gerardus Mercator develops a map projection that allows navigators to plot straight-line courses without having to adjust compass readings.

1600
William Gilbert publishes *De magnete (On the Magnet)*, a study of electricity and magnetism.

1644
René Descartes, in his *Principia philosophiae*, presents his theory that the Earth could have started as a molten mass, the crust forming as part of the cooling process.

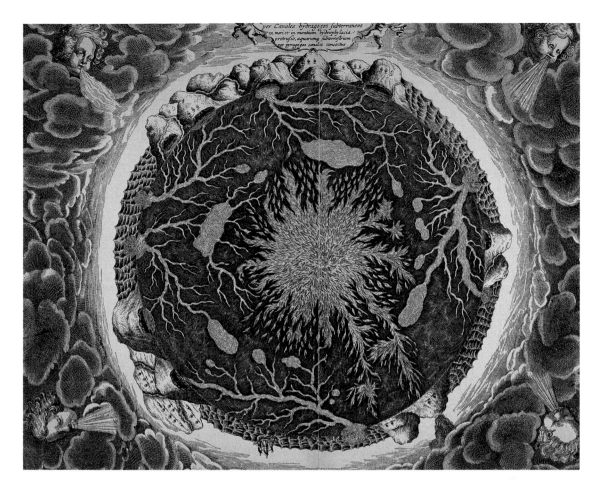

per Canales hydragogos fubterraneos
ex mari et in montium hydrophylacia
protrufio, aquarumq subterrestrium
per porrogatos canales concoctus

the northern horizon), the observer is at 45° north latitude. When Polaris is right on the horizon (0° above the horizon), the observer is at the Equator. Polaris isn't even visible to someone who has sailed into the Southern Hemisphere. In fact, seafarers at southern latitudes have no single bright star that points due south. The bright stars

1666
Danish geologist Nicolaus Steno begins to formulate the law of superposition, which states that older rock always appears below younger rock in sedimentary strata.

1686
British astronomer Edmond Halley creates a world map depicting prevailing wind directions in different regions—the first meteorological chart.

1735
English meteorologist George Hadley describes atmospheric circulation in terms of large-scale cells that move air from the equator to the poles.

1785
Scottish geologist James Hutton expresses the uniformitarian theory that the Earth's landscape was formed gradually by processes that can still be seen today.

that form crosshairs of the constellation Crux, the Southern Cross, point to the south celestial pole, the point about which the stars in the southern sky appear to rotate.

According to the Alexandrian poet Kallimachos, writing in the third century B.C., Thales of Miletus taught Ionian sailors to navigate using the constellation Ursa Minor, the Little Bear. The brightest stars in Ursa Minor form a grouping of seven stars known as the Little Dipper or the Little Wagon. It serves as a good celestial guide in the Northern Hemisphere, since Polaris is the last star in the Dipper's imagined handle.

Later great seafarers included the Vikings. At high northern latitudes, summer months find the days long and the nights short. When the sun does set, it's not for long, and at even higher latitudes the night sky never gets truly dark in the summer months. Instead, the glow of twilight illuminates the sky, blocking the stars from view.

Sailors in the far north had to find navigation methods other than celestial observation. One such method included birds. As wisdom had it, if a seabird had a full beak, it was no doubt headed toward land and its nest. If its beak was empty, it was headed out to sea. Some Nordic ships even brought birds on board that they surmised to be land-loving, like ravens, and deliberately starved them, believing that their flight upon release would show the direction to the closest land.

From the islands of the South Pacific came some of the greatest oceangoing voyagers in history:

the Polynesians, Micronesians, and Melanesians. In relatively small, hand-hewn boats, the early Polynesians covered thousands of nautical miles and spread out to populate many remote islands.

Like peoples of the north, the Polynesians used bird behavior to find their way. They also created elaborate star maps with detailed drawings of constellations that included the parrot and the trigger-fish, gourds and the chief of sharks in the Milky Way.

Although birds and stars helped guide their way, the Polynesians were also astute observers of the ocean's behavior. They were able to harness the prevailing winds and interpret changes in wave patterns along currents and near land.

VOYAGERS
Phoenician merchant galleys such as this sailed Mediterranean trade routes in the seventh century B.C.

Western-tending currents in the Indian Ocean may have aided the explorations of early Indonesians, to whom the people of Madagascar, some 4,000 miles southwest, can trace their lineage.

Maps of the world from the time of Homer, circa 1000 B.C., extend no farther than the countries that ring the Mediterranean Basin. People of this region believed that their landmass was surrounded by water, called Oceanus Fluvius, the ocean-river.

Eratosthenes, sometimes called the father of geography, created the first known geographic map of the world in the third century B.C. The *Hypomnemata geographica* had three parts: historical introduction, mathematical geography (including measurements of Earth), and a map with descriptions of the countries it contained.

The historical introduction highlighted geographical ideas from Homer and Hesiod, then expanded upon them with the knowledge of world geography gained up to Eratosthenes's time. The mathematical section elaborated on the principles of mapmaking, based on the assumption of a spherical Earth. It outlined zones, including the Tropics of Cancer and Capricorn, as well as the poles.

The final section included a detailed map extending west to the Pillars of Hercules, or Gibraltar, and east to unknown lands. As in Homeric maps, a world ocean surrounded the known landmasses.

ERATOSTHENES
Despite his important contributions to the study of geography, Eratosthenes's life ended tragically. He was stricken with blindness in his later years and finally committed suicide by starving himself to death.

But Eratsothenes's map extended much farther east, south, and north than anything conveyed by Homer. It included crude outlines of England, Ireland, India, and a land that may be Sri Lanka or Madagascar.

Each country or region was shaped according to received descriptions and not by any mathematical methods. Italy appeared to be a boot, Spain an ox hide, and Sardinia a human footprint. In other words, for his map, Eratosthenes had gathered knowledge of the known world to date and compiled it. In the same way, he included information of the flora, fauna, and products each country or region produced.

In the second century A.D., Ptolemy created the first world atlas, which contained 27 maps defined with lines of latitude and longitude. Astronomical observations by his predecessors gave him enough information to plot lines of latitude fairly close to their actual positions today. Ptolemy's world map was still centered on the Mediterranean, though, and became increasingly unreliable out toward its far edges. *Terra Incognita*—unknown lands—ring its periphery. Yet Ptolemy's is the first known map without an ocean encircling the central known landmass. It identifies individual bodies of water by name, too, including Oceanus Indicus (the Indian Ocean) and Oceanus Occidentalis (the Atlantic).

Like his geocentric model of the universe, Ptolemy's atlas remained the gold standard for centuries. In the tenth century, the Italians were producing charts that held fairly detailed directions and included measurements of ocean depths and coastline descriptions. Three centuries later, nautical charts with distance scales and bearings appeared. Despite fairly accurate charts, though, navigating at sea still required dead reckoning until the late 1700s. A vessel's latitude could easily be determined by the position of the sun or stars, but accurately determining longitude was altogether another matter.

MEASURING LONGITUDE

The earliest known methods of determining longitude stem from Hipparchus, in the second century B.C., who realized that lunar eclipses could act as time signals simultaneously visible at several points on Earth. Through the ages, lunar eclipses had been observed, their local start and end times recorded. Because Earth makes one rotation every 24 hours, one hour clocks its motion through one twenty-fourth of a circle, or 15° (360° divided by 24). Theoretically, the recorded time differences between one location and another could be used to calculate their respective longitudes, or distances going east and west around the sphere.

In 1631, astronomer Henry Gellibrand requested that Capt. Thomas James, who was sailing for the Northwest Passage, record the time of an eclipse that would occur during his voyage. Using the captain's observations, Gellibrand calculated the difference in longitude between London and Charlton Island in James Bay, Canada. His answer: 79°30', just 15' off.

During the 16th and 17th centuries, well-equipped mariners tried to determine their longitudinal positions by calculating the difference between true north and magnetic north—Earth's geographical pole and the pole indicated by magnetic compasses. In 1600, physician William Gilbert published *De magnete (On the Magnet)*, in which he

COMTE DE BUFFON

Natural historian

1707
Born Georges-Louis Leclerc on September 7 in Montbard, France.

1717
Studies at the Jesuit college in Dijon.

1723
Studies law in Dijon for three years, but decides to pursue the sciences instead.

1728
Studies mathematics, medicine, and botany at Angers.

1734
Elected to the Royal Academy of Sciences in Paris.

1739
Appointed keeper of the royal botanical gardens.

1740
Publishes French translation of Newton's *The Method of Fluxions and Infinite Series*.

1749-67
Publishes first volumes of *Histoire naturelle*, all current knowledge in natural history, geology, and anthropology. Proposes 50 volumes; ultimately produces 36.

1753
Elected to French Academy; presents "Discourse on Style."

1770-83
Publishes nine volumes of *Histoire naturelle* on birds.

1778
Publishes *Époques de la nature*, in which he reconstructs geologic history in stages.

1783-88
Publishes five volumes of *Histoire naturelle* on minerals.

1788
Dies on April 16 in Paris.

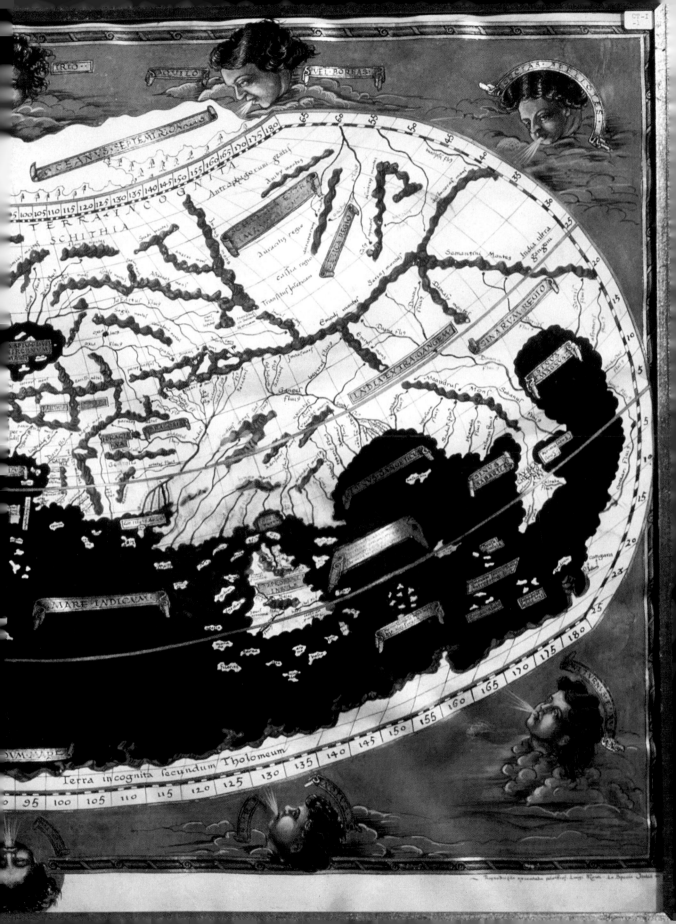

described Earth as a large magnet whose field was similar to that of a lodestone. Gilbert began amassing data on the difference between the magnetic and geographic north poles, which change as one moves east or west. It would be another two centuries, though, before such knowledge could really help mariners at sea.

The hazards of navigating beyond the sight of land were great.

Merchant ships and warships were routinely lost. For a seafaring nation like Britain, such perils threatened national security. In October 1707, a fleet of British warships began their trip home from a battle with the French, only a day's sail from home. As they reached the latitude of roughly 50°N, believing they were in the English Channel, the fleet began sailing east toward Portsmouth. Instead, they found themselves sev-

THE CAVENDISH EXPERIMENT

In the late 1700s, Henry Cavendish confirmed Isaac Newton's law of universal gravitation, expressed as $F = GMm / r^2$, where G is the gravitational constant; M and m are two point masses; r is the distance between M and m; and F is the gravitational force between them. It shows that large masses attract small ones.

Born on October 10, 1731, Cavendish was the first son of Lord Charles Cavendish, also an experimental scientist. After attending Cambridge, Cavendish moved to his father's home on Great Marlborough Street in Soho, London, in 1753. The two men conducted experiments on electricity, magnetism, and heat. Upon his father's death in 1783, Cavendish moved to Clapham Common and continued to work.

Henry Cavendish measured Earth's average density.

He created a torsion balance, based on a design by geologist John Mitchell, composed of a six-foot wooden rod that held two spherical masses at either end. Looking somewhat like a dumbbell, the bar and two spheres hung from the ceiling by

a quartz fiber with a mirror attached. A second dumbbell, holding two 350-pound lead spheres, was placed near the smaller dumbbell so that each large sphere could swivel closer to the smaller dumbbell.

The gravitational attraction between the large and small spheres exerted a torque on the quartz fiber, causing it to twist. Cavendish used a beam of light to measure this twist. He pointed the light toward the mirror, which reflected the beam back at a 90° angle.

As the smaller dumbbell was attracted toward the larger dumbbell, it rotated slightly causing the beam of light to be deflected. Cavendish carefully measured the angular difference in the deflection of the beam. In the process, he not only proved Newton's theory that large masses attract smaller ones, but also determined Earth's average density, which he expressed as specific gravity—a ratio of Earth's density to water's density.

eral degrees west of the channel just off of the Cape of Cornwall. One by one, four ships came to a violent end on the Isles of Scilly. In a matter of minutes, because of navigational error, 2,000 men were lost.

In 1713 a schoolteacher named Humphry Ditton, working with a colleague named William Whiston, developed a scheme to solve the longitude problem. They proposed the idea of anchoring ships at set points across the oceans. At midnight, every ship would fire a large rocket. The explosions would be heard for at least 100 miles in all directions, alerting mariners to the time in Greenwich, England. Theoretically, by comparing Greenwich time with local time, a captain could determine his longitude.

Although an impractical solution, Whiston and Ditton's idea spurred British Parliament to create a Board of Longitude. In 1714, the board established the Longitude Prize, offering the hefty sum of £20,000 to anybody who devised a realistic method for determining a vessel's longitude while at sea to within half a degree, £10,000 for accuracy within one degree, or £15,000 for accuracy within 40 minutes. Techniques deemed feasible by the board would be tested on voyages to the West Indies. The lure of such sums brought out many longitude lunatics, as they were called at the time, who offered up an array of half-baked ideas.

Through all the madness, only two methods were in serious contention. The first method was astronomical. Mariners already determined their latitude by the heavens; it was assumed that a similar method could be devised for determining longitude. Several astronomical methods emerged, including one that relied on the position of the moon relative to the stars and another that relied on the position of Jupiter's four largest moons. Each required careful observation and accurate measurements of heavenly objects, next to impossible on a ship rocking at sea.

JAMES HUTTON

Father of geology

1726
Born on June 3 in Edinburgh, Scotland.

1749
Receives medical degree in Holland.

1750
Decides not to practice medicine; takes up farming on family land. Interest in geology is sparked.

1754
Travels to Holland, Belgium, and France to improve his knowledge of agriculture.

1768
Gives up farming and moves to Edinburgh to pursue his scientific interests.

1783
Royal Society of Edinburgh founded; becomes active member.

1785
Writes "Abstract of a Dissertation Concerning the System of Earth, Its Duration, and Stability," describing his theories of geological processes.

1788
Elected foreign member of French Royal Society of Agriculture.

1788, 1790
Publishes papers on meteorology with Royal Society of Edinburgh.

1794
Publishes three-volume treatise on metaphysics and philosophy, *An Investigation of the Principles of Knowledge*.

1795
Publishes his book *Theory of the Earth* in two volumes; elaborates on earlier claims, provides extensive evidence.

1797
Dies on March 26 in Edinburgh, Scotland.

LEGACIES

This pen-and-ink drawing of John Harrison's H4 time-keeper, right, shows its internal movements. Charles Lyell, pictured opposite, was famous for his influential *Principles of Geology*, which he was in the process of revising for a 12th edition when he died in 1875.

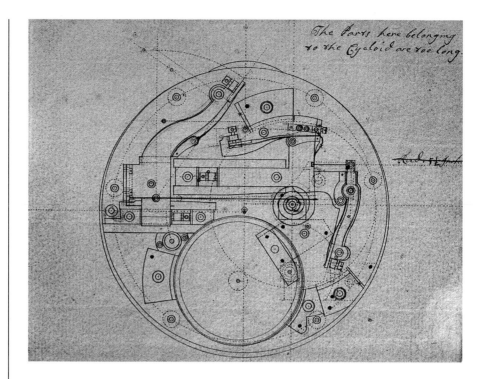

The Parts here belonging to the Cycloid are too long.

The second method depended on time and Earth's rotation on its axis. Clocks of the day were driven by pendulums, which could not keep accurate time on a ship as it rocked, especially during a gale, when navigation was most critical. The problem was how to tell time on board a ship at sea. A young English clock-maker, John Harrison, found the problem most intriguing.

Born in Foulby, a village in the north of England, Harrison was an inquisitive young man. A carpenter to begin with, he had become interested in the inner workings of clocks and began building and repairing them in his spare time. Harrison knew the properties of individual species of wood, and he used this knowledge as he built his wooden clocks. To reduce friction,

1798 – 1920

1798
English physicist Henry Cavendish calculates the average density of the Earth, concluding that the core must contain very dense, heavy metals.

1830-33
English geologist Charles Lyell publishes *Principles of Geology* in three volumes, containing many ideas based on earlier work by James Hutton.

1855
Italian Luigi Palmieri invents the electro-magnetic seismograph.

he made washers and pivots out of lignum vitae, a tropical wood from the Caribbean and South America that contains natural lubricating resins. Harrison's wooden mechanisms constituted an enormous improvement over contemporary metal clocks, which required oil that gummed up and dried out quickly. He also refined the works of the clocks he built, making them accurate to within one second per month. He grappled with the question of whether he could build a clock that would work at sea.

The challenges seemed insurmountable. Humidity and changes in atmospheric pressure and temperature would expand, contract, and eventually warp the mechanism. Since the force of gravity is different at different latitudes, a pendulum's motion would not work consistently. There was also the ever-present question of how to design a pendulum to function well even when tossed about on the waves.

At a young age, Harrison had become a bell ringer in the village church. As he pulled the rope, he would watch the bells swing in graceful arcs. This experience was

1862
Scottish engineer William Thomson (Lord Kelvin) estimates the age of the Earth to be 100 million years.

1872-76
The British ship *Challenger* performs the first major oceanographic expedition; its survey initiates the new science of oceanography.

1912
German geophysicist Alfred Wegener puts forth his theory of continental drift.

1920
Serbian mathematician Milutin Milankovitch shows that Earth's climate goes through periodic changes owing to variations in the planet's orbit.

brass and iron compensated for each other, creating a pendulum that was more stable than it would have been if made of either one of the metals alone.

Next Harrison built two identical clocks. He placed one in a very cold room and the other in a room with a roaring fire. He stood in the doorway between the two rooms, listening to the tick-tock of each clock. He altered the combination of brass and iron wires until the two clocks in the two rooms beat simultaneously. Now he had a pendulum that would be fairly resistant to changes in temperature.

In 1730, Harrison collected all his data showing the effects on clocks of temperature, friction, and gravity, and he headed to London. Quite certain that he now knew enough to build an accurate and reliable sea clock, he presented his findings to Edmund Halley, then the astronomer royal.

Halley introduced Harrison to George Graham, an acclaimed clockmaker in London. Harrison felt a bit mistrustful of Graham, worried that he would pirate his findings. Instead, he found Graham to be a "very honest man" who was so impressed by Harrison's work that he offered Harrison a loan so that he could complete his clock.

Harrison spent the next six years building his first sea clock, known as Harrison One or, today, H1 for short. In place of a pendulum, he devised a balancing mechanism that used springs to create a steady and continuous motion. That way, the clock's operation would not depend on a pendulum or gravity, and wound

invaluable in designing pendulum clocks. Harrison knew that for timekeeping accuracy, the pendulum needed to maintain a constant length in all conditions.

He experimented with different materials. In the process, he noticed that wires made of brass and iron expanded at different rates when heated. He experimented until he came up with just the right combination of wires made of the two metals. Wound tightly together, the once a day, its regular movement would continue, even on a boat as it rocked on the waves.

Harrison carted his prized instrument off to London, where Graham arranged to have it displayed to the scientific community. The clock became an instant celebrity. It soon underwent its first test—a stormy, five-week voyage to Lisbon, Portugal. H1 performed very well, but Harrison felt he could do even better. Suitably impressed, the Board of Longitude advanced Harrison £250 to work on a second model.

Early in the process, Harrison discovered inherent problems with the design of H2. Subjected to certain extreme movements, such as those in rough seas, it lost accuracy. So he began began working on a new model, H3. For 19 years he built and rebuilt this clock, supported by grants from the Board of Longitude, although after a while board members began to question whether he would ever produce his much anticipated marine timekeeper.

Ultimately Harrison decided to abandon large sea clock designs and consider pocket watches instead. In 1753 he designed a small watch and commissioned clockmaker John Jefferys to produce it. Harrison tested the watch, whose accuracy was so sharp that he realized he had spent years on the wrong path. He began designing and making even smaller timekeepers.

Completed in 1759, H4 became the forerunner of all precision watches yet to come. It performed well on its first voyage. The Board of Longitude ordered a second test, a voyage across the Atlantic, from Portsmouth, England, to Barbados. Harrison, now 71 years old, asked his son, William, to take the trip for him.

Before the boat set sail, the watch was calibrated to Portsmouth time, using the sun's position at noon. It was locked in a protective box on board and removed only once a day for careful rewinding. Over the next 46 days, the watch traveled from the chilly climate of England to the steamy Caribbean (roughly 50°F of temperature change). On the morning

HENRY CAVENDISH

Discoverer of hydrogen

1731
Born October 10 in Nice, France.

1749
Enters Peterhouse College, Cambridge.

1753
Leaves Cambridge, without a degree.

1760
Elected fellow of the Royal Society.

1764
Conducts experiments on arsenic.

1766
His discovery of hydrogen is published by the Royal Society in a paper on factitious airs, for which he receives the Copley Medal.

1772, 1776
Publishes papers on electrical phenomena.

1773
Elected fellow of the Society of Antiquities and trustee of the British Museum.

1784-85
Discovers that water is a compound of hydrogen and oxygen.

1784–89
Publishes a series of five papers describing his astronomical inquiries and experiments.

1798
In a paper published by the Royal Society, gives his measurement of the density of the Earth; concludes that Earth's core must be made of very dense metals.

1803
Elected a foreign associate of the Institut de France.

1810
Dies on February 24 in London.

STRATA SMITH

One hundred years after Nicolaus Steno described his principles of super-position and original horizontality, English geologist William Smith was born in Oxfordshire, England. Known as the father of English geology, Smith began life on his family's small farm. With little formal education, he spent his spare time exploring and collecting fossils. He studied geometry, surveying, and mapping, and became proficient enough to work as assistant to surveyor Edward Webb at the age of 18.

In 1791, Smith traveled to Somerset to survey an old estate. While working at one of the estate's mines, he noticed a pattern in the rock layers and discovered that certain layers held specific kinds of fossils.

William Smith's love for geology led him to draw the first large-scale stratigraphic maps.

Smith traveled a great deal for his work. By the time he was 25, he had toured across the entire country. He began to notice that the same ordered fossil groups appeared across England. Fossils in one sedimentary rock were always in succession from bottom to top in that layer. He repeatedly saw the same rock and fossil patterns.

As he traveled the country, Smith collected samples and mapped the various locations he visited, earning him the nickname Strata Smith. It was through this work that he developed his principle of faunal succession. If sedimentary rocks in one location contain fossils in a definite sequence and rocks at another location hold the same sequence, you can infer that the strata are related. This principle allows geologist to define increments of relative time and to date strata relative to each other.

Smith's discovery may seem like common sense, but it was extremely important. In Smith's day, strata were classified into four groupings, proposed by the German geologist Abraham Gottlob Werner. William Smith developed a new system, from which a geologic calendar could be developed.

In 1799, Smith's travels, provided him with enough data to produce the first large-scale geologic map of the area around Bath, Somerset. Sixteen years later, he published the first geologic map of England and Wales. It was enormous—eight feet tall and six feet wide. In 1817, he drew a geologic cross section of the strata from Snowdon to London.

But by 1819, Smith was in debtors' prison. His maps had been plagiarized, leaving him penniless and unrecognized for such breakthrough work. Once released from prison in London, he wandered the north of England, a homeless itinerant surveyor. A few years later, one of his old employers recognized him. Sir John Johnstone helped Smith reenter the Geological Society of London. In 1831 he received the first Wollaston Medal for his lifetime achievements.

DATING EARTH

Six thousand years seems like a long time, but the span of recorded human history on Earth is but a blink on the scale of geologic time. One intellectual challenge has been to find ways to describe and measure that longer span of time, the lifetime of the Earth, which goes back so much further than any human memory.

Up until the 1800s, Western notions of Earth's geological history largely conformed to biblical accounts. One of the most famous of these was that of James Ussher, Anglican Archbishop of Armagh, who boldly announced that he had calculated when the Earth was created: 4004 B.C.

Born in Dublin to an affluent Anglo-Irish family, Ussher was a devoted scholar and a passionate Calvinist. He believed in the predestination of souls, the complete sovereignty of God, and the utmost authority of the Bible. His published work reflected his scholarly interest in church history, and his ideas often showed a pronounced anti-Catholic bent.

In 1648, Ussher published a treatise on the calendar. His most famous work, *Annales veteris testamenti, a prima mundi origine deducti (Annals of the Old Testament, Deduced from the First Origins of the World)*, was published two years later. Ussher followed that work with another, *Annalium pars postierior (Later Additions to the Annals)* in 1654. It was in this volume that he presented his calculations, based on the ages of men in the Old Testament, for the date when the Earth was created.

In today's world of supercomputers, carbon dating, and satellite-generated images of Earth, it seems a bit overly zealous to have made such a claim. Yet when viewed in the context of Ussher's time, it was quite the scholarly feat. Ussher not only added up the successive generations recorded in the Bible, but also matched these events to those recorded in ancient texts. His task had required deep knowledge of languages, the Bible, and ancient history.

Not until the late 18th century did people begin to question received notions about geological history, which, thanks in part to Ussher, included the concept of a 6,000-year-old Earth. Marine fossils found in the Alps and elsewhere were considered proof of Noah's great flood. Earlier civilizations believed fossils grew naturally in the rocks, while some ancient Greeks interpreted dinosaur bones as remnants of a giant race of humans.

See pages 86-87 for more information on Leonardo da Vinci.

Leonardo da Vinci was one of the first to suggest the true origin of fossils. He argued that they were the remnants of ancient marine life and that groups of fossils found in strata were actually living communities of organisms similar to those he had observed on the coast. Leonardo also noticed that some layers were rich in fossils while others held none. This led him to the conclusion that each layer was deposited under different conditions, such as seasonal floods, and not by one big deluge. Da Vinci also believed that fossils found in northern Italy, far from the coast, could not have traveled that far in just 40 days, as in Noah's story.

More than a century after Leonardo, 17th-century naturalist Niels Stensen (known by the Latin version of his name, Nicolaus Steno) was given the head of a large shark

ANCIENT EARTH HISTORY

Walter and Luis Alvarez, son and father, peer through a star dome that shows the location of stars in our sky. The Alvarezes proposed that a cataclysmic meteor caused mass species extinction on Earth.

caught off the coast near Livorno, Italy. A Danish anatomist living in Florence, Steno noticed that the shark's teeth resembled triangular pieces of rock, commonly called *glossopetrae,* tongue stones, that had been found in fossil remains. The tongue stones must actually be shark's teeth, he realized, but how did they turn to stone and how did they lodge in a layer of rock and keep their shape?

Steno lived during a time when 17th-century naturalists were just beginning to understand the properties of matter. They believed solid matter was composed of tiny corpuscles. (Today we would call them molecules.) Steno argued that mineral corpuscles must have replaced corpuscles in the shark's teeth, turning them to stone. The process was so slow, the teeth kept their natural shape. When the shark died, its flesh decomposed but its teeth fell to the ocean floor, where they began to transform into rock. More sediment was deposited on top of the teeth and, over time, this sediment became the rock in which the teeth were embedded. Steno published these ideas in his work, *De solido intra solidum naturaliter contento dissertationis prodromus (Preliminary discourse to a dissertation on a solid body naturally contained within a solid),* in 1669.

Steno not only interpreted fossils correctly; he also discovered some important ideas on how layers of rock, or strata, form. The first is his principle of superposition.

Steno reasoned that in a series of rock layers that weren't severely deformed, the bottom layer was deposited first and therefore is the oldest. Knowing this basic principle, a geologist can determine relative ages of each layer.

Steno's second law is called the principle of original horizontality. Because particles in a fluid settle as a result of gravity, the original layer must be horizontal. Any layers that are steeply inclined must have been disturbed after they were deposited. Steno's final law, called the principle of original lateral continuity, asserts that geological layers originally extended in all directions until they thinned to nothing or butted up against the edge of earlier deposits (as in a depression or a basin).

British scientist Robert Hooke, Newton's nemesis, also argued the organic nature of fossils and challenged the idea that they were all deposited in a single biblical flood. Instead, Hooke suggested that fossils held information about Earth's natural history, and that they could be used to make chronological comparisons of rocks of a similar age. Many of the fossils he studied had no living counterparts, so Hooke stated that some fossils had a "fixed life span"—an early version of the idea of extinction of species.

By the mid-1700s, naturalists in Germany, France, Italy, Scandinavia, Switzerland, and England were illustrating, describing, and naming natural rock divisions. Ordering the strata soon followed.

Johann Gottlob Lehmann, an 18th-century German mineralogist and doctor, was one of the first to put rock types into a chronological order. His three chronological divisions were directly related to the

LAW OF SUPERPOSITION
In undisturbed sedimentary rocks, the law of superposition states that older rocks overlie younger rocks.

See page 48 for more information on Robert Hooke.

THE MOON AND OCEAN TIDES

Nineteenth-century scientists, chief among them Lord Kelvin, sought physical and mathematical laws to describe the rise and fall of the tides. This undated illustration shows the influence of the cycles of the moon on tides on Earth.

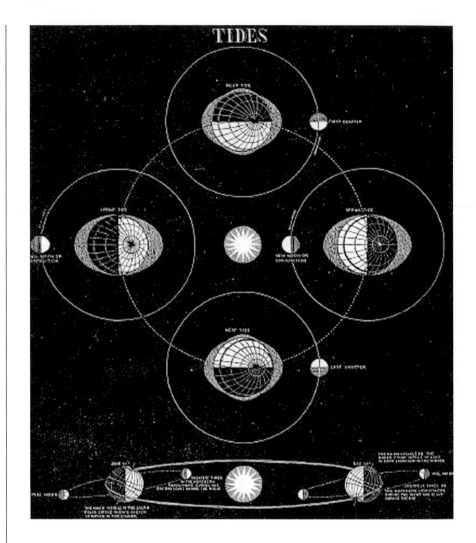

three primary epochs in the Book of Genesis: the creation of man, the corruption and destruction of man, and the dispersion of man. Under Lehmann's classification, the most primitive deposits were fossil-free, steeply tilted, and cut by volcanic dikes and ore veins. He believed these were laid down during the chaos of early creation. Layered, fossil-rich, gently tilted deposits (*Flözgebirge* or layered mountain strata) he considered the result of the great biblical Flood or Deluge. The third division held the youngest

deposits, rocks resulting from earthquakes, volcanic eruptions, after the Flood. Differences in the mineral composition and structure of different layers resulted from ocean fluctuations, he surmised. Lehmann's classification and chronology relied heavily on the belief that catastrophic events changed or formed Earth's surface. Dubbed catastrophism, this theory of sudden, short-lived, violent change harmonized with biblical accounts.

In 1787, Abraham Gottlob Werner took Lehmann's work further by publishing a general theory of the origin and sequence of rocks in Earth's crust.

Werner was born in Wehrau, Prussian Silesia (now Poland), an area rich in deposits of coal, iron, and other minerals. He was educated at Freiberg and Leipzig, studying law and mining, and was appointed inspector and teacher of mining and mineralogy at the Freiburg Mining Academy in 1775. An excellent instructor, Werner attracted students from throughout Europe, many of whom became his disciples.

Werner's predecessors had assumed the existence of an all-encompassing universal ocean that gradually receded, depositing rocks and minerals in its wake. Aptly dubbed Neptunism (for Neptune, the ancient Roman god of the sea), this theory relied heavily on catastrophic events such as the Deluge. Werner adapted many of the tenets of Neptunism into his own theories, but Werner was not a catastrophist. He also believed Earth was older than humanity and did not rely on Scripture to decipher Earth's stratigraphic history.

Werner expanded Lehmann's sequence, dividing the layers of Earth's crust into four successive formations. The first, most primitive series was called *Urgebirge*, or primary mountains. It contained predominantly intrusive igneous and metamorphic rocks (granite, schist, slate, and gneiss, as well as the hydrous magnesium silicate mineral, serpentine). It held no fossils. Werner believed the rocks in these layers were chemically precipitated out of the ocean. Because they were often found high in mountain ranges, the Urgebirge series was considered Earth's original surface.

The second group, called *Übergangsgebirge,* transition mountains or transition series, held slate and some limestone and did include fossils. These rocks were inclined or tilted along the slopes of mountains. Contrary to Steno's principle of original horizontality, Werner believed this incline was the result of having been deposited on Earth's primitive, irregular crust as water was subsiding. Most of these

EUGENE SHOEMAKER

Astrogeologist

1928
Born on April 28 in Los Angeles, California.

1947
Graduates with a bachelor's degree in geology from California Institute of Technology.

1948
At 20, graduates with a master's degree in geology from the California Institute of Technology. Begins working for United States Geological Survey (USGS), exploring for uranium.

1952
Visits Barringer Crater in Arizona.

1960
Earns Ph.D. degree in geology at Princeton University.

1962
Begins teaching at the California Institute of Technology.

1963
Diagnosed with Addison's disease. Establishes USGS Center of Astrogeology, Flagstaff, Arizona; serves as chief scientist.

1973
Initiates Palomar Planet-crossing Asteroid Survey.

1983
Initiates Palomar Asteroid and Comet Survey.

1992
Receives U.S. National Medal of Science.

1993
With his wife, Carolyn, and astronomer David Levy, discovers Comet Shoemaker-Levy 9 at Palomar Observatory.

1994
Watches Comet Shoemaker-Levy 9 explode into Jupiter.

1997
Dies on August 28 in Australia, in a vehicle accident.

rocks were considered chemical precipitates, but early mechanically deposited rocks (such as a hard, impure sandstone called greywacke) also belonged to this group.

Secondary rocks were part of the third series, called *Flöz* or layered strata. This category included sandstones, limestones, gypsum, rock salt, coal, and the fine-grained volcanic rock basalt. Werner argued that basalt sandwiched between other sedimentary layers had precipitated out of the ocean, while basalt that looked like lava flows had come from burning coal beds.

The fourth category filled the lowlands and valley bottoms. Called *Aufgeschwemmte* (water sediments), these alluvial rocks held loose gravel, sand, peat, and some limestones, shales, and sandstones.

Behind all the categories, Werner's concern was to correct Neptunism, which suffered from several theoretical shortcomings. The most obvious was water: Where did all of the water go when the ocean receded? Some Neptunians suggested it flowed to Earth's center, but Werner dismissed that idea as too speculative.

Werner also struggled to account for basalt. He believed that volcanic eruptions could be explained as the combustion of buried coal seams. To Werner, volcanoes were newcomers to Earth's history, dating from after the deposition of secondary coal layers. Despite clear evidence of volcanic island formation witnessed by the Italians for generations, Werner held to this belief.

The Renaissance gave us great minds that began contemplating origins and ideas that differed from those found in the Bible, but not until the late 18th century did scientists begin firmly rejecting Scripture as a source of geologic insight. One of the first to do this was the Scottish philosopher and gentleman farmer James Hutton.

Hutton was trained as a lawyer and a doctor but never practiced either profession. A private income allowed him to pursue his passion, natural philosophy. Although a devout Christian, Hutton ignored geologic lessons of the Bible as well as the idea that Earth's form and features resulted from catastrophic events like the Deluge. He opted to view Earth and its landforms with an impartial mind.

Considered the father of modern geology, Hutton spent years exploring the Scottish highlands and coastlines. While hiking the Cairngorm Mountains in 1764, he found granite intrusions that looked as though they had flowed into the surrounding rock. The texture and complex mineral content of the granite indicated that it must have crystallized from molten rock and did not form by chemical precipitation out of a universal ocean.

The idea that granite originated in hot, molten lava differed greatly from the Neptunian ideal. Hutton's observations also convinced him that the granite was much younger than the rock that surrounded it. In Werner's classification, the two rocks would have been roughly the same age.

On the Berwickshire coast, Hutton found gray shale tilted almost vertically and capped by horizontal layers of red sandstone. This observation led him to conclude that several cycles of deposition, erosion, and uplift had occurred. Such complex features would have taken an enormous amount of time to form. He began to believe that Earth must be older than 6,000 years.

With each successive observation, Hutton became more obsessed with discovering a geological mechanism that could produce the features he saw. He understood that, exposed to the elements, rocks decompose into gravel and eventually soil. He saw the cyclic nature of geologic processes—destruction of old rocks produces new rocks—and believed that the processes observed in the present also occurred in the past, a concept called uniformitarianism. In stark contrast to Werner, Hutton recognized that Earth is dynamic and ever changing.

In 1785, Hutton addressed the Royal Society of Edinburgh. He announced that Earth was infinitely old and outlined his theory that volcanic activity was the primary source for rocks on Earth. Hutton's ideas were presented at the height of Werner's influence. They were dubbed Plutonism—after Pluto, the ancient Roman god of the underworld—and they received a great deal of criticism. Some accused him of poor logic; others declared him a deist or an atheist. This criticism only spurred Hutton to look for geologic

TECTONICS

Wegener's idea of continental drift was first presented in 1912, but it wasn't until the 1960s that it gained wide acceptance. This current map illustrates plate tectonics, which provided an explanation for Wegener's theory.

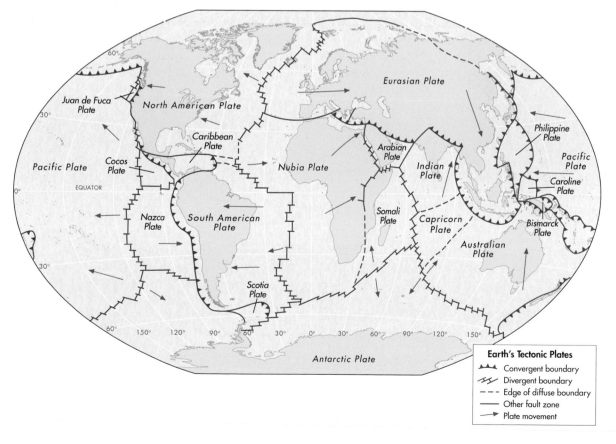

Earth's Tectonic Plates

- ▲▲▲ Convergent boundary
- ⌇⌇ Divergent boundary
- − − − Edge of diffuse boundary
- —— Other fault zone
- ⟶ Plate movement

See pages 260-61 for more information about Buffon.

formations that would prove his theories and sway his detractors. In 1795 he published his two-volume *Theory of the Earth with Proofs and Illustrations.* The book contained not only Hutton's ideas but also those of Georges-Louis Leclerc, Comte de Buffon, and others.

Like Hutton, Buffon believed that Earth had a molten origin. In his 1749 book, *L'histoire naturelle (Natural History),* he suggested that comets hitting the sun had caused solar material to break away; this material formed the planets.

Buffon believed Earth was this kind of cosmic artifact and that, over time, it had undergone six distinct epochs of cooling over some 75,000 years. Buffon also rejected

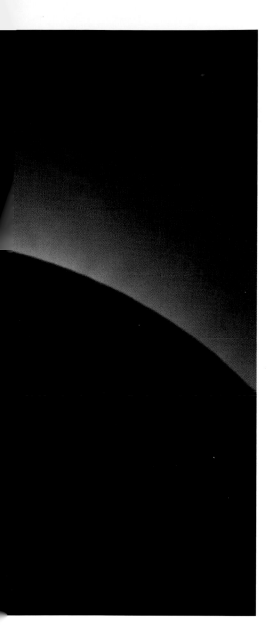

erosion, and deposition. A religious man, convinced that Earth was made with some grand design, Hutton sought meaning in the world around him. Yet his idea of an ageless Earth was blasphemy to many. Although his ideas closely paralleled the Newtonian view of a clockwork universe, his theories and contributions to geologic science were not widely accepted until well after his death.

Born the same year that Hutton died, in 1797, Sir Charles Lyell was also a Scotsman, a lawyer, and a natural philosopher. The eldest of ten children, Lyell began collecting insects in childhood, and it was an interest he pursued throughout his life. In 1816, he entered Exeter College, Oxford. He studied law, but his interest in science continued to occupy him. He joined the Geological Society and soon those interests overshadowed his legal pursuits. By the early 1820s, Lyell was firmly ensconced in his own geological research. He published his magnum opus, *Principles of Geology,* in 1830.

Revised 11 times over 42 years, Lyell's *Principles* synthesized the increasing mass of data supporting Hutton's interpretation of geologic processes. The book outlined in detail the concept of the uniformity of natural processes through time, providing numerous manifestations of those processes.

Lyell took Hutton's uniformitarianism one step further. He argued that the intensity, number, and circumstance of natural processes varied little over time. Catastrophic events like earthquakes

catastrophism, believing that the processes that formed the Earth in the past were still at work in the present day.

Hutton ended his *Theory of the Earth* by stating that Earth offered "no vestige of a beginning, no prospect of an end." For Hutton, the planet was timeless—forever moving through a cycle of volcanism,

RADIOACTIVITY

In a Paris laboratory in 1896, physicist Antoine Henri Becquerel, along with Marie Curie and her husband, Pierre, discovered radioactivity. A tightly sealed canister of photographic film had been placed next to a uranium-bearing mineral, which exposed the film with some kind of "invisible light." Marie Curie recognized that the reaction was due to an atomic process, not a chemical one. She eventually discovered new elements: radium, polonium, and thorium.

Radioactive decay occurs when parent isotopes with unstable nuclei spontaneously transform into one or more different nuclei. The nuclei continue to decay until a stable configuration, called a daughter isotope, is reached. These transformations produce one of three types of emissions: alpha (a helium nucleus), beta (a free electron), and gamma ray (high-energy photons, similar to x-rays).

British physicist Ernest Rutherford extended knowledge further when he discovered that thorium decayed at a fixed rate over time into a series of other elements until it finally comes to rest as a stable form of lead. This discovery led to the idea of a radioactive half-life—the time required for one-half of a radioactive substance to decay. It was also discovered that an isotope's rate of decay could not be altered by heat, cold, change in chemical state, or change in pressure. Because the rate of decay is consistent for any given isotope, the process can be used as a chronometer, or highly accurate timekeeper.

By 1930, decaying uranium isotopes were being used to date early rocks relative to each other. In 1934, the first timescale based on isotopes was published. Through the late 1930s and 1940s, more radioactive series were discovered, their decay process mapped.

Today's geologists use a range of decaying isotopes to date rocks. Rubidium-87, which has a half-life of 47 billion years, ultimately decays to strontium-87, and so this series is used to date objects older than 100 million years.

Radiocarbon dating helps date the most recent organic objects: those younger than 60,000 years. All living things incorporate a fixed ratio of carbon-12 and carbon-14 as long as they are alive, but once an organism dies, carbon-14 decays to nitrogen-14 at a known rate. After 5,730 years, only half of the carbon-14 remains; after another 5,730 years, a quarter of the carbon-14 remains. Now scientists use a simple mathematical formula to determine an artifact's age by measuring the carbon-14 remaining in it.

Becquerel's experiments with radioactivity were crucial for later work by Marie Curie in Paris and Ernest Rutherford in Cambridge.

occurred no more frequently in one epoch than in another.

Lyell became zealous about the idea of uniformity in geology, believing it was his mission to "free the science from Moses." His idea of an efficient, orderly, cyclic, steady-state, dynamic Earth contradicted several basic laws of physics, though—in particular, ideas erupting in the burgeoning field of thermodynamics. The eminent physicist William Thomson, Lord Kelvin, recognized this discrepancy and challenged Lyell on it.

Lord Kelvin argued that it was physically impossible for Earth to behave as a perpetually dynamic, consistently ordered machine. From his knowledge of physics, he believed the planet had changed considerably over time. Scientists in 1846 knew that temperatures increased as you went deeper into the Earth. Kelvin argued that Earth began as a molten sphere and had steadily cooled. The rate of change of temperature, going into the Earth, could be estimated by studying deep mines. With that information, Kelvin extrapolated the rate of cooling backward and calculated Earth's age at 20 million to 30 million years, a time during which the planet had gone through tremendous changes.

Modern geology still includes a theory of uniformitarianism, but not in the strictest Lyellian sense. Catastrophic events have occurred in Earth's recent past, some reminiscent of the Deluge. Catastrophic floods formed the Scablands of western Washington State, for example. Present-day geologists assume a uniformity of cause and effect through time, but understand that rates, intensities, and locations of geologic processes can vary. This concept, called actualism, allows us to coordinate knowledge about the past, the present, and even the future in Earth's history.

See pages 206-10 for more information on Lord Kelvin.

ARCTIC TRAVELS
Alfred Wegener travels by dogsled on his last expedition to Greenland in 1930.

EARTH'S INTERIOR

Through the 18th and 19th centuries, the science of geology developed rapidly. While most discussions focused on Earth's crust and surface features, Buffon, Hutton, Kelvin, and others also worked on theories of the planet's inner workings. It was an American geologist, however, James Dwight Dana, who shed the greatest light on Earth's interior. In 1873, Dana suggested that at its core, the Earth's composition might resemble that of various types of meteorites.

Born in Utica, New York, Dana had an early interest in both geology and zoology. In 1830 he entered Yale, where he studied chemistry and natural history under Benjamin Silliman, founding editor of the *American Journal of Science.* Graduating in 1833, Dana went on to become a mathematics instructor in the Navy. He sailed to the Mediterranean, where he studied Vesuvius. He worked as Silliman's chemistry assistant for two years, beginning in 1836, and published his *System of Mineralogy* in 1837. He was 24 years old.

The next year, Dana joined the team of the United States Exploring Expedition as geologist and mineralogist and embarked on a scientific and surveying expedition of the Pacific Ocean. Beginning in August 1838, the four-year journey took Dana from Virginia, down the eastern coasts of North and South America, then up along the western coast to Chile and Peru, then west across the Pacific to Samoa and Australia. In December 1839, the six-vessel expedition sailed farther south to explore the Antarctic continent west of the Balleny Islands. Then it headed north to the Hawaiian Islands and subsequently up to the Pacific Northwest.

Next Dana became part of an overland party that made its way south toward San Francisco Bay, the first official scientific team to visit and study the Mount Shasta region in northern California. Dana's notes and his sketch of the volcanic mountain were published in the *American Journal of Science and Art* in 1849, during the height of the California gold rush.

Reuniting in San Francisco, the full expedition headed back to the South Pacific, through Polynesia, the Philippines, Borneo, and Malaysia, around the Cape of Good Hope, and north to New York, where they arrived on June 10, 1842. Dana settled in New Haven, Connecticut, and married Silliman's daughter. In 1850 he succeeded his father-in-law at Yale as professor of natural history and geology, a position he held until 1892.

It took the better part of 13 years for Dana to compile the material he gathered during the voyage into a series of scientific papers. He had gained a unique view of Earth and its inner workings, visiting many of the world's most volcanic regions as well as Antarctica, where blackened meteorites are often spotted resting atop the icy-white terrain.

There are two types of meteorites. Roughly 25 percent are metallic meteorites, made of iron, nickel, or some combination thereof, while 75 percent are nonmetallic, or stony, meteorites. Stony meteorites have a

THREE TYPES OF ROCKS

There are three types of rocks: igneous, sedimentary, and metamorphic. Igneous rocks are formed from magma and lava; examples include granite and obsidian. Sedimentary rocks are formed from the compaction and cementation of sediment; examples include limestone and sandstone. Metamorphic rocks are formed from extreme heat and pressure; examples include gneiss and schist.

chemical composition similar to the rocks that make up Earth's crust, except that meteorites contain about 30 percent less oxygen and 40 percent less silicon. Dana suggested that metallic meteorites, with about 80 percent more iron than Earth's crust, are probably representative of Earth's interior.

In the late 1700s, the French physicist Pierre-Simon Marquis de Laplace had theorized that the solar system began as a cloud of gas and dust, spinning off a rotating nebula. "The outer parts of the nebula broke into rings," he wrote, "and the rings rolled themselves into globes—the planets." By the early 1900s, this idea was widely accepted. Geologist Thomas Chrowder Chamberlin and astronomer Forest Ray Moulton, both at the University of Chicago, thought differently. They proposed in 1904 that the planets formed as a result of the sun's encounter with a passing star.

MELTING PEAK

Rising some 19,453 feet above sea level, Kilimanjaro is Africa's highest peak. Recent satellite images reveal rapid snowcap loss, a casualty of global warming. At this rate, the glacier at this mountain's peak will be gone by 2020.

Chamberlin and Moulton thought that the intruding star's gravitational field must have ripped enormous amounts of matter from the sun. These gaseous fragments condensed to form planetesimals (small celestial bodies) and, over time, coalesced to form the planets. This catastrophic planetesimal hypothesis requires that the ejected material be flung from the sun at a very high velocity—too high, studies have since shown, for this to be a valid explanation for the origin of the solar system.

In 1944 Gerard Peter Kuiper and Carl Friedrich von Weizsäcker modified the planetesimal model, resulting in a theory that is widely accepted today. Their theory holds that if a gas cloud, slowly rotating, were disturbed by turbulence—such as a passing star or shock wave from a supernova explosion—vortices might develop within it. They would gather surrounding material, eventually coalescing into planetesimals. Smaller planetesimals would be swept up in the gravity of larger ones, thus forming protoplanets.

Temperatures near the newly ignited sun would have vaporized volatile substances, like hydrogen and helium, which have proved to be a large component of outer planets of the solar system. As the rotating, molten protoplanet Earth cooled, elements began to condense out of the cloud. Dense elements such as iron and nickel migrated toward Earth's core, while lighter elements such as silicon, calcium, aluminum, oxygen, and others began forming the crust. Based on seismic data, modern geologists partition Earth's interior into four primary zones: the crust, the mantle, the liquid outer core, and the solid inner core. Each division is characterized by a particular sort of rock and mineral deposit. Earth's crust holds primarily silica-based rocks, for example. The mantle contains magnesium, iron, calcium, sodium, iron, and silicon oxides. The outer and inner cores contain primarily iron and nickel.

PLATE TECTONICS

In the late 19th century, geologists began to develop theories to explain the formation of mountain ranges and geosynclines—layers of rock that curve or warp downward. It was widely assumed that Earth was in the process of cooling. Dana suggested that, like the shriveled skin of a dried apricot, Earth's rigid crust had wrinkled as its interior shrank during cooling. By measuring folded geosynclines, Dana estimated the crust had contracted by a several hundred kilometers along each mountain belt. With no knowledge of radioactive heating in Earth's interior, this seemed a plausible explanation.

Eduard Suess went further, suggesting that contraction caused rapid, catastrophic changes in Earth's crust. Periods of dramatic mountain building had been followed by long periods of calm, he suggested, and Africa, India, and Australia were once part of a large landmass he called Gondwanaland. As Earth's interior cooled and contracted, the crust wrinkled, forming mountains. Other regions sank, forming oceans.

ISOSTASY

Isostasy is the term used to describe the gravitational equilibrium maintained by Earth's crust on top of its liquid mantle. Since continental crust is less dense than oceanic crust, the continental crust floats on the mantle higher than the oceanic crust.

In 1908, Frank B. Taylor suggested that continents had drifted, wrinkling the crust into mountains. Oceans were folded depressions, made by the leading edges of the moving continents. Earth's crust continued to move, folding up and then uplifting sediments to form mountain ranges and geosynclines.

By 1912 Alfred Lothar Wegener, a German astronomer and meteorologist, staunchly advocated the theory of continental drift. Born in Berlin, the son of a pastor, Wegener was an interdisciplinary scientist, bringing geology, geophysics, climatology, and biology together into a comprehensive theory of Earth's inner workings.

After receiving a Ph.D. degree in astronomy, Wegener began working at the Aeronautic Observatory in Lindenberg, Germany, often doing atmospheric research with his brother. In 1906, the twosome broke the world's record for balloon travel by spending 52 hours in flight. After studying atmospheric phenomena in Greenland, Wegener published *The Thermodynamics of the Atmosphere* in 1910. In a letter to his fiancée, Wegener remarked that the east coast of South America looked as if it fit up against the west coast of Africa. By 1912, he had announced his theory of continental drift.

Wegener began studying rocks from the late Paleozoic era, roughly

DEFORESTATION

As vast expanses of forest and jungle land are cleared of vegetation, Earth's ability to recycle carbon dioxide back into oxygen dwindles. As carbon dioxide increases in the atmosphere, it traps in heat: the greenhouse effect.

200 million to 250 million years ago. He noticed that similar rock deposits could be found on continents that were separated by vast oceans, deposits linking dissimilar regions: South America, Africa, Australia, and Antarctica; North America, Scandinavia, Scotland, and Ireland. He proposed that Earth once held a single supercontinent, which he called Pangaea (from the Greek, meaning whole land). In 1915, Wegener published *Die Entstehung der Kontinente und Ozeane (The Origin of Continents and Oceans)*.

Wegener believed that despite the viscous nature of material below the crust, small forces acting over long periods of time could slowly move blocks of crust. He thought that centrifugal force, tidal forces, and Earth's wobble as it spins on its axis were all plausible contributors to the motion.

One of Wegener's staunchest supporters was a South African geologist, Alexander Logie du Toit. By 1921, du Toit was fervently searching for detailed geologic and fossil evidence in support of Wegener's theory. He discovered that the fossil records showed that the same ancient land plants had grown on continents now separated by vast oceans. Their seeds were enormous, too large to have been transported by the wind. If Wegener's theory was incorrect, how did these plants migrate across such distances? In 1937, du Toit published additional examples to support the theory of continental drift in *Our Wandering Continents*.

Hutton and others had suggested the idea of thermal convection, but it wasn't until a Scottish geologist, Arthur Holmes, began studying radioactivity in Earth's interior that a likely mechanism for continental drift was developed. In 1928, Holmes proposed that an irregular distribution of radioactive isotopes in Earth's lower mantle would disproportionately increase the temperature in that region. The hot mantle material would rise slowly toward the crust, where it would cool and move laterally, carrying Earth's crust along with it.

Over the years more supporting evidence was uncovered, but most American geologists were not yet convinced. Passionately debated throughout Wegener's life, the argument cooled down after his death. It wasn't until the 1950s, when new evidence for it emerged, that the debate resurfaced.

By then, exploration of Earth's oceans was expanding. A vast mid-ocean ridge, 50,000 kilometers in length, was discovered. Physicists were investigating Earth's magnetic field, and airborne magnetometers, submarine detectors used in World War II, were adapted to map magnetic variations of the ocean floor. The maps revealed a pattern.

By the early 1960s, a striped pattern of alternating magnetic fields had been discovered, laid out in rows on either side of the ridge in the middle of the Atlantic. One stripe reflected Earth's current magnetic field; the other reflected the reverse field. This so-called magnetic stripping is created as the seafloor spreads: Mid-ocean ridges mark areas where Earth's crust is being ripped apart. As the seafloor

spreads, lava rises, creating ridges on either side of the opening. As the rocks cool, their magnetic particles align with Earth's magnetic field, creating a magnetic imprint. The zebralike stripes represent magnetic reversals that occur about every million years, with some occurring as frequently as every 10,000 years.

In 1961, Princeton geologist Harry Hammond Hess reasoned that if Earth's crust spread along oceanic ridges, it must collide elsewhere. He suggested that the Atlantic Ocean was expanding along the mid-Atlantic ridge. If that were true, then, to compensate, the Pacific Ocean must be contracting. Hess theorized that the Pacific crust was descending into deep, narrow canyons along the ocean basin's rim. Seismic data gathered with newly

BLUE DOT

Some 93 million miles from the sun, Earth is a watery oasis in a solar system filled with desolate planets.

347

developed instruments of the 1960s revealed earthquake zones in the same areas where Hess predicted spreading and shrinking.

Today we recognize four types of plate boundaries. Divergent boundaries, like the mid-Atlantic ridge, are areas where new crust is generating as plates pull apart. Convergent boundaries, the second type, occur where the heavier oceanic crust subducts, or sinks, under the lighter continental crust, creating volcanic mountains, such as the Andes, along continental margins.

Another type of convergence is continental-continental, where two continents collide and neither crust is subducted, because the two have similar densities. In this case, the crust buckles and contorts, pushing upward or sideways. The Himalayan Mountains are a striking example of continental-continental convergence.

In transform boundaries, plates slide past each other horizontally. The San Andreas Fault zone, 1,300 kilometers long, is an example of such a boundary. Finally, plate boundary zones are areas where plate boundaries and interactions are unclear. The Alps are a result of such a boundary.

THE ATMOSPHERE AND HYDROSPHERE

Astronomer George Ogden Abell wrote, "We live at the bottom of the ocean of air that envelopes our planet." This life-sustaining ocean is composed of 78 percent nitrogen, 21 percent oxygen, and 1 percent argon, with traces of water vapor, carbon dioxide, and other gases. Our current atmosphere, though, is very different from the one that enveloped primordial Earth.

As Earth began forming in the solar nebula, it probably had a primitive atmosphere of hydrogen and helium. Comparatively rare on Earth, these gases are quite abundant in the universe, so it is likely that they were components of Earth's early atmosphere. Earth's gravity is too weak to hold on to hydrogen and helium gas, though, so these light elementes would easily have reached escape velocity. And once the sun's internal furnace ignited, the solar wind would have swept away any remaining traces of these two gases in the inner solar system.

In 1951, geologist William Walden Rubey suggested that volcanic processes created the gases that make up our atmosphere. About 3.5 billion years ago, Earth's surface would have cooled enough to form a crust. Still replete with volcanoes, Earth would have developed its next atmosphere through the release of gas from molten rock during volcanic activity, in a process called outgassing. The resulting primordial atmosphere would have been composed of water vapor, carbon dioxide, and ammonia, which would have released some nitrogen, but it would have held little or no free oxygen. Over time, Earth continued to cool and to build its atmosphere. Eventually water vapor began to condense, forming clouds and rain that produced the oceans.

There is also speculation that comets bombarded Earth heavily at this time. These dirty snowballs may have seeded the planet with more water and carbon dioxide, as well as other chemicals needed to form primitive amino acids, the building blocks of life. As water began to accumulate, it formed oceans. These large bodies of water dissolved roughly 50 percent of the atmosphere's carbon dioxide—which would later form into carbonate rocks, like limestone.

Fossil evidence reveals that early life, such as cyanobacteria, began to appear around 3.3 billion years ago. Such organisms converted carbon dioxide into oxygen, first oxygenating the oceans and then the atmosphere. As more primitive plants appeared, more carbon dioxide was converted to oxygen, dramatically increasing the overall oxygen levels in the atmosphere. This oxygen also reacted with ammonia to create nitrogen. Soon there formed a layer of ozone—an allotrope, or atomic variant, of oxygen—that served to protect the Earth and the primitive forms of life on it from ultraviolet radiation. Now a third atmosphere, rich in nitrogen and oxygen, had begun to envelope Earth.

PLANETARY SCIENCE

For most of history, astronomers were the ones who studied the objects of our solar system. One of the first was Galileo, who pointed his new telescope toward the moon in 1609, naming the moon's darker areas *maria* (sea in Latin) and its lighter areas *terrae* (land in Latin). Galileo's studies included numerous drawings and detailed measurements of the moon's features. He even used the length of shadows cast by lunar mountains to calculate the mountains' heights.

As the moon makes its way around our planet, it spins on its axis at a rate that matches the speed

See pages 36-37 for more information about Galileo's heavenly finds.

EARTH'S ELEMENTAL COMPOSITION

Only one-quarter of the more than 100 known elements are common on Earth, and more than 95 percent of the universe is composed of the two lightest elements, hydrogen and helium.

As knowledge in the fields of nuclear and stellar physics developed in the mid-20th century, researchers determined that most elements form during the explosive death of stars. Our own solar nebula, from which Earth and the planets formed, was cloud filled with the remnants of dead stars. Practically all the atoms on Earth, scientists now believe, were formed deep inside stars, long before Earth began to come together in that cloud.

As the molten protoplanet Earth cooled to temperatures of 1300°C to 1500°C, the first elements to condense were likely aluminum and titanium, followed by iron, nickel, silicon, cobalt, and magnesium at temperatures of 1000°C to 1300°C. Elements such as oxygen, sodium, and potassium likely condensed at temperatures between 300°C and 1000°C. Earth had to cool down to below 100°C before water formed.

of that monthly journey. Thus the moon's orbital period is the same as the length of its day—27.32 Earth days—and thus it always presents the same face toward Earth. Small variations in the moon's orbit allow us to periodically glimpse just around the corner, but no more than 60 percent of the entire surface can be seen from Earth. As a result, the moon's near side has been extensively mapped.

By the late 1950s, lunar features nearly as small as a kilometer across could be seen with the best Earth-based telescopes. Craters speckled the surface, some as large as 160 kilometers across. From their earthly vantage point, most astronomers believed these craters were volcanic in origin—remnants of the volcanic eruptions presumed to have also created the large black maria. It wasn't until 1960, when Eugene Merle Shoemaker presented his doctoral dissertation, that the true origin of lunar craters began to take shape.

Gene Shoemaker's love for rocks and minerals started at an early age. When he was seven years old, his mother gave him her father's child-hood marbles. The set included some agates and other brightly polished jewels, which captivated the young geologist. Soon he began collecting rocks around his neighborhood and on family trips to places like the Black Hills of Wyoming. In high school he took a job working for a lapidist. There he learned the art of cutting, polishing, and engraving precious stones.

One year before the end of World War II, Shoemaker entered the California Institute of Technology, a 16-year-old freshman. He graduated three years later and in the next year earned his master's degree. In 1948, he joined the United States Geological Survey (USGS) and began searching for uranium deposits in the Colorado Plateau. He also studied volcanic features at Hopi Flats. He also became enthralled with the moon and the idea of traveling there to do research.

A visit to Arizona's Barringer Crater in 1952 put Shoemaker on a lifelong quest to study craters and their origins, but he put that work aside in 1956, when the USGS assigned him to work on a project

ca 1930 – 1985

ca 1930
The first meteorograph is developed by the U.S. Weather Service.

1935
American physicist Charles Richter develops his scale for measuring the magnitude of earthquakes.

1964
The U.S.'s Ranger 7 spacecraft relays the first close-range photographs of the moon.

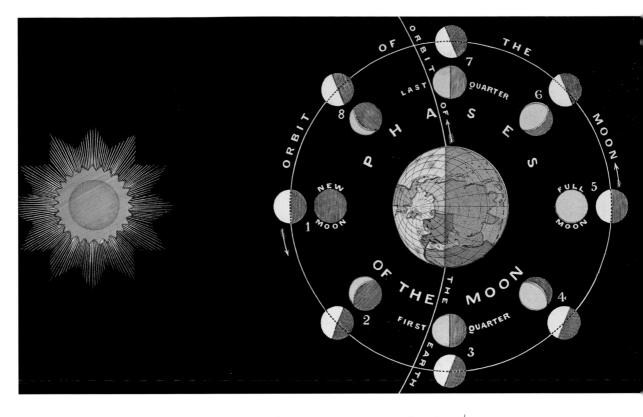

of more pressing national interest: the production of plutonium.

Shoemaker joined a team that was endeavoring to create plutonium by wrapping uranium around a one-megaton nuclear device. His task was to explore the feasibility, nature, and impact of such a large explosion. He visited the atomic bomb test site at Yucca Flats in Nevada, exploring craters there that had been created by kiloton nuclear explosions during tests conducted just a few years earlier. In the midst of this research, Shoemaker noticed the resemblance between the nuclear craters at Yucca Flats and the crater in

MOON PHASES

As the moon circles the Earth, it goes through eight phases: new, first quarter, full, and last quarter, with crescents in between.

1966
The Soviet Union's Luna 9 spacecraft soft-lands on the Moon and relays the first pictures directly form the lunar surface.

1972
The U.S.'s Landsat 1 is launched. It is the first satellite meant to survey the earth's resources from space.

1980
The U.S.'s Magsat satellite completes its mapping of the Earth's magnetic field.

1985
Scientists detect for the first time a hole in the ozone layer above Antarctica.

OUR CHANGING CLIMATE

Diagnosing past climates is a complex task. It consists of gathering statistics and averaging the effects of many meteorologic changes in a given area. Sediments and fossils can be indicators of certain conditions: hot versus cold, wet versus dry, for example.

Glaciers represent one of the best sources for clues to our climatic past. Ice in glaciers hardens into identifiable patterns through time. Petrified tree rings provide indicators of past temperatures and rainfall. Sedimentary rocks provide another long view of a region's climate history, each sedimentary stratum representing a change in conditions.

Perito Moreno Glacier in Argentina is just one of many receding glaciers worldwide.

Our planet has seen ice ages, mini–ice ages, and warming trends. The medieval climatic anomaly, from roughly the 10th to the 14th century, involved a warming trend that partially coincided with increased solar activity. Data for this period point to prolonged droughts in the western United States and alternating droughts and floods in equatorial East Africa.

A little ice age appears to have followed the medieval warm-up, lasting through the middle of the 19th century. Atlantic pack ice grew, warm summers were infrequent in northern Europe, and North America and Europe experienced icy-cold winters. The Thames River in England and canals and rivers in the Netherlands often froze. Even New York Harbor froze during the winter of 1780.

Today our concern is global warming. Prior increases in temperature were most likely part of Earth's natural climate cycles, but the current temperature rise is happening at a much faster pace, very likely exacerbated, if not caused, by human influences. It coincides with the industrial revolution and the use of large quantities of fossil fuels. Carbon emissions have been skyrocketing, increasing atmospheric carbon dioxide by more than 31 percent, methane by 150 percent over pre-industrial times.

As the sun shines on Earth, it heats the surface. When the sun sets, a portion of this heat normally radiates back out into space. Carbon dioxide forms a blanket, trapping excess heat and producing what is now called the greenhouse effect, a major factor in climate change and global warming today.

Glaciers are melting at unprecedented rates. Before the industrial revolution, more than 150 active glaciers occupied the area now designated Glacier National Park. Today there are 27, and even they are at risk. Glaciers in the South American Andes are melting three times faster than they did 50 years ago. The peak of Africa's Mount Kilimanjaro in Tanzania, covered with ice and snow for nearly 11,000 years, is rapidly losing its snowcap, according to satellite images. At this rate, it will be gone by 2020.

At least 25 percent of world's 4,000 mammal species are threatened or endangered, and two out of three bird species are in decline worldwide. Climate change—and habitat destruction by humans—are prime causes. Researchers estimate that half the world's wildlife could become extinct in the 21st century.

This theory proposed that early in its formation, Earth was spinning so rapidly that a chunk of the planet ripped away to become the moon. In 1882, geologist Osmond Fisher suggested that the scar from this rip formed the Pacific Ocean Basin.

The problem with this idea rests in the motions required to rip a chunk of Earth off, then toss it into orbit. Earth would have to spin around once every 2.6 hours for a piece to have been torn away. Both the Earth and the torn chunk would have had far too much angular momentum to produce today's Earth-moon system. Nevertheless, the Darwin-Fisher theory became accepted model for the moon's origin into the 20th century.

The second argument was proposed by astronomer Édouard Albert Roche and others, who argued that the moon and Earth formed together as a double planet. But their rotational and orbiting motions occur too fast for them to have formed at the same time.

In 1909, astronomer Thomas Jefferson Jackson See suggested that the moon and the Earth formed at the same time and in the same vicinity. The moon ventured close enough that it was captured by Earth's gravity. This is an interesting idea, but the Apollo missions revealed that the moon's rocks contain little iron. They do, however, hold each of oxygen's three isotopes, and in amounts nearly matching those found in the Earth's mantle.

In 1974 two geologists, William Kenneth Hartmann and Donald R. Davis, presented a theory that is widely accepted today. At a conference on satellites, they suggested that while Earth was forming in the solar nebula some 4.5 billion years ago, a smaller planetesimal hit it, propelling large amounts of material from its mantle into space.

As the system settled, the ejected material coalesced and formed the moon. Dubbed the "big whack," this theory explains why the moon has a similar composition to rocks found on Earth's surface but not to those found deeper. It also agrees with the Earth-moon system's angular momentum and can explain Earth's 23.5-degree tilt.

The space age began on October 4, 1957, when Russia launched Sputnik 1, the world's first artificial satellite. The size of a baseball, it weighed only 183 pounds, but its significance was profound. It marked the beginning of human investigation of the solar system from outer space, not just from our vantage point on Earth.

Since then, researchers have launched probes to the sun and to every planet in the solar system. Spacecraft carry instruments that draw upon centuries of work in physics, mathematics, and chemistry. They have penetrated the cloud layers of Jupiter, flown by Saturn's moon Titan, examined passing comets, and collected samples from the moon and Mars.

Launched on September 5, 1977, the U.S.'s Voyager 1 spacecraft visited Jupiter and its moons

VOLCANISM ON MARS
Mars has the largest volcanoes in the entire solar system. They are shield volcanoes, the largest type of volcano found on the Earth. Some of the volcanoes on Mars are more than three times as high as the tallest volcanoes on Earth. The biggest volcano on Mars is Olympus Mons, which is 27 kilometers high. By contrast, Mount Everest (not a volcano) is approximately nine kilometers high.

355

ANATOMY OF AN IMPACT

On a warm summer's evening in June 1178, five British monks saw the moon's waxing crescent appear to split in two. According to records kept by a monk named Gervase in Canterbury, England, the moon's northeastern limb appeared to sprout a cloud of "fire and hot coals." Meteor scientists today link this account with the 125,000-megaton explosion that carved the crater known as Giordano Bruno at roughly 36° N, 102° E on the moon.

The study of such craters began in 1609, when Galileo Galilei pointed his telescope toward the moon and realized that the spots he saw were actually depressions. Galileo even observed the craggy rims of moon craters. Nearly 60 years later, Robert Hooke suggested in *Micrographia* that the moon's craters could have been caused by either internal volcanic activity or impact from an external object. Hooke made experimental craters with musket balls in mud, but he decided that the moon's were volcanic in origin. Hooke could not imagine anything flying in at the moon from outer space, then presumed to be empty.

Today we know that most of the moon's surface formed more than three billion years ago, when the solar system was full of asteroids. Scientists now distinguish simple craters, complex craters, and basins on the moon and other planets. Simple craters tend to be bowl-shaped, with smooth, unterraced rims. Complex craters have scalloped inner walls and a central peak (or peaks) lifting from a broad, flat floor. Several impact basins on the moon have been identified, including the Schrödinger Basin and the multiringed Mare Orientale or Eastern Sea.

In this artist's conception, a meteor strikes the Earth, possibly creating our moon.

The moon isn't the only place with craters. Jupiter's moon Callisto is a heavily cratered world showing one prominent impact, the Valhalla Basin, as large as the United States north to south. Mimas, a moon of Saturn, has a large impact crater named Herschel, spanning one-third of its diameter.

Earth has experienced several impacts, too. In 1902, geologist Daniel Moreau Barringer studied a crater 35 miles east of Flagstaff, Arizona, then known as Coon Mountain. Most geologists considered it the result of a volcanic event, but Barringer was convinced it had been formed by the impact of a meteor. He founded a company to mine the meteoritic ore. Today the site bears his name: Barringer Meteor Crater.

On June 30, 1908, in Tunguska, Siberia, a brilliant fireball cut through the daylight sky and exploded before hitting the ground. It left no crater, but shock waves registered on seismographs in Europe. By far the loudest bang, though, occurred 65 million years ago when an asteroid struck Earth, sending a cloud of debris into the atmosphere that shrouded Earth for months, blocking the sun and killing off 75 percent of all species then on Earth. The event marks the Cretaceous-Tertiary (K-T) boundary in Earth's geologic history.

Geologist Walter Alvarez and his father, Luis Alvarez, a Nobel Prize–winning physicist, discovered geological strata containing a clay layer with high levels of iridium, an element common in asteroids but not on Earth. Many now believe that the layer, found worldwide, corresponds to the massive impact event millions of years ago.

in March 1979 before heading to an encounter with Saturn's system in November 1980. On February 14, 1990, some four billion miles from Earth, Voyager 1 turned its cameras toward home.

In contrast to the bright blue world seen by the crew of Apollo 8 some 22 years earlier, Voyager saw Earth as a tiny point of light shaped ever so slightly like a crescent. Surrounding the pale blue dot was a faint red beam of scattered sunlight, a photographic anomaly caused by Earth's proximity to the sun. Now, more than eight billion miles from home, Voyager 1 and its companion, Voyager 2, are at the farthest reaches of the solar system. Both carry disks with sounds and images of Earth. Envoys of our early space explorations, they have also provided us with better understanding of ourselves. No longer do we view our world as the center of the universe. To paraphrase T. S. Eliot's *Four Quartets*, the end of all our exploring brings us back to where we started, so that we may know the place for the first time.

NIGHT SKY

The Milky Way contains several billion stars—most of which are visible from Earth with the naked eye. This star field represents only a tiny fraction of the stars in our galaxy, of which our sun is one.

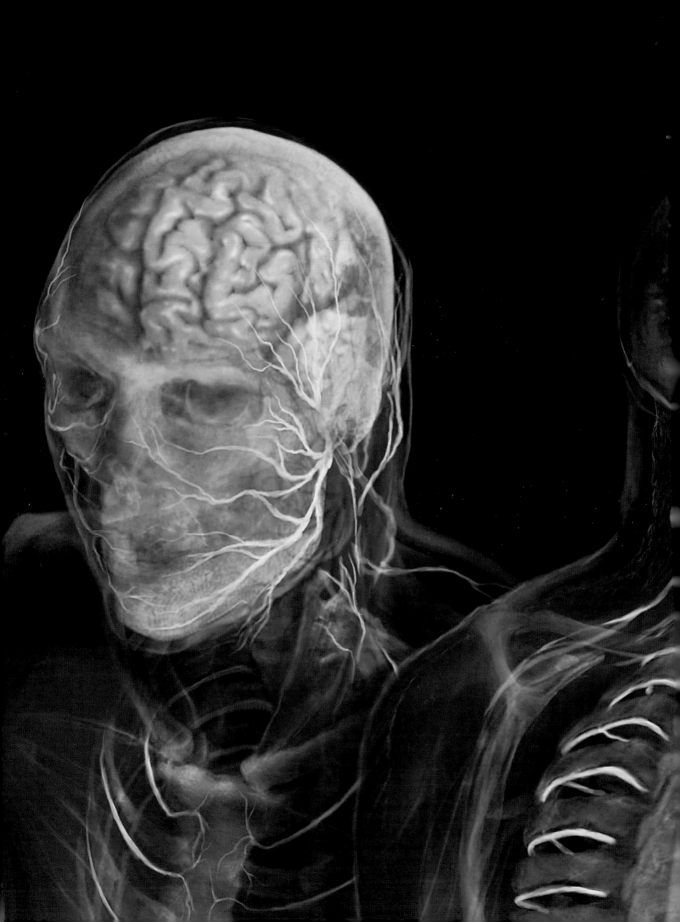

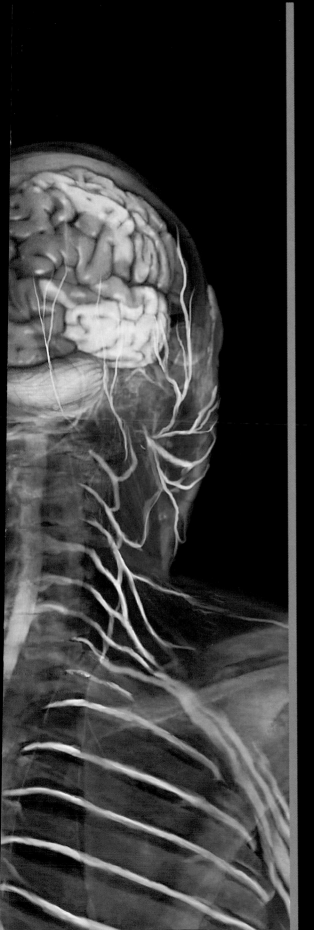

Mind & Behavior

6

TODAY'S SCIENTISTS, ARMED WITH AN ever increasing array of sophisticated instruments and techniques, can map and measure the minute electrical discharges in the brain associated with perception and thought. At the same time, cognitive scientists are studying how we learn, perceive, and process information. Psychologists and psychiatrists endeavor to uncover the causes for our behaviors and often seek ways of altering the less healthy of them.

Modern researchers struggle to answer many of the same basic questions posed by some of the earliest medical and philosophical texts that have come down to us from Greek antiquity: What is the mind? How is it related to the body? How does consciousness arise? How do we actually perceive, think, imagine, and dream? What are the causes of our behaviors and our responses, and to what extent do we control them—or do they control us?

Millennia ago, Greek philosophers observed that life and mind were not the same thing. In those who had suffered head trauma, perhaps in battle or by accident, many vital functions persisted, but consciousness and all that comes with it did not. Other unfortunates who received serious chest wounds or who spilled a great deal

PRECEDING PAGES
Seat of so much that we consider human, the nervous system is really the final frontier of science.

EPILEPSY
Approximately 50 million people in the world are known to have epilepsy, a neurological disorder distinguished by frequent, unexpected seizures. Persons with epilepsy may at times exhibit strange behavior and peculiar body movements.

See pages 26-27 for more information about Aristotle.

of blood lost both consciousness and life. Thus, two centers—the chest and the head, or more specifically the heart and the brain—emerged as likely candidates for the seat of life and mind.

A Greek physician living in southern Italy, Alcmaeon of Croton, performed numerous dissections in the sixth century B.C. and noted, among other things, the connection of the eye to the brain by means of the optic nerve and linked sensation with the brain.

A generation later, one of the authors of the writings attributed to the physician Hippocrates went further. In his treatise *On the Sacred Disease* (that being the disorder we call epilepsy today), he argued that the brain is the center of consciousness, emotions, and thought.

We may say we "feel" emotions in the heart, but the brain is the physical seat of mental experiences in this brain-centered, or encephalocentric view. "Men ought to know," the treatise says, "that from nothing else but the brain come joys, delights, laughter and games, as well as sorrows, griefs, despondency, and lamentations. By means of the brain, in a special manner, we acquire wisdom and knowledge, and see and hear, and know what is foul and what is fair, what is bad and what is good, what is sweet and what is unsavory. I am of the opinion that the brain exercises the greatest power in man."

But in the following century, Aristotle pointed instead to the heart, not the brain, as the seat of sensation. Indeed, the heart, with its never ceasing motion, seemed the most alive part of the body to Aristotle; when it stops, so does life.

The brain by comparison seemed inert and lifeless, its function predominantly to temper the heat of the heart by cooling the blood, according to Aristotle. Yet he did not locate mind in the heart. The mind or soul (*psyche*, in Aristotle's Greek) was the actualization of the entire functioning body, its purpose and its true form. This psyche was not localized anywhere, not a physical part of the body, but it was not separable from the body, either.

Aristotle's heart-centered, or cardiocentric, view of consciousness became widely accepted in antiquity. Echoes of this belief

ca 4000 B.C. – A.D. 1000

ca 4000 B.C.
Ancient Sumerian records, the first known writings about the brain, describe the sensations caused by eating the mind-altering poppy plant.

ca 2500 B.C.
Egyptian papyruses contain the first written anatomy of the brain. The papyrus documents 26 cases of brain injury and treatments for it.

ca 2000 B.C.
Trephination—drilling the skull for medical or spiritual reasons—is practiced in Europe and South America.

ca 500 B.C.
Greek physician Alcmaeon concludes that the brain, not the heart, is the central organ of sensation and thought.

resound today in our common speech, when we speak of sorrow as a "heartache" or of feeling like a "broken-hearted" lover.

But further studies, especially the exploratory dissections carried out in Alexandria, modified such views. As investigators explored the nervous system, the newly observed anatomical links between the brain and the rest of the body directed more attention to this wrinkled, gray, rather neglected, and seemingly quite dull organ.

The physician Galen, drawing on discoveries by his predecessors

THE LYCEUM

Aristotle was a keen naturalist, as portrayed in this 18th-century etching. He opened his own school in 335 B.C. in an Athenian grove.

ca 400 B.C.
Hippocrates describes four personality types, harmonizing with the four humors and four elements.

ca 350 B.C.
In *De Anima (On the Soul)*, Aristotle defines the mind as the rational, thinking part of the soul.

ca 220 B.C.
Greek physician Erasistratus shows that the human brain has more wrinkles than that of other animals, correlating this feature with higher mental capacity.

ca A.D. 1000
Arab physician Avicenna connects three ventricles of the brain with five functions: common sense, imagination, cogitation, estimation, and memory.

and on his own observations,
provided a more complex scheme.

Plato had divided human mental
life into three distinct faculties:
mind, spirit, and desire. (He also
equated these with the three
groups of people needed in a perfect society: intellectuals, soldiers,
and merchants, in decreasing order
of virtue.) Galen borrowed Plato's
divisions and located each faculty in
a particular organ. The higher functions of reason and intellect he
placed in the brain, the passions in
the heart, and the appetites and
urges in the liver. When we tell a
friend "think with your head, not
with your heart" we are repeating
Galen's and Plato's ideas, by locating

knowing and feeling in two different parts of the body.

Early dissections of the brain
revealed hollow cavities called
ventricles. Today we know these features to be the sources and reser-
voirs of cerebrospinal fluid, a liquid
that cushions and cleanses the brain,
but the ancients associated them
with higher brain functions. Writing
in the fifth century A.D., for example, the Christian theologian and
philosopher St. Augustine reported
that medical men of his day counted
three ventricles. The first, closest to
the face, was the seat of sensation;
the next one back, controlled memory; and the third, located near the
back of the neck, governed motor

functions. The exact number, arrangement, and particular roles of these ventricles varied over the next thousand years as the theory strove to encompass new ideas and observations.

Important developments in the Middle Ages included the idea that an anatomical feature called the vermis (literally, worm), a small spur of brain tissue, acted as a valve to open and close the ducts between the ventricles, thus allowing alternation among the mental activities of sensing, imagining, and reasoning. One medical writer of the tenth century used this theory to explain why people tend to look up when trying to remember something. The muscles that move the eyes upward, he explained, help open the valve to the ventricle controlling memory. Although ultimately erroneous, the ventricle theory is evidence of an early and continuing desire to localize mental functions into particular physical regions of the brain. Such work continues to this day.

Plato distinguished the mind from the body. When the body died, the mind or soul survived, personality intact, and eventually went to be housed in another body. Aristotle disagreed with his teacher on this score. He considered the psyche inseparable from the body, even though his writings are ambiguous about whether any part of the person survives death. St. Augustine, while citing the ventricle theory, argued that these anatomical features were themselves neither the soul nor the permanent seat of the soul, but only the location where it exercised its powers.

The full disjunction of mind and body occurred centuries later, when René Descartes, the French mathematician and philosopher, developed a theory so central to his work that it is now named after him: Cartesian dualism.

Descartes saw the world and human life as divided in two. On the one hand, there is matter, the stuff we see all around us, characterized by its property of always taking up space. Matter is made up of minute atoms in motion and is lifeless and inactive. On the other hand, there is another kind of stuff that does not occupy space. No atoms or matter compose it, and its central property is thinking. Thinking stuff—*res cogitans* in Latin—is what Descartes called it. It is what the soul, or the mind, is made of.

Descartes's distinction between mind and body is so engrained in our thinking that it is sometimes hard to think beyond it. But the idea left us with some problems. For example, if mind and body are totally different in substance, how can they interact? How does a desire in the mind, say, to wave hello to my friend, actually make my arm rise into the air? For Descartes, the pineal gland, a small mass of tissue in the brain, was the site where the soul "drove" the body. Few of his contemporaries were convinced, and many ridiculed the idea.

THE ELECTRICAL CONNECTION

Discovered slowly by anatomists from antiquity to the Renaissance, the nervous system connected the brain, the spinal column, and

See page 90 for more information about René Descartes.

BRAIN FUNCTION

This drawing from René Descartes's *De homine figuris* shows the pineal gland (labeled with an H) as the link between vision and a corresponding movement of the body.

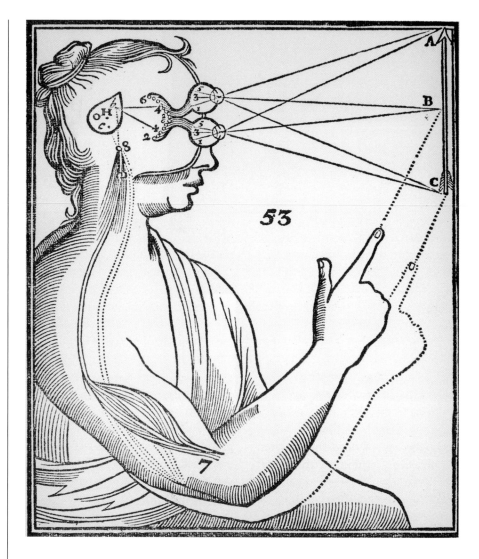

a system of nerves together into a network by which the brain could extend its influence throughout the body. But how? What carried information or commands back and forth through this system?

One frequent answer was that the nerves were hollow and filled with some subtle substance or fluid. Thus in this version, the nervous system was like a mass of plumbing or a complex hydraulic machine. The circulating nervous fluid was often called animal or vital spirits, the term spirits meaning a subtle material, not spiritual entities or ghosts.

The movement of these animal spirits through the nervous system allowed communication from the body to the brain (for example, "Foot feels hot!") and commands from the brain to the body (like, "Move that foot out of the fire!"). Mechanical views of the body proposed in the 17th century showed a system of valves that controlled the flow of spirits. These spirits in turn actuated muscle contractions, thus resulting in motion. Descartes and others used purely mechanical processes to explain reflex actions— actions, like pulling back suddenly after touching a hot stove, that don't require deliberate thought.

Although we now know that nerves are not hollow vessels containing fluids, these early theorists were on the right track. A network of nerves does carry signals throughout the body, but they are electrical signals, not animal spirits. But not until some 18th-century experiments were actually carried out in Italy did this refinement come to be made.

A connection between electricity and muscle movement was made in the 1770s and '80s by Luigi Galvani, a professor at the University of Bologna in Italy. Galvani discovered that he could make the legs of dead frogs twitch by touching them with metal instruments in the presence of static electricity generators or during nearby lightning storms. He became convinced of the existence of what he called animal electricity. Generated in the brain and conducted through the nervous system, animal electricity was the cause of muscle contraction, according to Galvani.

Alessandro Volta, Galvani's contemporary at the University of Pavia, Italy, was intrigued but skeptical. Learning from Galvani's frog experiments, in 1800 Volta built a battery by piling alternating disks of different metals atop one another. The device was later named after him, called a voltaic pile. Likewise the term galvanism, coined by Volta himself, referred to the response of muscles to applied electrical currents, as first shown by Galvani.

Galvani's nephew, Giovanni Aldini, literally took the show on the road, delighting and horrifying spectators across Europe. By sticking wires from Volta's battery into various body orifices, Galvani managed to elicit grimaces and eye movements from the decapitated heads of dogs and oxen and from the corpses of executed criminals.

It was not only sensational, though, for Aldini also used electricity therapeutically. His first patient, an Italian farmer suffering from severe melancholy, held a voltaic pile in his bare hand. A wire from the top of the pile was pressed to the top of his skull. After regular treatments, the patient's mood gradually improved, and after several weeks the man was fully cured.

The concept of electricity as therapy was not original to Aldini. In the first century A.D., the Roman physician Scribonius Largus had applied live electric eels to patients in an attempt to cure headache and gout. But Aldini's application of electrical current to sufferers of depression was the first clear practice of what would come to be called electroshock therapy.

THE AILING MIND

Throughout the long centuries of inquiry about the mind and its seat in the human body, a mind that was not in good health always presented a challenge. Mental illness was well recognized by ancient physicians.

See pages 193-95 for more information about Alessandro Volta.

ANIMAL ELECTRICITY

Luigi Galvani made dead frogs' legs twitch by probing them with metal instruments. He wrongly believed that muscle generated electricity. His idea of animal electricity became popular nonetheless. It carried a kernel of truth on which science still depends today.

A Hippocratic writer is clear in his diagnosis of its source and causes. It is from the brain, he asserts, that "we become mad and delirious, and fears and terrors assail us, some by night, and some by day, and dreams and untimely wanderings, and cares that are not suitable. . . . All these things we endure from the brain when it is not healthy, but is more hot, more cold, more moist, or more dry than natural . . . and we become mad from its humidity."

While the "divine madness" of the ancient oracle at Delphi or the prophetic Sibyl at Cumae was attributed to the inspiration of the gods, ancient Greek and Roman physicians regularly attributed madness and mental disorders to physical causes. They strove to treat mental ailments with regimens of diet and medicine. The root of white hellebore, for example, was considered a medical treatment for madness. Asclepiades, a Greek physician of the second century B.C., prescribed fresh air, good diet, massage, exercises to improve the memory, music, and wine—few of which we could argue with today.

There is a popular view that in medieval times, people were superstitious and attributed mental abnormalities to supernatural forces like demons or witches, but in fact, throughout the Middle Ages, physicians continued to study the physical causes of and cures for mental illness. Nor did medieval philosophers and theologians view mental illness as evidence of sin and its punishment. The actual records that survive

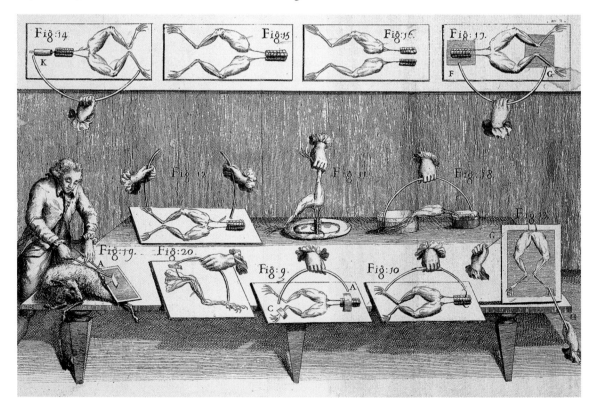

show that by and large, medieval physicians sought physical cures for mental ailments, observing diet, stress, living conditions, humoral imbalance, or physical injury as the causes of distress.

It is also a modern myth that medieval Europeans practiced trephination, the surgical removal of a piece of the skull, in order to "let demons escape" and treat madness. No literate person of the Middle Ages would have imagined for an instant that an incorporeal demon or spirit could be trapped by a shell of bone. Trephining was practiced from antiquity up to the 17th century, but its purpose was to relieve pressure or treat head injury.

The skull of a peasant trephined in the 11th century was recently unearthed in England. Forensic evaluation shows that he had suffered a blunt force trauma to the head, possibly from a brawl. The operation was apparently intended to relieve pressure on the brain, caused by his cracked skull. The presence of healed bone shows that this medical procedure—obviously horrific, given the lack of anesthesia—saved the man's life, and he lived many years afterward.

The incurably mentally ill received special care during the Middle Ages. English law recorded in the 13th century distinguished between those born with impaired mental faculties and those who later developed mental disorders. For the latter, boards of inquiry determined a person's competency, using the common-sense method of asking simple

questions: What day is it? What is your son's name? How many pence in a shilling? Those judged incapable of caring for themselves became wards of the state, their property protected for their heirs. In the hundreds of surviving documents from such inquiries, symptoms are described that seem remarkably similar to those of insanity, senility, postpartum depression, and other mental afflictions of today.

Special hospitals or asylums for the mentally ill began to be built in the late Middle Ages. At least five were founded in Spain the first half of the 15th century. Mental hospitals did not necessarily guarantee humane treatment, however, and treatments that we today would consider inhuman were common in the 17th and 18th centuries.

Among the most notorious of these institutions was the infamous hospital of St. Mary of Bethlehem in London. Originally a monastery, the building was converted into a prison for lunatics in 1547. Its shortened name, Bethlem, was even further

MEDIEVAL MEDICINE

Ortis Sanitatis, The Origin of Health, a 15th-century medical handbook, compiled cures from herbal tinctures to superstitious rituals.

BEDLAM

Bethlem Hospital at Moorfields, London, later called Bedlam, became a prison for lunatics in 1547. In the 17th century, ladies and gentlemen paid a small fee to tour the building and view the inmates.

The HOSPITAL _of_ BETHLEHEM.   _L'_HOSPITAL _de_ FOU.

Printed for John Bowles & Son, at the Black Horse in Cornhil.

corrupted to Bedlam, a word that has come to mean a scene of wild uproar and chaos. Early descriptions of Bethlem Hospital suggest that the place must have been just that. John Evelyn, an English author and diarist, visited the place in the late 17th century. "I stept into Bedlame," he wrote after, "where I saw several poore miserable creatures in chaines."

Despite the demoralizing treatment of people who were mentally ill, attitudes toward them gradually changed for the better. In 1793, a French physician, Philippe Pinel, dramatically dared to remove the chains from inmates in the dungeonlike cells of an asylum in Paris. In England, members of the Society of Friends ran more humanitarian mental

1543 – 1890

1543
Italian anatomist Andreas Vesalius publishes _De humani corporis fabrica_, with major sections on the workings of the nerves and the brain.

1690
English philosopher John Locke's _Essay Concerning Human Understanding_ introduces his theory that the newborn's mind is a blank slate and that all ideas come from the senses.

1791
Italian physician Luigi Galvani proposes that animal tissue generates electricity. His experiments contribute to the understanding of neural activity.

hospitals, and their successes influenced others in the field.

In mid-19th-century America, where conditions had greatly improved, Dorothea Lynde Dix of Maine became a stalwart reformer. She recalled that once, while visiting women inmates, she noticed that the mentally ill were locked into cells in a cold, damp cellar. She asked why there was no stove and the keeper simply responded, "Insane people do not feel the cold." Dix devoted her life to establishing insane asylums and educating others in treatment practices beyond simply jailing the mentally unbalanced.

HEALING STRATEGIES

Even with better hospitals, few caretakers really knew how to cope with severe mental illness. Distinctions were made between broad categories such as mania, melancholia, and schizophrenia, but no one really understood these illnesses or their causes. Efforts to understand the nature of mental disorder became paramount, and they went in two directions, the physiological and the psychological.

German psychiatrist Hans Berger began examining brain activity, recording the first electroencephalograph in 1929. At the same time, others were investigating electroconvulsive therapy (ECT, or electric shock)—a harsher variation of the procedure discovered by Aldini in the late 18th century. Electric shock did seem to alleviate many symptoms temporarily. The procedure is still in use and has been proved effective for certain types of depression. Treatment today involves applying electrodes to the temples and passing a 110-volt current into the brain for only a few seconds. Ten to twelve treatments are generally required to deal with depression. Temporary amnesia occurs after ECT, a side effect that sometimes develops into permanent memory lapse if too many treatments are administered. Today's theory behind ECT is that it increases neurotransmitter, enzyme activity, and blood flow in the brain and also releases natural antidepressants. Critics consider the procedure dehumanizing, but to those whose depression has been lifted by it, the treatment is a blessing.

1837
Czech physiologist Jan Evangelista Purkinje discovers the large nerve cells with branching extensions found in the cerebral cortex, now called Purkinje cells.

1861
French surgeon Paul Broca identifies the brain's speech center.

1879
German psychologist Wilhelm Wundt sets up his laboratory, the first to study human behavior as a science.

1890
American psychologist William James publishes *The Principles of Psychology*, asserting that human behavior is not random but serves a function.

MENTAL ILLNESS

Into the 19th century, the shape of the human head was considered a clue to the character of the mind within. Exacting measurements of the skulls of mentally ill patients, criminals, and individuals representing racial types were used to seek the causes of behavior.

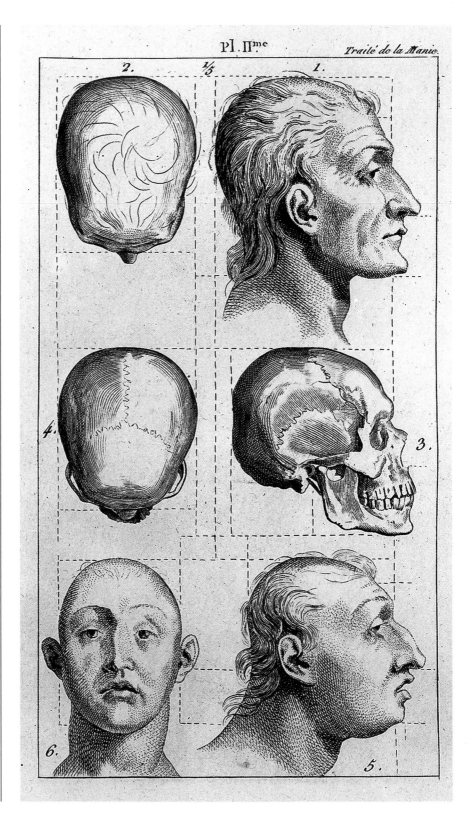

TREATING MENTAL ILLNESS

The Book of Deuteronomy minced no words when it proclaimed that violators of the law of God would be struck down with "madness and blindness and fury of mind." That the mentally ill had been punished by a god or possessed by a demon was a popular belief, wides-pread for centuries, even though attempts to explain mental and emotional disorders as natural occurrences, medically treatable, date back to Hippocrates.

Cicero, Roman statesman and philosopher of the first century B.C., was among the first to describe human emotions in terms that today we would call psychological. He listed four perturbations, or passions, central to human feeling and behavior: fear, sorrow, joy, and libido, or violent desire. Diseases of the soul, akin to diseases of the mind, arose from excess passion and a lack of judgment and reason.

Galen, on the other hand, drew on his theory of health as a balance of the humors to suggest that the mind's health depended on a harmony of the passions. If errors in judgment were made, education could correct them.

Later generations built upon these classical foundations. Medieval physicians regularly sought natural explanations for mental illnesses. They focused on humoral imbalance, emotional and physical stress, and improper diet as causes. Accordingly, they proposed cures based on diet and medicines, particularly herbs.

In the 17th century, Jan Baptista van Helmont observed and described behavioral abnormalities, including some, such as aphasia, that stem from brain injury. He sought to explain their origins according to new principles of scientific investigation.

In the absence of scientific treatments, the mentally ill sought miracle cures.

In the 1800s in America and Europe, meanwhile, the mentally ill were often confined to cellars and even cages, their ailments treated by techniques that today would be called physical violence and abuse. One reformer in Massachusetts reported observing mental hospital inmates being "beaten with rods and lashed into obedience." Government reforms in Europe and the U.S. dictated more humane treatment practices. In 1865 in the U.S., for instance, the Willard Act mandated that chronically insane persons be lodged not in poorhouses but in state-run asylums. Those who improved were assigned to colonies, farms, and foster homes.

As neuroscientific research advanced, and as the practices of psychiatry, psychotherapy, and psychoanalysis developed as acceptable and scientific procedures, the treatment of the mentally ill improved.

Psychoactive pharmaceuticals now play significant roles in the successful treatment of emotional ills. Despite side effects, psychotherapeutic drugs have been used successfully to treat depression, eating disorders, panic attacks, and obsessive-compulsive disorders, to name but a few.

Chief among these drugs are antidepressants and tranquilizers. Serotonin reuptake inhibitors (SRIs) temper depression by increasing available serotonin, a natural brain chemical that helps maintain mental balance. The tranquilizer class of drugs is used to reduce fears, anxiety, tension, and agitation. Antipsychotic agents, or neuroleptics, are used to treat schizophrenia and other psychoses; minor tranquilizers, or anxiolytics, are used to treat milder forms of anxiety.

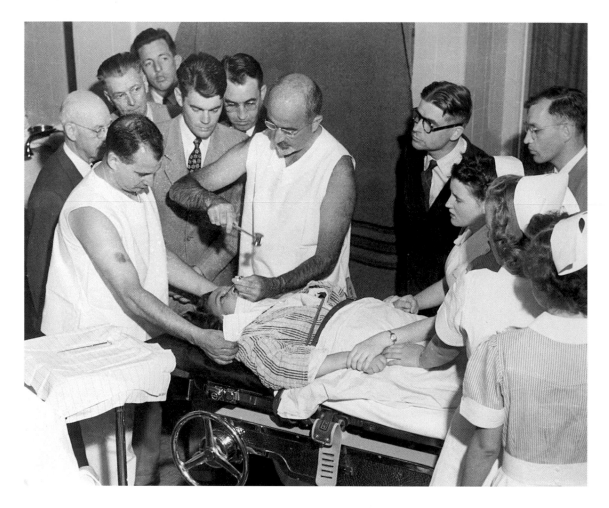

LOBOTOMY

Observers lean forward to watch medical practitioners perform a lobotomy, a surgical procedure of the 1940s and 1950s that denatured or severed the prefrontal lobes from the rest of the brain in order to calm an anxious patient.

A far more drastic approach developed in the early 20th century: the lobotomy. When late 19th-century experimenters had surgically disconnected the frontal lobes from the brains of dogs, the animals turned benign. The procedure left people thinking whether the same could be done on the human brain. Perhaps disconnecting the prefrontal lobes—the very front portion of the brain, seat of emotion, learning, and social behavior—might actually improve the lives of people who suffer from extreme anxiety, pain, traumatic memories, violent inclinations, or other mental states that diminished the quality of life for them and their loved ones.

Portuguese neurologist António Egas Moniz was willing to give the procedure a try, and in the 1930s he pioneered the lobotomy. Egas Moniz developed a technique of drilling holes in each side of the forehead to access the tissue between the central brain and the prefrontal lobes. At first he killed the tissue by infusing it with alcohol; soon he turned to slicing it with a thin wire.

Egas Moniz's surgeries did seem successful in cases of overwhelming fear, tension, and anxiety, as well as in some forms of schizophrenia and paranoia. He received the Nobel Prize for medicine in 1949, honoring the therapeutic value of his innovation, but the procedure he developed has met with vigorous opposition from the beginning. Across the world, laws and regulations minimize the use of lobotomies. Soon a new technique for calming the behavior and improving the lives of the mentally disturbed developed: drug therapy.

By the 1950s, it was accepted knowledge that the brain teems with message-bearing chemicals, which transmit nerve impulses and control thought and mood. Researchers became interested in the possibility that psychoactive drugs could help control severe mental conditions. Salts of lithium, a common metallic element, was developed for manic-depression, thorazine (or chlorpromazine), an antipsychotic agent, for schizophrenia. Slowly a vast arsenal of drugs developed that could elevate mood, depress mood, alleviate the tremors of Parkinson's disease, and calm hyperkinetic children. For a brief time during the 1960s, Valium, a mild tranquilizer, wasthe most prescribed drug in the United States.

As more was learned about the brain's messenger chemicals and the special receptor sites to which they bind, pharmaceutical chemists could see new ways to mimic or block natural neurotransmitters. Brain and nervous system physiology was essential to the design of this new wave of psychoactive drugs. Antidepressive agents like Prozac, which caused a sensation during the 1990s, for example, increase the availability of naturally occurring serotonin, a neurotransmitter, in the tiny spaces between nerve cells. Some experts believe that chemical compounds will eventually be able to control all but the most unusual sorts of mental illness in the century to come.

Physical and pharmaceutical therapies proved beneficial in mental health treatment during the 20th century, but so did the treatment methods that relied on talking, listening, analysis, and personal interaction. All are components of what became known in the early 20th century as psychotherapy, a blanket term that now includes a number of techniques using verbal or nonverbal communication to normalize abnormal behavior.

Totally different from drugs, shocks, or surgery, psychotherapy tries to reform the disordered mind by helping patients understand why they behave the way they do or by helping them identify and change troublesome behaviors. In some techniques, patients are instructed to freely associate and report their thoughts without reservation. Through conversation with the therapist, a patient externalizes his or her troubles, an act of ventilation that, with reassurances from the therapist, may be all that is required to deal with mild depression and what some call normal neuroses. When talking therapy is not fully effective, some believe in a more intense form, psychoanalysis, through which a patient delves into his or her past and seeks deeper root causes of emotional problems.

PSYCHOSURGERY
From the 1940s into the 1950s, when psychoactive medications came into use, lobotomies were carried out extensively. Today, psychosurgery is still performed on much smaller areas of the brain, but only in rare cases, when all other alternatives fail.

The most famous proponent of psychoanalytic theory was the Austrian neurologist Sigmund Freud, who exercised enormous influence on 20th-century ideas of human behavior and how the mind works. Freud introduced a new idea, which he called the "unconscious," a sort of force or organ within the human consciousness that exerts strong influences and often evokes patterns of neurosis, the least severe form of mental illness.

Freud theorized that no one says or does anything accidentally. Slips of the tongue, misunderstandings, and mistaken perceptions all arise from the unconscious, a reservoir of

FREUD AND JUNG

The psychoanalytic theories of Sigmund Freud and Carl Gustav Jung had enormous influence over 20th-century ideas of human behavior and mental aberrations. While the psychoanalytic method is generally attributed to Freud, it got its impetus from the "talking cure" of his colleague, Josef Breuer, who relieved hysteria in his patients by guiding them to recall and confront traumatic memories. Breuer used hypnotism in treatment, a practice that Freud decided to abandon because he believed that it encouraged dependency. His version of the talking cure, which he first called psychical analysis, allowed patients to view and share their thoughts freely, allowing them to be observed and interpreted by the therapist.

Freud himself went through intensive psychoanalysis, delving deeply into his past, his hidden feelings, and his dreams. Dreams, he concluded, were associated with conscious and unconscious desires, especially sexual desires, and were the gateway to the mind and its hidden motivations. Thus the psychosexual development of children, from an infantile oral phase, through strong attraction to a parent of the opposite sex during early childhood, through detachment from the par-

Carl Jung believed that shared symbols ruled much of human behavior.

ents during adolescence, became one keystone of his psychological theories.

Jung, a pupil of Freud, founded his own school of analytic psychology, placing less emphasis on sexual factors in psychoneuroses. Jung decided that the instinctual biological drive called libido involved not only sexual drives but also the creative force, a natural energy that guided all human conduct. Unlike Freud, Jung believed that sexuality does not become an important force in behavior until just before puberty.

Jung believed that the unconscious mind contained personal drives and experiences of which individuals may not be aware—attitudes inherited from ancestors, a collective racial consciousness. The collective conscious included ancestral thought patterns called archetypes, a repository of shared images and symbols that surfaced in dreams and myths and contained wisdom that directed all humanity.

Freudian and Jungian ideas reached their apogee in the early to mid-20th century. They have encountered decreasing acceptance among mental health professionals since then, but their influence still extends far and wide, not only in therapy but also in other disciplines and in popular culture.

feelings and attitudes often disregarded even by the person involved. For Freud, dreams were "the royal road to a knowledge of the unconscious activities of the mind," and their analysis revealed a great deal.

Freud posited the theory that the mind was divided into three parts: the id, the ego, and the superego. The id is totally unconscious and the source of instinctual impulses and demands for immediate satisfaction of primitive needs. The ego is conscious; it is the aware sense of the self, and it expresses itself in thought, behavior, and decision-making. The superego is the judge and rulemaker; it is the part of the mind that tells right from wrong, and it often comes into conflict with the other two parts of the mind, especially the id.

Serious conflicts, Freud said, cause emotional difficulty. For Freud, many of those conflicts stemmed from early sexual desires, which society marked with shame and judgment, often causing the desires to be repressed—shunted into the unconscious, Freud would say—only to come out in later behaviors and attitudes that might be antisocial or self-destructive.

Freud strongly emphasized sexuality in his psychological theories, while his pupil Carl Gustav Jung believed that other factors of human existence stimulated behavior just as forcefully. One of Jung's most celebrated contributions was his theory that people can be categorized as either introverted or extroverted: those who depend mainly on themselves to satisfy their needs, compared with those who seek out others for personal fulfillment. To Freud's three parts of the mind, Jung added the collective unconscious, for he believed that all humankind shared an underlying repository of myth, symbols, and belief, always operational in every human behavior.

THE ROOTS OF BEHAVIOR

In the latter part of the 19th century, the study of human cultures expanded with the flowering of a new field of study, anthropology.

SIGMUND FREUD

Pioneer of psychoanalysis

1856
Born on May 6, 1856, in Freiberg, Moravia.

1873
Graduates summa cum laude from secondary school and enters Vienna University to study medicine.

1881
Employed as a clinical assistant to a psychiatrist in Vienna.

1885
Researches medicinal effects of cocaine; discovers its analgesic effects.

1892
As therapist, begins use of free association, a technique used for psychiatric evaluation and treatment.

1895
Works with Josef Breuer on *Studies in Hysteria.*

1897
Begins self-analysis.

1900
Publishes *The Interpretation of Dreams,* presenting theory of the unconscious.

1905
Publishes *Three Essays on the Theory of Sexuality, Jokes and Their Relation to the Unconscious,* and *Fragment of an Analysis of a Case of Hysteria (Dora).*

1919
Becomes a full professor at the University of Vienna.

1935
Elected honorary member, British Royal Society of Medicine.

1938
Fleeing the Nazis, leaves Austria and resettles in England.

1939
Dies on September 23 in London.

YELLOW   BLUE   RED   GREEN

SKINNER'S PIGEONS

American psychologist B. F. Skinner used pigeons to test his ideas of behavioral psychology. Carefully designed schedules of reward and punishment allowed him to train the birds into complex behaviors.

Influential anthropologists, such as Franz Boas at the turn of the 20th century and Claude Levi-Strauss half a century later, argued that societies must be understood as organizational systems that regulate and give meaning to human life. Each culture has devised different but equally valid means of achieving those goals. Culture thus influences human development, mind and body. "The behavior of an individual," Boas wrote, "is determined not by his racial affiliation, but by the character of his ancestry and his cultural environment."

A structural anthropologist born in Brussels and educated in Paris, Lévi-Strauss saw culture as a system of communication, analogous to language. Much of his work was an attempt to identify universal structures in the human mind. He believed he could identify them by finding them reflected in myths, symbols, and forms of social organization. "I claim to show not how men think in myths," Levi-Strauss once observed, "but how myths operate in men's minds without their being aware of the fact."

At the same time that anthropologists turned their attention to cultural behavior, psychologists were seeking new ways to study the behavior of species, animal and human, asking what operated during such universal experiences as learning and mating. Insofar as animal behavior was concerned, investigators wanted to determine which behaviors were attributable to genetic inheritance and which were the products of individual learning.

Konrad Lorenz, the Austrian zoologist considered the father of ethology, the study of animal behavior, inclined to the first view. He showed, for example, how a young bird identifies the first large moving object it sees—whether bird, human, or otherwise—as a fellow member of its species.

Perhaps the most provocative and controversial synthesis of studies in behavior, genetics, and evolution emerged in 1975, when Harvard biologist Edward O. Wilson proposed that a good deal of animal behavior—from the organization in ant colonies and turkey flocks to human social organization and customs—could be understood as the result of evolutionary adaptations and genetic history. According to Wilson's theory, human acts of altruism, once honored as human nature, might not be all that different from instinctual cooperation among termites. Human courtship pat-

terns appear strikingly similar to those of porcupines and peacocks. Although intellectually intriguing, Wilson's view was widely assailed on humanistic grounds.

Another behavior scientist who found himself no stranger to attack was the American psychologist B. F. Skinner. Skinner argued that behavior is largely learned as a result of positive and negative interactions with one's environment. He insisted that external influences, not internal ones, are what mattered in shaping human behavior, and that the concepts freedom and free will—long held as internal motivators essential to the best of human behavior—were merely illusions.

Humans are really controlled by rewards and punishments, Skinner asserted. He designed scientific experiments to demonstrate the power of conditioning in shaping behavior. Investigators succeeded in modifying the actions and directing the learning of various animals— mice, rats, pigeons, and humans— through a simple regimen, rewarding desired actions and withholding rewards or responding negatively to undesired actions.

These methods form the basis of behaviorism, a theory of human and animal psychology associated directly with Skinner. Behaviorism goes back to the work of the late 19th-century Russian neurologist Ivan Pavlov, a meticulous experimentalist who explored the connection between the nervous, circulatory, and digestive systems.

Pavlov fitted several dogs with stomach shunts, which allowed

PAVLOV'S DOGS

Russian physiologist Ivan Pavlov found that once dogs associated the sound of a bell with food, they would salivate whenever they heard the sound of the bell, even if no food was present.

him to collect their gastric juices for further study. During this work, Pavlov noticed that the dogs salivated whenever they anticipated food—a normal reflex. He then discovered that he could train the dogs to associate some other stimulus—the chime of a bell or an electric shock—with food. When the stimulus occurred, the dogs would salivate, whether in the presence of food or not. The animals had acquired a conditioned reflex, intrinsic to Skinner's behaviorist psychology.

In general, Skinnerian forms of therapy deemphasize the Freudian unconscious and discount what lies buried in the patient's past. Behavioral therapists concentrate instead on current behavior and difficulties experienced in the present. Neuroses and psychoses do not come from unconscious repression, according to this theory; they are bad habits that the

patient has learned, and they can be changed. Like Pavlov's dogs, the behavior of the troubled patient can be conditioned. In fact, according to this line of reasoning, people need not enter a doctor-patient relationship to gain mental health. They can learn how to extinguish undesirable behaviors on their own. Not surprisingly, many of Skinner's ideas fueled controversy. Critics found his ideas cold-blooded and questioned whether human beings could or should be conditioned like the pigeons he had trained to walk in precise figure eights. Moreover, his critics contended, he was wrong to ignore modern learning theories and the natural stages of development.

The Swiss psychologist Jean Piaget promoted a theory of human psychology in which the stages of childhood development were central. A pioneer in studying the intellectual and cognitive development of children, Piaget said that all human beings went through universal and identifiable stages in the course of adapting to the world.

For example, they went from manipulating things to manipulating abstract ideas; from demanding satisfaction to learning how to accommodate one's needs with society's demands. Piaget identified four stages of child development: a sensory and motor development period, through the age of two; a pre-rational stage, up to the age of seven; a stage of perfecting concrete operations, ages seven to eleven; and a stage of learning more formal or abstract operations, up to the age of seventeen.

Unlike Skinner, who focused on environmental issues, and Freud, who emphasized emotions and instincts, Piaget emphasized thinking and the manipulation of things and ideas: cognition, in other words. He based his sense of universal stages of development on the patterns of growth in a rational, perceptive child eager to make sense of the world. "If only we could know what was going on in a baby's mind while observing him in action," Piaget once said, "we could certainly understand everything there is to psychology."

But plenty of psychological challenges arise at the other end of life. One out of six elderly Americans suffers from depression, one out of fifty from psychotic disorders. Of those aged 85 and over, 35 percent suffer from some form of dementia, including Alzheimer's disease.

In ages past, it was standard practice to treat the emotional problems of the elderly lightly. Tiberius Caesar allegedly remarked that it was foolish for any man over 60 to ask a physician to take his pulse. For many years, senility was a catch-all term used for any mental deterioration in old age. Until recently, various forms of dementia were unclassified and little known about the chemistry of the brain as it ages.

One of the few early psychologists who took an interest in geriatric development was Erik Erikson, who constructed an eight-stage

IVAN PAVLOV

Discoverer of conditioned reflexes

1849
Born September 14 in Ryazan, Russia.

1875
Graduates from University of St. Petersburg; takes assistantship at Imperial Medical Academy.

1879
Completes course of medical study, receiving gold medal.

1883
Discovers dynamic nerves of the heart; submits thesis for degree of doctor of medicine.

1890
Becomes chair and professor of pharmacology at Imperial Medical Academy.

1890
Becomes director of department of physiology, Institute of Experimental Medicine.

1897
Publishes *Lectures on the Function of the Principal Digestive Glands*, which presents his research on digestion.

1903
Reads paper on "The Experimental Psychology and Psychopathology of Animals," which includes findings on conditioned reflexes.

1904
Receives Nobel Prize for physiology or medicine for his work on digestive glands.

1921
Awarded special government decree, signed by Lenin.

1935
Laboratory built by Russian government for work on conditioned reflexes.

1936
Dies on February 27 in Leningrad.

WHO ARE THE MENTALLY ILL?

Some years ago Dr. Jonathan Cole, the superintendent of the Boston State Hospital, a psychiatric facility, was asked to define mental illness. His response was indicative of the complexity of the subject. "Mental illness," he said, "is something that even psychiatrists have trouble defining today. The definition is in a state of acute confusion. . . . Many of our clients are people in distress."

Today that distress has been analyzed in broad categories and specific classifications of diseases and disorders of the brain and mind. Neuroses, which may be caused by various psychological factors like childhood abuse or emotional deprivation, are the most common of the many forms of mental illness. They are generally regarded as mild disorders, more treatable than others. Everyone experiences occasional bouts of anxiety or depression—they are normal, physical responses to the ups and downs of daily life. Everyone undergoes occasional fits of jealousy, hatred, fear, guilt, and inferiority. These experiences can be mild enough to be called normal neuroses, not needing professional treatment, or they can get out of hand and overwhelm the sufferer, as in the case of clinical depression, paranoia, and psychological disorders such as obsessive-compulsive disorder and post-traumatic stress syndrome.

Psychosis is a more severe state of mental illness characterized by delusions, hallucinations, and the inability to comprehend reality or to control impulses. Schizophrenia—a mind-crippler that splits the afflicted from normal everyday life—and bipolar disorder—marked by alternating periods of mania and depression—are among the major psychoses. Some of these illnesses—schizophrenia, for example—seem to be caused by inherited genetic factors; others—mania and depression, for instance—by imbalances or improper activities in certain neurotransmitters. Alzheimer's disease, caused by an organic disease in the brain, is a degenerative affliction characterized by microscopic brain lesions and clumps of microscopic fibrils that run through neurons and affect their normal activity. The result is mental disorder: confusion, disorientation, memory loss, speech disturbances, and, eventually, full loss of mental capacity.

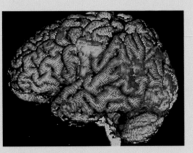

PET—positron emission tomography—pictures the brain in action.

Some mentally ill people suffer from what psychologists now call personality disorders. The most severely afflicted are the sociopaths and psychopaths, many of whom are never diagnosed or hospitalized. Some end up in jail because of antisocial behavior: writing bad checks, drug abuse, sexual deviance. The emotions of love, loyalty, sympathy, or remorse are alien to the psychopathic mind. Sociopathic behavior involves a persistent pattern of maladaptive acts, a classic example of a mental illness that is probably a combination of biochemical and social influences in varying proportions.

It used to be that experts included on the list of the mentally ill those called feeble-minded or mentally retarded (or now, more delicately, the mentally challenged): those whose brain development has stopped or whose learning ability has been impaired by organic deficiencies present at birth or by head traumas. Today we know that subnormal intellectual development often results from congenital causes, brain injury, or disease. Neuroscientists continue to seek causes and cures, while treatment paradigms attempt to provide these people the best quality of life possible.

scenario of human life and suggested that each stage consists of a crisis—a turning point, not a ruinous event—that has to be confronted and resolved. Upon each resolution, healthy development proceeds. In Erickson's eighth and final developmental stage, a person faces the conflict of integrity versus despair. This challenge comes in the later years of life, a time when people evaluate their lives. If all goes well, wisdom is the reward.

Other psychologists doubted that internal impulses alone explain our behavior. They established the field of social psychology, the study of how others influence an individual's behavior. Kurt Lewin, a Prussian-born American, studied group dynamics and became known for his field theory of behavior. Lewin held that to understand and predict human behavior fully, one has to accept the totality of events in a person's psychological field, or life-space, as he also called it. Our psychological and environmental surroundings, including the people and social groups we associate with, contribute to our personalities and shape our behaviors.

Lewin was also a proponent of the theory of psychology known as Gestalt, which stressed that every structure of psychological, physiological, and behavioral experience was experienced, and needed to be analyzed, as a gestalt, a word taken from the German and meaning an integrated whole.

According to Gestalt theory, the mind perceives integrated wholes, not discrete parts. A triangle is perceived as a triangle, not the three lines that shape it. The mind hears a symphony as a whole before deliberately dividing the performance into notes or instrumental parts. Behavior should also be seen as an integrated, unified response to a situation. Gestalt therapy involves treatment of the person as a whole, including biological components and their organic functions, interrelationships with the external world, as well as inner psychological experiences.

JEAN PIAGET

Father of developmental psychology

1896
Born on August 9, in Neuchâtel, Switzerland.

1918
Publishes *Recherché*, a philosophical novel.

1918
Receives a Doctorate in Science from the University of Neuchâtel where his thesis is on mollusks of Valais.

1921
Begins work in child psychology.

1924
Publishes *Judgment and Reasoning in the Child.*

1926
Publishes *The Child's Conception of the World.*

1929
Appointed professor at the University of Geneva.

1936
Publishes *The Origins of Intelligence in Children.*

1940
Becomes director of the Psychology Laboratory and the president of the Swiss Society of Psychology.

1955
Creates and directs the International Center for Epistemology in Geneva.

1972
Defines the four stages of intellectual development.

1972
Awarded the Erasmus prize.

1974
Publishes *The Grasp of Consciousness.*

1980
Dies on September 16 in Geneva.

For all its legitimate theories and therapies, dating from the 20th century on, psychology has had its detractors. It has occasionally been denigrated as an inexact science replete with hasty generalizations and assertions that cannot be empirically proven. As medical investigators have learned more about the chemical and physical operations of the brain and the nervous system, drug therapy has become as necessary to psychiatry, the medical treatment of mental illness, as psychotherapy was in years past.

Some years ago, psychiatrist Ronald D. Laing aroused the ire of his peers by suggesting that individual madness was but a reflection of society's ills and evils. Laing considered schizophrenia not a mental illness but a "breakdown in interpersonal relationships." John Dewey, the American educator and philosopher, also held a skeptical view of psychology. He once remarked, "Popular psychology is a mass of cant, of slush, and of superstition worthy of the most flourishing days of the medicine man." Up against such seering criticism, psychological theories have persisted.

TUNING IN TO THE BRAIN

Neuroscience is the scientific study of the brain and the nervous system. Neuroscientists emphasize the biochemistry, anatomy, and electrical connections of the brains and the network of nerves connected to it. Neuroscience research and neurosurgery have opened up new realms of understanding and practice about certain behaviors and conditions once defined as entirely psychological. The field has also promised—and in many cases delivered—methods for treating brain injuries or nervous system disorders.

Neuroscientists continue in the tradition, from Hippocrates to Galvani, of seeking to understand the physical corollaries of mental states. One early precursor to today's neuroscientists, Franz Josef Gall, a German physiologist born in 1758, believed that the skull held information about the brain, and thereby information about the personality.

A distinguished physician who ultimately practiced in Vienna, Gall invented phrenology: the study of the skull's shape, based on the

1891 – 1987

1891
Russian physician Ivan Pavlov begins research on conditioned reflexes.

1900
Austrian neurologist Sigmund Freud publishes *The Interpretation of Dreams*, arguing that dreams serve as fulfillment of subconscious wishes.

1913
American psychologist John B. Watson introduces behaviorism as a school of psychology, later developed by B. F. Skinner.

theory that its distinctive features can reveal details about the individual's character and mental capacity.

Gall identified and named more than 20 organs within the human brain. These, he believed, corresponded to 20 faculties of the human personality. The combination of a person's faculties was set at birth and could be only slightly modified by education. With this concept of faculties, Gall's theory connected the personality, the brain, and the skull, which he believed was a physical match for the brain it contained, and hence a mirror of the individual's distinctive personality.

Gall associated the shape, bumps, and indentations of a person's skull with specific moral, sexual, emotional, and intellectual characteristics. Pleasing the theologians, he even identified lumps that were linked to goodness and religious sentiment. Soon quacks had seized on his theory—which in Gall's hands was based on study and observation—and they used it in traveling medicine-show therapy sessions, offering to tell people's personalities, like their fortunes, by reading their skulls. But in a strange twist, phrenology—by bringing attention to psychology and the mental condition of individuals—helped bring about more enlightened treatment for criminal offenders and the mentally ill.

Gall may have been off the mark, but his ideas of various cerebral regions would have a counterpart years later in studies of the brain's hemispheres and lobes and their specific roles in human behavior. Indeed, modern renditions of cerebral architecture and the specialized functions within belong to the venerable tradition of medieval ventricular theories.

Essential to perception, communication, memory, to our ability to understand science and to appreciate a tune, the cerebral cortex appears as a deeply folded orb, front and center in the brain. Its right side directs movements on the left side of the body, left side governs right. This fact was observed even in ancient Greece, and Aldini noted that shocks administered to the right side of a cadaver's brain caused muscular motions in the left side of the body.

1929
German physician Hans Berger develops the electroencephalograph to measure electrical activity in the brain.

1936
Swiss psychologist Jean Piaget publishes *The Origins of Intelligence in Children,* featuring what he calls genetic epistemology.

1950
English mathematician Alan Turing develops a method to measure artificial intelligence, later called the Turing test.

1987
Antidepressant drug Prozac introduced to the market by the Eli Lilly Corporation.

Language disorders occur after injury to the left hemisphere; memory impairment occurs after injury to the right. Beneath the cortex, more primitive brain structures control bodily functions.

Neuroscientists study not just the brain but the entire nervous system. Santiago Ramón y Cajal, a Spanish neuroanatomist, conducted a systematic study of all its interconnections, overlaps, and extensions. Deft of hand—perhaps the result of his early years as a shoemaker and barber—Ramón y Cajal was skilled at sketching what he saw during dissections and under the microscope, which was of great value in preserving his findings. He developed a silver nitrate stain to be introduced to minutely thin sections of brain or

THE SYNAPTIC NETWORK

The human nervous system is often compared to the system of interconnected electrical conductors embedded in computers or telephone networks, with its complex mass of nerve-cell circuitry and its countless flashing electrical signals. Where chips and transistors do the job in machinery, neurons, or nerve cells, are the central operators of the nervous system. Billions of impulse-bearing cells, made up of a nucleated cell body with extensions called dendrites, send and pick up the signals. The first neuron, scientists believe, appeared in animals some 500 million years ago, about 3 billion years after the initial appearance of the DNA molecule.

Besides the basic cell with its nucleus, a neuron has a single axon, a long nerve fiber that connects to a neighboring cell and conducts impulses from the body of the nerve cell. A neuron and its axon can range in size from a tenth of an inch to three feet; the entire system, if stretched out, might measure three million miles.

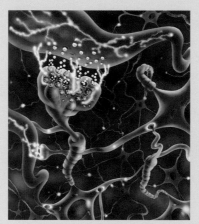

Nerve cells include axons, long fibers reaching out to other cells, and dendrites, or receptors.

But without a biological switch to transmit electrochemical messages, the system would be as immobile as a car engine with no ignition device to make a connection in the electrical circuit. The nervous system's switch is a synapse, a minute gap about a billionth of an inch wide, between the axon terminal and a target cell. Across this junction, nerve impulses pass. When nerve impulses reach a knoblike synaptic bulb at the end of the transmitting neuron, tiny globules inside the bulb, holding thousands of neurotransmitter molecules, spill their contents into the gap. The neurotransmitters bind with receptors on the target cell. This opens certain receptor channels, which allow sodium ions to rush into the target cell and potassium ions to leave. Within this electrochemical reaction, the flow of ions excites an area of the target cell membrane and generates electrical impulses in the cell. It all happens in the nerves and the brain, but we experience it as a thought or perception, a feeling or a dream.

nerves that he viewed under the microscope. The stains showed nerve cells and fibers with unprecedented clarity. Ramón y Cajal described what he saw as a network of lianas and mosses in a tropical forest.

He recorded touchstone descriptions of the developmental and structural basis of the neuron, the basic cell throughout the nervous system. He detailed how nerve impulses are transmitted, neuron by neuron, and how parts of the nervous system degenerate and regenerate. There is little doubt that Ramón y Cajal's observations made possible the modern theory of nerve function and the astonishing discoveries of 20th-century neuroscience.

Far more observations, of course, had to be made before researchers could fully grasp the significance of the neural system, understanding its bewildering, branching parts in light of the findings about living cells of Virchow and Schwann. Slowly the fundamental structure of nerve cells and their connections, the synapses, emerged.

Nerve cells send and receive ceaseless chemical messages, triggered by electrical impulses. Signals travel among the cells, adding up to communications that can instigate physical mental, and internal bodily functions. Minute amounts of chemicals travel between cells through long connecting fibers, called axons, and across the tiny spaces between cells to receptor cells called synapses. Cells release chemical transmitters, in turn picked up by receptors, and sent along the network to long chains of nerve cells. Brain scientists began to catalog the features of the organ's anatomy, learning that a sea snail has only 20,000 brain cells, whereas a newborn human has 100,000,000. As Ramón y Cajal once remarked, "We understand in proportion as we study ourselves."

As more and more was learned about the intricate neurotransmission network, it became clear that diversity aplenty was nestled within it. For one thing, some neurons communicate using several different neurotransmitters. For another, a certain neurotransmitter might not be matched in strict lock-and-key fashion to only one or two receptor proteins; it could actually work with up to several dozen or more. The ramifications are striking. Such chemical variation suggests that brain cells are capable of greater subtlety of response than suspected, which is why our senses are capable of sifting out finely tuned differences in color, sound, flavor, odor, and texture.

This electrochemical versatility may also pave the way for a future generation of psychoactive drugs tailored to target specific receptors that control a given symptom, thereby eliminating adverse side effects. Already, researchers have identified different receptors for the neurotransmitter dopamine, which has been linked to schizophrenia; for norepinephrine, another neurotransmitter associated with anxiety disorders and depression; and for serotonin, also tied to depression, whose operations are key to the effects of today's antidepressants in

See pages 219-23 for more information about particle physics.

the class of serotonin reuptake inhibitors, or SRIs.

Early neuroanatomists, limited though they were by their instruments, managed to identify certain neurons, tracts of nerve fibers, and specific cells in the gray matter. They knew that paraplegia was localized to the spinal cord, and one researcher even created an elaborate cytoarchitectonic map—literally, a map of cell architecture—of the entire cerebral cortex. But all the hands-on anatomical digging and naked-eye observations could never match the sophistication of late 20th-century instrumentation, which produced views of the brain no one had ever dreamed could be possible.

The electroencephalograph (EEG) was the first instrument of the modern age to offer images of brain activity. A descendant of the galvanic instruments of the 18th century, the EEG measures electrical impulses as they travel through the brain. First developed in the 1920s, it consists of a set of sensors attached to the head, which transmit impulses from the brain to a machine that plots them out as lines on a graph. Normal, abnormal, or excited brain behavior figures forth as different line shapes on the graph. A related technique, magneto-encephalography (MEG), records electrical signals from the brain based on changes in magnetic fields.

Positron emission tomography (PET), in common use only since the early 21st century, requires sophisticated technology that applies the principles of radioactivity and particle physics to the problem of generating images of the brain and other internal organs. Controlled radioactive substances are administered to the patient. A scanner can pick up energy emissions released by the radioactive substance in the brain and gene rate from those emissions an image of the sections of the brain. Healthy tissue absorbs the radioactively tagged substance better than depleted tissue does, and screen images show these distinctions in vivid colors.

Even higher resolutions of activity deep in the brain can now be achieved with functional magnetic resonance imaging (fMRI), a scanning method based on differences in the magnetic resonance of certain atomic nuclei in areas of neuronal activity.

In 2005, researchers at the University of Pennsylvania School of Medicine exhibited a striking example of fMRI's power. This non-invasive technique helped them see the effects of psychological stress in an area of the brain linked to anxiety and depression. With fMRI, they were able to observe an increase in blood flow to the prefrontal cortex in individuals subjected to stress. They also watched as the increased blood flow remained, even when the source of stress was removed, suggesting that the effects of stress last longer than once believed.

When used together, such techniques produce unparalleled views of how different parts of the brain process information. Imaging technologies now let scientists peer deeply into the mysterious organ of thought within the human skull.

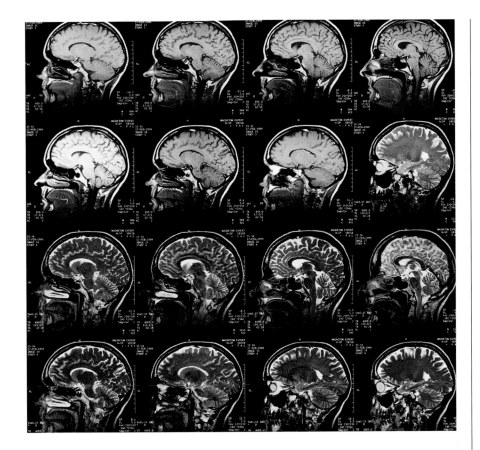

INTELLIGENCE OR MIMICRY?

The mind will continue to make decisions so long as human beings remain human beings, and the brain will continue to be the repository of the intellect and specialized faculties such as calculation and memory. But ever since computer technology arrived, science has taken up the challenge to synthesize the human talents of calculation and memory—if not the gift of reasoning—in the workings of a machine.

The earliest computing machines were designed for counting. The bead-operated abacus led the way. The first practical machine that one could call a calculator was invented in 1642 by Blaise Pascal, the French mathematician and philosopher.

Numbered wheels were moved with a stylus. The device was made to be used for counting monetary sums by simple addition and subtraction. Soon, new inventions performed multiplication by adding repeatedly. By the end of the 19th century, a variety of manually operated calculating machines were on the market. First they operated with cogs and levers, then electrical devices, and later the electronic models that we know today.

The slide rule, a calculating device consisting of a ruler with a moveable section in the center, was once a necessity for every engineer. Both parts were divided with hatch marks indicating logarithmic scales, and informed manipulation

COMPUTER GENIUS
Alan Turing and colleagues work on the Ferranti Mark I Computer for the British government. This computer became the prototype for a commercial version, which was delivered to the University of Manchester in February 1951. Previously, Turing had done work on Colossus, the world's first electronic programmable computer, in 1943.

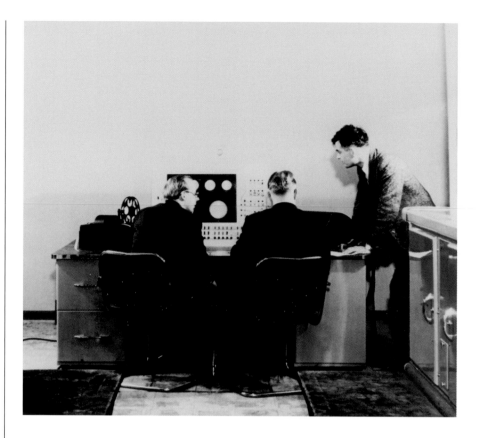

of the two rules resulted in answers to problems in multiplication, division, and higher-order mathematical operations.

The binary system of numbers was itself an invention of the mathematician and philosopher Gottfried Wilhelm Leibniz in the late 17th century. Intellectually, the binary, or base-two, number system transformed every number into an expression consisting of either 1 or 0. Practically, it was the principle that allowed Leibniz to invent one of the first calculating machines, the stepped reckoner.

And, in the long run, the binary system reduced problems to a logic on which inventors could base a calculating—one might even say thinking—machine.

The notion of a thinking machine, or the creation of artificial intelligence, captured the imagination of one English mathematician. Alan Mathison Turing, a logician, set his mind to work during World War II cracking German codes and later pioneered computer theory. At a time when even calculators were rare, Turing believed in the prospect of designing computers that could think.

"My contention is," he said, "that machines can be constructed which will simulate the behavior of the human mind very closely. They will make mistakes at times, and at times they may make new and very interesting statements, and on the whole the output of them will be worth attention to the same sort of extent as the output of a human mind."

World War II presented the impetus for engineers on both sides of the Atlantic to begin developing the thinking machines that Turing envisioned. Even in World War I, German intelligence officers had used machines to generate messages into binary code to transmit among military personnel. British forces could intercept but not understand the communications. They retaliated by inventing Colossus, an electronic digital computer that received paper tapes punched with holes that signified strings of 1s and 0s and, performing 5,000 calculations per minute, transformed code into language.

Two years later, engineers at the United States' Ballistic Research Laboratory built ENIAC, short for Electronic Numerical Integrator And Computer, as a tool to do the complex calculations required in the testing of ballistics. A 30-ton, multi-machine monster, ENIAC's inner working relied on the movement of electrons, atomic particles, through a massive complex of metallic circuitry configured so that the movement of electrons mirrored logic.

ENIAC, and all computers coming after, depended on a variation of the binary system called Boolean algebra, the invention of a 19th-century mathematician, George Boole. Boole reduced all decision-making to a set of three mental operations—"and," "or," and "not." These operations could be neatly expressed by the two numbers of the binary code: "and" represented by 1 and 0; "or" represented by either 1 or 0; and "not" represented by neither 1 nor 0. With Boolean logic, higher order questions could be reduced to binary operations.

The concept seems simple, but the machines required were at first gigantic. ENIAC weighed three tons. Its inner workings included 19,000 vacuum tubes, 1,500 electronic signal relays, and hundreds of

ALAN TURING

Father of computer science

1912
Born June 23 in London.

1931
Enters King's College, Cambridge, as mathematics scholar.

1935
Elected fellow of King's College for his dissertation, "Central Limit Theorem of Probability."

1937
Publishes "On Computable Numbers, with an Application to the *Entscheidungsproblem*"; wins fellowship at Princeton University.

1939
Is instrumental in breaking the German "Enigma" codes.

1940
Conceptualizes programmable computer; named Colossus, the first such machine is built three years later, based on his theories.

1943
Works at Bell Laboratories on speech encypherment.

1945
Begins designing a stored-program machine (MOSAIC), which will store data and programs in its electronic memory.

1948
At Manchester University, works on MADAM, a prototype computer.

1950
Publishes *Computing Machinery and Intelligence*, introducing what comes to be known as the Turing test of artificial intelligence.

1952
Publishes *The Chemical Basis of Morphogenesis*.

1954
Dies by suicide on June 7 in Wilmslow, Cheshire, England.

ULTIMATE CHESS
World-class chess champion Garry Kasparov faces off against Deep Blue, an IBM computer that could calculate 200 million moves a second. Kasporov tricked the computer initially, but was later defeated in subsequent matches.

thousands of internal devices that manipulated the pathway of electrons. It required 200 kilowatts of electricity to run.

It took years to perfect ENIAC in all its operations, but by 1949, observers determined that it could calculate the trajectory of a missile in 30 seconds, half the time of the actual event. The same calculation would take a human being 20 hours. By the mid-1950s, ENIAC's usefulness had been extended by the U.S. government to problems in meteorology, atomic energy, aerodynamics, astrophysics, and many other fields. Soon business saw the promise. In

1949 Texas Instruments produced its first integrated circuit—a much miniaturized version of the internal workings of a large machine like ENIAC. In 1964 IBM (International Business Machines) introduced its first standard office computer, the System/360, called a mainframe after the cabinets needed to house its multiple units.

As advanced in behavior as computers have become in the half-century since, their operations cannot be equated with human intelligence, in the view of many scientists. A computer that plays extraordinary chess and can trounce a master is still not human. It has no consciousness in the classic sense that would be understood by early psychologists like Freud and Jung.

In 1996, IBM's much touted computer, Deep Blue, beat world champion Gary Kasparov at a game of chess. The machine had been programmed to analyze some 200 million positions per second. It lacked intuition, but made up for this deficiency by brute force in its ability to perform iterative calculations at lightning speed. The challenge remains for researchers in the field of artificial intelligence, still seeking ways to build a machine that can reproduce the sort of thinking that appears to be uniquely human, such as complex decision-making, visual pattern recognition, intentionality, and even the use of natural language.

John Searle, an American philosopher best known for his investigations into the human mind and consciousness, has put the quest for artificial intelligence in a rational context. All that computers will be able to achieve, says Searle, is mimicry, fooling us into thinking they actually understand. A human being follows rules consciously, but computers, despite appearances, do not. They behave as if they follow intellectual rules, but in fact, they operate according to the laws of physics and mechanics. In the human brain, information connects with other mental operations, whether thought or perception. In the computer, Searle writes, "The level of information processing which is described in the cognitive

INSTINCTS

English surgeon and sociologist Wilfred Trotter popularized the phrase "herd instinct" as it applied to sociable animals, including humans. His book *Instincts of the Herd in Peace and War*, a seminal work in socio-psychology, was published in 1916.

science computational models of cognition, on the other hand, is simply a matter of getting a set of symbols as output in response to a set of symbols as input." Perhaps a computer can be made to learn without thinking or think without learning, but mathematical, programmed logic is not the same as the complicated mental processes that take place in the human brain.

Wilfred Trotter, an English surgeon and sociologist, called human reason "the indispensable agent in everything man has accomplished. It enables him to learn, to add knowledge and preserve it, to build up arts, sciences, and civilization without limit." His comment can apply not only to the thought processes that computers attempt to replicate, but to the search that has gone on throughout human history: the attempt to observe, measure, and understand—in other words, the perennial search for theories for everything.

FURTHER READING

B ecause of the often swift changes in science, the best and most reliable resources and readings will usually be either the primary works by the scientists themselves or, since even the understanding of science history changes over time, the most recent accounts and analyses on a particular subject. While the Internet has taken much abuse as a reliable source of information, there are many reliable sources online, and once one is found—one with good bibliographic citations—the best advice is to follow the recommended links from that site. The Internet also now provides many primary readings, from ancient Chinese, Greek, and Arab sources to the writings of Charles Darwin and Albert Einstein.

Aquinas, Thomas. *Selected Philosophical Writings,* edited by Timothy McDermott. New York: Oxford University Press, 1998.

Aristotle. *The Basic Works of Aristotle,* edited by Richard McKeon. New York: Modern Library, 2001. Reprint edition.

Aristotle. *Historia Animalium, Vol. I: Books I-X: Text,* edited by Allan Gotthelf and D. M. Balme. Cambridge, U.K.: Cambridge University Press, 2002.

Aujulaut, Norbert. *Lascaux: Movement, Space, and Time.* New York: Harry Abrams, 2005. The complex of caves in France whose wall art captivated several generations is no longer open to the public. This book combines excellent photography with the most recent research findings.

Bernstein, Jeremy. *The Merely Personal: Observations on Science and Scientists.* Chicago: Ivan R. Dee, 2001. For many years Bernstein wrote on science and scientists for

The New Yorker. This book collects some of those essays, which combined an understanding of the work of science along with an eye for the sometimes odd lives of scientists.

Browne, Janet. *Charles Darwin: Voyaging.* New York: Alfred A. Knopf, 1996. *Charles Darwin: The Power of Place.* New York: Alfred A. Knopf, 2003. These two books make up the most definitive biography of Charles Darwin. They are also excellent reads, full of the drama of discovery and Darwin's personal trials.

Bryson, Bill. *A Short History of Almost Everything.* New York: Broadway Books, 2003. Bryson doesn't often delve too deeply, but his lively writing carries the reader through sometimes difficult scientific ideas.

Burenhult, Goran. *The First Human: The Illustrated History of Humankind.* New York: Harper Collins, 1993. This is a lavishly illustrated book with excellent graphics that chart the development and taxonomy of the human species and how only one species of the many that evolved came to survive.

Darrigol, Olivier. *Worlds of Flow: A History of Hydrodynamics from the Bernoullis to Prandtl.* New York: Oxford University Press, 2005.

Dawkins, Richard. *The Selfish Gene: 30th Anniversary Edition.* New York: Oxford University Press, 2006. *The Selfish Gene* introduced Dawkins as an imaginative thinker and literate writer. He remains, along with Stephen Jay Gould (the two disagree about much), at the top of the reading list for those interested in modern considerations of Darwin and evolution.

Dowden, Bradley, and James Fieser, editors. *The Internet Encyclopedia of Philosophy,* http://www.iep.utm.edu. This is an excellent online compendium of philosophers' lives and thought.

Einstein, Albert. *Ideas and Opinions.* New York: Modern Library, 1994. Reprint edition. While there are several books about Albert Einstein, he himself was not loath to write down his own thoughts on subjects ranging from physics to world peace. Physics and philosophy are often much closer than we think.

Farber, Paul Lawrence. *Finding Order in Nature: The Naturalist Tradition from Linnaeus to E. O. Wilson.* Baltimore, MD: The Johns Hopkins University Press, 2000.

Feynman, Richard P. *The Feynman Lectures on Physics: The Definitive and Extended Edition,* edited by Robert B. Leighton and Matthew Sands. New York: Addison-Wesley, 2005. Although Richard Feynman became famous as a character in his own books, he was idolized as a teacher of physics. These lectures can be hard going but are always relieved by moments in which something difficult suddenly becomes clear.

Frazer, James George. *The Golden Bough: A Study in Magic and Religion.* New York: Macmillan & Co., 1922. James Frazer worked for 30 years on this great comparative study of myth and religion. Gathering myths from all over the world Frazer sought to find connections among them all, especially the myths related to spring and rebirth. While his sometimes too willing suspension of critical analysis has been criticized, there is so much in these volumes that is fascinating that it's worth diving into. (Available online at *http://www.bartleby.com/196/.*)

Gleick, James. *Isaac Newton.* New York: Vintage, 2004. Newton was an odd character even for a scientist, and Gleick's book gives us a very human look at a man who could not keep himself from investigating the world around him.

Greene, Brian. *The Elegant Universe.* New York: W. W. Norton, 1999. Greene has been the most visible proponent of string theory, but this book also serves as an excellent introduction to the development of quantum theory and why it clashes with relativity.

Halsall, Paul, editor. *Internet History of Science Sourcebook.* Fordham University, 1998-2001. *http://www.fordham.edu/halsall/science/sciencesbook.html*

Hawking, Stephen. *A Brief History of Time.* New York: Bantam Books, 1988. *The Theory of Everything: The Origin and Fate of the Universe.* New York: New Millennium Press, 2002. While *Time* became a bestseller, Hawking's most recent book, *The Theory of Everything,* is far more exciting reading since, in it, he revisits his cosmology in light of quantum physics. His gentle and persuasive writing carries the reader along on his adventure.

Margulis, Lynn. *Symbiotic Planet: A New Look at Evolution.* New York: Basic Books, 2000. Margulis delves deeply into the evolutionary possibilities presented by her studies of microbial life. Was there a period in life's history that preceded Darwinian evolution?

McEvoy, J. P., and Oscar Zarate. *Introducing Quantum Theory.* Cambridge, U.K.: Icon Books Ltd., 1996. A short, lively book whose casual language and cartoon illustrations belie its depth. A good introduction to the major players in the development of quantum theory.

Michielsen, Kristel, and Hans De Raedt. *Quantum Mechanics.* University of Groningen, The Netherlands, 2006. *http://msc.phys.rug.nl/quantummechanics/intro.htm.*

Moore, Walter. *Schrödinger: Life and Thought.* Cambridge, U.K.: Cambridge University Press, 1989. Although not as well known as Albert Einstein to those outside the world of physics, Austrian-born physicist Erwin Schrödinger (1887-1961) was nearly alone responsible for developing the theory and mathematical proofs of wave mechanics needed to explain motion in the quantum world. Since Schrödinger's life and work paralleled the development of atomic theory and quantum mechanics, this well-written book covers the development of 20th-century science. Since Schrödinger was as much a philosopher as physicist, the book also serves as a history of ideas.

Museum of Paleontology. University of California, Berkeley. *http://www.ucmp.berkeley.edu.* A very good primer on the various taxa of species.

The Nobel Foundation, *http://www.nobelprize.org.*

Nurse, Paul. *The Great Ideas of Biology: The Romanes Lecture for 2003.* New York: Oxford University Press, 2004.

O'Connor, John J., and Edmund F. Robertson. *The MacTutor History of Mathematics.* School of Mathematics and Statistics, University of St Andrews, Scotland, 2006. *http://www-history.mcs.st-andrews.ac.uk/history/index.html.* With both well-written biographies and analyses of the works of the great mathematicians, this site also provides excellent bibliographies of sources both online and off.

Paustian, Timothy, editor. *Microbiology and Bacteriology: The World of Microbes.* University of Wisconsin, 1999-2006. *http://www.bact.wisc.edu/Microtextbook/index.php*

Penrose, Roger. *The Road to Reality: A*

Complete Guide to the Laws of the Universe. New York: Knopf, 2005.

Pliny. *Natural History: Books I-II, Books III-VII,* edited by H. Rackham. Boston: Harvard University Press (Loeb Classical Library), 1989.

Project Gutenberg Literary Archive Foundation, *http://www.gutenberg.org.* This website is an extraordinary resource, holding original texts of the writings of scientists from Aristotle to Darwin. All of the latter's major works—*The Descent of Man, On the Origin of Species,* and *The Voyage of the Beagle*—and his letters and other scientific writing can be read on this site. Other major works here include Charles Lyell's *The Antiquity of Man,* Francis Bacon's *The Advancement of Learning* and *New Atlantis,* Rene Descartes' *Discourse on the Method of Rightly Conducting One's Reason and of Seeking Truth in the Sciences,* and Malthus's *An Essay on the Principle of Population.*

Quammen, David. *The Reluctant Mr. Darwin: An Intimate Portrait of Charles Darwin and the Making of His Theory of Evolution.* New York: W. W. Norton, 2006. An excellent science writer, Quammen here explores the years in which Darwin procrastinated over committing to paper his theory of natural selection.

Rae, Alastair I. M. *Quantum Physics: Illusion or Reality?* Cambridge, U.K.: Cambridge University Press, 1986. A classic presentation of the world of quantum physics from a writer who seems sympathetic to the reader trying to make some headway through the odd world being described.

Ridley, Matt. *Genome: The Autobiography of a Species.* New York: HarperCollins, 2000.

Ronan, Colin A. *The Cambridge Illustrated History of the World's Science.* Cambridge, U.K.: Cambridge University Press, 1983.

Segre, Emilio. *Enrico Fermi, Physicist.* Chicago: University of Chicago Press, 1995.

The Tree of Life Web Project, *http://tolweb.org/tree.* Want to find out what's known about a species or where it belongs in relation to others? This is the place to go. A resource with much to offer and always adding more.

Torrance, Robert M. *Encompassing Nature: A Sourcebook.* Washington, DC: Counterpoint, 1998. Torrance provides readings for those interested in a literary view of science and natural history from ancient Hindu and Chinese texts up to modern times. Insightful introductions examine the relationship between science and culture.

Tyson, Neil deGrasse. *Universe Down to Earth.* New York: Columbia University Press, 1994.

Zalta, Edward N., editor. *The Stanford Encyclopedia of Philosophy.* The Metaphysics Research Lab, Center for the Study of Language and Information, Stanford University, 2006. *http://plato .stanford.edu/contents.html*

INDEX

Illustration Credits

COVER: The Granger Collection, NY.

FRONT MATTER: 2, The Wellcome Library, London; 6, Archivo Iconografico, S.A./CORBIS; 9, The Granger Collection, NY; 10, Bettmann/CORBIS; 12-13, The Granger Collection, NY; 15, The Stapleton Collection/CORBIS; 17, The Granger Collection, NY.

CHAPTER 1, THE HEAVENS: 18-19, NASA, ESA, and The Hubble Heritage Team (STScI/AURA); 21, Erich Lessing/Art Resource, NY; 23, Bibliothèque des Arts Décoratifs, Paris, France, Archives Charmet/The Bridgeman Art Library; 24, The Granger Collection, NY; 26, HIP/Art Resource, NY; 28, The Granger Collection, NY; 29, Bettmann/CORBIS; 31, Jean-Leon Huens; 34-35, The Granger Collection, NY; 36, The Granger Collection, NY; 39, Erich Lessing/Art Resource, NY; 40, The Granger Collection, NY; 42-43, Bettmann/CORBIS; 44, William Schick/CORBIS; 46 (upper), Fitzwilliam Museum, University of Cambridge, UK/The Bridgeman Art Library; 46 (lower), Clayton J. Price/CORBIS; 47, CORBIS; 48, Bettmann/CORBIS; 51, Mansell/Time Life Pictures/Getty Images; 52-53, Bibliothèque des Arts Décoratifs, Paris, France, Archives Charmet/The Bridgeman Art Library; 54, Robert Gendler/www.robgendlerastropics.com; 55, Bettmann/CORBIS; 57, Courtesy of the Archives, California Institute of Technology; 59, Mary Evans/Photo Researchers, Inc.; 61, Science Museum/Science & Society Picture Library; 62, Robert Cummins/CORBIS; 65, Bettmann/CORBIS; 66, Shigemi Numazawa/Atlas Photo Bank/Photo Researchers, Inc.; 67, Bettmann/CORBIS; 68, T.A. Rector/University of Alaska, Anchorage and WIYN/AURA/NSF; 70, Julian Baum/Photo Researchers, Inc.

CHAPTER 2, THE HUMAN BODY: 72-73, Araldo de Luca/CORBIS; 74, The Wellcome Library, London; 75, College of Pharmacy/Washington State University; 76, Stock Montage/Getty Images; 78, Wellcome Library, London; 79, North Wind Picture Archives; 80, The Granger Collection, NY; 83, CORBIS; 84, National Library of Medicine/Science Photo Library/Photo Researchers, Inc.; 85, The Granger Collection, NY; 86, The Wellcome Library, London; 88, Erich Lessing/Art Resource, NY; 90, Bettmann/CORBIS; 92, Scimat/Photo Researchers, Inc.; 94, The Wellcome Library, London; 96-97, Jean-Loup Charmet/Photo Researchers, Inc.; 98, The Wellcome Library, London; 101, The Wellcome Library, London; 102, Bettmann/CORBIS; 105, The Wellcome Library, London; 106, The Wellcome Library, London; 108, Stefano Bianchetti/CORBIS; 110, Visuals Unlimited/CORBIS; 111, Oxford Science Archive/HIP; 113, Bettmann/CORBIS; 115, The Wellcome Library, London; 116, Bettmann/CORBIS; 118, Bettmann/CORBIS; 119, Biophoto Associates/Photo Researchers, Inc.; 121, CDC/PHIL/CORBIS; 123, Hulton-Deutsch Collection/CORBIS; 124, The Wellcome Library, London; 126, Don W. Fawcett/Photo Researchers, Inc.; 128-130 (all), The Wellcome Library, London; 133, Paul Almasy/CORBIS; 134, CORBIS; 136, Ted Spiegel/CORBIS; 138, Bill Nation/CORBIS SYGMA; 139, Sheila Terry/Photo Researchers, Inc.; 140, Stephen Ferry/Liaison/Getty Images; 142, Rick Friedman/CORBIS; 145, Ernesto Orlando Lawrence Berkeley National Laboratory.

CHAPTER 3, MATTER & ENERGY: 146-147, CORBIS; 148, Bettmann/CORBIS; 149, Allan H. Shoemake/Getty Images; 150, The Granger Collection, NY; 152, The Granger Collection, NY; 153, David Lees/CORBIS; 154, The Granger Collection, NY; 156-157, Kimbell Art Museum/CORBIS; 159, The Wellcome Library, London; 160, Hulton Archive/Getty Images; 161, The Wellcome Library, London; 162, Archivo Iconografico, S.A./CORBIS; 164, Ann Ronan Picture Library/HIP; 165, The Granger Collection, NY; 166, The Granger Collection, NY; 168-169, HIP/Art Resource, NY; 170 (upper), IIHR, History of Hydraulics Collection; 170 (lower), The Granger Collection, NY; 173, Ann Ronan Picture Library/HIP; 175, Jim Sugar/CORBIS; 176-177, Private Collection/The Bridgeman Art Library; 178-180 (all), The Granger Collection, NY; 183, Science Museum/Science & Society Picture Library; 184, Science Photo Library/Photo Researchers, Inc.; 186, Science Museum/Science & Society Picture Library; 187, Baldwin H. Ward & Kathryn C. Ward/CORBIS; 188 (upper), Science Museum/Science & Society Picture Library 188 (lower), NASA; 189, Mary Evans Picture Library; 190, The Granger Collection, NY; 192, Science Museum/Science & Society Picture Library; 193, The Granger Collection, NY;

194, Science Museum/Science & Society Picture Library; 196, The Royal Institution, London, UK/The Bridgeman Art Library; 198, The Granger Collection, NY; 199, Ernesto Orlando Lawrence Berkeley National Laboratory; 200, Bettmann/CORBIS; 203, Science Museum/Science & Society Picture Library; 204, Science Museum/Science & Society Picture Library; 207, Roger Ressmeyer/CORBIS; 208, Ernesto Orlando Lawrence Berkeley National Laboratory; 210, The Granger Collection, NY; 213, DOE/Science Source/Photo Researchers, Inc.; 214, Carl Anderson/Photo Researchers, Inc.; 216, Novosti Photo Library/Photo Researchers, Inc.; 218, Douglas Kirkland/CORBIS; 220, Ralph Morse/Time Life Pictures/Getty Images; 222, Danny Lehman/CORBIS; 224, NASA/SAO/CXC; 227, Everett Kennedy Brown/epa/CORBIS; 228, Kevin Fleming/CORBIS.

CHAPTER 4, LIFE ITSELF: 230-231, Mediscan/CORBIS; 232, The Granger Collection, NY; 233, CORBIS; 234, The Granger Collection, NY; 238, Bettmann/CORBIS; 240 (upper), Topkapi Palace Museum, Istanbul, Turkey/The Bridgeman Art Library; 240 (lower), The Wellcome Library, London; 243, Explorer/Photo Researchers, Inc.; 245, The Granger Collection, NY; 246, The Granger Collection, NY; 247, Gianni Dagli Orti/CORBIS; 248, The Granger Collection, NY; 250, Stock Montage/Getty Images; 252-256 (all), The Granger Collection, NY; 258, Mansell/Time Life Pictures/Getty Images; 260, Mansell/Time Life

Pictures/Getty Images; 262, Ann Ronan Picture Library/HIP; 266-267, The Granger Collection, NY; 268, The Wellcome Library, London; 270, The Granger Collection, NY; 274-275, The Granger Collection, NY; 276, John Durham/Photo Researchers, Inc.; 278, The Granger Collection, NY; 279, Mansell/Time Life Pictures/Getty Images; 280-281, The Wellcome Library, London; 282, Science Source/Photo Researchers, Inc.; 283, Lee D. Simon/Photo Researchers, Inc.; 284, Kurt Hutton/Picture Post/Getty Images; 286, Michael Freeman/CORBIS; 289, Michael A. Keller/CORBIS; 290, Bettmann/CORBIS; 293, Digital Vision/Getty Images; 294, Photo Researchers, Inc.; 296, Ralph White/CORBIS; 297, Stephen Ferry/Liaison/Getty Images; 298-299, Henry Groskinsky/Time Life Pictures/Getty Images; 301, O. Louis Mazzatenta/NGS Image Collection; 302, NASA.

CHAPTER 5, EARTH & MOON: 304-305, The Granger Collection, NY; 306, Gianni Dagli Orti/CORBIS; 306-307, Mary Evans Picture Library; 309, SuperStock, Inc.; 310, Robert Magis; 312, Mary Evans Picture Library; 315, The Granger Collection, NY; 316-317, Bettmann/CORBIS; 318, Musée des Arts Décoratifs, Paris, France, Lauros/Giraudon/The Bridgeman Art Library; 320-321, Gianni Dagli Orti/CORBIS; 322, The Granger Collection, NY; 324 (upper), The Worshipful Company of Clockmakers' Collection, UK/The Bridgeman Art Library; 324 (lower), Bettmann/COR-BIS; 325, The Granger Collection, NY;

326, Bettmann/CORBIS; 328, Science Museum/Science & Society Picture Library; 330, The Granger Collection, NY; 332, Roger Ressmeyer/CORBIS; 334, Bettmann/CORBIS; 337, NGS Maps; 338-339, Roger Ressmeyer/CORBIS; 340, Bettmann/CORBIS; 341, The Granger Collection, NY; 343, Kazuyoshi Nomachi/CORBIS; 345, Skyscan/COR-BIS; 347, R. Russell/PanStock/Panoramic Images/NGSImages.com; 350, NASA; 351, Science Museum/Science & Society Picture Library; 353, NASA/Roger Ressmeyer/CORBIS; 354, Francesc Muntada/CORBIS; 356, Don Davis/NASA; 357, P. Stattmayer/PanStock/Panoramic Images/NGSImages.com.

CHAPTER 6, THE MYSTERY OF MIND & BEHAVIOR: 358-359, Anatomical Travelogue/Photo Researchers, Inc.; 361, CORBIS; 362, Ted Spiegel/CORBIS; 364, Hulton Archive/Getty Images; 366-368 upper (all), The Wellcome Library, London; 368 (lower), Bettmann/CORBIS; 370, The Wellcome Library, London; 371, The Wellcome Library, London; 372, Bettmann/CORBIS; 374, Central Press/Getty Images; 376, Bettmann/CORBIS; 378, Novosti/Photo Researchers, Inc.; 380, D. Silbersweig/Photo Researchers, Inc.; 382, The Wellcome Library, London; 383, James Leynse/CORBIS; 384, Jim Dowdalls/Photo Researchers, Inc.; 387, Simon Fraser/Photo Researchers, Inc.; 388, Science Museum/Science & Society Picture Library; 390, Louie Psihoyos/CORBIS; 391, The Wellcome Library, London.

Theories for Everything

An Illustrated History of Science

John Langone, Bruce Stutz, and Andrea Gianopoulos

Prepared by the Book Division

Kevin Mulroy, Senior Vice President and Publisher

Leah Bendavid-Val, Director of Photography Publishing
and Illustrations

Marianne R. Koszorus, Director of Design

Barbara Brownell Grogan, Executive Editor

Elizabeth Newhouse, Director of Travel Publishing

Carl Mehler, Director of Maps

Staff for this Book

Garrett W. Brown, Editor

Peggy Archambault, Art Director

Jennifer Davis, Illustrations Editor

Susan Tyler Hitchcock, Developmental Editor

Judith Klein and Margo Browning, Contributing Editors

Karin Kinney, Proofreader

Richard Wain, Production Project Manager

Meredith Wilcox, Illustrations Specialist

Cameron Zotter, Design Assistant

Suzanne Poole, Research Assistant

John Baldridge and Michael Greninger, Editorial Interns

Al Morrow, Design Intern

Rebecca Hinds, Managing Editor

Gary Colbert, Production Director

Manufacturing and Quality Management

Christopher A. Liedel, Chief Financial Officer

Phillip L. Schlosser, Vice President

John T. Dunn, Technical Director

Vincent P. Ryan, Director

Chris Brown, Director

Maryclare Tracy, Manager

Since 1888, the National Geographic Society has funded more than 13,000 research, exploration, and preservation projects around the world. National Geographic Partners distributes a portion of the funds it receives from your purchase to National Geographic Society to support programs including the conservation of animals and their habitats.

National Geographic Partners
1145 17th Street NW
Washington, DC 20036-4688 USA

Get closer to National Geographic explorers and photographers, and connect with our global community. Join us today at nationalgeographic.com/join

For information about special discounts for bulk purchases, please contact National Geographic Books Special Sales: specialsales@natgeo.com

For rights or permissions inquiries, please contact National Geographic Books Subsidiary Rights: bookrights@natgeo.com

ISBN: 978-1-4351-3339-6 (special sales ed.)

Library of Congress Cataloging-in-Publication Data
Langone, John, 1929-
    Theories for everything : an illustrated history of science / by John Langone, Bruce Stutz, and Andrea Gianopoulos. -- 1st ed.
        p. cm.
    Includes bibliographical references and index.
        ISBN 0-7922-3912-1 (cloth : alk. paper)
        1. Science--History. 2. Science--History--Pictorial works. I. Stutz, Bruce. II. Gianopoulos, Andrea. III. Title.

Q125.L29 2006
509--dc22
                        2006021419
Printed in China

19/RRDS/2